Table of Contents

Prelude

The material in this book would have never been born without the friendship and help of Bob McCaffray-Lent, liturgical musician extraordinary. When actually preaching, I never used a text, and rarely even notes. Each Wednesday, while working with Bob at St. Leo parish in Tacoma, WA., I gave him an early rendition of how I would approach the scriptures for Sunday, so he could match the liturgy and music to the direction I was going. Divested of any text, I went over and over my remarks in order to preach while moving around the sanctuary. At my going-away party from St. Leo in 1995, Bob surprised and delighted me with an enormous pile of notes – every homily during our 8 years together. Those notes formed the basis for my re-construction and eventual finalization of the material in this book. I offer unending thanks to Bob for this and a thousand other signs of friendship over the past 35 years.

For the past three years I have been offering one homily each week to a variety of friends, especially a group called Companeros, made up mostly of former Jesuits, many of whom I have never met. I am grateful for comments. both complimentary and otherwise. from this group, and especially grateful to one never-met friend, Jim Brown, who carefully corrected and edited the 3rd, or C-Cycle section of this book.

Despite Bob's notes, and three years of homilies after I left St. Leo, there remained holes – Sundays in the year for which I had no material. For some of these, I created anew. For two, I borrowed homilies from friends, both superb preachers – Fr. Mike Ryan, pastor of The Seattle Cathedral for more than three decades, and Fr. John Coleman, S.J., a renowned sociologist of religion, now associate pastor at St. Ignatius in San Francisco. Buried unobtrusively, these gems are worth discovering on your own.

Finally, I am grateful to many friends, many readers of, or listeners to, my words over the years. They have encouraged me to being this material to print, helping me believe them a likely source of nourishment to others and not just an egotistic exercise. I count first among such encouragers, my wondrous wife, Dee McQuesten, who has kept alive and grateful for the past twenty years. She insists my words are significant; I hope you do also.

L. Patrick Carroll
January 2019

BOOK ONE
The A Cycle

Preface

Some years ago I began to be pastor in a new parish I faced a serious personal dilemma. I knew the reputation of the parish, knew most of the staff people there, and knew my own aspirations and limitations. I was aware that almost everything I had done as a priest was already being done by someone else in that parish, and being done well. I had begun and developed the RCIA program in my previous parish; here the woman that began that program in the archdiocese already worked. I had organized and done most of the adult education in my previous two positions; here an excellent staff person already facilitated adult education. I prided myself on liturgical planning, and implementation. Here a musician and liturgist were well in place. For some years I had felt lacking in a direct contact with the poor, and a ministry that opted for the poor. This parish was inundated with social ministries, and people dedicated to a gospel rooted in the Twenty-fifth chapter of Matthew. I spent a restless summer wondering prayerfully what my role would be.

When I arrived in September, I very carefully crafted my first homily, honestly sharing with parishioners my concerns about "fitting in" and "helping out." I made a pledge to them that I would try, if I did nothing else, to tell the story of Jesus. I foresaw that my task was to tell the story of Jesus, over and over until I got it right, until we got it right.

Perhaps a year earlier, I had attended a workshop by John Shea in which he began one of his wonderful stories playfully saying something like this:

> I wasn't there; I didn't see him. I never witnessed a miracle, never heard a sermon that he preached, never rejoiced in his presence. I wasn't there, didn't see him, didn't hear him, didn't touch him. But some other people did, and they told their friends, who passed it on to other friends still, who shared it with their children, through generation after generation, one telling another until, thank God, someone told me. And now, I'm telling you, so that we will never forget. It's the story of Jesus.

I passed on to the parish this approach of John Shea's, promising to do my best to tell that story. I have tried to be faithful to my pledge. My role in the parish was to be the primary teller of the story, in preaching, teaching, presiding, celebrating, mourning, and, yes, even in living. I have failed as often as I have succeeded, certainly, but I have discovered over and over the importance of that pledge. In both honesty and humility I have heard people tell me too often that I give the best homilies they have ever heard. I know my intelligence, my voice, my depth of faith, my personal integrity cannot account for such compliments. I come to believe the praise comes because what I am trying to do is, at least, the right thing to try.

After nine years at St. Leo I had the opportunity to take three months off from the parish, to read, sleep, write, fill up my head and heart, and empty out my fatigue. During those months I visited various churches and heard many preachers, both Catholic and others. Some were very good, some horrific, but all have helped me appreciate the significance of my initial pledge to a parish in which I regularly preached to tell the story of Jesus. As a person in the pews then, and in the two decades since I left active ministry, I have experienced that homilizers tend to talk about everything else but Jesus, his life, his message, the connections between his life and words and our own struggles, sorrows, joys, hopes dreams.

There are many books on, approaches to, theories about preaching. All of them, I'm sure, have some merit. I would like to add one simple approach to the mix. I offer a series of homilies rooted in this approach.

I assert boldly that what Christian people want, need, thirst for, is a deeper understanding of Jesus. We want to know, to feel, to experience how Jesus makes a difference, changes things, saves us. We desperately long to understand how the ancient story intertwines with our own.

Any preacher, invited to say what he or she spoke about on a given weekend, ought to be able to respond, "I talked about the Gospel." The subject of the homily is not some other topic, however important. People do not need yet another talk on abortion, or social justice, o, certainly on tithing. These subjects and many like them mingle with our lives, and need to be preached in ways that connect our story with the story of Jesus. How does this transforming Word relate to the realities of my life?

I do not perceive a passionate interest in exegesis of the biblical text for its own sake. I more than suspect that people come to our Christian communities with a deep longing for meaning, to somehow be touched with the hope that their individual lives carry, in their fierce particularity, some transcendent significance. We all want to know that what we are about is both saving and being saved, freeing and being set free, loving and being loved, and that, somehow, it all counts for something. The story of Jesus, when it becomes, indeed, our story, provides such poignancy.

On some deep existential level we ask two simple questions of scripture: *Is this story true? Does it matter?* Is there something about human life that this story illuminates, and can it make a difference in my life.

Let me make this more specific. I do not believe that it much matters whether Jesus walked on the water two thousand years ago, and that Peter walked with him. What matters is whether when I am sinking, someone will lift me up. What matters is whether I have the courage to step out of the boat, into the teeth of the storm, because it seems, strangely, as if Jesus is inviting me to do so. What matters is whether I can invite others to take new, bold steps into unfamiliar waters with confidence in the Jesus in whom we both believe. What truly matters is preaching that can help people connect the story that is supposed to enflesh the Word of God for us with the stories they are living, today, here and now.

Every Sunday a homilist faces the task of reflecting, out of his or her personal faith, on the Good News of Jesus. We may escape into philosophical, or theological truisms, even brilliant fresh truths. We can transfer our attention to topical issues of the day, surrounding them with faith-filled direction. Or we can enter into the mystery of Jesus and see if his life, his words, his facing of death, his overcoming death, has anything to do with the topics of the day, the lives of people, the fears of nations.

Obviously, even an entire book, cannot suggest the gamut of possibilities for telling the story of Jesus, and relating it to the real stories of real people. But we can, more modestly, more simply, provide some sign posts, some directions.

First, I suggest that in every passage of the Gospel, a person can take one of three stances. We can be a bystander, watching the scene, letting it occur in the life of someone else. We can be the object of the words or ministry of Jesus, letting him speak to, or act on us. We can, most difficult of all, be the subjects, the perpetrators of the ministry of Jesus, inviting him to act in and through us. Each of these "stances" provides a homiletic possibility. Each provides an entree for different human stories, different facets of human experience that may help the ancient text put on flesh.

Thus in the story of the cure of a paralytic in Mk. 2, we may stand and watch as Jesus cares for the paralyzed woman or man. We can stand in wonder and hope, placing someone we love on that mat, and letting this be a way for us, today, to pray for healing for another. The preacher, the teller of the story, can invite a community, each in their own hearts to put before Jesus an uncle, a friend, a child, a parent in the midst of illness, and let them lie on that mat; we can be the carrier of the pallet, bringing the loved one before the enfleshed word.

Perhaps more pertinently we can place ourselves on that mat. We can acknowledge the truth that this story is not just an old one, a long time ago, about someone else, but is my story. For *I* am paralyzed. I am not able to love as I want, to walk where I want, to be as free, as lively, as able to dance as I would wish. I lie, always, on some mat, and I can ask for the healing that Jesus wants to give. I can cry out with this paralytic, and so many others, "If you want to you can heal me." I can wait and be still enough to hear Jesus say to me the words, "Get up and walk!" I can hear a homilist, out of his own healed faith, encourage me to believe I do not have to be paralyzed in the same old way anymore. I can walk.

With far more difficulty, but, at times, equal importance, every Christian can be invited to stand before the paralyzed world, or any individual in it, and be the presence of Jesus. We can assume the power that is given us as the Body of Christ, and speak, and enact the healing word. We can look at those in our various communities who suffer, and cry out in love, "Get up!" We can take on the pain of Jesus for those lost in our neighborhoods and cities, paralyzed by addictions, or poverty, or mental illness and undertake the long-term miracle of healing, in Jesus name. We can stand before God's Body, our world, wracked with ecological irresponsibility, and assume the Christ-like responsibility of healing the earth.

This and every story of Jesus is relevant today; the preaching task is to make connection between the story, and each specific community. Every Gospel story submits of entrance; one who would speak of it can go in and live there, tasting, touching, smelling, hearing, letting it become her or his story, then exit and tell what has been seen.

I remember entering into that other story of a storm, in Mark's gospel. The disciples are tossed about by waves and wind, and Jesus seems asleep in the back of the boat. I recall becoming furious at Jesus, crying out as did his friends of long ago, "Don't you care that we are drowning?" I felt with them the waves overwhelming me and the community of which I am a part.

Don't you care that we spend millions for arms, while children starve?

Don't you care that the mentally ill wander the streets of our cities?

Don't you care that our nation pretends to be concerned with peace, but provides armaments for the world, and has been responsible for the deaths of so many who share your name in El Salvador, or Guatemala, in Syria and Iraq.

Don't you care about an elderly parishioner who's wife is suffering from Alzheimer's disease, and who is losing his own mind caring for her?

Don't you care,... don't you care,... .don't you care!

The homeletic experience was real, vivid, immediate. Every member of the community could add a personal lament, a resentment towards an apparently sleeping, impervious Jesus. When Jesus does wake up and act, however, it is not a long time ago, but can only be the Body of Jesus now able to act,... you and me and us!

We learn, over and over, how to make similar connections between the words of Jesus, his sermons and parables, and our own and other's lives.

Jesus spoke, not so much to a crowd, as to individuals in turn. It was as if said:

> "Steve, you are so able to live without a lot of stuff, you will surely be blessed.
> Sally, you have such a passion for justice, you will certainly be satisfied.
> Betty, one day your tears will be wiped away, and because you care so deeply, you can be deeply comforted."

An individual message spoken to individual people. I have come to suspect that every word of Jesus can be so particularized, for what he says in general, he says also to the individual trying to believe. I have heard Jesus say to me, "I have played Pipes for you and you wouldn't dance." I have listened to others for whom I knew Jesus says, "As my father has loved me, so I have loved you; live in that love."

Though we all experience it differently, personally, each member of the community needs to hear the call to mission, to service, to "laying down our lives," a message that flows from almost every passage of the story of Jesus. Often that preaching is not merely personal, but communal.

Clearly the ideal homily speaks not only to individuals within a community, but, at times, to the community as a whole, standing in need of comfort or conversion. Each entire community, each privileged enfleshment of the Body of Christ, has a story crying out for relevance derived from The Story. I vividly recall preaching to our community as we grieved our collective way through the Gulf War. It could have been any lent, any war -- true, sadly, in almost any age!

The topic of preaching was not the war itself, but the graced time of Lent. The story of Jesus Tempted in the Desert was instantly appropriated to our national temptation to change the world in splashy, heroic ways, rather than a more mundane, slow messianic pattern. The tale of a man born blind, Pharisees who claimed to see, parents who did not want to get involved, and the apostles wondering who to blame . . . all spoke directly to the reality of our seemingly blind national tendency to violent solutions.

I believe passionately that the gospels can, and deserve to be preached with an immediacy for today, and a particularity that allows the story of Jesus to touch and transform the stories of an almost infinite variety of listeners. We have all experienced ourselves collapsed beside the well, unable to go on, when yet another person in need comes up looking for living water from our empty, or missing bucket. We have, each one of us, felt dead, buried within a tomb, and longed for a voice crying out in our direction, "Unbind him/her and let him/her be free." We have all hung on a personal cross, and cried out, "My God, my God, why have you abandoned me?" And who has not known tears turned into laughter and celebrated that this second wine was greater than the first?

I delight that I was invited years ago to enter, as priest, into a community which having very little need for me forced me carefully to wonder what I could provide. My experience there suggests that every community, whatever else it may have or not have, needs first and above all someone or several to tell the story of Jesus to this people, in this place, today. I hope that all who preach to our communities may discover new and fresh ways to let the story be true in the lives of our listeners. That search, especially for the stories that give the gospel hand and ear, heart beat and elbow grease must emerge from the community where they are preached, and the experience of the story-teller.

I offer these homilies of my own not merely so others will use them, but so that all who listen, waiting for a word to feed them can discover their own. Everyone can take them home, and make them personal -- something that matters.

I offer a mixture, of scriptural insight and storytelling, hoping both can refresh the reader, initiate a group discussion, even, perhaps, resource other's called to preach this word.

1) The First Sunday of Advent

Rooted in: Is. 2:1-5; Ro. 13:11-14; Mt. 24:37-44

In Dante's <u>Divine Comedy</u> a sign hangs over the entrance to the Inferno:

> "*Abandon Hope all you who enter here ...*"

As we the followers of Jesus enter in to the Season of Advent we say, loudly, the opposite:

> "*All who enter here must Hope!*"

All who enter into this Advent community are invited to be people of hope, as we wait together for Christmas, a fuller birth of Jesus.

We need to be honest about the difficulty of hoping. I was brought to this awareness just before one Advent. In a session of Remembering Church (a community of people pondering their return to the Church) we discussed somewhat piously the readings for the Feast of Christ the King. We spoke about the kingdom of Christ, the reign of God, the longed for reign of justice, love, peace. One of the women present began to speak of a strong experience of renewed hope and energy she and her friends were experiencing in the wake of a recent election. She was wild with enthusiasm for a newly elected official who actually walked among the poor, touched their poverty, their hearts, their hopes. She was truly excited and mirrored the excitement of others.

Personally, I was amazed. I had seen the same phenomenon, but had remained cynical. I had seen it before and it had come to naught. Perhaps that is the function of advanced age, perhaps it is realism. What crashed into my face was the deep realization of my more pervasive cynicism, a personal reluctance to "get my hopes up." I have done so too often, and been disappointed. I am perhaps too much like the man in the gospel who has been coming to the waters for 18 years but no longer seems to have any real hope for himself being cured. He comes only out of habit.

As I enter into Advent again, I fear I may have carved out a little niche for myself where I can work very hard to keep things from getting worse, but no longer truly believe that things can change, can improve beyond belief. I may have a kind of transcendent hope; things will certainly be all right hereafter. "Don't cry; there will a pie in the sky when you die, by and by!" But I do not often have the kind of expectant, immediate, "we can do it with God's power," hope

But this is what Advent is about. A time to restore, recuperate, rekindle that excited expectant hope.

The biblical message today insists that now is the hour to wake up for salvation is closer that when we first accepted it. The day draws near. "Stay Awake!" cries Jesus.

For most of my life I had never liked the final image of the gospel comparing Jesus to a thief in the night, coming when we least expect it.

Then I had a cardiac arrest; I died without warning.

Resuscitated, I know, now first hand, the truth. The point is not that Jesus is like a thief, but that we would do well to be ready, anticipatory all the time.

God does not want us to be caught surprised, doesn't want us to be overwhelmed, doesn't want us to be afraid or neurotic.

God does want us to be awake, ready, excited, hopeful, longing for God's final coming, and God's coming every day.

I want to look more carefully at the reading from the Hebrew scripture today. Isaiah proclaims "the day is coming." The mountain for the Lord's house will be established; nations will stream toward in and finally learn from God. Today the promise is that nations will quit fighting, will not raise the sword against each other, "will beat their swords into plowshares."

As we listen to the Advent promise, we look forward to Christmas. But we not await an innocuous little child in a warm blankie. We await the very real possibility of peace, because God is bursting into our world. We rekindle our hope for peace, and our own commitment to bring that peace about.

I was a peacenik years ago; I marched, demonstrated, wrote letters, called Congress, but I fear I may have ceased to believe that anything can truly happen. I need to rediscover hope. I need to believe that peace can be a reality. And I need this Advent season

—perhaps this year, more than ever – to be helped to see the seeds of hope, to trust that life can come out of an apparently lifeless stump.

Everything in the culture around us argues against Advent, invites us to celebrate Christmas from Thanksgiving on, the famous "holiday season." We are already, at the outset of Advent, besieged with the trees, the carols, the frantic shopping, the endless TV commercials, and at least four Christmas movies are on TV each night.

But we cannot get to Christmas without Advent.

Our faith, at its best, invites us to wait, to feel our emptiness, our cynicism, our despair … and out of these to choose to hope, to let Christmas happen in us and around us, this year, because slowly honestly, over the next four weeks we learn again to hope, and are given new eyes – Christmas eyes.

I remember early one Advent spending about ten minutes in the free kitchen connected with the parish where I worked, just hanging around, familiarizing myself again with that painful reality. I found it incredibly depressing. I saw fewer of the mentally ill than I remembered, fewer elderly, fewer families with little children waiting for a hot breakfast. What I saw was mostly African American men between 35-50, at the height of what could be expected to be their "productive years." They were sitting, waiting. A pall of sadness, a cloak of despair hung over the room. Something was terribly wrong. I carried the darkness all day.

That very afternoon I was given a paper to read, written by a woman who had been doing an internship in that kitchen for Catholic Community Services. She told several stories in her reflection paper, stories of individual people she had come to know, love and to have hope in and for. I discovered an Advent truth in the experience of *my* dismal feelings challenged by *her* paper. There is something about looking at the macrocosm, the big picture, that if left alone can paralyze, overwhelm me, fill me with gloom. But it is in the ability to see the microcosm, the small frame, in seeing Joe, and Bill, and Easy Ed, and Mickey, in seeing individuals that allowed her, and can allow me to hope

Peace comes, Jesus comes, not because the whole system works perfectly, but because here and there, and over yonder, hope happens. I restore my hope when I talk to someone whose life was a mess and now it is better. If I see the incredibly lovely faces of the kids in a head start program, or appreciate the wonder of a housing complex being raised up in the neighborhood, or remember Henry who used to have to eat in our kitchen for years and now no longer does.

I want this Advent to learn to stay awake as Jesus insists. I need to see the single sword that has become a plowshare. I need a season, a time, a month of serious prayer and reflection to prepare for Christmas.

So please come with me into a renewed hope, a renewed commitment with all who choose to enter our narrow doorway this Advent. We will help each other to see with new eyes, Hope-filled eyes, and, who knows, but in a month we may be able to say, with honesty, "Merry Christmas!"

2) Second Sunday in Advent: A Playful Alternate

I wasn't there. I didn't see this. Like the stories of Jesus himself, I heard it from another, who had heard it from another before, until finally someone told me, and I pass it on to you now, so that we won't forget.

But this is not a story of "Once upon a time," in the distant past, but a future story that I am sure will happen "not long from now," and "not far from here." It is an Advent story, speaking of how all our seeds of promise can lead to the fullness of life. Just a little story, but such a big promise.

When he woke up that morning it was as if from a dream, or perhaps still in a dream. The words that frame today's prayer, words from the letter of Paul were in his ears . . .

"Rejoice always, . . . give constant thanks. . . don't stifle the spirit . . .

May the God of peace make you perfect in holiness, . . . Rejoice."

He looked out the window and saw just beyond his house a marvelous sight. He saw as if in a vision the parousia, the final Christmas, the Kingdom of God:

The poor, still dressed in rags though now the rags were shinning, sat at a sumptuous feast.

People in prison stripes were dancing freely in the streets,

Crutches of the lame were piled by the roadside as their previous owners joined in the dance. Those blind before were looking everywhere with eyes of wonder.

A great white robed throng of martyrs joined in the feast, for he could spy the faces many who had given their lives in service of the poor.

It was surely the messianic banquet, the fulfillment of all our Christmas promises, the fullness of which all our hopes, our lives are but a seed. For truly:

> "the eyes of the blind were opened,
> the ears of the deaf unstopped,
> the lame were leaping like deer,
> and the tongue of the speechless were singing for joy,"

Surely this was good news to the Poor!

He raced from his room, ran outside rushing towards the feast, but between him and the celebration the mountains were too high, the valleys too low, there was no highway to this God. The blockage came, in fact in the form of an enormous wall between the fellow and the feast.

Atop the wall he saw a vision of a man, dressed in camel's hair, a scraggly beard, wild eyes, a ringing voice. As he looked at this prophetic presence on top of the wall, a voice cried out, "Don't look to me, I'm not the light. I can only show you the way to the light. I can only point the way to the feast."

The man began to walk around the wall, but the figure on top yelled down to him, "It's too high, you can't get around it!"

He tried to dig under it, but the voice said, "It's too low, you can't get under it!" And when he tried to climb over it, the voice said again, "That's not the way either! You have to get help."

Of course, he thought, "I need help." We can't get to this banquet without community! If I get some friends we can boost each other up and over the wall, then pull the others up behind us."

So he ran into the streets of the city looking for help. He rapidly found three good friends who came to help him over the wall into the fulfillment of all our Christian dreams, into the city of God, into Christmas.

The three friends joined him and they began to form a human ladder to lift the first one over the wall, but, alas, they were not high enough. They needed one more helper. He went back to the neighborhood to get one more person to help.

But the only person he could find was Bernie Jones.. Distraught, he tried looking everywhere else, but the only one around was Bernie Jones, and he hated Bernie ... He had always hated Bernie Schwartz.

Bernie had hit him with a snow ball in the fourth grade, and they had been enemies ever since.

Bernie had formed a committee and not asked him to join.

Bernie had married his first girl friend, stolen his first job.

In high school, once he loaned Bernie Jones his car; Bernie wrecked it.

Bernie and others like him had ruined his neighborhood.

Bernie Jones was a different ethnic group, a different religion, a different political party, ...sexual orientation, . . . Sufi number, . . . Myers-Briggs profile.

But he couldn't get over the wall without Bernie .

He could not get into the fulfillment of God's promises without Bernie Jones!.

All his desires for life could not be achieved without relying on Bernie

It was Bernie Jones or nothing.

And so our Advent Hope.

Who is Bernie to me? Individually, or as a group?

How did he/ she become so? What would change it?

3) The Third Sunday of Advent

Scripture Readings: Is. 35:1-6, 10; James 5: 7-10; Mt. 11:2-11

I want to plant an Advent bulb, a thought that has been growing in me.

Doubt will not destroy me; indifference will!

The second reading for this Sunday contains a metaphor that captures much of the season. It has become one of the best of Advent Songs.

See the farmer patiently tending the soil, waiting for its precious yield, waiting through the winter and the spring rain. Waiting patiently.

So it is, the metaphor suggests that we wait for the coming of Jesus. We plant bulbs and wait for them to burst to life. We do not wait passively only; we water, incense, reverence, toil with them, trying to foster that life. But finally we know their sprouting is not up to us.

And doubt will not destroy them; indifference will!

The final line of that reading from James invites us to take as our models of patience, the prophets. so, again, all through Advent, we listen to the voice of the prophets, especially Isaiah. Today we listen to a vision, a hope, a dream, really an undying expectation, foretelling a better time, when God will burst in full bloom into our life. A time when parched land will bloom with flowers, when the weak will no longer be victimized, when the blind will see, the deaf will hear, the lame will leap like a stag, and those who could not even speak will break into song

Christmas in just a few days is supposed to be the reminder, the celebration that this vision has been fulfilled, that God is indeed in our midst. There is in me, perhaps in you, much doubt that this is true. So the Church and Jesus offer to us John the Baptizer as the last and greatest of the prophets. Great because he too had his doubts.

We are invited to consider John, doubting John. So let us sit with him in prison for a moment.

John has been a full speed ahead, an "in your face" kind of guy. He has ranted and raved, eaten scraps of food, worn scraps of clothing. He has insulted tax collectors representing the Romans, called the Pharisees a "brood of vipers," has railed against the military, and finally he has criticized the life-style of Herod, the local potentate. Not unexpectedly he has been imprisoned for his intemperate remarks. And now, he experiences some doubt as he faces death in prison.

John is not blind. He can look around, as we can, and see clearly that the world is a mess. This Jesus, to whom he sent his followers is certainly inspiring, but:

a lot of children were slaughtered at his birth,
a lot of sick people still suffer and die,
the Roman rascals still overrun Palestine,
Poor people still abound,
lepers are not all cleansed,
and everything but religion takes place in the temple

John has reason to doubt.

He sends people to Jesus on his behalf to ask, "Was I right? I gave it my best shot. I tried my best. Was I on the right track? Was any of it true? Are you the One who is to come?"

John, doubting John. Our best and final prophet. Our Advent Prophet, whom we are to take as a model of patience.

Jesus tells John, tells us, to look again, keep looking, look closely. He tells John's friends to go back and tell John what they see. Not everything is fixed; all pain is not removed, but the signs are there to see if you will.

Yes there is violence, but there are heroes struggling for peace.
There is hunger, but many are truly trying to feed.
There is ignorance, but some are searching, trying to teach.
There are people ravaged with disease, and those who would wish to deny them, but some of my followers are with them, loving them.

Jesus says the, says now, if I am not yet fully here, *I Am Here!*

And he goes on. He points to John and says, it's people like this, greatest of the Prophets who help me come, who prepare my way.

John is our Advent hero because despite enormous gobs of doubt, and lack of perfect evidence, he prepares, waters, reverences the soil.

He Acts! Doubt would not destroy him. Indifference will!

So John does not passively await the coming of Jesus; he hollers out that the coming is near to all who will hear. He is no reed swaying in the wind, no weak skinned dandy dressed in finest Christmas linen; he comes with his sleeves rolled up, his work shirt on, trying to make that coming happen, even to the point of prison, even to the point of death.

Advent Grace is the grace of John the Baptizer, waiting working patiently despite uncertainty for a different world, not dismayed by the time it takes in coming.

As the old song says: *He shall not, he shall not be moved; he shall not, he shall not be moved.*"

There are numerous modern heroes, modern Johns, Committed Christian people who usher in Christ's coming heroically, as Desmond Tutu helped to do in South Africa, or Oscar Romero in El Salvador, but I think a lot about a lesser known heroine, a friend named Jeannie. I remember getting a pre-Christmas letter from her telling me she had fallen and cracked her head, sustained a concussion. She apologized, saying she'd be inactive for awhile.

The week before Jeannie had delivered a huge box of hand knitted gloves, caps, sweaters, scarves for me to pass out to the people who came to our Food Bank. A couple weeks before Jeannie had sent down two boxes of Christmas gifts and toys.

I am invited to trust in the presence of Jesus even when he apparently is not in the story.

So we look at the trust of Joseph, as Matthew tells this story. In both Matthew and Luke's gospels, the early chapters are told, whether rooted in history or not, primarily to set up the themes of the entire gospel. Two things especially stand out in Matthew's version of the pre-Jesus story: Where he was before the dream, and his trust in that dream.

First, the gospel writer is careful to point out that Joseph had "already decided to put Mary away quietly." Joseph, we realize, has already decided not to subject Mary to the law that should apply to an unmarried, pregnant woman. He will not report her, will not follow the law and allow Mary to be an outcast, or worse be stoned to death. Joseph is ready to receive the promise of Jesus because he has already made a person, Mary, more important than the religious law. He already knows what Jesus will proclaim throughout Matthew's Gospel, that he is the fulfillment of the law.

Whether we decide to break the speeding law to get to the hospital to be with a sick spouse, or let ourselves be arrested protesting on behalf of immigrants, or continue to speak on behalf of full acceptance of women into Church ministry, we need to be willing to step outside legal boundaries to prepare the way for Jesus ... who came not to destroy the law but to fulfill it, that is, to help us reach its deepest meaning, the challenge to fully love.

More central to the heart of the gospel is Joseph's radical trust in the impulse, the urging of God. Joseph is told in a dream not merely not to let Mary get hurt, but to "not fear to take her as his wife," despite the evidence against her. And Joseph woke from the dream and did as he was told.

Maybe that's what Advent, in preparation for Christmas, is always about -- waking from a dream and doing what we are told, so that God can take on flesh in our world! I believe such prompting happens all the time, in large and small ways, recognized or not. More importantly, I believe the on-going reality of Christmas, the possibility of Jesus being born over and over in our midst, depends on such acts of trust in the voice of God within us.

We are all, as Joseph, invited to trust in the reality of Jesus, of God with us, even when he doesn't seem to be in the story. We trust voices urging us to heroism, dreams in the quiet of the night, telling us to marry this woman, go to this school, don't be afraid to fight for this cause, this issue, this unfulfilled dream.

For this trust to be realized we need to catch here, at the very beginning the over-arching theme of Matthew's Gospel. This telling of the story of Jesus begins and ends with a promise: *Emmanuel*, God with us. At the outset, Joseph is told the child's name will be "God with us." At the end of the story Jesus tells his followers, "I will be with you, till the end of the World."

Trust in the presence of Jesus, even when apparently absent, seems to say what Advent, Christmas, and the entire Christian story are about.

So I relish the example of people all around me, trusting in the presence of Jesus: A wife, mother of three, who risks going to graduate school despite already being overwhelmed with responsibilities at home, and church and school because God will be with her.

Or a woman willing to risk entering into marriage again, even though she has been hurt so badly twice in the past. She is able to risk loving again, because God is with her.

Or a man who uproots his family, leaves a good job, familiar surroundings, and moves from northernmost Canada to come to Portland to help create a center of spirituality because he knows God will be with him.

Or two religious women who try to do short term foster care only to discover that they are now and will be for years parents of two very troubled youth. They accept the responsibility and do it well because they believe that God is with them.

I am grateful that I live in the midst of people who take such risks, trust such dreams . . . and so do you! We are together an Advent people, helping each other to hope, to listen, to visions and dreams and trust that Jesus is with us, even when he is not terribly visible. So we let him be born over and over and over again. Christmas is just a few short days away, but before it gets here I invite each of us to stop a moment and remember our Joseph experiences -- moments in the past when we have been called, asked, challenged to take a major risk, and we woke up, and trusted in the dream. Remember such times.

Then, quietly, slowly, notice where we might be urged right now, "not to be afraid," to risk, step out . . . to put Jesus into the story, to let Jesus be born.

5) Christmas

Scripture Readings: Is. 9:2-4, 6-7; Titus 2:11-14; Lk. 2: 1-16

I was quite flattered one year when our Archdiocesan paper published reflections of mine on "Where God May Be Found." These thoughts were intended to help us look, as we try to do all through Advent, for the signs of God's presence, the signs of hope around us. Advent celebrates our desire to trust the unlikely, the impossible, that God is in our midst.

Most of the reflections in those articles, and most of our reflections through the Advent season look outward, away, distant from ourselves to see God's presence. That is good, but tonight it feels that such outward gaze may miss the main, the most important point.

The God we look for is not outside ourselves. The Birth of Christ we celebrate is not merely the birth of Jesus of Nazareth two thousand years ago in a small, obscure village, in the city of David, in a guest house of strangers shared with animals.

How different Christmas might be if we thought of it not just as the birthday of Jesus, but as a day of birth for us!

The Advent wreath, now fully lit, hovers over the baptistery; Christmas and Easter, birth and Baptism into life and death are one.

On the final week of Advent we remembered that the Annunciation to Mary was also an invitation to us, individually and as a body of believers, to accept the invitation to give birth to God's love in our world . . .

> in the unlikely city where we live,
> in the neighborhood of our very real, concrete lives,
> in the old or new, modern, or traditional church where
> we worship.
> Right here, Christ can take flesh.

Nothing is impossible to God.

We need to get very quiet for a moment. We need to smell the hay, to feel the arms of Mary holding not just Jesus but us. We need to hear the angel's songs, need to imagine that this celebration is for our birth . . . your birth, my birth.

What we celebrate, and try to renew each year is our sharing in this mystery. We remember not only what happened to Jesus, but what happens to us because of Jesus. We are born more deeply into the mystery. Advent marks our pregnancy, our waiting, our getting ready to give birth to hope, so that tonight we experience ourselves as this child.

Our prayerful task tonight is to name and accept and run with this birth that is happening in us, large or small, this very moment, this season, in this stage of our lives.

I remember how I very clearly, once, celebrated Christmas this way. I had been wrestling for months with an invitation from my Jesuit provincial to accept a new position. It meant leaving a warm wonderful parish to risk re-birth in late middle-age in a new place. It meant trusting in the possible new action of God in a new community, ... in a new me. It was admittedly very difficult to see how it might work, or why I should try it. But that Advent helped me to say "Yes" to yet another birth another new beginning, another effort to let whatever was grace in me be born in new people, new ways. I had morning sickness, night sweats, but finally the birth happened.

Another time, after being critically ill, I found Advent the season that helped me decide not to be an invalid, not to let myself die before death came. I wrote that Christmas a poem that seems in its own way true of all of us:

Fresh out of hope,
Expectations dimmed by dark of age and illness
Weary of an inner/outer world gone mad ...
When, despite the bumper stickers,
"Birth Happens!"

Heart starts again,
Blood pumps through brain and body,
Spirit stirred by stable full of promise.
"Birth Happens."

The Jesus story, told again,
Denies my darkness,
Will not let me fold my tent
When love is pitched beside it.
"Birth Happens,"
In me and around me.

So I will live while life endures
And love as best I can
And tell the Jesus story
To myself and you.
The story starts each time
"Birth Happens"

"Merry Christmas"
From an Easter point of view
From one, if not exactly risen from the dead,
Still, close enough to say
"Birth Happens."

But this is not just my story. In its own way, Christmas is the story of each of us, all of us together. Somewhere in you, your life, your family, your job, your relationships, Christ is, or can be born tonight. Where is it? What is new, what is breathing, booming, birthing in you?

" ... for Christ plays in ten thousand places,
Lovely in limbs, and lovely in eyes not his
to the Father, through the features of (our) faces"

These immortal lines from a far better Jesuit poet capture our Christmas celebration. Tonight each of us play, dances, celebrates our new life together before God. We sing, we laugh, perhaps we cry, and tomorrow we will be the only Christ some people will ever meet.

A few days before one Christmas we found, down in the basement of St. Leo's old rectory, an ancient statue of our patron, St. Leo the Great. The statue was severely broken. A chunk had gone from the head of the statue; it had no lower arms or hands. Just after Christmas we took that statue over to a food bank the parish ran and draped the battered form of our patron in the green work jacket that the Food Connection workers and volunteers wear. The statue stood there for years, perhaps still, as a beaten up reminder that those workers and volunteers are St. Leo's hands now, the only hands he has. This ancient saint still feeds the poor through them.

So it is Christmas and all of us are born today;

We are the saints; we are the minds, hands, hearts, voices, lips; we are the enfleshment of God; we are the Body of Christ, born anew, born again, this Christmas night!

6) The Solemnity of Mary, The Mother of God—January 1

Scripture Readings: Num; 6:22-27; Gal:4:4-7':1 2"16-21

I remember once gazing at a reproduction of a famous paint-ing of today's gospel scene, <u>The Adoration of the Shepherds,</u> by Bartolome Murillo which hangs in the Wallace Collection in London. Murillo must have been somewhat taken by the scene since he painted at least six different versions of the shepherds at the crèche. The dominant color of the painting is of shades of brown. The ox and the donkey are in brown as, in a lighter brown, is the straw in the manger and on the floor. Joseph wears a brown cloak as do two of the shepherds kneeling and gazing at the baby. On the left hand side of the painting is a woman (a wife of one of the shepherds, presumably) not looking at the crib but at a little boy, her son, who is smiling broadly back at her. She and the boy also are dressed in brown.

Mary stands out wearing a red gown and she is looking at the baby, not at the shepherds. Both Mary's face and the fragile body of the baby in the feeding trough are translucently and brilliantly white. Clearly, in many ways, the picture is a story of a mother's love, the shepherd's wife's love for her son and Mary's for her tender babe.

Hans Urs von Balthazar once wrote:

After a mother has smiled for a long time at her child, the child will begin to smile back; she has awakened love in its heart and in awakening love in its heart, she awakes also recognition.

Awakening love and recognition within a child's heart is a result of more than just a mother's smile, her voice is also important. Mothers don't just cuddle babies and smile at them, they also speak to them. This hearing the mother's voice beckoning the child to come outwards towards a bigger world even when there isn't yet any real understanding of what is being said, is vital to bringing a child to self-awareness and speech.

We come out of the darkness and chaos of infancy precisely to the extent that we are called out of the darkness and chaos of infancy by the voices, especially our mother's voice, that cajole, caress, reassure and keep forever luring us beyond ourselves. During the critical early months of a child's life, it is the mother's voice that does most of this. That is why the first language we learn is called our 'mother tongue'. There are no father tongue languages. It's the mother's voice that first caressed us and lured us out of unthinking, inarticulate darkness. Rainer Marie Rilke says that an infant's journey into human awareness depends upon the mother's voice displacing " the surging abyss."

In this Sunday's gospel Luke presents Mary, just days after the grueling journey to Bethlehem and the amazing birth, carrying out the promise she had made to Gabriel. The child is healthy and cuddly, and the angels, unable to contain their joy, have once more danced hugely into Mary's life through the shepherds to whom the angels appeared. Even the animals seem to understand.

Mary is presented to us by Luke as a woman of deep prayer, reflection and being present to God in the moment. We are told that she quietly" kept all these things, reflecting on them in her heart," a phrase we meet again when Luke tells of Jesus lost in the temple at age 12. This reflectivity is told to realize a most reflective son.

Today's feast is of Mary the mother of God. It can be hard to understand that phrase since all Christians agree that God is without beginning. It seems that a God without beginning cannot be born.. But Jesus is fully human and as a human, a man, so has to be born like any child. Mary, whom the early church proclaimed, theotokos—bearer of God.

We can connect this gospel also with our reading from Paul about crying Abba, Father. If we take seriously the incarnation, along with the full divine "emptying out' it entails according to Paul, we can wonder how this child Jesus came to be nurtured in his Jewish faith. Given the culture of Jesus' time and place, the child was first nurtured in his mother's world and only later initiated by his father into the world of men. Jesus almost certainly (as most children do) learned to pray on Mary's lap. So, it is not too great a speculative leap to conjecture that Jesus' striking way of addressing God with that intimate term, Abba (something like our Daddy or papa) was also something learned from his mother. What a powerful testimony to the power of a mother's intimate moments with her child. We might remember this when we pray later the Our Father which in its original language was Abba.

In a moving musical composition, Like Winter Waiting, John Foley S.J. has Joseph sing about Mary, "Who is this women?". The question for Joseph and for us, of course, is really: "Who is this woman for me?" For us too we know that who Mary is for us depends on us, on our care for her and commitment to her as our mother. You might ask, "How much care and commitment should I have for Mary? But isn't that a backwards way to think about our relationship to any person, especially Mary. Maybe this is a better to answer the question in the Foley song. Elizabeth said to Mary, "Who am I that the mother of my Lord should come to me?". Maybe that is what we should ask and say to Mary our mother today:" Who are we that the mother of our Lord should come to us?"

I stressed Mary as prayerful, a mother who taught Jesus how to pray as a human infant and small baby. As our mother we can also ask her to teach us how to pray. Archbishop Fulton Sheen, in his famous television broadcasts in the 1950's, used to always end with a request for Mary to teach us to pray, using Mary Dixon Thayer's poem:

> Lovely Lady, dressed blue, teach me how to pray!
> God was just your little boy, tell me what to say!
> Did you lift Him up sometimes, gently on your knee?
> Did you sing to Him the way my mother did to me?
> Did you hold His hand at night?
> Did you ever try telling stories of the world ? O! and did he cry ?
> Do you really think He cares if I tell Him things—Little things
> that happen ?

And do the angels' wings make noise ? And can He hear me
if I speak low ?
Does He understand me now? —Tell because you know.
God was just your little boy, and you know the way.

Another Mary, the poet Mary Oliver, also tells us how to pray:

Praying doesn't have to be the blue iris, it could be weeds in a vacant
lot, or a few small stones; just pay attention, then patch a few words
together and don't try to make them elaborate, this isn't a contest but
the doorway into thanks and a silence in which another voice (it could
be Mary's, it could be Jesus') may speak.

7) Feast of Epiphany

For many years, believing it could not be improved, upon I simply read, or recited the following poem, which captures the mystery and the challenge of the manifestation of Jesus in our midst. No more apocryphal than the gospel story itself, the poem is, you may say "satisfactory.

A quite brief reflection follows the poem

The Journey of the Magi
T. S. Eliot

'A cold coming we had of it,
Just the worst time of the year
For a journey, and such a journey:
The ways deep and the weather sharp,
The very dead of winter.'
And the camels galled, sore-footed, refractory,
Lying down in the melting snow.
There were times we regretted

The summer palaces on slopes, the terraces,
And the silken girls bringing sherbet.

Then the camel men cursing and grumbling
And running away, and wanting their liquor and women,
And the night-fires going out, and the lack of shelters,
And the cities hostile and the towns unfriendly
And the villages dirty and charging high prices:
A hard time we had of it.

At the end we preferred to travel all night,
Sleeping in snatches,
With the voices singing in our ears, saying
That this was all folly.

Then at dawn we came down to a temperate valley,
Wet, below the snow line, smelling of vegetation;
With a running stream and a water-mill beating the darkness,
And three trees on the low sky,
And an old white horse galloped in
away in the meadow.
Then we came to a tavern with
vine-leaves over the lintel,
Six hands at an open door dicing for pieces of silver,
And feet kicking the empty wine-skins.
But there was no information, and so we continued
And arrived at evening, not a moment too soon
Finding the place; it was (you may say) satisfactory.

All this was a long time ago, I remember,
And I would do it again, but set down
This set down
This: were we led all that way for

Birth or Death? There was a Birth, certainly,
We had evidence and no doubt. I had seen birth and death,
But had thought they were different;
this Birth was
Hard and bitter agony for us, like
Death, our death.
We returned to our places, these Kingdoms,
But no longer at ease here, in the old dispensation,
With an alien people clutching their gods.
I should be glad of another death.

In this time, these days, if we have glimpsed the mystery, if sometime in our lives, no matter how long ago, we met and even fell in
love with our incarnate God, have we become "at home with an
alien people clutching their gods."

Perhaps, as we end this Christmas season, we would be glad of
another death.

8) Second Sunday of the Year

Scripture Reading: Jn. 1:29-34

We know, but sometimes forget that the early church didn't celebrate Christmas. For centuries the feast was that of Epiphany. The important reality was not that Jesus was born, but that he eventually, gradually became manifest, visible to us. So the celebration of the wise men coming to the crib expanded into the Baptism at the Jordan, the wedding feast of Cana, and every other telling of the initial appearances of Jesus in our midst. Although, this Sunday, we are, back into green vestments and "Ordinary time," we really continue in the spirit of Epiphany. We celebrate the gradual revelation of Jesus as one of us, in our midst.

Specifically, this Sunday we listen to the evangelist John's version of the baptism of Jesus. We do not witness the event, but are told of it through the eyes of the Baptizer sometime later.

What a marvelous scene! Jesus comes up the road towards John and a group of his disciples. John points at Jesus and tells them who this young man is, "The lamb of God." "An amazing event happened not long ago at the river when he and I met. This Jesus is eminently worth knowing, worth following. He is the servant, the Messiah for whom we have been waiting for ages."

The synoptic versions recount the baptismal event as essentially a profound religious experience of Jesus: God speaks to him telling him he is Son, he is beloved. This experience impels Jesus to beginning his public ministry.

In John's gospel the event is rather a manifestation to John the Baptizer of the identity of Jesus that frees him to send his followers to become disciples of this Jesus.

I am fascinated by the way John's Gospel always contains everything in every event. John tells us everything he knows and everything about Jesus is known from the outset. For example, he names Jesus "The Lamb of God." What would that title have meant to the disciples at the beginning. "Lamb of God" is a title that will only make sense in the context of the Paschal mysteries. It will only have meaning when Jesus transforms the Jewish feast into the sacrament of a new covenant between God and us. Only when Jesus has become a lamb that was slain, and the sacred meal is not a sacrificed animal, but his flesh, his blood. Only at the end of the story, will this title John gives at the beginning make sense.

But perhaps there is more to that title. Perhaps John teases his readers with a deep biblical awareness of one of our primary stories. Hidden in this title is a reminiscence of Abraham walking with his son, Isaac, up the hill, God's mountain. Abraham dreads the prospect, but is willing to sacrifice Isaac back to God if that is necessary for the fulfillment of the very promise built on Isaac's existence. Abraham cannot see how he can be the "father of many nations" if Isaac is dead; still he moves towards that mountain altar. As they climb Isaac asks "Where is the animal for sacrifice.?" Abraham replies, "God will provide a lamb." In the story God doesn't. What they find is a ram. The lamb comes later. 2000 years later God provides the lamb; the lamb of God is Jesus, son of the Father, sacrificed. John plants that, providing historical, covenant awareness here at the very beginning of the Jesus story.

Also, John knows and tells his disciples here in the very first scene, "I have seen and have testified, that this is the Son of God." In Mark, the earliest Gospel, only at the end, at the cross, is the Centurion able to assert with authority, "Truly, this is God's Son!" In John's telling we know all about Jesus already.

So what does this epiphany, this manifestation mean for us today?

Let me go back to the beginning. Imagine John, here with us, pointing out Jesus. Here, right at the beginning of the new year, the liturgical year, John points out to us Jesus! For the rest of the year we will be looking at this Jesus. And right here the question arises. Am I willing to follow him? Because we have been through it all already, like John, we know the story even at its beginning.

Am I willing to risk everything, to stake everything on following this Jesus? Am I willing to take seriously the story that this is the one who will set me, set us free? Put with more challenge, am I willing to listen to the voice, the words, the message of this Jesus rather than all the cultural voices that surround me, inviting my fidelity?

Am I willing to select my family choices,, my job, where I live, who I relate to, how I spend my leisure time, what I read, . . . everything to the values and vision of this Jesus.

Throughout this coming year we will be listening to the story of Jesus as Matthew's gospel tells it to us. In this telling Jesus will invite us to be happy, to find human blessedness in ways so different from our world. Our world tells us we will be happy if we get enough stuff. Jesus says, "Happy are the poor in Spirit." Our world tells us we will be happy if we can avoid pain and suffering by using the right deodorant, or getting in "the club," or a tax sheltered annuity. Jesus says "Happy are they who weep," for only those who weep can finally be comforted. Jesus invites us to be vulnerable in a world that says, "Be strong."

Am I willing to hear this story over again, and risk my life on it this year?

At the end of Matthew's Gospel Jesus tells us how our lives will finally be judged. Did we get it right? We religious folks might rather be judged on religious grounds. Did I go to Church? Did I say the right prayers? Did I have the right ideas, orthodox ideas, in my head? Did I read and believe The New Catechism? Did I insist on the Real Presence and insists that women were incapable of making that presence real? And Jesus says "I was hungry did you feed me, thirsty, naked, in prison, on the margins of your world; did you care?" If we follow Jesus he will insist that our lives matter not because of what we believe, or our religious practices, but whether or not we love. Especially whether we love those most in need.

Perhaps, right here at the beginning of the gospel of the year, I need to acknowledge that I want to look for an easier path, an easier person to follow. Or, perhaps, I am ready to follow John's finger pointing at Jesus, willing to come to this altar and eat his flesh, drink his blood, risk his vision.

Will you come with me into this liturgical year, this not so ordinary time?

9) Third Sunday of the Year

Readings: Is: 8:23-9:3; I Cor. 1:10-13,17; Mt.4:12-23

I was in the bank one day when a teller asked a client in line if he had any plans for the day. He replied, "I hope to see Bill and Hilary sent to jail." Clearly this Trump supporter wanted his new president to fulfill his harshest promises.

Outside a group of about 20 women with pink hats on were waiting for a bus on their way to join some 50,000 others who were desperately hoping president Trump will not do most of the things he said he would.

Two camps, two ideologies. As Paul lamented in the 2nd reading today, some are in one faction, some in another, but all ought to belong to the one same body. That's very difficult to come by.

Choosing to follow or be unwilling to follow a Trump is, or can be, for us, rooted in how we see following Jesus. What values do we give ourselves to? What values do we live for? What values would we die for.

I was struck by the recent powerful, if painful movie Silence in which naive idealistic young Jesuit missionaries go to Japan hoping to find a lost or perhaps apostate brother and to serve the handful of hidden poor people trying to be Christians in that land still. They start with a passion, a certainty that still astounds me. They will go through any suffering to bring Christ to these people . . .even as they see these people die to protect them.

With these thoughts and feelings in my mind and heart.... The passionate reactions to our most reactionary president the fanatic passion of those young Jesuits, I come to today's gospel, to Jesus, calling his first followers as Matthew tells the story . . . apparently eventually his story, as the writer of this gospel.

Imagine, if you will, Jesus walking along the beach. He sees two brothers and, although apparently a total stranger to them, he bids them follow him and change from fishermen to fishers of men and women, whatever that means. And there was such a power in his manner, his words, his very being that they drop everything and follow him. Could anyone have such magnetism to evoke such immediate and total response? Apparently Jesus did

And then his ministry begins....He goes about preaching, healing, inspiring people wherever he goes.

You and I come here as followers of Jesus. What does that mean to me.

Obviously to many I know that meant to go for a long walk with other people in silence, being willing to stand up for the rights of women, minorities, the poor that seem under threat today.

For many it seems to be willing to speak out, speak up for young people here in our nation illegally, but who have never known any other home whose presence among us is threatened.

For some it means insisting that health care is a right, not a privilege and that any decently human nation would help to provide that care for all its people, or that our nation thrives because we welcome those from other nations and try to build bridges to help them come and grow among us rather than walls to keep them from us. Some walk in silence, believing they are followers of Jesus when they want to insist that we are one world on one planet and that we need to protect our planet and also care for all the people who inhabit it with us....For followers of Jesus it cannot be 'America First,' but all of us together.

Come after Jesus means many things, daily, everyday things, like providing for our own family, but looking out for our neighbor too, like paying workers a fair wage, giving our employer a full days' work.

I invite us know to simply, quietly imagine ourselves on that beach
See Jesus walk up and begin to walk by, then
Turn, and invite us to come with him . . .
How do I respond?

10) Fourth Sunday of the Year

<u>Readings</u>; Zeph.. 2:3; 3:12-13; 1 Cor. 1: 26-31; Mt. 5:1-12

Not long after I became a priest, a Methodist minister and myself were doing a workshop for parents on teenagers and drug use. It was a most difficult time of enormous change in the Church, in our society; the toll on families was great. One of the parents kept insisting on telling the kids what God's commandments were. I remember saying, in the course of the evening that we Christians, both in our own living and in teaching our children, had to get the emphasis off the commandments and onto the beatitudes which were Jesus life directions for us. A man in the assembly stood up and yelled at me to take off my collar for I was a disgrace to the priesthood for undermining the commandments.

I have since thought deeply about the relationship, the similarities and differences between our ancient rule of law, the Ten Commandments, and the new law of Jesus, what we call the Beatitudes, which we just heard proclaimed again today. I still stand by my earlier contention.

Indeed there are many similarities.

The entire passage and the gospel of Matthew itself are deliberately framed to present Jesus as a "new Moses," one who has been led out of Egypt, coming down from the mountain to tell God's people a vision for them.

The text supports the theory that Matthew intended there to be 10 not 8 beatitudes, echoing deliberately the Decalogue that Moses gave to the people.

The entire "sermon on the Mount," of which the beatitudes are but the beginning, is rooted in God's promise. We heard again today in Zephaniah, that those who are gentle, lowly will inherit the land, will enter into the promised land, will finish with jubilation this Exodus journey . . . the journey we call "Life."

Finally, Jesus like John before him, and all the prophets of the Hebrew scriptures from Moses on, speaks of reforming our lives because the "kingdom of God is at hand." Every sentence of this message is about reform for the reign of God, an outline of how God's reign can take possession of our lives.

Still, If there are similarities, the differences are profound:

This new message is rooted in the prophetic word of Jeremiah of a day when God will put his law not on stony tablets, but in our hearts. Every word of this mountain sermon speaks to converted hearts, not merely modified behavior.

The message of Jesus is positive, behavioral. With the exception of the positive command to honor our father and our mother, the rest of the Decalogue tells us what *not* to do. We could apparently best keep these commands by doing nothing, by being dead. The invitation of Jesus is to life, to an active, assertive doing of love, in a series of invitations we can **never** measure and **never** finish. We can know whether we have ever born false witness or kept the Lord's Day holy, but we will never be able to honestly say that we have mourned enough for human suffering, or hungered sufficiently for what is right, or finally and forever brought about peace.

The commandments can be heard as a *mirror* held up to life with which we can see our good or bad reflection, see how poorly we may have done. The beatitudes are a *prism* through which we can hear the invitation of God to happiness, beatitude. They do not tell us as much about ourselves as they do the values of God, the vision of God.

The commandments are something we can apparently do on our own, by will power. The beatitudes are something we need to be converted into, things God does in us as we put on the mind and heart of Christ.

The commandments offer a series of proscriptions taken for the most part from the surrounding cultures, reasonable rules for a well ordered society on which every right thinking person may agree. The beatitudes are paradoxical, not reasonable. They are counter cultural to our world, or any human world so far. They don't make immediate apparent sense. They turn the world upside down, invite us to look at everything differently. The are the message of one who says "die to find life, take up a cross, go an extra mile, turn another cheek." How can those who weep, or those who hunger and thirst, or those who are persecuted be happy? It does not, at first blush, make sense.

The beatitudes are also, perhaps, not so much a list of an entire gamut of things to do. I suspect we are invited to discover one out of which we most live our lives. Some will be known as gentle, some as compassionate, some as living very, very simply. Others will be passionate for peace; some most willing to suffer for what they know to be right. Perhaps we only embody them all as a community of the followers of Jesus, each individual living one beatitude more than the others. Yet no one can live any beatitude fully without including the others since they are not disembodied, but enfleshed attitudes towards life that spill over into one another in any real person living them.

Finally we do not have here a blueprint for success in any worldly way. In the deepest sense a life lived out of these beatitudes will not "work" in human terms. The fruit promised in them, that we will be blessed, will be happy, involves insistence that we will weep, be persecuted, judged, condemned . . . yet somehow in the midst of that, happy.

All of which leads us, has lead me, at least, to a life long of wondering whether what Jesus proclaims is true? Is this message credible? Is this indeed where happiness lies? And I invite you to wonder the same. Do the people you know who live out these values seem happy?

I remember asking a group of high school seniors who they knew personally that they thought was really happy. All of them wanted to be quite rich, or great athletes, or find themselves in some other arena that the world judges success. The people they saw in their experience as most happy were, for example, teachers who gave hundreds of extra hours to help them, or a mother who truly laid down her life for her children, or a generous and unselfish friend. Amazingly they saw but could not accept the paradox.

Who do you see who is happy, blessed?

Each time I preach on this gospel I know I am delighted to have known a poor Sanctuary family from El Salvador who enriched our parish with their poverty of fact and spirit.

Recently, I spent an hour with a wonderful woman who works with street people, especially prostitutes. As we spoke, she wept deeply because one of "her" women had disappeared. Her very sorrow, her ability to feel the pain, is, ironically the source of her deepest joy in life.

One of the happiest people I have known was a Jesuit friend of mine who spent many hours, days and weeks in jail for various demonstrations -- to stop the war in Vietnam, or halt the building of nuclear submarines, or to close the School of the Americas. Every fiber of his being hungered and thirsted for justice, and was willing to suffer persecution to slake that hunger. And he was happy to his core, perhaps the most humorously delightful person I have ever known.

I will be forever grateful to have lived and worked alongside Archbishop Raymond Hunthausen who endured persecution, in-sults, slander with an incredible peace and blessedness.

These and so many invite me to trust the message of Jesus (a message so much more demanding than that of commandments) the paradoxical message of the Beatitudes, to reform my life, and to enter the promised land of God's incredible happiness.

11) The Fifth Sunday

Scripture Readings: Is. 58:6-10; I Cor. 2:1-5; Mt. 5: 13-16

In an old Hasidic legend a Rabbi was quizzing his pupils:

"How can one determine the hour of dawn, when night ends and day begins?"
One student replied: "When from a distance you can tell the difference between a dog and a sheep."
"No," answered the rabbi.
"Is it when you can distinguish between a fig tree and a grapevine?" asked a second.
"No!"
"Tell us then, Rabbi!"
"When you can look into the face of any human being and you have enough light to recognize your sister or your brother .... Until then it is night and darkness is still with us."

Religion is relationship, not rules

We are still listening to the Sermon on the Mount. Clear, simple terribly straight forward. Today we heard the brief section between the beatitudes and a long passage with 7 parts (that is, <u>all possible truth,</u> in Jewish numeration) that transposes the old law into the new. Every section will begin "You have heard it said, . . . " and move to ". . . but I say to you." In every instance Jesus will move the old law on stony tablets into a new law written on fleshy hearts, offering a new light to the world.

At the heart of each section moving from an old teaching to a new one, as in the beatitudes we reflected on last Sunday, is the simple truth:

Those who walk in Christ's life have light to see that every man is brother, every woman, sister.

Religion is not rules but relationships.

The Gospel statement today is unusually simple, clear direct. You can search the commentaries if you want but none say much of anything except what the gospel itself says. You <u>are </u>the salt of the world. You <u>are </u>the light of the world. You <u>are</u> a city on a hill. Jesus insists that who we are and what we do as his followers needs to be seen, that real religion is relationship, not rules. You are to be seen not so people praise you, but so they can praise the God who has changed your hearts. It's very, very clear.

Let us take a moment and consider the wonderful first reading. "Deal your bread to the hungry," Isaiah says. "Shelter the homeless, clothe the naked," that your light can shine. "No oppression, no false accusations, no malicious speech. Your light will shine in darkness."

In the sacred scripture of our Hebrew ancestors concern for the needy of our world is a central proof that light shines in darkness, that dawn has come ... when we can see a human face as the face of our brother, our sister. When we can see that religion is relationships, not rules. Social Ministry is not an adjunct, not peripheral, not extra in our church life. It is not a requirement if our parish happens to be in a poor part of town. Care for our sisters and brothers is at the very heart of our life as a church.

Two blocks down from a parish where I used to minister, in a store front, the "Metropolitan Church," gathered each Sunday. As in most cities this was an ecumenical Church ministering to gay people. One weekend as we listened to this gospel that community was having a three day vigil for victims of AIDS. How important it was for our Catholic community to gather with them in prayer, to be with them, holding before God the victims of this terrible disease; our sisters, our brothers, suffering.

That same weekend was also "U. S. World Marriage Day. In the light of this gospel, how important to see that the sacrament of marriage especially invites men and women together to become light, salt, city to each other and to all. Marriage is called sacramental precisely because it makes holy relationships, witnesses to God's light, God's covenant with us.

In marriage two people have courage to stand before each other and all of us and say not just "friend," not just "brother," or "sister" but "flesh of my flesh, bone of my bone." They say "I want to be a sign to you of God's faithful love, in good times and bad, in sickness and health, even when you let me down. I want to be sacrament to you."

And this couple joins hands together and takes this gospel very seriously, saying to the rest of us:

"We want our love, over time to become a sign to you that love can last, that fidelity is possible, that God's covenant is fleshed out, that religion is relationships, not rules."

This doesn't always work in marriage, and it is never easy. But we can thank God today and pray for those married couples in our midst who are muddling through, not just surviving, but thriving, as they mirror to us the enfleshed love of God, the light of the world.

As we continue with Eucharist today, in a variety of ways, we let light shine, and we look into each other's faces and say: "My sister, my brother, my husband, my wife, my friend . . . ." We celebrate in Eucharist that our religious conviction and commitment is about the constant building of deeper and deeper relationships with one another in ways that become salt to our earth, light to our world, a city on a hill

12) An Alternate Homily: For a Parish Baptism

Salt of the Earth! Me? Light of the World! Me? Let my light shine so that people will bless God! Not Me.

Into what do we baptize children? Into what do we invite parents to make a deeper commitment and offer to help them live it out? Salt? Light?

Let me offer some vignettes from a period in my life.

First story. At a Religious Education Congress in Los Angeles I heard "Tony," an increasingly famous guitar player/ singer. Tony has no arms. He plays the guitar with his feet. He was invited to sing at the opening session of the Congress on the theme of Evangelization. He bounded on stage, sat down, took the guitar in his feet and played beautiful music, then sang gloriously. He told us about his experience of singing for the Pope. After he sang the Pope applauded, then bounded across the stage to embrace him. Tony said he wished he had arms! John Paul II kissed Tony on the cheek then turned to go back to his seat. Suddenly the Pope turned around and said to him, "Keep giving people hope!" Tony said this word changed his life. He saw now who he was and why he was alive; to give people hope. That's why he spoke first at a conference on Evangelization. Spreading the Gospel is about giving people hope!

Second story. Flying home from that congress I read <u>USA Today</u>. In the financial section I discovered a not quite sad story about a couple in Pennsylvania trying to make it on two incomes, just getting started in marriage. In 1990, they *only* had a combined income of $78,000 between them and it was so tough to make ends meet and at the same time to save money for a down payment on a house. They were only able to set aside $25, 000 per year and they needed $100,000! Their income statement indicated a combined $10,000 for entertainment, and something called "mad money." Their contributions to church and other charities was $150.00 (even less than the 1.5% that is average for most U.S. church goers!)

Third story. Two weeks before I listened to parents preparing for their children's baptisms in our parish as they responded to the question: "What do you ask of Christ's Church for your child?" The simple answer is "Baptism." The longer answers were more complex, more beautiful. Each parent spoke in their own way about needing help offering to their children a vision, a way of life, a light, a taste of salt. Each wanted a community to help them to be a sign, to be a taste. They hoped we would be that community for them.

Fourth vignette. Also at one of the baptismal sessions. A parent talking about the baptism of their first child. As they prepared to come to church they got a phone call telling them that the baby's grandmother, the mothers' mom, had just died! As they drove to Church for the baptism they reflected on birth and death. The baptism became a profound experience of the cycle of life, death, new life that is so quintessentially Christian. In every parish we celebrate funerals during the week, then change our mood and come and baptize on Sundays. We acknowledge that life and death are very close, interweave, overlap. We keep wrestling with the question: What is life about? What does it mean?

Is it about playing the guitar with your feet, and giving hope to others?
Is it about saving $25,000 a year, giving nothing away, and getting your first house?
Is it about being light? Salt?

Fifth reflection: I had gone to the Southern California Religious Education conference to give two talks. I'm not sure why. It is a prestigious place to talk. Many big names are there. They pay well. I have relatives in the area that I don't see often and it is convenient to have my way paid. I love to talk. Did I go because I wanted my light to shine so people would see and praise me? Or so they would praise God? My motives were quite mixed; I simply wasn't sure.

In one talk I spoke about religious experience, how we might recognize God's presence in our lives. When I finished my remarks I invited questions. The first respondent, rather than asking a question, told the audience of about 600 people about an experience of her own – an experience of God. When she finished another person rose and did the same. Then another, and another. In all about ten people stood and praised God for God's amazing presence in their lives. It was an awesome experience for me, and, I suspect, the entire room. At the end they clapped, ostensibly for me, but really for God and though I am never really sure deep down why I do things, I know I want to speak of God, speak for God, give witness to God's love. It was good to see that here, at least, it happened.

Out of these stories a simple piece of Gospel wisdom is revealed. Jesus' very honest, very simple, very personal invitation to each of us (yes, to other apostles, to holy folks, to special people) but also *personally to each of us* to be light of the world, salt of the earth. To be that light, that salt by the witness we give of care for the hungry, the homeless, the afflicted, the oppressed, that is, by the way we give people hope. And we are invited to give a public witness, not hiding our action or our faith. We are not to hide our good deeds, not to avoid being noticed lest others think us better than we are. We are to love deeply and honestly and let others see that love so they can be led to the God who inspires us.

And honestly my friends, this is what baptism is about. In a very public, community celebration we invite children to share in the vision, the values, the guitar playing, the singing despite the pain ... all the values of Jesus. We look death in the face and keep affirming life. We keep pulling people out of the baptismal waters, re-born and trusting that this re-birth lasts forever. We commit ourselves to acting and loving and doing so publicly because we want God to be praised, the same God who works in us even when we are not very sure why were are so acting.

13) The Fifth Sunday
of the Year Alternative

(This homily is a gift from a friend, Fr. Michael Ryan, pastor of St. James Cathedral, in Seattle, given on Feb. 5. 2017)

Last Sunday, a parishioner expressed to me his disappointment that I hadn't addressed in my homily the current situation in our nation with regard to immigrants and refugees. He thought that the gospel of the Beatitudes presented the perfect opportunity to do so and he was probably right. All I could tell him was that the news about that highly controversial executive order didn't break until very late in the week and I had no time to prepare a new homily. I suppose I could also have told him that I was wary of speaking from the pulpit about a subject that some would regard as purely partisan politics which, current headlines not with standing, have no place in the pulpit. Political controversies come and go – one minute they flourish and the next they fade – but God's Word endures forever. And the pulpit is for preaching God's Word. Right?

But what happens when the Word of God clearly clashes with the word of our political leaders? What happens when the moral imperatives of God's Word – and our deeply held beliefs as Christians - are at odds with positions espoused by our elected leaders? What happens when to pretend otherwise or to look the other way would be nothing short of cowardice? That's the time, I would say, when a preacher finds his deepest calling, and when a community finds its greatest challenge. It's also when we realize that the Word of God doesn't live in isolation from the lives of the people to whom God speaks: on the contrary, it is in those very lives that God's Word comes to life. God's Word gets its fullest meaning when it makes great demands, disturbs consciences, and stirs people into action. And while that may involve at times what sounds like partisan politics, it's really advocating for justice. If we look to the scriptures, it is precisely this sort of thing that made life dangerous and difficult for the prophets of old. Isaiah is a good example. In today's first reading we heard him challenging people to share their bread with the hungry, to shelter the oppressed and the homeless, and to clothe the naked. But why didn't Isaiah stick to a purely religious message? Why, for instance, didn't he stick to preaching strictly 'spiritual' things about the Covenant or the Commandments? For one reason only. God. God inspired him to speak out against people who thought they were fulfilling their religious obligations by simply saying their prayers, keeping their Sabbaths, doing their fasting, offering their sacrifices, painstakingly and piously performing their religious rituals -- all the while turning their backs on the poor, the hungry, the homeless, and the dispossessed. In God's name, Isaiah exposed that hollow religiosity for what it was and he challenged the people to make their religion real by caring for the poor, feeding the hungry, sheltering the oppressed and the homeless, clothing the naked. Only then, he told them, would they be truly honoring God. Only then would their light break forth like the dawn, their wounds be healed, their prayers be heard on high. Only then would the Lord listen to them when they called for help.

Fast-forward to today. The way we deal with immigrants and refugees may sound like partisan politics but it's not. It's a matter of faith, of justice. To turn away refugees and immigrants, to close our borders to people because of their religion or national origin – people, many of whom are fleeing violence, oppression and persecution - is in direct opposition to our most deeply-held values as believers. As believers, the words from the Book of Exodus should ring in our ears, "You shall not oppress the alien... you shall befriend the alien, for once you too were aliens in the land of Egypt."

All of this is in opposition, too, to some of our most deeply held values as Americans. Our country, as you know, has a long and glorious history of welcoming refugees and immigrants – 'the tired, the poor, the huddled masses yearning to breathe free.' Our own parents and grandparents were among those huddled masses, and so are many of you! And that's not to say that reasonable precautions shouldn't be taken for the safety of all. Of course they should and they already are. Our nation has one of the most rigorous screening processes for immigrants and refugees in the world. But when reasonable precautions turn into a paranoia that whips up suspicion toward an entire population or religious group, we believers need to speak up and speak out.

My friends, this message is not about politics, it's about principle. It's about basic Christian morality. Pope Francis says it so well, "It is hypocrisy to call yourself a Christian and chase away a refugee or someone seeking help, someone who is hungry or thirsty. If I say I am a Christian but do these things, I am a hypocrite." And Pope Francis is far from alone here. St. John Paul II, in calling the

Church to reach out to refugees said – in the strongest possible terms (and, I would say, in light of recent developments, quite prophetic terms), "It is necessary to guard against the rise of new forms of racism or nationalism which attempt to make any of our brothers and sisters scapegoats."

In today's reading from Matthew's gospel, Jesus challenged his disciples to engage with the world around them. He didn't want timid followers who would tiptoe around – quiet, cautious, fearful. No, he wanted his followers to make a difference in the world around them – to add the flavor and zest that salt adds to food. He also wanted them – wanted us – to be light: to bring light to the dark, muddled and confused world around us, the light of his gospel, the light we dare not hide under a bushel basket, the light that reveals, in this present moment, ugly things like nativism and nationalism, calling them what they are; the light that is willing to challenge every injustice where we find it, beginning with threats to life in the womb and including every other threat to human life and livelihood, including the threat of deportation that hangs over millions of mothers, fathers and children; the discrimination and even persecution that our Muslim brothers and sisters are currently experiencing.

My friends, on the day of our baptism we were each given a lighted candle and told to keep it burning brightly and to walk always as "children of the light." That is our calling, our sacred calling. We do it alone and we do it together, but do it we must, for we are the light of the world. And the world is waiting, my friends. The world is waiting! The world is waiting!

14) The Sixth Sunday of the Year

Scripture Readings: Sir. 15:15-20; 1 Cor. 2:6-10; Mt. 5: 17-34

Perhaps the major temptation of Christianity is our inclination to adore the messenger and ignore the message! It is, after all, far easier to worship Jesus than to listen to what he says and let it direct my life!

Throughout these weeks we listen to the Sermon on the Mount, the central presentation of the message of Jesus in Matthew's Gospel. Matthew frames the message of Jesus as fulfillment of Jewish hopes and promises, directed primarily for Jewish Christians, or prospective Jewish converts to the Christian community. As we have already begun to see in this liturgical year, Matthew uses a clever consistent literary device, presenting Jesus as the "new Moses, " the first greatest leader of this Jewish people.

Throughout the Sermon on the Mount, Matthew's Jesus parallels Moses giving the commandments to the people on Mt. Sinai, now a law no longer written on stone tablets, but on hearts of flesh. The section offered to us today spells out what the witness of the followers of Jesus will look like, and how this might be a more "blessed," or "happy" way to live than that of the former covenant. The new message is couched entirely in terms of the previous relationship between God and God's people.

Seven times Jesus says: "You have heard it said . . . . but I say to you." Seven times Jesus recalls one of the original ten commandments, or some derivative from them, only to indicate how his message fulfills, brings the true life, true meaning, invites a "heart of flesh," out of those ancient, revered directives.

No accident that, Numerically seven, for Jesus' Jewish listeners, means "whole, "full," "complete." In fact, these seven new renditions of the law invite consideration of a new creation, a new seven days.

This section of the Sermon is intimately connected with all that precedes it as Jesus offers life, a message that comes from and touches into the heart, a message meant to lead us to "blessedness" to "happiness." The message is not expressed in the negative terms of "thou shalt nots, . . ." but in the positive invitation to full and complete life.

This is a message inviting its hearers to be salt, light, witness to a world in darkness, a message calling to holiness "beyond that of the scribes and Pharisees."

The specifics of the message proclaimed today is not as harsh, or even as disturbing as it may at first appear, nor as absolute and condemnatory as oft presented by interpreters. By paraphrasing we can arrive at the heart of each of the invitations.

You have heard it said, "Don't kill." Jesus invites us not even to be angry, not to abuse another person. Rather, reconcile and make peace as quickly as possible; live non-violently.

You have heard it said, "Don't commit adultery." Jesus encourages his followers not to even look at another person as an object of lust. People (women) are not objects. Lust destroys us as people, destroys relationships, and it would be better to lose a part of ourselves than our entire person-hood. We want to see each other as person, as friend, as sister, as loved one.

You have heard it said, but previously only to men, "Don't Divorce," (except for very good reason). Jesus says to men, do not even treat women as property of yourself or anyone else. There is no reason at all to justify treating woman as if she were something you owned. Jesus speaks more to relationship than to issues of marriage and divorce.

Finally, this week, you have heard it said, "Don't swear false oaths in God's name." Jesus insists that we not swear at all. Say what we mean, be honest, straightforward, not political, not bureaucratic. Each new formulation, and those we will hear in the gospel next week, are demanding, but reasonable, and more humanly captivating than their abstract predecessors.

Two other important comments on the specifics of today's text. They have to do with Jesus relationship with laws and rules . . . a distinction our wonderful Pope Francis understands and some rebellious church leaders do not!

First, we cannot legitimately make one of the parts of this sermon more important than the others. We cannot absolutize one teaching unless we are willing to do the same with every other teaching. We cannot make *war* all right sometimes, but *divorce* never! It seems more faithful to Jesus to acknowledge that Jesus consistently speaks a very lofty moral heroism, invites us constantly to heroic sanctity. We should never kill; we should never divorce; we should never view people as objects of our sexual desires; we should never speak untruthfully. We should never approach the altar if someone has a grudge against us. All of these injunctions are equally serious.

But we will fail. *And in the face of every failing Jesus, who calls us to sanctity, will be gentle with the human inability to realize our and his ideals.*

Secondly, and perhaps most important in understanding of the entire Sermon on the Mount, this is not a new law! It is not law at all. As a teacher of ethics, Jesus does not substitute one law for another. He does not offer us a new, better, more exact entree to legalism. He does not invite us to be even exacting than the Scribes and Pharisees excoriated in Matthews' Gospel. Whenever we as a church take this sermon and turn it into rules, laws, we miss the point. Laws and rules about just wars, or capital punishment, or about divorce, or sex outside of marriage, or legitimate dishonesty miss the point of Jesus teaching. This is terribly important in the Sermon on the mount, or any other place where Jesus teaches the moral law. Jesus is not a lawgiver; Rather, he offers constantly a moral ideal, challenges us to live up to that heroic standard, and then appears ready to comfort who ever fails to do so.

Jesus suggests, invites, even demands that we cannot separate our relationships with God from our relationships with each other. He wants us to live up to our best and truest selves, to fulfill all the potentiality of being human. He insists that we acknowledge the connection between offering the gift of ourselves to God, and giving that gift to others. Jesus moral teaching is not about law, but about relationships, not about following abstract, disembodied laws, *but about being head-over-heals-in-love because we have first been loved.* It invites us to incredible generosity because we are called to be "blessed", "happy," "salt," "light," witness to the continued presence of that Jesus still teaching more by example than by word.

This homily has been somewhat academic, more a class in scripture than an inspiration perhaps. But it flows out of a need to clarify how we can take the <u>message</u> of Jesus, and <u>not just the messenger,</u> with absolute seriousness!

15) The Seventh Sunday

Scripture Readings: Lev. 19:1-2:17-18; 1 Cor. 3:16-23;Mt. 5:38-48

We continue this Sunday to listen to the Sermon on the Mount, We continue to try to accept the message as well as reverencing the messenger. We continue today the section in which Jesus 7 times teaches the fulfillment of the Hebraic covenant, saying: "You have heard it said, . . .but I say to you."

This is a most difficult passage. Difficult because it has been taken too literally, unreflectively by some; difficult because it has been totally ignored by most. This passage has been used to justify telling a wife to stay in an abusive relationship and continue to be hit, beaten, abused. It has been used to give too painless forgiveness and exoneration to sexual, psychological, verbal abusers. People have given away too much, too easily, missing the point of a kind of confrontational non-violence that marked Jesus own behavior.

Others have have pretty well decided that the words of Jesus are unrealistic, impossible, unfeasible. Catholics support capital punishment in about the same numbers as others. Christians, absurdly, generally believe war, more violence, is a legitimate way to stop violence . We are as likely as anyone to act on the theory that if you step on mine I will kick yours! Catholics in majority numbers voted for a president for whom being vindictive is the norm. These words of Jesus just don't compute, in our day, perhaps in any day.

Let me share three images as we move into the gospel today:

First, a scene from the movie Ghandi, in which an entire phalanx of Indians walk up to the British militia in an act of non-violent resistance. They are struck, clubbed, knocked to the ground. They retreat, only to re-group, bandage their wounds, get their wind, and then to come again to be struck, clubbed, knocked to the ground again. They do not resist, but neither do they turn back. This overwhelming scene is etched forever in my imagination. Perhaps in yours.

Second scene. During the struggle for civil rights in the U.S. in the late 60's, a Quaker young man named David went with a black friend to a restaurant in the deep south; he ordered a coke. Shortly, he felt a sharp point in his back and turned to see the angriest eyes he had ever beheld. When he turned around the knife was pointed at his heart. He spoke: "Friend, whether you put that knife in my heart is up to you, but in either case I want you to know, I love you!" The man dropped the knife and ran from the restaurant.

The third image. A friend of mine went to visit the Cathedral in Mexico City, a visit that became for him a kind of metaphor for life. He wanted to go to the Cathedral to pray, to be with God in a lovely and famous place. But to get to the Cathedral he had to pass through more than a hundred beggars spread all over the Plaza, each asking something of him. What to do when we want to get to a God blocked from us by so many poor people? Three choices seemed possible then, and, in hindsight, in life:

> He could walk right by, ignoring the beggars in order to visit an abstract and uninvolved God, divorced from the surrounding, pervasive suffering.

> He could try to give something to each beggar until, in a short time, he would be one of them, sharing in their poverty -- not a bad choice and perhaps a necessary one for some.

> He could arbitrarily pick one and make that one his beggar, helping in whatever way he could at least a single person. Outside the immediate scene he could try to understand why there are so many beggars and try to address that.

These three stories present what it feel like to me to talk about "turning the other cheek," of "loving your enemies" or "giving to whomever asks of you." The words are challenging, but somehow we can feel life in them. These words need not be inducements to guilt, held up like a mirror before us, showing us how bad we are. Rather these words can serve as a filter through which Jesus offers us a life we had not hitherto imagined.

The ordinary human response to violence is more violence. Faced with violence coming at us we can fight, flee, or surrender, but Jesus offers another option . . . Love Back! Go beyond what is asked. React to power with another kind of power. This response is not natural, not easy, not practical. It may not "work," and it certainly

will never be popular. Like the rest of the Sermon on the Mount it
is a word inviting us to a kind of paradoxical blessedness, happiness.
Though not apparently so, it just may be right, true, human, perfect.

If we want to make sense out of this passage we need to look
carefully, even critically at its final line about perfection. Some
translations say "Be perfect as your heavenly Father is perfect."
An excellent formulation of the Pelagian heresy which maintained
that we could make ourselves perfect, lift ourselves up by our own
bootstraps, as if we did not need love, need God's graciousness.

The New American Bible reads more accurately, "You must be
made perfect as your Heavenly Father is perfect." Perfection happens to us, not by us!

I have heard that a proper rendition of the Greek would probably
be paraphrased, "You must be perfected as your God is perfected," that is, you must become as completely who you are meant
to be, you must be as fulfilled in your being uniquely you, as God
is perfectly who God is. I'm not supposed to become God. I'm
supposed to become Pat Carroll . . . totally, fully, completely, even
perfectly Pat Carroll, a still awesome, but more manageable task.

The major point is that becoming perfect is not something we
do, but something that happens to us, over time. We do not make
ourselves perfect, we get loved into it.

"Turn your cheek," "love your enemy," "be perfect!" Tall orders
and something we can only do as everyone begins to be seen as
friend, brother, sister -- part of my family, part of my community.

I love what happened in the first session of a small faith-sharing
group in a parish where I served. As the people arrived that first

evening at an apartment house where one group was to meet, a very inebriated man entered the building with the others coming to join the group. Everyone presumed he must have come along with someone else as part of the group. They entered the apartment. The man fell down and slept, un-moving, un-moveable, soundly throughout the meeting. At the end when people went to leave each presumed whoever brought the man with them would take him home, but no one had, so no one did. Eventually all realized that the man they had simply accepted as he was did not belong there in the first place!

More recently I am deeply moved by the story of members of a black church welcoming a young white man into their bible study class . . . a man who had come to kill them.

There is a weird symbol in these stories . . . we are able to be our best and most accepting, most forgiving most perfect selves when it involves people we see as sisters, as brothers . . . people whom we have told ourselves we want to love. We love, forgive, and grow with those who have become somehow part of our community, our family, our home.

Jesus words were spoken to us as a single human family, brothers and sisters all, to one another and to Him. It is important to hear them again as we gather as a family around our Eucharistic supper!

16) The Eighth Sunday

Scripture Readings: Is. 49:14-17; I Cor. 4:1-5; Mt. 6:24-34

One thing I most like about Jesus is his oratorical style. It's like my own sometimes. I call it the "Why use one word when five will do?" approach. If a thing is worth saying one way, it's worth saying several other ways too! The gospel today, and really the entire Sermon on the Mount utilizes this approach. Jesus keeps saying the same thing, over and over, in different ways, from different directions.

Today's Gospel is yet another way of summarizing the same thing: Jesus is the fulfillment of the entire Hebraic law, the messianic completion of all that Matthew's Israelite readers had previously believed. He is the new Moses; what he says completes what Moses said before.

Today the entire Decalogue is summed up in the first commandment. "I am the Lord Thy God, thou shalt not have strange Gods before me," i.e. there is no other God but God.

The entire Sermon is summarized in this line. You cannot have two Gods, two masters. Nobody can serve, be faithful to more than one God.

Everything Jesus has said in the Sermon so far, everything we've heard over the past several weeks invites us to trust in this God more than we do in stuff (i.e. not just money, but mammon, or things).

Let me summarize the Sermon on the Mount so far.

I know it may not look or feel like it sometimes, but I have a path for you that will bring you happiness, blessedness, life, the fulfillment of all your human potential.

To achieve it you are invited to be poor in spirit, to be able to weep, to hunger and thirst for Justice, to be meek, and to be willing to be persecuted.

You are invited to be public about your good deeds, to be salt, light for the world. You are challenged to forgive injuries, to go beyond measure in sharing what you have with others, to treat other people as your sisters and brothers.

To be able to live this out you are challenged to trust that God is right and the world is wrong.

Finally, today, Jesus says the same thing from another direction; You will find your security in God, in God's love for you, and in nobody, nowhere else.

I do not by any means think it is easy to trust in God, to stake one's life on the truth of Jesus' words in this Sermon. We, like our

Hebraic ancestors, have a life-long challenge to overcome idolatry, to cease worshiping other Gods. We may not build statues of gold (though we build Pentagons) and Kingdoms to worship, but we do put our security and our hopes in all kinds of things, one at a time, or together, and thus make them our little gods. And we/ I usually try to do so alongside our worship of the real God. But the heart of today's Gospel reminds us that we can't have two Gods, two masters.

In order to understand where we really worship, who, or what we, in fact, honor as God in our very real lives it is helpful to respond to questions like these:

> Where do I give my heart? Faith, after all means *do* (give) *cor*, (heart,) to give my heart.

> What gets me up in the mornings?

> When I go to bed exhausted at night, what wore me out? Was it worth being worn out for?

> To what do I give my time, energy, my money.

> What captures my emotional life? That is, what do I dream about, worry about, fret about, long for?

Most of us, facing such questions, must acknowledge that we have a whole pantheon of little gods, capturing bits and pieces of our heart; family, job, security, sports, hobbies, material possessions, even sex, money, power, control.

Certainly as a nation, collectively, we spend an awful lot of time, energy, talent, money on our national security no matter what the cost to our own children, women, our poor, and no matter what the cost to other people, refugees, immigrants, people of poor nations. How can we consider spending billions of dollars on a wall while 15% of children are hungry in our land. How hire 10,000 more border guards when schools are without books? We have a lot of gods.

I say this not just to beat ourselves up, but just to acknowledge the reality that we spend our lives trying to serve two or more masters, and Jesus today invites us into the integrity of total trust in one, true God, a God whose care for us is total.

As we come to the end of the Sermon on the Mount and prepare for Lent, what do we hold onto? An invitation to radically trust God, the God we have met and been loved by, in Jesus. And to radically build our lives on that trust!

I once heard a wonderful story on the importance of Canon Law in the Church. It speaks also to the importance of Old Covenant in relationship to the Sermon on the Mount: Let me end these several weeks of consideration of that sermon with the story.

Once upon a time there were five rabbis arguing about what was the most important part of the revelation of God to the Jewish people.

The First rabbi maintained that the most important part was the Pentateuch, those first five books of the bible. If we knew what was in them, and lived by that, we would have everything.

The second Rabbi insisted that we did not need so much. Just the decalogue. If we knew those ten commandments, and followed them, everything else would follow.

The <u>third Rabbi</u> said we did not need so much. If one knew and followed only the first commandment -- one God, no strange or foreign Gods -- if one knew and followed that, everything else would surely follow.

The <u>fourth rabbi</u> was sure we did not need so much. If one knew only the first two words of the first commandment, "I Am" that was enough, for if one knows God, and adheres to that knowledge everything else will follow.

And the <u>fifth rabbi,</u> scratching his head for a long time, finally spoke. He was sure we did not need all those words. He reminded his fellow rabbis of the little aspirant, the ' sound, a kind of "hshhh" over the first letter of the first word of the first commandment. That's all we need, for that, "hshhh " he said is the sound Elijah heard when he met God calling him out of his cave, and if we have met God, then everything else will follow.

The Sermon on the Mount suggests simply: If we meet Jesus, everything else will follow.

If we have met God, met Jesus and let him be our master, everything else will follow. During the coming Lenten season, we enter more fully into that meeting with God in Jesus. We do that in Eucharist now.

17) The First Sunday of Lent

Scripture Readings; Gen. 2:7-9, 3:1-7; Ro. 5: 12-18; Mt. 4: 1-11

Recently I re-read *Franny and Zooey*, J.D. Salinger's great novel. I loved it. I remembered much of it, but it seemed a completely different book than the one I had loved thirty years ago. The novel hadn't changed; I had. As we begin Lent, it strikes me that the liturgical year is like reading a great novel over, year after year. We do Lent again not because Lent changes but because we do. In fact we celebrate Lent over each year to help us change, help us become more truly who we are, who God invites us to be.

We listen to the same stories, like that of Adam and Eve and they help us to change, remembering that "the problem was not the apple on the tree, but the pair on the ground." When I was young I wondered why we all have to suffer because of what Adam and Eve did. As I get older it is clear that *we are all effected* by each others' choices. This story is just about the reputed first dumb choice. But each failed relationship touches any number of lives.

Statistics tell us a single alcoholic disturbs at least five families. Every lie I tell undermines another's ability to trust. Every selfish, self-serving, human choice, every choice in which anyone tries to become "like God" (totally in charge of even our small part of the universe) effects others, effects all!

So we hear the story of human frailty and human fall differently at every stage of our lives because we keep changing.

The same is true of the Gospel story, about Jesus in the desert being tempted by his demons, wrestling with his inner voices telling him he cannot be who he thinks he is. . We begin every Lent with a version of this story. It is a Lenten passage. Forty days and forty nights of prayer and fasting. Forty days and forty nights of trying to internalize the baptism he had just experienced. Forty days and forty nights of change -- for Jesus will come out of the desert a different person, ready to begin a public life that will change the face of heaven and earth.

Just before this Gospel scene, Jesus has been with the followers of John at the River. He has joined in this baptism, this ritual of commitment, of covenant fidelity. While in the water Jesus has an overwhelming experience of God. He hears a voice telling him "You are my son, my favor rests on you."

I imagine Jesus after this event wondering how to live out the experience. How to trust this voice? What does it mean? he goes to the desert to fast and pray. At the end he is tempted. The temptations are stylized, poetic, symbolic. They say that what happened to Jesus is what happens over and over, always and ever to all of us.

Jesus was tempted not to believe what happened in Baptism! Tempted not to trust his experience of God. Tempted not to believe that he is indeed uniquely God's child, God's beloved. Jesus is tempted to have to prove it to himself . . . simply to not believe.

Jesus is tempted not to believe that he will have the bread he needs to live by, and so to make stones into something they are not.

Jesus is tempted not to believe that he is loved by God, held in God's hand, and, since he will never be harmed, to go high on the temple, so high that people look like ants . . . rather than to stay with those people, and see them, and himself as human.

Jesus is tempted not to believe that he already possesses the earth in all its fullness. This last temptation is the most pernicious. His demons take him up on the mountain, where God is revealed, the mountain from which he will teach in God's name, tempted to use that mountain top as a place of power and control, rather than revelation and service.

In all of these Jesus is tempted to prove something by a bizarre act that tempts God, that pushes God to the wall, rather than to trust what God already said to him in the waters. Jesus is tempted not to believe! Every temptation is the temptation not to believe.

In the story of Adam and Eve, the man and the woman, our mythical ancestors were tempted not to believe that everything was already theirs, that they would learn and grow and possess all they needed. They were tempted to skip a step, to go beyond human boundaries, to be something they were not. Not happy with being loved, being human, being God's so special children, they wanted to **be** God. They failed where Jesus did not. They said yes; Jesus said no.

Where sin abounds, grace does more abound, and we are faced with these two stories and the question is ours. Do we want to believe, with Jesus, who we are and are becoming? Or do we want to question and ultimately deny it with the Man, the Woman?

Often early in Lent Jesuit parishes offer a Novena of Grace in honor of St. Francis Xavier. Francis incarnates many of the themes of Lent, certainly the temptation scene today. There is a famous story of how Francis and Ignatius of Loyola met at the university of Paris, after Ignatius' conversion, but before Xavier's. Francis was apparently a "big man on campus," a dashing romancer a star athlete, successful and vain. The story says Ignatius used to walk by him and whisper in his ear, "What does it profit, Francis, if you gain the whole world and lose your soul?" A contemporary translation would say, "lose yourself in the process." What good will it do to get all those prizes and not be faithful to yourself, your integrity, your giftedness? Eventually Ignatius succeeded in getting Francis to join him and become his first and greatest follower, the first to bring the Christian message to India. Like all of us Xavier was tempted no to be his best and truest self.

This is how temptation always works with me. It invites me to be less than my real self, to deny who I really am, to deny in a sense my baptism, forgetting that I am a child of God, favored by God, with all that favor entails.

I am tired at the end of a day. I have a drink to relax. I am tempted to have five and blot out the world. If I am faithful to myself, I will come to peace with my world, not deny it. I won't need or want to blot it out

I am hurt by a friend or family member. I am tempted to rule them out of my life, my heart. I am tempted to deny the reality that they are precious to me, for they are precious to the God who is love.

I am tempted to hoard, to get more stuff, more land, more water, more property, more food ... forgetting what my native American brothers and sisters always knew, that the land is ours (or rather we are the lands) completely already.

We are tempted as a people to search for bargains, inexpensive coffee, inexpensive tennis shoes, less expensive golden do dads, though the laborer in El Salvador, India or Taiwan suffers. We are tempted to forget or deny our power over other people in a way that denies who I am, who they are . . .my brothers and sisters, sharers of this planet.

I could go on and on with the deep truth of this temptation scene. It is a truth we will spend all of Lent preparing to rediscover. The point is simple. Every temptation is the temptation to deny our humanity, to deny the truth about ourselves, to deny the baptismal reality that tells me, as it did Jesus that I am beloved son or daughter. On our journey to Easter we will keep deepening this baptismal reality until we renew it again at the Vigil.

If I believe myself to be beloved son, beloved daughter I do not have to prove it to anyone, not even myself.

People in our midst in this parish are hearing this Lenten invitation for the first time. These catechumens, today to become "the Elect." They invite us to change with them as they prepare for Baptism. We say today that we are willing to change, to take away something of whatever keeps us from being fully human, from fully believing in God's love for us as we move through Lent towards Easter.

18) The Second Sunday of Lent

Scripture Readings: Gen. 12:1-4; 2 Tim. 1:8-10; Mt. 17:1-9

A wonderful Rabbinic legend suggests that Abram was the 12th man asked to be the beginning of the Jewish tribe. The 12th one asked to pick up, in old age, and start over, start elsewhere. The 12th one asked to trust the bizarre promise that came from God. Though the 12th asked, Abram was the first to say "Yes," and with that Yes become our original "Ancestor in Faith." He was joined by his wife Sarah who is noted for laughing -- laughter being the appropriate response to God's behavior in our regard!

Because of this wonderful and obviously true legend, the line that most strikes me in the readings today is the one that says "Abram went as God directed him." The author adds the footnote that he was 75 years old when he set out, underlining what a courageous (or foolish) thing Abram was doing.

The message of the scripture today is *simply the invitation to trust our experience of God as Abraham did, and perhaps as so many* others have not!

Why does Dorothy Day totally change the direction of her life to start the Catholic Worker movement? Why does Mother Theresa leave her original religious community which she loved to form another new community? Closer to home, why does a young family with slender resources begin to take in foster children? Or why does a lay woman ministering in the church give up a job she is excellent at to take over more responsibility with less security as the head of a parish, even though she cannot fully be pastor, in an entirely new Church career? Why does a mother with small children decide to go back to school, adding to her already too full life?

Do each of these in their own way, like Abraham before them, hear a voice somehow calling them to leave behind what is familiar and go to a new place that God will show them?

Why did St. Francis Xavier, whom many Jesuit parishes honor around this time of year, leave a career of scholar priest in the safety of Post-Reformation Europe to go across the globe in poverty and misunderstanding to speak of Jesus to those who would otherwise never have heard the name. Or why did Oscar Romero, in mid-life, change his entire ecclesial orientation and move from and institutionally conservative scholar to become the simple Bishop of the poor? Why move from chancery security to martyr-inviting prophet? Closer, again, to home why does a young man return to a church he never much liked or understood after his mother's death? Or how does a man consider leaving a career of 30 years to begin a new life of service to the Church? Do they hear, somehow, God's inviting voice?

And why on earth do we have, year after year, people coming to our unlikely community to be baptized? Or move from another tradition to join our family of Faith? What is it that they see? What do they hear? How are they invited to leave whatever is familiar, comfortable, normal in their lives?

I cannot help but wonder whether for everyone who responds as any of the above, there are not 11 who never heard, or hearing, never listened. I cannot help but wonder whether in myself, or in each of us, for every time we have managed to hear and respond whether we did not miss at least 11 other chances to say "Yes!"

We come then to this Sunday, this Lent, this preparation for Easter, invited to become less bound up, less unfree, more able to let our Baptism, our immersion into Christ take over all we are. We try to become in George Maloney's marvelous phrase, "totally Fire!"

The story of Jesus in the Gospel today can help us respond to what we hear the quiet of our hearts, the voice, urging us to say our fiery "Yes." What does Jesus nourish us with today?

Last week in the temptation story, Jesus was taken in a final temptation to the top of a mountain, invited to kneel down, surrender to the demons, and win the world. Despite all odds, Jesus trusted that everything was already his! He had heard a voice at his baptism telling him he was God's favored Son. Like Abraham before him, Jesus trusted that voice and began to live it out.

Now, again in the Gospel today, Jesus is on a mountain top, in the middle of his story. He is on the way to Jerusalem, and he is touched again, consoled again, reminded again that he is indeed God's favored son. And, again, Jesus trusts what he believes God has said to him, called him to.

Like Abraham before him and all of us after him, Jesus is invited to trust and follow without turning back. To trust his unique experience of God. And he will trust that God even though it leads him to another mountain, to Calvary ... and beyond, to resurrection.

In that trust lies our salvation!

Peter stands always in the Gospel for all of us. Today Peter is like all of us one who had experienced something profound, and he wants to stay and savor the experience, live it over and over. Jesus knows that we cannot hold onto the moment that inspires and fosters our faith, but rather we need to go down from the mountain and live out the experience in the market place where misunderstandings, dissension, even crucifixion occur. When Peter and his friends go down from the mountain, they do not speak about the experience, and so they forget its power. When the passion comes, they panic and run.

I deeply believe that every person in this church today has met the God of Abraham, the God of Jesus – probably more than once. Perhaps the meeting was powerful in a moment of grace, of vocation, with dazzling clarity. Perhaps it was very quiet, with only small hints, invitations, but for a second, clear. Without some experience of God (even if we never name or own it as ours) we would not be here today.

Lent invites us,
this weekend invites us,
the history of the great heroes of our faith invites us,
Baptism and its Lenten renewal invites us,
the possibility of Easter invites us
to listen to God's voice.

All of these invite us to listen to that voice and trust that what we hear truly is from God. This is not the fervor of a moment, not a touch of flu, not the first stages of psychotic break, but the voice of GOD. And we are invited to respond wholeheartedly with Abraham, to go where God directs us.

For a moment, we quietly reflect on what that means to me this Lent.

19) The Third Sunday of Lent

Scripture Readings: Ex. 17:3-7; Ro. 5:1-2,5-8; Jn. 4:5-42

A priest friend told me of a young drug addict whom he got to know in the drop in center where he worked. The man was well educated, married with family, yet squandered everything and found himself for several years on the streets, living from hand to mouth, buried in his addictions. One day as the priest and the wounded young man talked, my priest friend asked him when he was going to get his life together. The young man voiced despair, acknowledged that he did not know where to turn, how to start over. He had no funds, no hope. The priest offered to help him get into a treatment program if he really wanted to. Astounded, the man said: "Would you really do that for me?" His "For Me?" was riddled with self-hatred, mixed with overwhelming gratitude.

That "For Me?" is perhaps the Lenten cry of all of us. The story of our ancestors in Exodus is the story of all of us. We are all in the desert, half way to we know not where, dying of thirst, longing to return even to the slavery of Egypt if it meant food and water for us. Clamoring out to Moses and to God, the people want to know, "Is God in our midst, or not?" In our thirst we all want to know if God is with us. Will this God do anything for us?

The assertion of Paul to the Romans that "While we were still sinners Christ died for us," suggests that yes, indeed, Jesus would do that for us.

The Samaritan woman in the gospel is in the story because she is me, she is you, she is out catechumens moving towards the Easter waters. Hers is the story of us all, terminally, congenitally thirsty human beings. She comes to the well at an hour when no one else will see her, apart from the crowd, hating herself, distrusting everyone else. She comes not believing that God or anyone else is there for her, but Jesus is.

She is all of us.

She is a *woman*, one that Jewish men did not talk to in public. The oppressed victim, then and now, of a patriarchal world. She has become the symbol of women whom Jesus loves and treasures, even if the Church does not. The woman who becomes a missionary, an apostle to her people, though neither ordained, nor appreciated. Jews did not talk to women. Rabbis did not acknowledge women.

But Jesus did; and does.

She is also a *Samaritan*. A member of an outcast tribe, unfaithful to the law of Moses. Jews did not acknowledge Samaritans, nor believe that God was there for them. This woman carries on her shoulders all the opprobrium of any outcast people, in any age ...

she is the black the Hispanic, the Asian, the native American, the Cuban, the mentally or morally defective; She is the Moslem -- whoever it is we see as other than, less than, worse than ourselves.

Jews did not talk, were not there for, would do nothing for Samaritans.

But Jesus did!

The woman is also a *sinner*. She has made a mess of her life. She has gone through relationships without constancy or hope. She bears on her shoulders the self-hatred of all of us who have been less than we wanted, failed in our commitments, hurt those most dear to us, experienced the disgust, distrust, or alienation of others. She is me; she is you.

Perhaps good people do not embrace sinners.

But Jesus does.

I see Jesus lifting himself up out of his own fatigue, as he lies exhausted against the well. Too tired to go to town for food, he sends the apostles without him as he collapses at an hour when no one should bother him. Then here comes this woman! I imagine Jesus looking up, feeling his fatigue, saying to himself, "Oh, no, here comes another one!" But he overcomes this initial reaction and meets her, knows her, loves her, brings her back to life.

This is a story for our elect, those preparing for the Easter sacraments. It is a story for that part in all of us that longs for the waters of life, waters because of which we will never be thirsty again. This water comes from a well so deep that all our thirst can be quenched.

Is God there for her, for us? Would Jesus do this for her, for us? And the answer in this baptismal story is a resounding "Yes!"

Today the elect experience the first of three scrutinies. The Church invites them to let this gospel to help them look into their lives, examine their hearts, to know and name where they thirst. Where do they cry out, "Is God there for Us?"

All of us with the elect are invited to let this story touch us, as we feel the longing of this woman, of that man at the drop in Center, of every living man or woman who has ever known to their toes a deep, pervasive, existential thirst.

Let me honestly tell you that I find this difficult. All week sitting with these readings I find myself aware of what I thirst for, for others, for the world, for our parish. But I do not easily name, touch, own, feel my own deep thirst. If I know my own emptiness there may be no one there for me. I am afraid. I pray for the courage here in this Eucharist to name my own deepest thirst, and more importantly to believe that Jesus can fill it.

Before we close, notice that this story does not end with the woman caught up in a nice warm, safe, cuddly relationship with Jesus. Rather it ends in mission. this woman goes back to her town where she was an outcast, and proclaims to them, Good News! Satisfied herself, she invites others to name their thirst, so it can be quenched. she is not the quencher. Finally they believe because of what they see and hear, but she is the one who leads them to the water. She is healed herself when she can do what thousands of addicts call their 12th step, and reach back to those who share her thirst.

We are all addicts, compulsives, attached, broken people who have been plunged into the waters and now invite others, as best we can, to truly know that God is there for them, That Jesus will do everything he can for them.

20) The Fourth Sunday of Lent

Scripture Readings: I Sam. 16:1,6-7, 10-13; Eph. 5:8-14; Jn. 9: 1-41

Lent is entirely about Baptism. The Readings of each Sunday are the final words to those preparing for Baptism at Easter and, by extension, words central to the renewal of Baptism in every disciple. These words tell us what it means to be unbound and set free, to be overwhelmed by and assumed into the life of Jesus Christ. These words on successive Sundays:

> Challenge us, after wrestling with demons, to emerge trusting in the name God has given each of us, "Son," "Daughter," "Beloved."

> Take us to the mountain top to get a glimpse of the eventual glory of Jesus and then to let that glimpse empower us to return down the mountain, to Jerusalem, to death, and to the fullness of life.

Invited us to know our deepest thirst and have it slaked by the living waters of Love.

Lent is about Baptism and the gradual unbinding of everything that keeps us less than free, so that we can plunge into those waters again at the Easter Vigil.

Today' story invites us into a different metaphor: Baptism is like being blind, then being touched by waters that open our eyes to new vision, helping us to see everything more clearly. Darkness turns into light; a metaphor that will dominate the Vigil, as we light a new fire against the pitch black night, let our individual candles remind us of our baptismal reception of this light of Christ.

Today we admit that we do not need this baptism, do not need this gospel, do not need this entire Lenten season *unless we know ourselves as blind*. We are even encouraged by the gospel to stand first with the Pharisees more than with the man born blind -- they think (Perhaps like us) that they see just fine already.

This gospel passage recalls for me a favorite story from my youth – one that is being referred to a great deal lately. Hans Christian Anderson tells the tale of a vain King who commissioned a special set of golden clothes. Though very vain, and very powerful, the king was not very smart. So the spinner of this new suit told the king that his new outfit, made of finest gold, was invisible to the wearer, but lovely to everyone else. Their fear of the power of the king kept all the people blind, as he pranced around in what he thought to be a new suit, but was indeed his birthday suit exactly as old and wrinkled as the King. It took the unshrouded eyes of a small boy to point out the obvious:

"Look at the king, he's altogether, yes altogether, as naked as the day that he was born."

The Emperor had no clothes

A contemporary spin off of that famous story offers the political biography of a recent president entitled "The Clothes Have no Emperor!" There was a suit for sure, but no one was in it. No one was home.

Whether we stay with the metaphor of an emperor who has no clothes, or clothes that have no emperor, we point to a possible blindness in us that helps us enter the gospel story today.

What is frightening to is the blindness that is willed, chosen, because to see what is very plain will ask too much of us, will be too great a risk. Those who would have pointed out the King's nakedness risked death, so they did not see it. Frightening repercussions kept them, and can keep me blind. The Pharisees in today's story would have had to disrupt their entire religious conceptual framework to acknowledge that Jesus actually worked the miracle they could not help but see . . . so they steadfastly refused to see!

Each year around this time we cannot help but remember the saintly, soon-to-be canonized heroic Oscar Romero, Archbishop of El Salvador, shot while saying Mass just before Palm Sunday in 1980. It helps to remember also that for years Oscar Romero did not see the poverty of his people, did not see his Church's collusion in that poverty. Only when his friend Jesuit Fr. Rutillo Grande was killed because of his care for poor parishioners did Romero's blinders lift. He saw. And this sight changed him, as he became aware of the plight of the poor. He saw the rulers of his land differently. He saw Church and society with new eyes. This new sight, new vision led Oscar Romero to speak and act in ways that eventually made him a martyr. And it is this martyrdom that makes it so difficult for all of us to let ourselves see.

To see the *naked* truth and to proclaim what one sees was as dangerous for Oscar Romero in reality as it was for the King's people in that fairy tale. For "Fairy Tales," even in their ugliest parts, "do come true!"

I find myself praying during Lent to see what is directly before my eyes, with more than a fleeting glimpse. I am haunted by the request that Romero made to our nation to see what we were doing to his people, his land, as he requested then president Carter to quit financing the Salvadoran government and their military, pleading with us to intervene for peace. And briefly, under Carter we did. But as administrations changed we quickly supported the war again as 30,000 people were killed including American Church women, and a number of Jesuits. At the time we knew what was happening. We, the followers of Jesus, saw this war going on, as we have so many others like it, but if we really saw we would have been forced to change our lives.

It is not easy to "See." It is not easy to speak out loud what we see! And when I preach words like this someone is always upset confirming why it is so difficult to 'see."

Similarly, we hear frequently of our nations' quite difficult effort to count the homeless people in our midst. How see the 1 million starving in Central Africa. How see the 33, 000 killed by guns each year in our nation – many of them preventable suicides if guns were not so available. Our nation risks a collective blindness to poor immigrants already in our midst and even more poor refugees from Syria.

If we really see the faces of the homeless, the hungry, the hopeless in our land, we will be forced to change. If we see the truth before us, and proclaimed with that small boy's courage before the emperor, our lives would be transformed.

Can we pray today, this fourth Sunday of Lent for this deep penetrating sight?

And we do not need to deal only with huge swooping political, world issues to feel the truth of today's gospel. In the quiet of our personal lives we know it is difficult to look with honesty at the reality of all our relationships and to tell the truth about them. How hard it is to admit that a particular relationship is cruel, unforgiving . . . and then to take the steps to change it. How challenging to own another relationship as disordered, dishonest, manipulative, unloving, and then take the steps to change it.

In the Gospel story today _the hero_, the man born blind was ruthlessly scrutinized, asked over and over and over again, what happened, and how, and by whom. Finally, unwilling to believe this formerly blind man, the Pharisees who see so clearly throw him out of the temple. When the man born blind meets Jesus he meets him as savior because this now seeing servant tells the truth . . . what he saw, what he knew, no matter what. I was blind; now I see.

The goats of the story, the Pharisees refused to see what was right before their eyes, refused to accept the naked truth, and even Jesus can do nothing for them.

Today with the elect we let this story scrutinize our lives. We long to have our eyes opened on every level, stripping away relentlessly whatever keeps us from seeing with the very eyes of Jesus.

21) The Fifth Sunday of Lent

Scripture Readings: Ez. 37:12-14; Ro. 8: 8-11; Jn. 11: 1-45

"My Life closed twice before its close—
It yet remains to see
If immortality unveil
A Third event to me ...

(Emily Dickinson)

Emily Dickinson's lines wring in my ears as I hear the Gospel and celebrate this Sunday against a personal backdrop of amazement to be alive. Twice now, my life has almost closed.

I have lived most of my life aware that I could easily have died when I was eight. I had polio before there was a known cause or cure, and survived by what I believed then, and perhaps still to be a miracle -- if nothing else a miracle of love on the part of my parents. The sense that I could easily be dead haunted my early years and I wrestled to come to grips with that as an adult, dancing a fine line between discounting the event and being overwhelmed by it.

Then, in 1995, I died again. I experienced cardiac arrest while saying Mass during a retreat in Missoula, Montana, but was lucky (or unlucky) enough both to have two doctors and four nurses in the retreat community, and to be 100 yards from the hospital. I survived again. As an adult this experience has made me vividly, undeniably aware that life is a gift.

That truth, so deep now in me, is equally true for everyone.

We do not deserve, or earn life. It is entirely gift; every day, every moment. And if we reach down to touch the experience every single one of us knows this is true. We can recall a real or near accident, an illness, a plane we didn't catch, a wave we escaped from, a situation that could have meant our demise but did not.

If this is a physical truth about every human being it is even more a psychological, spiritual reality. We have survived broken families, being disappointed by our children, or our parents, lost jobs, addictions, disillusionment with family, church, political life. We have known the death of loved ones, relationships, communities. For the most part, we have survived them all and come back to life.

The story of Lazarus is the story of every one of us, and in order to really listen to it, we need to remember the moments when we were entombed, wrapped up, dead -- and Jesus called us back to life. Against this backdrop of our most intense human experiences of pain, and loss and death, we listen to this gospel story for a word, a reminder of hope.

Step back for a moment and put this story of Lazarus in context. The Church offers this passage today as the last major instruction to the Elect, the final word that scrutinizes their hearts preparing them for the baptismal waters. Leading us to Easter, the Elect are invited to look at how this story is theirs, to know where they have died and come back to life already.

Moreover this story is part of a Gospel that describes a "new Creation." John starts his Gospel story (as the bible itself begins) "In the beginning. . ." He moves through six signs, six days of creation, of which this is the last. The Death/Resurrection of Jesus will be the final sign, final day, establishing that new creation, changing absolutely everything.

Remember the Baptismal font is meant for immersion, not just sprinkling – we are buried in the water and lifted up, out to new life.

As with the Elect, we are all invited to remember today the various ways we have already experienced an escape from death. We are not now resurrected, but *resuscitated*; we will have to die again, as Lazarus did. But we have already passed over, passed through death, and, in Jesus, we can look at the world differently. We renew in Lent to Easter this vision.

This remembering is not always easy. Something in us resists. We hold onto the death.

I find myself wondering whether the stone before the tomb is one that keeps Lazarus in, or one that keeps Jesus out. Perhaps this Sunday, this final Week of scrutiny of the elect and ourselves, we ask which side of the stone we look from. Each of us has stones that keep Jesus from getting at us, keep us from being free with the freedom of those who know they are lucky to be alive. All of us are bound up in various fears, and struggles, needing to hear again the cry of Jesus "Unbind him, unbind her, and let them go free!"

Part of each of us want to stay in the tomb; it's dark and quiet and safe. We may be bound up, tied in knots, and not much use to anyone else, but no one can hurt us, nothing can get at us. John Shea suggests that: "It is the sound of Jesus tears that fall on ground that wake Lazarus up." Jesus calls out to us, keeps yelling at us, "Pat, come forth!" "Unbind him and let him go free!" And we return. We start over, begin to face the light, and live again. It is the deep, personal, agonizing love of Jesus for me that calls me back to life.

Recall the key lines that Jesus responds to Martha and Mary's similar lament: "If you had been here, my brother would not have died." We all cry the same thing: If you were here, were really God, if you really cared, loved, noticed, this or that would not have happened. I wouldn't be sick, my job would have continued, our church wouldn't be so messed up, our country so oppressive to the poor, our political leadership so contrary to everything that speaks of life . . .

If you had been here . . .

If you had only been here . . .

If you had been here . . .

And Jesus says (not just about the end of life, but right now):

"I am the Resurrection and the life. Anyone who dies believing in me will live. Anyone who believes in me will never really die. Do you believe this?"

In the early Church the newly baptized came into the on-going Easter Vigil Service drenched with water, saturated with oil, robed in white, looking like ghosts. They came in reminding the community that we all have survived death.

We here today, coming to the end of Lent renewing our Easter faith, are a people preparing to respond to Jesus question: "Do you believe this?" We remember how the story of Lazarus is the story of each of us. We are close to Easter. Everything about Lent and Easter invites us to a renewed and deep "Yes." to this question. We believe already that the deepest thing about us is that we are people who have already been raised from the dead, people lifted out of a watery baptismal tomb, who have come back to life. We are almost ready to say our "Yes."

22) Passion / Palm Sunday

Scripture Readings: Is. 50:4-7; Phil. 2:6-11; Mt. 26:14-27:66

We have listened to a lengthy reading of the Passion of Jesus as it is told to us by Matthew, a story that both needs to be broken open with loving care, and yet resists commentary because it speaks so powerfully. We will hear another telling of the story, by John, on Good Friday; on that day we focus on the reality of the passion and death itself. Each of our four gospels are unique. Each tells the story of Jesus, and specifically the portion of the passion and death in at least slightly different fashion and the differences are precious!

On this Passion/Palm Sunday we are invited to hear what Matthew's Gospel uniquely tells us about Jesus, and especially how he views the passion and death of Jesus. We will hear the same from Luke, or Mark on successive years.

Allow me to just hint at some of Matthew's central desires in his passion narrative. Out of myriad possibilities let me mention just three today.

First, a small but lovely point. At the last supper with his disciples what we have come to call the words of institution are remembered, Matthew's Jesus adds to the earlier Markan version the simple words "with you." "I will drink new wine *with you* in my Father's reign." Jesus is, for Matthew, *Emmanuel*, God with us, and the entire Gospel begins and ends with this theme, from "His name will be Emmanuel," (God is with you) in chapter one, to the final lines "I will be with you until the consummation of the World." Planted here, as we begin the Passion narrative, is that promise again. Jesus will always be with us. Our God will always be with us.

Secondly, we "chosen people," can miss our messiah's coming.

I find myself most captivated by the dream of Pilate's wife. A dream began Matthew's telling of the story as wise men, Gentiles from the East, followed their vision and acknowledge the new born "king of the Jews," while the Jewish people themselves remain oblivious to what has happened in their midst. Here at the end a Gentile woman listens to her dream, warning her husband to have nothing to do with the death of this "King of the Jews," while Jewish people plead for his death. In both the beginning and the end, the Gentiles get it; tragically the Jewish people do not.

Here and throughout the passion narrative Matthew (himself a Jew) is concerned to explain how his Jewish family by and large, missed the messiah when he came. He needs to explain the phenomenon already happening by the time the gospel is written, that the message is "for the nations," not just for Israel. Through Israel, God's love is revealed to everyone and the message of salvation is now universal … a message Matthew delights in revealing, even as he mourns the blind, deafness of his people.

Throughout the gospel Matthew is concerned with showing Jesus as the fulfillment of all the prophecies given to the Jewish people. He continues that theme throughout the passion. Over and over again we are told that this or that event happened in fulfillment of the scriptures. Matthew keeps insisting that Jesus is the fulfillment of everything his people had hoped for, dreamed about for centuries, as he laments their inability to recognize this Messiah when he comes.

And we, today, are deeply reminded in this Matthean telling that we can miss its point, miss its power for us. We call *ourselves* "chosen people, a royal priesthood, a people set apart." but we now are perhaps as likely to fail to see the importance of Jesus in our midst as Matthew's beloved, initial chosen people were then.

Third, in the notions specific to Matthew's telling of the Passion, the reaction of every individual character is significant. Matthew takes care to emphasize every character in the story in relationship to Jesus as instructive. Each actor in the passion drama tells us something about ourselves.

Thus a woman lavishes expensive oil on Jesus, wastes it in love. A disciple prepares to betray Jesus for money.

Each person's response invites us to look at our response to these events. This is seen most centrally in the reactions of Judas and Peter to the results of their betrayals. Judas hangs himself in despair; Peter weeps bitterly in repentance.

Two possibilities are always present for sinful disciples; repentance or despair.

We could go on with details special to this telling of the painful story of our salvation. But perhaps these hints are enough to invite us to stay with the story, to make it our own, to let it challenge us and change us as we move towards the Sacred Triduum, the High Holy Days of our Tradition. This is not a story, only for others a long time ago, it is for us.

The Passion narrative reminds us that God is with us, now and forever despite, or rather perhaps because of this tragic death.

The Passion narrative reminds us that though we are a chosen people we can still miss, ignore, discount the need to perhaps uproot and reconsider absolutely everything we have been told and come to hold dear because of this story of Jesus. The Death of Jesus always invites us to change, to conversion.

The Passion narrative reminds us that our reaction to each event, like those who experienced it first hand, can be acceptance or rejection of God's love poured out for us in Jesus.

23) Holy Thursday

Scripture Readings: Exodus 12: 1-8,11-14; I Cor. 11: 23-6; Jn. 13:13-34

Each time I celebrate this feast, I recall a particular parish celebration. We had invited those preparing for entrance into the Church in full communion and also those who were formally celebrating a return to the Church through a liturgical process called "Re-membering Church" to take part in the washing of feet. Immediately after the proclamation of the gospel Ministers washed the feet of those entering or re-entering the Church, and they then went to the community and knelt to wash the feet of others. I was amazed to see how many refused to let them, and how even those who submitted did so with great embarrassment and reluctance. Even though all had just heard the dialogue in which Peter initially refuses to let Jesus wash his feet, many imitated Peter's reluctance.

I learned that evening, and have seen repeated many times since, how much more difficult it is to have our feet washed than to wash others, to be the *washee* than the *washer*. We discover something deep in each of us in Peter's refusal and Jesus insistence. I find myself musing ever since: **What is it in us that resists this washing of our feet, and why is it so terribly important to Jesus?**

We come to the end of the Book of Signs in John's Gospel and enter into the Book of Glory, preparing for this greatest sign, the death and resurrection of Jesus. The passage begins with the assertion that now, "the hour is at hand," and Jesus is "loving until the end." Here everything that has come before is crystallized. Jesus is going to perform a deep act of ultimate service.

We note that John has no institution narrative around the Eucharist similar to what we heard from Paul tonight. John substitutes the washing of the feet for the institution of the Eucharist. Perhaps they mean the same thing. In each Jesus hands himself over <u>to</u> and <u>for</u> his disciples. By each gesture (bread and wine shared; feet washed) Jesus characterizes his impending suffering and death as a work of service, a laying down of life for his friends. The terrible significance of this act will not be totally clear now, but only intuited: "You don't know what I'm doing now, but later you will understand!"

Peter does sense, intuit, his "ghost guesses," what this means. He is profoundly scandalized. "Lord, you will never wash my feet!" He objects to this reversal of roles between himself and Jesus. He refuses to accept what this reversal of roles implies. On a deep, intuited level Peter (and each one refusing to have feet washed in every Holy Thursday service since) realizes that this washing will turn the world upside down. Peter is not ready (we, today may not be ready) for this conversion.

Mark's gospel presents the same reaction when, after recognizing Jesus as Messiah, Peter is confronted with Jesus description of the kind of Messiah he would be. When Jesus begins to talk about the cross, Peter objects: "No, not that way, never!" And Jesus becomes terribly upset with him: "Get behind me you Satan!" There, and again here in John's supper scene, Peter's objections seem at first trivial, harmless. Still Jesus becomes passionate, strong, insistent. Jesus sees Peter reactions in each case as a fundamental rejection of the recognition that <u>service and suffering are the path to salvation</u>!

Service, and this sacrificial suffering, point to the same reality. In each, one person puts aside his or her own good for the good of another. One lays down one's life for another. Every service is some kind of self-gift, tending towards a more total self-gift.

Let me step back and reflect (with Sandra Schneiders) that there are three different ways of service .. actually two pseudo and one genuine.

Sometimes what passes for service arises out of a power relationship, and is in reality servitude . . .a child for a parent, a slave for a master, a woman in a patriarchal marriage for her husband. Such "service" arises from inequality in a structure of domination. The server has no real choice. I wash feet because I am expected to; I always wash feet, any feet. Give me a foot and I must wash it!

Another pseudo service is done by the one with power in a form of condescension, parent towards child, professional to client. Again the relationship is unequal. It can be good, but can also be controlling, manipulative, maintaining and deepening the inequality, not liberating the one served. A priest tonight can subvert the

Rite by washing feet in a ritual service and not truly serve the people, only impress them with his pretended humility!

But service done in the context of friendship and equality, service done freely exacts no debt, demands no return, invites reciprocity. Such service as that offered by Jesus to the disciples and to Peter is both non-exploitative and rare.

Here at the final meal as a gesture that encapsulates everything he has to say to us, Jesus invites us not to love of enemies, but to love of friends, even unto death. Jesus later will call his disciples not servants, but "friends." Jesus abolishes inequality, deliberately reverses the social roles by this washing of feet.

Return again to Peter's reluctant acceptance of this gesture and what it means to us. Peter realizes that Jesus overcomes the inequality between them, wipes it out, inaugurating a relationship of friends. In doing this, on a level that Peter somehow intuits, Jesus subverts, in principle all structures of power, and lays the ground work for Peter's (and his successors') own service, authority and power. In his initial rejection of this washing of his feet Peter rejects a whole new order that Jesus chooses to speak through this symbolic act. Jesus institutes an entirely new order of human relationship.

Jesus says, in effect; "I am Lord and Master, but I refuse to base anything on that. I will become your servant. I will lay down my life for you, as my friends." Jesus says to his followers, his church, that we should live among ourselves the love of friendship that delights in mutual service, and knows no order of individual importance. The Eucharist is dramatically enacted.

Peter and our own acceptance of the ritual washing here tonight at the beginning of the Triduum sets a framework for an entirely new order of things with endless ramifications ..

--for relationships within the church, where those who lead lay down life for friends, where men and women are radically equal in service.

--for those who join our communities as servants and invite the rest of us to do, or re-do the same,

--for all the communities, including national, of which we Christian disciples are a part, inviting us to adjust our relationships from dominance to friendship.

I am grateful to Peter and his resistance to this washing. He invites me and all of us to think what it is we do, who it is we are, as the followers of Jesus gathered around this table of equals to share in Eucharist tonight . . . the night before his death, the beginning of our days of celebrating his Resurrection.

24) Good Friday

Scripture Readings: Is. 52:13-53:12; Heb. 4:14-16, 5:7-9; Jn. 18:1-19:42

The powerful reading of John's Gospel that lies at the heart of our Good Friday celebration invites, mostly, a respectful silence, awe, gratitude. My remarks are brief, hopefully helping us focus on some of what is unique to this telling of the passion story by John.

There was an enormous shift in consciousness in the early Church between the writing of the Gospel of Mark in the mid 60's CE., and the version from John we just heard written probably after 100 CE. Everything in Mark underscored the humanity of Jesus; every word, every event in John lets divinity shine through. Here Jesus is in control, is calm, has power even as he goes to death. Jesus makes decisions, sees clearly what it all means and why it has to happen.

Mark's passion touches the human part of us that suffers, shares with Jesus, knows that God is with us even in the pain. John's touches that part that needs a God who knows what is going on, who has not lost control of the universe even in this or other tragedies.

I once enjoyed enormously the performance of a wonderful actor, Leonardo de Phillipis, who captured the "feel" of John's Gospel. Leonardo presented the entire gospel as an Icon . . . a glorified, wondrous image of God to be admired as from a distance. The impact was awe, wonder, admiration -- not imitation. Jesus was truly magnificent -- but distant.

Some elements of the story to hold in our minds/ hearts:

The Gospel of John is filled with images of light and dark. Remember "the light comes into the world and the darkness cannot blot it out." The entire gospel is a struggle between light and dark; recall the story of the blind man who saw and the sighted Pharisees who did not that we heard on the 4th Sunday of Lent. When Judas leaves the supper table, "It is night." On Easter the story begins "early in the morning, " that is at the first crack of dawn. Light wins! This triumph of light over darkness, a dominant metaphor in John, becomes the central image of the Easter Vigil which we begin by lighting an enormous fire, and a new candle against the darkness of the sinful night.

An historical problem occurs in John's gospel. We hear many bad things attributed to "the Jews." Because of the antisemitism spawned by a careless rendering of this text, we need to take care to trans-literate that to "(some of) the Jewish religious leaders," those who were concerned with ritual purity, keeping Jewish laws, etc. Clearly Jesus breaks some of the traditions of past, most recent Judaism and that is why he is put to death. But we cannot ascribe his death to "all Jewish people," even in his day, but rather to those leaders holding on to a power threatened by his presence. To continue to use the Jews as scapegoats for the death of Jesus is to let off the hook any in every age including our own those who put religious ritual, law, tradition before authentic religious values like caring for the poor, building God's reign, speaking the truth.

The scene in the passion most specific to John involves Mary and the beloved disciple. This passage *feels* like the announcement of the birth of the church. I am struck to recall that John only has Mary present twice in the gospel. She is present at the beginning, ushering in the story as she invites Jesus to begin his public life at the wedding in Cana. In her "Do what he tells you," Mary all but forces Jesus to inaugurate his miraculous ministry. She helps the story get started.

Beneath the cross she is entrusted to take care of and be in the care of John, the care of those loved by Jesus, the care of the Church. She is present at the birth of the mission of the Church as she was at the birth of the mission of Jesus.

In John's passion the final words, "It is finished," imply that this was something Jesus was doing, not something done to him. In some ways the word *passion*, does not fit the story at all. The passion is not something so much that Jesus endured, something that happened to him, as something he chose. Jesus hands over his Spirit to God, and in the central Resurrection scene he will breathe that same spirit back on the disciples, the Church. The Spirit Jesus lived with, the Spirit of God, is surrendered freely at his death so it can be given to the Church.

Finally, we are told that "Blood and Water flowed out," from Jesus side after his death. Water and blood flowed onto the earth, soaked into the earth, flooded our world. The water of Baptism, the blood of Eucharist are spilled on and for us in this most sacramental of gospels written when the early church had already been celebrating Baptism and Eucharist for two generations.

These are some details we notice in this telling. What do you notice? How does this story transform you? For we are gathered in this Triduum not just to recall, and re-enact what happened to Jesus, but more importantly to remember what happens to us because of Jesus!

25) The Easter Vigil

Scripture Readings: See Lectionary for Readings from Hebrew Scripture; some variance with each parish; Ro. 6: 3-11; Mt. 28: 1-10

Maybe it's from so much time spent in the Bay Area, and Seattle but I am fascinated by earthquakes. I notice that when Jesus died in Matthew's Gospel the earth quakes, trembles. And, again, here in the Easter Gospel, as day dawns there is a great earthquake. An Angel comes to roll back the stone, then sits on that stone in white baptismal garments as the guards faint in fear. An angel tells the barely believing women that Jesus is risen and they are assigned to spread the good, the earth shattering news.

It feels right to say that Easter is about the earth quaking, about rocks that were hardened being melted, splintered. Easter is about life beginning anew and again. It has begun again in the past and it is that way right now for our elect, for us in this Easter celebration.

Each year at the Easter Vigil we celebrate this quaking earth as our lives are split apart, begun anew. I remember many baptismal stories, stories of complicated lives that somehow came together in this sacramental moment, stories of people dying and coming back to life, many people rising out of shattered stories to start over and rebuild on a better, stronger rock.

I remember especially Audrey, a woman who waited seventy years for baptism, despite a number of futile tries over many years to get to the font. I can still feel Audrey literally shaking and shuddering in my hands beneath the waters, then coming out beaming, bawling, laughing, all at once. Stones that had battered her down for years and years were clearly lifted, shattered, and she was born anew to begin again.

Easter begins with an Earthquake. As we come here tonight to celebrate Easter the earth quakes again as we gather around the fire and light our candles against the night's darkness, singing and telling ourselves "This is the night!" We listen to our first best stories, stories of hope, of creation, good in the beginning and still today -- stories of people led from slavery to freedom, of new, fresh, abundant meals, new hearts. We celebrate not just what happened to Jesus as his tomb was broken open and he emerged alive, but what has happened and is happening to us who come here tonight a people already dead and buried, our tombs broken open so we can live in Christ Jesus.

Some years ago, I visited Memphis and the Civil Rights museum in the motel where Martin Luther King, Jr. was killed a quarter century ago. I walked those hallways, remembering the stories I lived through in the sixties that shattered my white, middle-class complacency. In King's death my personal world view was destroyed, shattered, utterly. I had to rebuild a new image of people, nation and self. In Memphis, I was touched again by the voice and the courage of King. He had been to the mountain top. He has seen the promised land, as he said the night before his death. He admitted he may not get there with his listeners, but he knew we will all get there! The earth-shaking Easter faith of King helped rebuild my faith and is the faith of this community who will not accept death, will not let defeat have the final word!

We gather as a people who have probably more than once had our lives shattered, who live in a world of uprooted dreams and lost hopes, who do not just celebrate but live Easter. We are a people of continual quaking, shaking, redistributing, who believe that stones can be rolled away, that angels robed in white garments can keep sending us on the mission. We believe that things _can_ get better, life _can_ come out of various forms of death, real and metaphorical. We _can_ recover from illness and rejection. We _can_ be part of service provided to the needy, or those with handicapping conditions. We _can_ teach the young, and comfort the elderly, the immigrant, the refugee. We _can_ work for affordable housing. We _can_ provide comfort and love to gang members, or those returning to our world from prison. We _can, we can, we can_.

Easter begins with the quaking of the earth. Stones roll away, tombs open, and life is proclaimed. Throughout Lent we have been aware of stones. Stones that we carry through life with us. Stones rolled up before the tombs where we are buried, either keeping us in or keeping Jesus out. We have been aware of life crushed out of us, weights we can't let go of. Now the earth recreates itself; the stones of death are rolled away. Life wins!

Each Easter around the Baptismal font we celebrate the earth moving in hope! The stories of each of those who come before us to be baptized or enter into a new communion with Jesus and with us brings with them a story ... an addiction finally overcome, a family lost but a new one found, one nation, or culture or style of life left behind, another begun. Some come new and fresh to us, others who have been here for years now formally join us. Every person has a story of stones rolled back by some shaking of their personal cosmos, and all of us are given new hope in our own dramatic lives. I know that I, and I suspect all of us find ourselves continually made new, filled with life and laughter because of the stories of the people that make up this Easter community.

There is something profoundly true about this Gospel. It is not an old story, but one true and worth celebrating right now! *Feel It!*

Feel it here in this holy place! The earth quakes, shakes, trembles. We can feel it under our feet, and under our hearts, deep down in our guts.

As we approach the womb/tomb/baptismal font we, like the women in the story, are half fearful, half joyful. All the little stones that we have noticed and assembled through our Lent are now put into one big stone, covering the dead body of Jesus. But the stone is rolled back. One robed in a baptismal garment sits on it and tells us Jesus is not dead. He is risen. So are we!

Though incredibly sacred and profound, defining who we are at our very best and deepest selves, this night does not exist for itself but for the world. We, like the women in the story, are sent back to our lives empowered by this vision. We will meet Jesus in the same places, our Galilee's, where we originally did. He'll come to us there or not at all.

How do we sustain our Easter Faith? How do we hold onto this conviction that in Jesus death and resurrection the earth has been moved and everything is new? We do so as we touch and cel-ebrate Easter, -- Baptism, light overcoming darkness, our sealing in God's Spirit, our communion with Jesus -- as well as we can tonight, and then hold onto the memory all year long.

We are like the small boy flying a kite. when a cloud comes and removes it from view. His grandfather teasing him suggests that maybe someone had come and taken the kite away. But the boy knows he still has firm hold on the kite, even though he cannot see it. How does he know? He tells his grandfather: "I can feel something you can't feel!"

In Seattle, we know that mountain is there even though we often cannot see it.

The earth has shaken. The stone of death has been forever rolled back. The white robes of baptism gleam before us. Easter is in our midst. We are willing to stake our lives on that felt fact.

We move now to celebrate with those who come before us to join the long line of those who have felt this shaking of the earth, a mystery not all can see.

26) The Second Sunday of Easter

Scripture Readings: Acts. 2:42-47; 1 Peter 1:3-9; Jn. 20:19-31

One Easter Sunday night, as I arrived home from a wonderful Easter dinner, a co-worker of mine in the parish met me at my door. Steve told me that he had just learned that his brother had died in a car accident that morning. He had come to implore me to come home with him to tell his mother who was visiting that her 40 year old son had just died.

This was how my Easter ended! After all the celebrations, the rejoicing and singing of Alleluias, after the candles lit against the dark night, the baptisms that said we had overcome death with Jesus, and all of us had risen to new life, after a wonderful day living in the glow of our Easter liturgical extravaganza, I faced this ultimate task.

As Easter ended I wept with a grieving family asking myself: Has anything really changed because of what we have been celebrating these past three days? Do we really believe all this? Do we really believe that Jesus is risen from death and all of us with him? Do we really believe that death is not the final word? Do we believe that everything about life and death is changed because of what we spent the previous night proclaiming and celebrating?

I do not pretend to know what happens after death. I do not know what heaven may be like I cannot describe in any concrete detail what it will mean for Steve's brother, or any of us to share fully in Christ's Resurrection. But I cannot celebrate this season without trying to look at reality with different eyes. I must assert that death does not win, death is not the end, somehow victory can come out of defeat, life comes (not just at the end, but all the way along) out of death. Everything is changed!

The readings this week, and all throughout the Easter season force us to acknowledge that Easter is not only, or perhaps even primarily about *what has happened to Jesus*. The larger theme is *what happens to us*, the community of believers. Easter is about how we are changed, made new, re-created. We are challenged to wonder how we will live in new ways that witness to the boundless hope this mystery gives.

The passage we hear today from the Acts of the Apostles presents that idealized vision of the early community in Jerusalem. They live in common and share everything. Each had everything each needed. They took meals in common and spent all day praising God. Because they lived a communal life so strikingly unique, others came to believe, and everyday more were added to their number. Granted it is easier to give everything away and share all we have with others when we expect the world to end momentarily, still the way these first followers lived stood in stark contrast to the world around them, and converts came because they could see the difference. They still will!

Peter's letter, probably among the final passages written in what we now call the New Testament, almost a century after the first occurrence of these Paschal Mysteries, speaks of a community experiencing a new birth because they believe what they did not see, and they live in inexpressible joy. The community of believers is changed because of the Resurrection.

The gospel of John presents the basis of that change, that re-birth. Jesus on the very night of Easter breathes the spirit, His Spirit, on the Church (note: not just on priests, not just officials, but on all the Church, the **disciples**, the followers of Jesus). Jesus gives them, gives us the power, the Spirit to be forgivers, to help people know they are forgiven -- forgiven of everything, forever. The breathe of a new creation changed the followers of Jesus then, changes us still.

Thomas wasn't there. He didn't hear the words or touch the wounds. He needed to experience the forgiveness. Thomas is in the story so that Jesus can act out towards Thomas the power he has just given his followers. Jesus shows what forgiveness looks like in the concrete specific. When Jesus sees Thomas a week later he is not petty or vindictive. He doesn't lambaste Thomas for his hard-headed, hard-heartedness. Jesus loves Thomas, becomes incredibly vulnerable to him, offers his wounds to be touched if this will help Thomas to believe. And, through Thomas, he invites us all to believe in the Spirit's power in us, to believe that we are changed, even when we do not feel or see it.

Out of all the possible points in this Gospel that surely bear deep-er reflection I want to focus on just one today. *Jesus shows Thomas his wounds.* These wounds are the very heart of what has changed in Jesus, and in us.

He proves who he is by showing the marks of suffering, now glorified. Who he is is certified by the undeniable marks of how he got there. These holes in side and feet and hands demonstrate what he passed through. What were signs of suffering on Friday, are, on Sunday, the marks of glory. However we phrase it, we who believe in Resurrection look at suffering, struggle, pain, and finally death differently because Jesus wounds are transformed. When I die, whatever I have passed through in this life will still be visible in or around me. I will be what I have passed through, survived, overcome.

We look at the same reality and perceive it transformed!

Returning to the death of my friend's brother that capped my Easter that fateful year, I remember what his mother said when told her son had died. Her first words were "He tried so hard!" I suggested then that she try to remember that. "He tried so hard!" Whatever life, Kerry, her son, is living now will be immortalized because he tried so hard. The signs of his struggle, so painful in life, become the marks of his glory now. The white robed army of witnesses are changed, are washed white in the blood of the lamb.

Everything in the human psyche tries to avoid suffering and pain. In the light of Resurrection we are empowered to face the suffering that life and love inevitably bring, trusting that we can pass through them, overcome them, eventually have them glorified. And people will touch our wounds to know it is still us.

I say this, not to glorify suffering, nor to encourage us to take on suffering we do not need. Rather I want to affirm our Easter faith … that if we try to love, to care for others, to feel the pain of our sisters and brothers as well as our own, the wounds we inevitably receive will be the source of whatever eternal life is ours.

The Resurrection is not just about Jesus, but about all of us who have died in these baptismal waters (point at the baptistery), and come back to life with Him. Everything has changed!

27) The Third Sunday of Easter

Scripture Readings: Acts. 2:14, 22-28; 1 Peter 1:11; Luke 24:13-35

The Jesus we meet in the Resurrection narratives is the same Risen Jesus we meet now.

These early stories gives us hints of where we can look today to discover Jesus. Those who had seen Jesus dead became vividly aware that he was still alive, still in their midst and, though the stories in Matthew, Mark, Luke and John don't easily mesh, in fact contradict each other, they do remarkably coalesce to help us find the Risen Christ, right now.

He still is present when two or three are gathered in his name. He comes veiled, un-recognized, appearing to be a gardener, a fisherman on the coast, a stranger walking along the road (a neighbor next to us in the super market, an elderly lady down the street, a man with Down syndrome in the pew in front of us.) He still breaks open the word for us, or sits and breaks bread at table, or sends us to our sisters and brothers with some mission of proclaiming Good News.

No story of the Risen Christ better captures the Jesus they met then and we meet now than the wondrous tale of the disciples on the road to Emmaus. The story is shaped by the telling and re-telling of that primitive community as they gathered for Eucharist. It becomes, in outline, a liturgical event . . . with gathering rite, liturgy of the word, offering of gifts, Eucharistic meal and dismissal.

Two are gathered in his name, walking along the road, speaking about this Jesus whom they "had hoped" was to be the Messiah, the one to set Israel free. And he suddenly is in their midst, unseen, but present, asking about their pain, their confusion, their muddled facts and fancies. They had heard rumors he was alive, but it seemed the prattling of women . . . no one (at least no men) had seen him. Despite the rumors, they were in pain, disillusioned, preparing for this meeting by their very need to be met, for Jesus Risen, as in his earthly life, apparently comes to us in our brokenness, our poverty.

Only the sick still need a physician.

When he joins this couple (probably a man and woman; the custom would have named the man, and left the woman anonymous), Jesus shares with them a long, seven mile liturgy of the Word. He takes the scriptures and breaks them open for these disciples explaining every passage of their sacred books that has to do with himself. He helps them re-tell their story, re-look at the striking events of the past three years, and, more, the past three days and see them in a new light. Jesus helps them connect the ancient story with their present reality. He helps them see things in a new light by a homily that brings the Word of God and the Word of life together.

When they arrive where they were headed *the disciples invite this stranger to be a friend*, to join them in table fellowship. They offer the gifts of hospitality and companionship, and discover who he really is in this "breaking of the bread." And, when their eyes are opened and they see Jesus, he does then what he seems so often to do to this day... he disappears.

Still this meeting has missioned them as meeting Jesus always does. They rush back to Jerusalem and form, instantly, the Church's first small faith sharing community.

Before they can tell how they met Jesus, they are told that he is risen and has appeared to Peter. Then, after the Jerusalem community has told their story, these two believers can tell how they met and recognized him also. Faith in the Resurrection is shared across time and space so that the witnesses can believe what they have seen. The Church is a community of people witnessing to the Resurrection ... to each other and to the world.

We meet Jesus where they did. We meet him still when we are walking along the roads, discouraged, disillusioned, hopes dashed, dreams delayed, but talking about Jesus. Two or three gather in his name, and he, as he promised, is in our midst.

We meet Jesus whenever the scriptures are opened up to us to help us look at our story in a new light, from a new vantage point, meshing our understanding with the Word of God, ever ancient, ever new. Remember the times You have come to Mass tired, defeated, discouraged, eager, hopeful, and the scripture read, or perhaps the homily preached seem picked and aimed exactly at you!

We meet Jesus when we have the courage to offer hospitality, to invite a stranger to be part of our community, an acquaintance to be a *companion,* literally a sharer of bread. When gifts are shared, Jesus is present.

We meet him still in the mysterious breaking of the bread; Eucharistic bread surely, other meals likely, when love is present and eyes are opened in the sharing.

And whenever and however we meet Jesus, if it is indeed the Christ, we are sent missioned back to believers and un-believers alike to tell something of the Good News that has opened up our eyes, our hearts, our lives.

And so the story goes on, and is retold in each generation as each believers faith builds on the faith of others throughout the generations.

28) The Fourth Sunday of Easter

Scripture Readings: Acts. 2:14, 36-51; 1 Peter 2:20-25; Jn. 10: 1-10

For most of my preaching life I was bothered by the insertion of the Shepherd image into the Easter season every year. This Fourth Sunday, in each year of the liturgical cycle, goes to the tenth chapter of John. I keep wondering why. Why not more stories of the Risen Christ? Why not stay with the scenes our imagination associates with Easter ... Christ not recognized, "Peace be with you," "Go to Galilee," "Feed my lambs?"

But each year the church invites us to think of the risen Christ in this image of the Shepherd, the *Good* Shepherd, the one who knows the sheep by name, the one whose voice we follow.

One year I celebrated this Sunday at a very small liturgy; myself and a couple, life-long friends at a cabin near the ocean. As we prayed together over these readings around the bread and wine that is at the heart of a then 35 year friendship I was struck with the appropriateness of this image. The glue that had held our love together through so much blood that had flowed under the bridges of our lives was our shared faith in and desire to follow Jesus, to listen to his voice and to go where he calls us . . . where he has gone ahead of us.

Oh yes , in the years we had been friends, we had all three of us heard other voices, ones that wanted to kill and destroy us. Each had from time to time begun to walk a misguided path. We had, as I Peter suggested, "gone astray like sheep," but deep down each of us are Easter people and we always returned to the Shepherd.

It is impossible to hear this reading about following the Shepherd during this Easter Season without knowing that this following is precisely through suffering and death, through pain and loss. Easter is not just about what happened to Jesus but is also, and perhaps more, about us and what happens to us because of Jesus. The promised fullness of life does not come without the letting go, the dying, the trusting as Jesus did.

I was struck in this simple Easter Eucharist not just with my love for these friends. I also know them as people who have followed Jesus through death to life. One of them had suffered an incredible blow to his ego and his image, lost a job he loved because accusations against his character. His world had been all but destroyed, but he remained faithful to his best and truest self and continued to work in ministry, touching hundreds of lives in loving, insightful ways.

His wife when I met her was among the most dynamic, fun filled, life affirming, playful people I have ever known. She has suffered with acute diabetes for the past many years, gradually losing weight, strength, ability to live fully as she would like. Several times a day she needs to pay close heed to her sugar count . . . before eating, or walking. She has lost consciousness through diabetic shock enough times to know how critical it is to keep careful track. She does this unobtrusively, calling no attention to herself, or her suffering. Limited by her disease, she still lives well, with laughter and gratitude.

As we listened to Jesus, the Good Shepherd together, I realized how both of them, quite unconsciously to either them or myself, had been Easter people to me. He has helped me to live with all the ways I have disappointed myself, let down those I loved, failed to live up to my best and truest self and still had the courage and the faith to go on, to minister, trusting in Jesus not myself.

As my health has waned, as my back gives out, my heart has failed me, my memory lags, She has helped me to refuse to focus on the health I don't have and be grateful for the gift of life I do still possess. Both live and love and go on embracing life out of their desire to listen to the voice of Jesus, to let him be their only gate. In a world riddled with ambiguity, both know to their toes that Jesus calls them by name, loves them, leads them.

I am grateful for Easter friends, and I know now why we listen to the words of the Good Shepherd during this Easter Season. I believe anew

> The Lord is my Shepherd, I shall not want.
> He makes me lie down in green pastures;
> he leads me beside still waters;
> he restores my soul.

29) The Fifth Sunday of Easter

Scripture Readings: Acts 6:1-7; 1 Peter 2:4-9; Jn. 14:1-12

Today's Gospel is a favorite selection for the celebration of funerals because it speaks so clearly of Resurrection. It is indeed an Easter Gospel though the context is at the final supper before the death of Jesus. My awareness of the Easter truth of this passage flows out of its connection with a significant celebration of a good friend's funeral. I cannot hear it without remembering one of the most profound experiences of my priestly life.

In the mid-1980's I was co-pastor in a parish. The day before one Thanksgiving the president of our parish council fell of his roof while cleaning gutters. He landed on his head, dying instantly. This family tragedy touched our entire parish deeply. The man was about 45 years old, had a wonderful wife, four children, many, many friends. As friend as well as pastor, I was asked to do the funeral and homily.

I still know of no way to make death, especially sudden, tragic death palatable. I worried and worried about what to say to help his family and our entire parish find hope in the face of this death, to celebrate a life so early quenched, to somehow bring our shared faith to touch this mystery of death so close to the dark bone of human experience. But before I could get to that homily I had to celebrate Thanksgiving, a series of weekend Masses, a wedding, and some commitments with my own family.

This loss had been on my mind, and in my heart throughout the weekend; the funeral itself was in place, with readers and readings, friends and family involved in the liturgy in various ways, music carefully picked out. But it was the Monday afternoon of the funeral before I was able to close my door and have but one solid hour to prepare my homily, still with no clear idea of what to say or how to say it. I remember being overwhelmed with the thought of some 2000 people present waiting for me to speak a word of hope and my fear of not having one to speak.

Just as I closed the door and began to pray I heard a knock. The deceased man's 17 year old son was at my door. He came, ostensibly to ask about taping the service, but really to talk about himself and his relationship with his father. I felt trapped . . . this was the only time I had, my last moment for preparation, but the need of this young man to talk seemed more important than the homily right then. I let go of my agenda, pushed things aside and invited him to sit down.

He told me about himself, his struggle with the practice of his faith, and how that struggle had built a wedge between himself and his father. The estrangement haunted him now that his father was dead. He wanted to know if he could still go to communion at the funeral, believing that to be terribly important to his father if not to him, for he was still unsure what it all meant. We talked beyond the hour I had. I knew that the most important thing I did that entire weekend was this conversation with this hurting, sensitive, questioning young man.

When he left I scarcely had time to grab a bit to eat before going to set up the Church for the service. As he walked out the door my eyes fell on the gospel passage the family had picked out and my homily came to me in less than an instant. The Gospel was the one we heard today from the fourteenth chapter of John!

Normally when I preach I fret and stew, write and re-write, and finally hammer out an idea. But this one <u>came to me.</u> I realized that what was needed were not my words of comfort or hope, but the words of Jesus, and the words of the deceased now caught up into the life of Jesus, spoken to his wife, family, grieving friends, and a wounded parish community. And to me!

I do believe that all of us are caught up into Christ when we are baptized. I believe that when we die we finally, forever, and totally put on Christ. The promise given in baptism is completed. I believe that all the readings of this Season, as we celebrate Easter over and over and over again, keep telling us that we celebrate not so much what happened to Jesus as what happened to us because of Jesus. All of this flashed through my heart, my brain at once as I framed the homily around listening to my departed friend speaking to his wife, to us, to me, saying (as Jesus did before him):

> **Do not let you hearts be troubled,**
> **Have faith in God and faith in me.**
> **In my father's house there are many mansions . . .**
> **I am going to prepare a place for you.**
> **I will come back to take you with me,**
> **so that where I am you also may be . . .**

These words became the funeral homily!

If we put on Jesus, as this fine man so clearly had, then the deeds, the works, the words of Jesus become our own. This "homily" was no exercise in rhetorical stretching, but the deepest truth of our Christian, Easter faith. Our assimilation into Jesus, begun at Baptism, completed at death.

The insight I experienced at this time of death is an enduring truth we are invited to celebrate each Easter season, to celebrate today! We celebrate what happens to us in germ as we enter into Baptismal waters; it is continually fleshed out as we move closer to our final fulfillment. This assimilation doesn't happen only at death, but all along as we put on the deeds and words of Jesus, as we make his life our own, eventually to make his death and Resurrection our own.

I have often said that our Easter faith reminds us that from now on the worst thing that can happen to us is that we die and go to heaven! At root we have nothing to fear. As we celebrate Easter again today we know that each of us facing death can put the words of Jesus in our mouths. Each of us can hear from those we love the very same words.

My prayer is that this belief gives us courage not just to face death, but to live with the courage, the integrity, the compassion of Jesus because we share now in the faith of Jesus, a faith that let him say, "Do not let your hearts be troubled or afraid!"

30) The Sixth Sunday of Easter

Scripture Readings: Acts 8:5-8, 14-17; 1 Peter 3:15-18; Jn. 14: 15-21

This is the 6th Sunday **of** Easter, not after Easter. We continue to celebrate Easter over and over; our attention gradually moves from looking back at the Easter event to forward towards Pentecost. Our focus remains on what happens to us because of what happened to Jesus in the Resurrection as we prepare to celebrate the continued presence of Jesus with his people, his Church, through his spirit.

As we begin to talk about the Spirit, I am reminded of a wonderful story about a missionary in China using art work to catechize his community. In a small chapel the priest designed three windows; in one he put an eye, symbolizing God the Father, in another a cross, symbolizing the Son, in the third a dove, symbolizing the Holy Spirit. An aging Chinese woman came to him and said:

> *"Honorable Father and his eye I understand; Honorable Father is always looking out; for us."*

"Honorable Son and his cross I understand; Honorable Son died for us on the cross.

*"But Hon*orable Holy Spirit and his bird I do not understand."

She spoke, perhaps for all of us. It is not easy to "explain" the Holy Spirit, and that Spirit's presence with us. John Shea captures the difficulty of this explanation perfectly when he (speaking very rapidly) suggests that Jesus was himself a bit stuck, saying to his followers . . .,

"I'm going away, but I'll stay, and I have to go, cause if I don't go I'll be gone and can't be here, but if I go I can stay because my spirit will stay so that even if it looks like I'm gone I'll still be here, or at least my spirit will be which is better than if I was, so I have to go, so I can stay. Even though it will look like I'm gone I'll still be here through my spirit! Got it?

A bit more slowly, the best image I manage for what Jesus tells us is to picture a dying parent, talking to a child:

"I have to go, but I want you to promise me one thing: Be good, love each other. Aunt Peggy will take care of you. Listen to her as you would to me. In that way I can continue to be with you."

Such a promise though not the same as the promise of His Spirit that Jesus leaves us, provides a feel for that promise in language we can understand: The promise of one who loves deeply to stay, in spirit, with the beloved. A promise that urges the beloved to go on with life knowing the lover is still present.

"You've got my Spirit; the Father's Spirit,
You are not orphans,
You won't see me, but you have my life.
God will love you just as God loves me...

In today's Gospel, the content of the promise is as important as the promise itself. As Jesus faces death everything becomes simpler, more focused. He invites us to continue to live in his Spirit, keeping the commandment of loving one another. The many and apparently varied commandments simplify down to one: Love each other. All he asks of those who live on in his Spirit is that we love. The experience of the ongoing love of Jesus is the sign that the promise is fulfilled. We know Jesus meant what he said because we experience its reality every time we experience the boundaries of love being broken.

The second reading today captures something central to this Spirit of Jesus. In one of my favorite New Testament lines the First Letter of Peter urges us "Always be ready to give your answer to anyone who asks you for the reason for the hope you all have."

The grounds of our hope is that we are not abandoned, are not orphans, the Spirit of Jesus lives in us, lives still. The task we have this sixth Sunday of Easter is to touch that hope, to look carefully for the grounds of our hope because that spirit is in us. We Easter people, looking forward to the celebration of Pentecost ask ourselves:

What is our hope?
Where do we experience that Spirit already?
What do we have to build on?

Every Easter Community these days has neophytes in their presence, newly Baptized people witnessing to the very new life of Jesus. Look at your new members and savor their presence. Look around at God's people, filled with God's Spirit and be given grounds for hope.

God's Spirit shows itself in children that join us for Liturgy, going out to reflect on God's word together, or bringing food for the poor to the altar, sharing in communion for the first time. Children bring hope.

God's Spirit shows itself in elderly parishioners continuing to give the gift of their presence and their prayers. I recall with wonder an older parishioner who at 80 recently bought 10 sewing machines and began to teach poor people in the neighborhood how to make their own clothes.

God's Spirit is manifest in the experience a young married woman who suffering from her and her husband's infertility despite her strong desire to be a mother. A teacher, she loves the children with whom she is entrusted. This year several of her students gave her a mother's day cards telling her that she is like a mother to them.

God's spirit is manifest in a business man who with others of like mind has gradually taken over most of a neighborhood helping to create shops, restaurants, a theater. In every business he and his visionary collaborators hire a percentage of people thought unemployable. The do all they can to create a community unlike those surrounding them, a community where people work, meet, talk, even pray forming a kind of base community of care in which God's Spirit is visibly present.

All of us can open our eyes, becoming aware of such manifestations of God's Spirit, the grounds of our hope. Recall and relish them today. We are only able to hope into the future because we know the "Paraclete" has been with us in the past.

We hear God saying over and over and over,

> *"I will never forget you my people;*
> *I have held you in the palm of my hand.*
> *I will never forget you,*
> *I will not leave you orphans.*
> *I will never forget my own."*

31) The Ascension of the Lord

Scripture Readings: Acts 1:1-11; Eph. 1:17-23; Mt. 28: 19-20

Happy Birthday!

Ascension Thursday, even when it is celebrated on a Sunday, begins our 10 day birthday party as Church. For Forty days plus we prepared to celebrate Easter. For forty more days more we have celebrated over and over not just what happened to Jesus in his Resurrection, but more importantly what is happening in us because of Jesus. From Ascension to Pentecost Sunday we culminate this extended jubilation as we commemorate our birthday as the followers of Jesus, taking on his mission and his message as our own.

Put simply. He goes; we stay to continue his work.

I have often been struck by the ironic contrast between today's scriptural message and the set prayers the Church provides for this feast. The opening prayer, the prayer over the gifts, and the prayer after communion all stress the point that where Jesus is going we will follow. We are invited in each of these prayers to keep our eyes firmly fixed on heaven, to goal of our earthly journey.

Yet, in the reading from Acts, the Apostles are chastised by God's messenger precisely for "looking up to heaven." The Gospel encourages them and us to set our gaze on this world into which we are to bring Good News. "Go, Baptize all nations."

It may be intriguing to look up, and look beyond this world, but I suggest that the point of this feast and the new birth it initiates is to call us to action here, and now and always. Throughout the entire book of Acts, Luke will retell the story of Jesus over, but now as it is lived out by his followers, and, by extension, by us today. We continue to preach, to be persecuted, to spread the news from Jerusalem, throughout Asia Minor, to Greece, and finally to Rome, to the cultural, political, religious heart of our world. Today in this unchurched Northwestern part of the United States, to Iran and, Iraq, Somalia and Syria, South Sudan and Manchester England -- wherever Good News is in short supply .

The most powerful part of the scripture readings today lies in the promise of the gospel, an apt conclusion to the entire message of Matthew's telling of the story of Jesus.

The Gospel began with a promise; "They shall call him Emmanuel, a name which means, 'God is with us." Today the gospel story ends with Jesus promise, "I shall be with you always." The Spirit whose coming we celebrate at the end of these days, on Pentecost, forcibly reminds us that though Jesus is gone, perhaps in a bodily form, he remains with us more powerfully than he has been before in the Spirit given to us. We are birthed, born again, made new, made into the body of Jesus continuing to act in his name, and in his Spirit's power.

This mission and this power are the meaning of this feast.

I had a priest friend who was fond of saying "I'm not trying to get to heaven; I'm just trying to get down to earth."

This might well be a summary of our challenge today. Are our feet firmly planted in this world? Are we reborn? Are we new? Am I? Do we look and act like people with whom Jesus (Emmanuel) is present always?

Lately, in the U.S. Church we have moved this feast from Thursday to Sunday so that the Church can truly come together to celebrate it. I contend that if any feast needs to be held in mid-week it is this one, for it is the challenge to be disciples on Thursday that the feast is all about. It is not about Church in Church, but about World, about being the presence and the sign of Jesus in our offices, our schools, our neighborhoods, our day care centers, our food banks, our health care clinics, our bookstores, our film centers, our computer developers and our political world, especially.

Too often we have heard, "She's a good Catholic, she goes to Mass every day." This feast invites us to hear "He's a great Catholic; he pays much more than the living wage and involves everyone who works for him in the decisions of the company." Or "they are a wonderful Catholic family; they never miss a school board meeting and are always ready to help with school projects." Or "She is a wonderful Catholic; in her work in Congress she speaks for the poor, the marginal, the ones most powerless in our society."

Before we move to Eucharist today, let's be still for a moment, letting our focus fall not on heaven, but on this earth, where Jesus remains with us. How and where do I want to enter this world more fully this year? What is your birthday wish this year as a member of the Church?

32) The Seventh Sunday of Easter:

Scripture Readings: Acts 1:12-14; 1 Peter 4:13-16; Jn. 17: 1-11

How are the Followers of Jesus supposed to live in the World?

As we celebrate the Birthday of the Church, a celebration that extends from Ascension Thursday to next Sunday's celebration of Pentecost, we ask ourselves what does this Spirit expect us to be, to do? What does it mean to live in the Spirit of Jesus in a very real, very messy world? Before I look at the readings specifically today I want to step back and try to feel deeply the questions they, and this birthday celebration raise for me. Only at the end will I return to the scriptures for whatever light they shine on these questions.

Again, what is our relationship with the world to be? Are we supposed to stand firmly against it, like a religious Ralph Nader, constantly in tension, fighting, asserting our values over and against those prevalent around us. Is our primary Christian stance to be "No!" in the face of the demons? Is our main voice the prophetic one of Dan Berrigan, or Dorothy Day? Archbishop Romero died for standing against the powers that were!

Or are we rather supposed to ignore the world, remove ourselves from it, like the Amish, or like Hasidic Jews, or monkish members of contemplative orders throughout our history? Is our struggle to not let the world effect or infect us at all? Simon Stylites was canonized for sitting for many years atop a pole, above and apart from the world.

Or are we rather to enter into it, work alongside it, run the risk of being co-opted by it? Joe Biden takes this risk, so did Paul Ryan, Nancy Pelosi, and every other Catholic politician. The Bishops in Germany in the 1930's let the values of Hitler overwhelm them, and Church leaders in every age have risked too close an association with power .

Whatever ideological stance we take, how are we to successfully converse with the world we inhabit? How do we enter the conversation about political, social, moral issues? Can we impose our value system on the systems that surround us? Or can we only hope to witness to something different and trust that the world will see us? Does it do any good at all to argue "Christians turn the other cheek, so we should not support war," or Life begins at conception, so we cannot have abortions," or "only God should determine when we die, so euthanasia is always immoral," when so many simply do not support our premises.

There are specifically religious groups like Habitat for Humanity that insist that everyone who works with them share their prayer before and after work, and in their liturgy of celebration when a house is finished. They are as concerned with keeping the community's Christian identity as with simply getting houses built. Which is most important for a Christian, getting the job done, providing housing, or risking everything to support the faith that nourishes the work and the people?

How is a Christian individual or group supposed to live in the world?

However each of us approaches the question, the question is real.

What about education? Should a parish struggle to help every parent send their children to a Catholic school, whether or not the parish sponsors that school? Or should we work to provide what religious education we can while at the same time hoping that our parents will be the kind of caring citizens that help to make the public school system all it can be, for the good of all? Should the Christian stance be better, but separate schools, or a commitment to the best possible public school system influenced by Christian folks? Every parish has people taking both stances. Is one right? Or better?

Certainly we have reached an absurd point when a receptionist at a clinic that offers abortion services is killed in the name of "The Right to Life," but such a painful fiasco raises the question whether we Christians should try to change laws, or forcibly stop those who are following what is legal, or spend our energy dealing with the problems that make abortion or euthanasia a seemingly good option. Or is our task to offer better options, whatever may be legal or illegal?

How should a Christian be in a complex world?

We have Catholics taking every side of almost every issue. Paul Ryan and Nancy Pelosi frequently disagree and neither ever agrees with Pat Bucannan. One Bishop key-notes the Call to Action convention believing that we need to raise all the questions in the world; another Bishop excommunicates members of the same group believing we should protect ourselves from conflict.

One bishop insists we cannot absolve nor anoint someone using Physician assisted suicide, others speak of compassion in every instance!

What should be our approach to solving the lack of available health care to so many people, or the disparity between Catholic teaching against the death penalty and the enormous support for it in our country, even among Catholics? Should we cooperate with military efforts to preserve our oil supply, or the same efforts to stop ethnic cleansing in a part of the world where we have no political interests? Can we support boycotts of enemy countries, like Russia or Iraq, when, due to the boycotts, children starve and are not educated? Can we refuse to admit refugees from lands where Military weapons we have provided are killing them by the thousands?

How am I as a Christian or we as a Christian community supposed to exist in the world? The question does not go away.

When we turn to today's scripture we do not get so much an answer as helpful approaches to deal with the question. In fact, I have maintained for years that while we may ask God for answers, God only *gives us a person to help us live with the questions*. The gift of that person, the Holy Spirit of Jesus, is what this entire Ascension-Pentecost reality is about.

The reading today from the Acts of the Apostles speaks of a community experiencing the absence of Jesus. These believers have had a profound experience of Jesus; their lives have been turned upside down. They have seen Jesus killed, and have experienced him risen. Still they do not know what to do, how to live out the implications of what has happened. They do not know how to live in the world, so they pray, and wait for the coming of the Spirit.

If we act only on our instincts, our unreflected, spontaneous biases we will probably be wrong. We too need to wait, to pray, to invite the Spirit to lead us to the marketplace. In almost every case I have spoken about above, I do not know what is best for me, and certainly do not know what you should do ... but I firmly believe we all need to pray, to wait, to listen, and to let the spirit speak to and guide us, and we need to do that together.

The second reading today from Peter suggests that those who will follow Jesus will have to suffer. We should never be ashamed or afraid to suffer because we are believers. Perhaps one infallible sign that we are following the Spirit of Jesus is that we are in fact misunderstood, or persecuted by someone. We can scarcely expect to follow one who was crucified for his involvement in the world and not be invited into some suffering on his behalf. It will not be easy to be a Christian in a broken world.

I repeat again my belief that the most deceptive myth we try to live with is the belief that if we are good people, doing what we are supposed to do, and saying what we believe, everything will turn out all right. The truth is unavoidable that if we are good, and do what we are supposed to do, if we act on our deepest beliefs, we will undoubtedly be crucified in one way or another, and only then will things turn out all right. We cannot skip that middle step.

Finally, the Gospel this Sunday: Everything I have said so far prepares us to hear these words. Jesus turns from talking to his followers at that final supper. He talks now in prayer to his God. He prays for his followers, for us.

He has finished what he was sent to do. God will glorify him. Eventually God will also glorify all of us, his followers, but meanwhile we remain in the world in all its complexity. Jesus does not ask God to take us out of the world, but to help us stay in the fray, as he himself did, faithful to the end.

Jesus invites us to love our enemies, lay down our lives, hunger and thirst for justice, care for the poor, the outcast the marginalized, as he did.

The gospel reminds us that, however we enter into our world, Jesus continues to pray for us, constantly intercedes for us, to live in his Spirit, with constancy and courage.

Once I have raised so many issues, and by implications so many, many more, it may be frustrating to realize that none of these readings solve our question. None tells us clearly how to live in the world. But they can help us not run from the question, help us to live ever more deeply the mystery of Christ in us, and we in him, and all of us in his Spirit.

I have been saying for weeks that we do not celebrate Easter for these seven weeks just to recall what happened to Jesus, but rather to sharpen our awareness of what has happened to us because of Jesus. How badly we need the Spirit of Pentecost, the Spirit of Jesus to live as he did in this World, "that the world might be saved ..."

33) Pentecost Sunday

Scripture Readings: Acts 2: 1-11; 1 Cor. 12:3-7, 12-13; Jn. 20: 19-13

Two Images wrestle with my heart as we celebrate this feast.

For many years I have held this first image in my soul -- a gathering of religious people praying, singing, listening to the Word of God, awaiting direction about where to go, how to act at a pivotal moment in their collective history. They are urged by their leader to remain faithful to his teaching. They wait apart, separated from the hostile world outside. Suddenly that outside world breaks violently into their midst. Tongues of fire lash their gathering. A mighty wind whips that fire into a frenzy and the entire community is tragically, senselessly destroyed.

This image from Waco, Texas in 1993 burns in my brain as a kind of counter-Pentecost, a constant reminder of a community at odds with the world around itself, evasive not embrassive, turned in instead of sent out. Fire and wind and Spirit for ill as well as good.

A Second Image. A parish church gathered in its Sunday celebration. Just after the opening prayer a group of people knock loudly at the door, interrupting the quiet before the first reading. The Presiding priest invites those knocking to enter. In the name of the community he inquires what they want. They reply that they are a group of people who have been looking into our Catholic faith. They want to be welcomed as Catechumens, want to join our ranks as we move together through the liturgical year. They desire to listen with us to the story of Jesus, eventually moving with us towards the Easter Sacraments. We applaud and welcome them. We do this, or something like it, every year.

Today, Pentecost, concludes the process of initiation that we began to solemnize with that autumn liturgy. These inquirers, then catechumens, now neophytes watched and walked with us through the year, through Lent, through Easter. With them we have renewed the Spirit of our own Baptism, Confirmation, Eucharist. Today they gather with us prepared to lead us in our recessional from this Church into the world from which they and we came.

Somehow these two images mesh, clash, and clarify each other. Their enormous difference lies in the great gulf between <u>separation from</u> and <u>insertion into</u>, between <u>coming in</u> versus <u>going out</u>, from a <u>fire</u> within us <u>for ourselves</u> and a <u>fire</u> going out from us <u>for others</u>.

In the light of these contrasting images, one dealing death, one offering abundant life, let me turn to the Readings for this feast.

From the Acts of the Apostles we hear the classic version of the Pentecost story. The Spirit bursts into the world healing the divisions caused by the origins of human sin at Babel. That mythological story speaks of the sin that decimates human speech, separating humans one from another, rendering communication impossible across ethnic, cultural, national, ideological boundaries. Pentecost restores the primordial harmony. One language unites all, every nation, every people, if only for a moment.

God's Spirit brings people together, unites, connects, invites, welcomes; it does not separate, divide, destroy.

In the First letter to the Corinthians Paul's central concern is the end of the divisions in that early community. Because the Spirit of Jesus lives in His followers there is no longer Jew or Greek, slave or free, young or old, black or white or brown, no Russian or Syrian or Cuban or Iraqi. We and *They* disappear. We are all parts of the same body, all needing each other's gifts if our own are to flourish in this Body, if our voices are to ring in harmony. Inclusion, acceptance, respect for differences become the ineluctable sign of the presence of God's Spirit.

The Pentecost scene in John's Gospel occurs not forty days later but on "that first day of the week," that first day of Resurrection. The breath of Jesus brings peace. This Spirit is not limited as we have too often imagined to a few, to priests, to the ordained, but is given to the Church, the disciples, all the followers of Jesus. This peace comes from healing and forgiveness, from a community whose main task appears to be letting people become unbound, letting everyone, always have the chance to start over, to begin anew and again. The gift Jesus gives to his followers is essentially to forgive as God does, with the same spirit God gave Jesus. Again we become a community not of the perfect standing over and against those who are less than ourselves, but a fragile gathering of the broken but forgiven; people no longer holding onto past hurts, ancient injuries, old wars.

It has taken me many years to learn this, but I am now convinced that the Church is not supposed to "work." I used to think it was an aberration that so much emotional, spiritual, psychological energy was expended getting along with the very people with whom we prayed and ministered. For years I have resented the infighting, the politicizing, the intramural wars that too frequently occur in every Church community. Why, I had wondered, could not we who professed to follow Jesus get along, agree to disagree, lend support to one another?

It now seems clear to me that the very point of the Church, the reason for our existence as a community of the fragile followers of Jesus, is that it is very difficult for people to agree, to get along, to manage to love each other no matter what.

The church exists as a sign that such a community is possible!

Living in God's spirit, belonging to the Church of Jesus seems sometimes like dancing in a circle; we never get anywhere, and we keep bumping into each other. Finally we may catch the harmony, and move in tandem . . . but meanwhile the important thing is to keep dancing, keep trying because the effort is more important than the outcome.

A great prophetic Jesuit who worked for nearly 50 years in a neighborhood where I was once pastor taught me this lesson. Out of deep concern for the poor and a passion for justice, this dedicated yet somehow playful priest undertook a hundred different projects, started fifty programs, invited literally thousands of people to join with him. By his own admission, nothing he ever did "worked." All the problems he has addressed -- hunger, homelessness, care for the mentally ill, substance abuse, military expenditures and training for war in the face of poverty -- all got worse not better. Still he went on because what matters is not the programmatic outcome but the quality of the relationships of the people engaged together. He struggles with others against injustice in the world not because doing so will change the world, but because if they do not the world will change them.

And this parish, this small church? Our Pentecost question becomes how can we celebrate our diversity and become more fully one? How make our diversity a gift, a virtue not something to be cleansed, expunged. In a world so riddled in divisiveness, conflict, violence, leading to conflagration, death and destruction, how do we witness to something quite different? How can we use our gifts to open doors, to welcome, to include? How celebrate and live our inter-dependent need for each other. We are young and old, black and white and brown, moderately rich and fairly poor. *If we can be one* there is hope for our world.

Months ago a few of our sisters and brothers knocked on our doors and sought entrance. We welcomed them, then moved with them through the life of Jesus, then through his death and Resurrection. Today that journey culminates in Pentecost and the gift of the Spirit. That Spirit constantly sends us out into our world to renew it in Jesus. We Pray:

Come Holy Spirit
Fill the hearts of your faithful people.
Kindle in us the fire of your love.
Send forth your Spirit
And we shall be re-created,
And we shall renew the face of the earth.

34) The Feast of the Holy Trinity

Scripture Readings: Ex. 34,:4-6, 8-9; 2 Cor. 13: 11-13; Jn. 3: 16-18

I am tempted to begin with a playful review of our catechism.

Remember: There are Twelve Apostles
                Eleven faithful ones,
                Ten Commandments
                Nine choirs of Angles
                Eight beatitudes
                Seven Sacraments
                Six Precepts of the Church (at least there were)
                Five decades of the rosary
                Four Gospels
                Three persons in God
                Two Natures in Christ
                One God,
                and no proof!

It feels equally flippant to start today saying something profound like: The Theme of Today's Mass is "GOD!"

Doesn't that sound strange? Both of these awkward beginnings testify to how difficult it is to preach about a dogma.

The scripture readings for this feast simply invite us to look from various angles at a dogma, a truth of our faith, inviting reflection on its importance in our lives. The first reading stresses the Lordship of the God we are inclined to call Father; the second reading stresses the harmony of the community that lives in the fellowship of the Spirit; the Gospel invites us to deeper faith in Jesus, the incarnate presence of God's love in our midst . . . the Trinity. A theologian friend of mine, Fr. Peter Chirico, constantly reminded people that any dogma, any credal statement, any Church teaching is only important in so far as it effects our behavior, helps us to live better more holy lives What's in our heads only matters if it changes our hearts!

So today we wrestle with not the fact of, but the importance of the Trinity. One of the finest books of recent years, **God For Us** by Katherine LaCugna, now deceased theologian from Notre Dame (who grew up in St. Joseph parish, Seattle) insists that the Church's teaching about Trinity is best concerned not with the life of the Trinity all by itself in some heaven, but with the God who relates to us. LaCugna maintains that our reflection on God remains always Christological or Soteriological, that is, it is important because it helps us understand Jesus and our own salvation.

Ordinarily a homily should not be a Theology class. Ten to fifteen minutes is not adequate to even begin a serious reflection on the central mystery of our faith. Still, given our feast today, let me share with you from LaCugna's book a caution, and then two simple insights. These are ideas that help me follow Jesus; I hope they help you.

First, then a caution. We need to begin with the profound awareness that everything we say about God is untrue! Everything is at least partial, a bit of a guess, imperfect, inadequate. The most true thing we can say about God is that no one word, no human language, no image, however biblical, sufficiently encapsulates God. God is, finally, not Father, not Spirit, not Son. God is not eagle, or rock, or compassion. God is bigger, fuller, more complex and at the same time more simple than any of our words or ideas. We can speak only tentatively of what God has shown us about herself/ himself.

Having said this, what is unique about our Christian Faith is our belief that God is Triune. Our God has revealed to us something about the Divine in our midst in three different, unique, wondrous personalities. We can be helped to know who we are by growing in our understanding of who God is revealed to be for us.

The first and most striking thing about this Trinitarian revelation involves our call as a people related to such a God to embrace diversity. We Christians recognize diversity as something profoundly true about reality, and about the God who creates this reality. Our God is revealed as marvelous in diversity, three persons, each totally yet uniquely God.

Just as every human being is completely unique, so each divine person is completely unique. Diversity is embraced as the one foundation of everything. This notion of Trinity invites us to preserve the essentially relational nature of human existence and the interdependent quality of the entire universe.

In terms less abstract, we are all called to love each other; we are all in this together.

We are not faithful to this God when we do not let creation image God, when we make some people better than others, or do not acknowledge, admit, celebrate the interdependence of every person and every part of this creation.

The second striking notion from La Cugna's reflection concerns the relational character of God as revealed to us. God's relationality invites us human beings to change the way we relate to each other individually and as nations. The inner life of God is neither a *monarchy*, nor a *patriarchy*, but the perfect harmony of diverse personalities. There is not one God over, or above other Gods; the Father is not greater than the Son (as God), nor the Son greater than the Spirit. Any human society that would image/ mirror God must involve diversity, harmony, circularity. God is simply not about *power over*, but *relationship with*. So, our Church , our parishes, or any other segment of the church fail to be the Church of Jesus when we act out of "authority over" rather than "relationship with."

In fact the most amazing thing to the followers of Jesus from Judaism was the realization that the distant, all powerful "Lord" that Moses met in the Exodus reading we heard today is not God all by God's self. "Jesus is Lord, "also. This scandalized them. And without the Holy Spirit empowering us we cannot even recognize this truth! Some inner harmony of love spills over to us inviting us to the same harmony, same love.

Maybe I can make all this more simple, more clear. We, the followers of Jesus are loved by and invited to fall in love with the God that Jesus reveals. This God of Jesus is essentially characterized as community, constituted in love, spilling over into creation. We image this God when we are loving, creative, interconnected.

Our Christian, Triune Faith tells us at its simplest and best:

- that we have met and we know God as one who creates and sustains us in life, while creating and sustaining a life that is full, vibrant, beautiful,
- that we have met and know God as our brother, our friend, our guide, our companion, our teacher, indeed, our savior. Jesus gets inside us and changes everything.
- and we have met and know, and celebrate God as a unique Spirit that binds us together, affords us insight beyond our own wisdom, gives us courage to follow Jesus despite our fears.

And in all of these, and the infinite variety of other ways God enters our life, God does so as community of love, inviting us ever more deeply into the creative, sustaining, familial community life.

This is, in part, what we celebrate today when the theme of our Mass is, simply, God.

35) The Feast of the Body and Blood of Christ

(Corpus Christi)

<u>Scripture Readings:</u> Deut. 8:2-3, 14-16; 1 Cor. 10:16-17; Jn. 6: 51-52

In the early 70's I was at a parish church when the pastor, delightfully, introduced the Kiss of Peace for the first time. By serendipity, he did so this very Sunday, the Feast of Corpus Christi. Referring to the second reading: "This bread we break is a sharing in the body of Christ; the loaf is one and so are we, etc.," he went on to elaborately remind the assembly that we are all one loaf, so we all share in the same bread, and we greet the members of the same loaf, etc. Then he said, quite solemnly, "So, let's all turn *to the crumb next to us,* and wish the peace of Christ."

That experience has forever shaped my understanding of this feast.

Corpus Christi, now called the Feast of the Body and Blood of Christ, grew up in the late middle ages as a celebration honoring the consecrated host. The host was placed in a gorgeous monstrance, carried in a solemn procession, with much incense, pomp, circumstance. Such celebrations stressed the least significant aspect of Eucharistic life in the Church, *a tendency to honor the host rather than eat it.*

At the time this feast began to be celebrated, people rarely received communion at Mass. Eucharistic devotion bowed and sang and genuflected but did not eat. Such practice stood in stark contrast with the readings for the feast, all of which challenge us to sincere eating and drinking.

Taken together these three short readings say about all there is to say about a more authentic, and even a more traditional approach to Eucharistic devotion.

First, the Eucharist is food for a journey, like the Manna in the dessert for our Israelite ancestors as they moved from Egypt to the Promised land, from slavery to freedom, from death to life! The Eucharist is food for those who know they are hungry, who need to be nourished, and who have used up every other option. We have no food to turn to than this!

Secondly, in a truth so sadly neglected for centuries, the Eucharist is not only communion with Jesus, but also with the Body of Christ, the Church. The context of the section of First Corinthians from which our short reading is taken underlines the need to recognize the *body* if we are going to receive the *body*. We are all *crumbs* of the same loaf. To receive Jesus "worthily" we need to take in the whole package, all the messy people who make up this body. We cannot come to this altar and receive Jesus if we are not ready and willing to receive into ourselves all the people who share this meal with us. That's why we have the Kiss of Peace before communion (or perhaps even before the gifts are offered at the table). If we are not able to greet each other in human warmth how will we receive each other in Divine friendship.

Paul's central theological insight is that the Church, the believers in Jesus, are, not just in metaphor but in fact, his Body! Remember how, when struck to the ground, Paul heard the question:

"Saul, Saul, why are you persecuting me?"

It's not in the book, but I imagine Paul responding with amazement:

"I'm not persecuting you, I'm just out killing a few Christians!"

And Jesus replies:

"They are me, and I am them, we are each other ... and you can't have one without the other!"

We are invited on this feast to take Paul's insight with absolute seriousness. To receive Jesus is to receive into our hearts, our lives, our very blood stream, each other. Should we not be open to doing so, we should not approach the broken bread at this altar.

The third reading, the Gospel offers a theology with which we are, ironically, more familiar, even more comfortable. Amazingly, we blanch less at the thought of eating the flesh and drinking the blood of Jesus than we do taking the life of one another into our hearts, our lives. It is amazing how have become familiar, even comfortable, with such an outrageous idea -- to receive communion is to receive Jesus into our lives, to let his blood be in our veins, his flesh be on our bones.

We can forget that the Jewish people presented by John as hearing these words were totally scandalized, and for the most part, "walked no more with him." Jewish laws had strict prohibitions against eating or touching any blood. The shock of Jesus words as John presents the story would force his hearers to listen in a new way. This new way would see Jesus suggesting himself as the source, the life force, of whatever is important in his listeners lives because he offers them a link to God. Jesus *is* a new covenant, a new pact, an entirely new relationship with the meaning of life, existence, everything. Jesus replaces all other covenants, all institutions, all religion, every other way of nurturing life.

For his hearers or for us to believe these words about eating flesh and drinking blood is to say that Jesus is totally, completely, irrevocably central to their lives, to our lives. We cannot hear these words casually, partially. To receive Eucharist is to give myself over completely, without reservation to the mystery into which I am entering.

These three readings then, together, constitute a tremendous and challenging commitment.

Together they mean that we are on a journey from slavery to freedom and our very lives are at stake.

Together they mean we are hungry on this journey and we can know and name our hungers. -- we risk dying if we are not fed mightily on the way.

Together they mean that we desperately want to be part of this family, this body with whom we travel and that we are completely available to all those who travel with us.

Together these readings mean that we are totally willing to let Jesus take over our lives, to live no longer ourselves, but to allow room for Jesus to live in us.

As I say this I picture of a young woman who suffered from multiple sclerosis who, over the strong objections of her family, joined the parish where I ministered. She did so out of a deep belief in and desire for the Eucharist. Shortly after Easter the very year she formally became part of our parish she became very, very sick, needing a nursing home that offered all but total care. Her family no longer accepted any responsibility for her, so this community she had joined had to take up that responsibility. She, and we risked everything on this mystery. She risked losing all affection and care but that of Jesus; we risked accepting responsibility for a stranger now become a sister!

We are terribly human and we will celebrate this feast as we do everything human, with some faltering, some backsliding. We will not totally live up to what we profess. In fact this feast of the Body of Christ is the feast of exactly that, this *Body*, not just the Eucharistic bread. We are indeed *crummy*, crumbling parts of the body of Christ, and we turn to each other with a smile as well as a conviction as we celebrate who Christ is, and who we are with him. We are people who want to be, but will always imperfectly be *The Body of Christ.*

36) The Eleventh Sunday

Scripture Readings: Ex. 19:1-6; Ro. 5:6-11; Mt. 9:36-10:8

Some years ago in our RCIA process a very intelligent young doctor was going towards the baptismal font kicking and screaming, looking for an excuse to avoid the direction faith was inevitably leading. He sought for any excuse to remove himself from the process he had promised his wife to pursue. He thought he had us one day for he had heard that Sunday the Preface in which we call ourselves " a chosen people, a royal nation, a Holy Priesthood, a people set apart." He began our Wednesday night session asking at the outset, almost with glee:

"What is this baloney about the "Chosen people; Who do you think you are?"

I was amazed to hear come out of my mouth a response more or less like the following:

"God did not choose the Jewish people, nor does God choose us now because we are so good, but because we are so needy. We are not the brightest and the best, but the weakest and the worst. Chosen because we need it so badly not because we deserve it so much! And besides everyone is chosen.!"

I recall that evening as I look at today's readings about call. Moses is called to lead this people, "God's treasured possession." Admittedly the whole earth is God's but this people shall be a priestly kingdom, a holy nation.

Paul reminds the first Christian community of Rome that it is while we were still sinners that Christ died for us ... called, loved, saved us way before we deserved it. It fact, Paul says, it is this Love before merit that proves God's love for us.

I am especially fond of the Gospel this weekend because of the kind of people Jesus apparently calls to a special share in his ministry. They are no community of saints, no community of brain surgeons or wise philosophers. They are, rather the kind of fragile, fallible people who have made up the disciples of Jesus ever since. People like ourselves.

Brash Peter, always leading with his clay foot, speaking more than he can live up to, jumping bravely out of boats, only to sink, fishing all night on the wrong side of the boat, cutting off ears when capitulation is called for, denying he even knows the one he promised to follow even to death. So human Peter.

And James and John who have the courage to leave net and family behind to pursue Jesus' invitation, but who will argue over who is most important, apparently even inviting their mother to intercede for them.

Matthew, who tells the story, had been a traitor, a tax collector living off the misery of his fellow Jews. And Judas, tragic Judas, who will finally give up on the vision.

I often wonder were Jesus powers of discernment so poor that he could not have chosen a better bunch out of the many who followed him? Or did he indeed choose the foolish of this world to confound the wise?

And does he not still do this? Look around at the community worshipping here today. I am not aware of anyone terribly famous or fantastically brilliant. I am not aware of anyone even who is ostentatiously holy, though I am constantly impressed with the deep, honest everyday holiness of so many in our midst. We are the community of Jesus, chosen not because of merit, but because of love. It was true in the beginning and it will be true forever.

But like that first community of the followers of Jesus the mission we are invited into is to proclaim good news, especially the good news of this freely given, undeserved, comprehensive love, first given to us. We are invited to "cure the sick, raise the dead, cleanse lepers, cast out demons." The very fact that we do not feel able to do such things is the point. We can't, God can, working in and through us.

We can love those who are sick in our parish, and if not bring them to life, ease their passage into eternal life. We can celebrate the deaths of our community with the kind of faith that raises them to life, and consoles those who mourn their loss. With the life of Jesus working in our midst, we can cast out the demons of ignorance, fear, poverty, in us, among us and around us.

The final line of the Gospel is, then, perhaps the line towards which our readings and all these reflections point. "What you have freely received, freely give." I am convinced that our God invites fairly fragile people to experience God's love and then to give it away. If we know that we don't deserve the gifts we have received, we are not inclined to hoard and hang onto them.

The counselor or teacher who never expected to have much money finds it fairly easy to give 10% of it away. The singer among us surprised, delighted to have the gift of song can share it easily with this community. The widow who survived her loss because a community surrounded her with care can easily spend her spare time now in a nursing home consoling others. That doctor who did not expect to find religious faith, who fought it strongly, now knowing a God who loves him deeply, undeservedly, can give every patient more than medical care, touching them with love that heals more deeply.

Those who did not deserve, or earn, or even expect to be called and gifted, those who were loved "while they were still sinners," those like us who are the called disciples of Jesus, can freely give, what was freely received and we wait to be told again today:

> **"You--a chosen race, a royal priesthood, a holy nation,**
> **a people set apart--you, go to love and serve! "**

37) The Twelfth Sunday

Scripture Readings: Jer. 20:10-13; Ro. 5: 12-15; Mt. 10:26-33

I have never been terribly consoled knowing that I mean more to God than "many sparrows." And, as the years pass by, numbering the hairs on my head becomes less of a task for anyone, never mind God! The metaphor gets in the way of the promise which does console me a great deal, namely that Jesus will stand before God on my behalf in the light of whatever suffering I might endure on his account. And that is the point of the Gospel.

It seems important to get inside what would have been the experience of Jesus followers at the time the Gospel is written, or the disciples to whom Jesus spoke something like the words of today's reading.

We can be deceived into imagining that it would have been great to have seen Jesus in the flesh, to have walked the roads with him, to have heard him speak and to have experienced the miracles first hand, and then to be sent out to do some of the work ourselves. Realism enters with today's word. Apparently it felt dangerous to follow him. Jesus tells his closest followers not to be afraid. Despite all the evidence that gives reason to your fear, don't be afraid!

You can be killed, but not really hurt!

These disciples shared the life and the lot of someone around whom trouble was brewing. If they stayed with him there was a good chance that the political and/or the religious authorities would punish them. They had reason to be afraid, these first followers of Jesus. Their leader was first vilified, then crucified and they had cause to believe they might be also.

It was scary to be a companion of this itinerant, radical preacher; it ought to be scary now. Is it?

I suspect that is the crunch point of today's readings. Do we share the reality of Jeremiah who initially in today's first reading laments that he was "seduced" (not just *enticed*, but the more graphic *seduced*) into speaking God's word to a people who didn't want to hear it? The keepers of the law, the religious folks of his day, were looking for every chance to get him and he was both angry and afraid. Jeremiah speaks confidently that God will be with him, but still, things are piling up; he is, quite naturally, afraid.

Am I afraid, precisely because I am a follower of Jesus? In my public life, my work life, my family life, does what I say or do disturb anyone? Do the values I espouse, my most dearly held convictions create any stir at all in the world in which I live and move and have my being? The readings today would seem to have no force unless I had cause to be afraid. Put another way, If I was arrested and accused of being a Christian, a follower of Jesus, would there be enough evidence to convict me??

The high school student, living his faith as he understands it, and so not messing with drugs when "everyone is doing it," risks the title "nerd." The Christian in business, law, medicine, Real Estate who refuses to take part in questionable practices, risks losing a job . . . and that can be very scary.

A politician today able to stand with Jesus clearly on the side of *all* the poor, whether on death row, unborn, more than two years on welfare, elderly, gay, or illegally in our country certainly needs to fear for re-election.

A Catholic, especially a priest, who, in the light of the Gospel, wonders out loud whether women could possibly be ordained, or whether gay couples shouldn't have legal rights to inheritance or sick room visitation, the basic right to marry, or raises the question of welcoming refugees from Syria and Iran, can reasonably fear being silenced or disciplined.

All of the above and so many other issues like them are important implications of following Jesus, and not being afraid. But none rise to the level of life-threatening. Not many of us risk the fate of Thomas Moore before Henry the 8th, or Oscar Romero before the El Salvadoran Military, or even Dorothy Day or Dan Berrigan before the Federal Government. Still we are invited, all of us, to wonder today about the cost of discipleship What is Jesus asking of me, where is the crunch; how does believing in and following Jesus both raise my fears and paradoxically invite me not to be afraid?

I think of Patty, a prophetic woman in today's so complicated church. After fourteen years of working as school teacher, musician, religious education director, RCIA coordinator, and almost every other imaginable parish position, Patty finished her theological education. Masters of Divinity in hand she was invited to become pastoral administrator of a parish that had always had a priest; now there were not enough to go around. She knew that this new position held a million risks. She gave up a secure job with decent pay and a community of people who loved her as she did them. She risked the anger of parishioners who did not like the direction the church was going, risked the possible financial failure of the parish, risked ecclesial disapproval when she preached or led the community in worship. Still her prayer led her to say "Yes," to forging a prophetic path not just for women in the Church, but because the community needed and deserved her gifts, and if Jesus was with her as he seemed to promise, nothing could finally hurt her. Though the past years have held enormous struggle and pain, she has survived and her community has thrived.

I think of Brian a financial consultant who five years ago made $150,000, and was miserable. He stopped cold and spent almost the entire year in retreats of one kind or another. He has re-entered the fray but now he invites people to socially responsible investments with less attention to earnings and more to justice making. He has committed himself to a simple style of life more dependent on peace than things. He pursues this path, the path of Jesus, partly for his own peace of mind, but largely to model prophetically an entirely different behavior to the world of finance in which he moves.

Each of us does have a prophetic call in our world. All of us are invited to some substantial risk as disciples of Jesus. Each of us ought, somewhere in our lives, to be afraid . . . and then to have the courage not to let the fear win. Remember: Our hairs are counted. We are worth more than many sparrows.

38) The Thirteenth Sunday

Scripture Readings: 2 Kings 4:8-12, 14-17; Ro. 6: 3-4,8-11; Mt. 10:37-42

The strongest liturgical impression I have from my many years of celebrating involves the second reading today and the Easter Vigil. Picture, if you will, a packed community huddled in a dark church. We have already heard the wonderful stories from the Hebrew scriptures, stories of creation, of Abraham and Isaac, of flood and Exodus and a promised messiah. Into the darkness a single light shines on a flowing baptismal pool. A lovely young woman, with no book in hand, steps behind the pool and tells us,

> "Do you not know that we who were baptized into Christ Jesus were baptized into his death ... so that just as Christ was raised from the dead, we too might live a new life.... If we have died with Christ we are also to live with him. ..."

This new life in Jesus proclaimed at the Center of the Easter Vigil readings is the center of everything we are, everything we do here around this altar, everything we are or do when we leave this place to transform our world.

The Gospel today speaks about this new life in challenging terms. It speaks about loving Jesus more than our families, speaks about taking up a cross, speaks about losing life, speaks the challenge of the call of discipleship. It is not an easy word to hear, but it is at the center of our lives, the light shining in the darkness.

This passage from "the hard sayings" of Jesus reminds me of the small boy trying to impress his teacher asking, "How do I know what Jesus want me to do?" The teacher suggested that he read the bible. A week later the teacher asked him if he had read the bible and the boy replied, "I did, but never again. You didn't tell me I might not like what Jesus tells me!"

Perhaps the boy read a passage like this one. Why does Jesus say things like this, and what does he mean?

Why does Jesus say "Whoever loves Father, mother, sister, brother more than me is not worthy of me?

Probably because it is true. It was true historically when Matthew's Gospel was written. Those who became Christians, either from Judaism, or from the surrounding pagan nations had to give up family roots, friends, all their identity, to follow Jesus. That's undoubtedly where the saying comes from.

But it makes sense on another level too. I remember a wife who told me her marriage never worked until she quit expecting her husband to be her savior, to be Jesus in a sense. Only when she acknowledged his frailty and fragility, his humanity, could she love him as he was. If we expect our loved ones to be everything we want or need we will stifle them with our expectations. If we put them into the context of a greater, deeper love of God for me, and me for God, then our human relationships can be whole, and full. They don't need to be in opposition, but they do need to be in perspective.

And why does Jesus say we need to take up a cross to find ourselves, to discover who we really are? Again, probably because it is true.

Jesus said what he believed; Jesus acted on his convictions. He lived as an honest, authentic, loving, fearless man. To live this way brought suffering, a cross for him. It will for us. If we are willing to be authentic, willing to love, willing to act and speak with courage, we will endure some cross. If we are not willing to so act, we will never find out who we are. Witness the martyred Jesuits of El Salvador; witness Martin Luther King, Jr. . . . or witness the many people of this Christian community who let Jesus be central to their lives and are willing to accept the suffering that their love brings.

Jesus challenge to take up a cross is personalized; take up *your* cross, not mine! He does not suggest that *any* pain will do. The Christian message is not masochistic, no matter how we paint it so. Jesus is not making a rule: "You must suffer!" He is speaking a fact that experience eventually teaches us all. We need to accept, embrace, move through the suffering that love brings into our lives. We cannot live and love and avoid pain.

The form pain takes will differ with each person and with each diverse demand of love.

I have known people who needed to stay with a pain filled marriage and work through the pain to new life. And I have known people who, with enormous suffering, have had to break out of a marriage to find any life for themselves or their family.

I personally experienced much suffering in struggling to stay faithful to my priestly call and ministry. And I have had to embrace a very real cross and undergo much suffering to move out of ordained ministry to discover and save my ability to live and love.

I have seen people stay in jobs, or leave them, seen people stay in one place geographically, or move across the country, seen people re-commit to significant relationships, and be forced by reality to move out of them. All, if for the good, with great pain. Most significant human choices can be done either to run away from suffering or to enter more fully into suffering because it was there and love seemed to demand it. **No one can say ahead of time, or for another what any individual person's life-giving-cross might be.**

The prophet, the holy person of today's gospel, the follower of Jesus is the one who loves as best he or she can, with all the gifts and courage one can muster, willing to enter into dialogue with community to discover how and where love leads, willing to face the hardship love brings. Jesus suggest that life comes from taking up the cross life gives uniquely to each of us.

There is another part to the Gospel today. The final paragraph speaks of the importance of those who try to be followers of Jesus not just doing things for others, but letting others do things for them.

"Whoever welcomes you welcomes me ..."

Receiving is as important as giving. The person who takes care of Elijah, or you, or me, because we are trying to be faithful to Jesus gets a reward as great as our own. We are all in this together, and we need each other. Following Jesus is not just doing things, but also receiving things, and sometimes that's harder.

I remember watching at a reception for a wonderful staff person leaving a parish where I worked. An older parishioner on a fixed and minimum income, a very poor, wonderfully simple woman tried to give her a five dollar bill. She tried to refuse it, and a small struggle took place. Finally the well paid professional woman received the poor woman's gift. Both are rewarded.

A priest friend who works on the streets tells me about a woman in a sheltered living situation who gives him a dollar each month for him in his ministry. He has to receive it.

It consoles me that Jesus today tells us not just to put him ahead of our families, or to take up a cross, but also to allow ourselves to receive the love that others want to give us.

All of this to remind us what we heard out of the darkness on Easter Sunday dawn, "We who are baptized in Christ are called to live a new life!"

39) The Fourteenth Sunday

Scripture Readings: Zach. 9:9-10; Ro. 8. 9, 11-13; Mt. 11:25-30

Many years ago, now, my father was dying. His aorta blood vessel on his neck had burst from a cancerous tumor; he would inevitably bleed to death. Doctors could sedate and bandage him, curtail the bleeding until he was about to lapse into a comma, then he would become more conscious, begin to bleed, come closer to death.

Because his wife, my step-mother, had had a biopsy that morning, we hoped to keep my father alive until she could get to the hospital to see him. Throughout the day the family experienced several intervals of quiet waiting as he was nearly comatose. Then my father would wake, becoming conscious of all of us gathered around him.

Several times over the space of hours he woke, looked at us and asked: "Am I really going to die?"

Everyone got very quiet. Eventually it seemed left to me, the family priest to say, "Yes, dad, you are really going to die."

Each time he said, "I'm so afraid."

I asked him, "What do you do when you are afraid?"

He replied: "I say, 'Sacred Heart of Jesus, I place my trust in you,' or 'Jesus meek and humble of heart, make my heart like unto thine.'" Prayers taken from today's Gospel.

In the moments before his death, as those who loved him wept, my father returned to the prayers that had sustained him all through life. In the moments before his death, my father, in the ultimate human weakness, was drawn to the weakness and vulnerability of Jesus, "meek and humble of heart."

By most standards my father had been a very successful man, in business, in the community, and with his family. Though a very religious man he was far from a saint. He knew human weakness. I have been struck ever since his death that my father's faith, finally, was not based in his strength, or power, or prestige, but was rooted precisely in the support God offered to him in his weakness.

God is not revealed to us in our wisdom and cleverness, but in our child-like questions and our emptiness. For my father, as for Jesus, and for us all, _fragility becomes strength_!

This is an important personal lesson to internalize and I am grateful to my father for modeling this insight. But, more important than my personal reflection, we celebrate this Sunday close to the celebration of our national birthday. I find myself amazed every third year that readings picked out for the entire world-wide church so appropriately invite reflection on "The Fourth of July," our nation, and its stance in the world.

Before we heard the Gospel we listened to the words of the Prophet Isaiah ringing out about a leader who will come to us "meek and riding on an ass." This king will

"... banish the chariots
and the nation's bow he will banish
as he proclaims peace to the nations."

As the gospel does on the personal scale, the prophet suggests on the larger world scale that power is found in meekness and fragility.

It is good, as Christians to listen to this truth, lest we see some virtue in midnight air strikes on Syria, or contemplate pre-emptive action towards North Korea foreseeing scores of civilians displaced or killed. How much more satisfying to a Christian it ought to be to be a peaceful presence in Somalia than a violent one in Korea, to enter into a violent situation as peacemakers, not just adding to the violence, to be part of a dialogue in the Holy land, rather than providing Israel with more and more armaments. Though often the way of Nations, meeting violence with more violence is not the Way of Jesus.

I am also struck that on this weekend after we celebrate our national independence Jesus invites us to take his **yoke** -- the ultimate symbol of <u>de</u>pendence -- upon us and learn from him. Though I firmly believe in the wonderful gift that it is to be a citizen of the United States, and am deeply grateful for our becoming an independent nation so many years ago, I am convinced of our absolute need to acknowledge not our independence but our interdependence in, and with, and on every other nation of the world.

Nations of the Middle East, or trading partners in Europe do not exist as pawns for our national self-interest—"America First," if you will" Our own deepest and best good is co-extensive with the best and deepest good of the people of even the most impoverished or alienated nations.

I suggest for our communal prayer after this Fourth of July, this consideration: It may only be on religious grounds, but I suspect even on pragmatic political ones that we as a nation need to ask, not the independent question: "**What is best for us?**" but the interdependent one, "**What is best for everyone?**"

Finally, I remember taking communion through the final weeks of June a few years ago to a wonderfully wise Native American Woman. Betty was, in the truest sense, an elder, an incredibly faith-filled woman with a wisdom and strength that comes only from one who shares in Jesus' humility and gentleness. There was in her a wisdom and even a cleverness that comes from one who manages to remain child-like. Though her burden in illness was indeed great, it was light because of her faith in Jesus, who carried the burden with her. In other words she made real and credible for me the truth of today's gospel.

Betty became for me a symbol of the need for those of us who call ourselves American, to learn from the first of us, those Indian people here before we came. Recently reading Sherman Alexi's "You Don't Have to Say You Love Me," a great new memory of his Mother and his own painful upbringing, and how we stifled in them what we must learn for ourselves.

We need to learn their deep reverence for the land we share,
to understand their strength in weakness,
to share their insight into God, who binds earth, people, sky everything together
A God, revealed to them in lovely but fragile natural beauty –
beautiful for spacious skies,
for many centuries before we came.

Then, perhaps, we can pray, as individuals, and as a nation, a people with one another:

"*Jesus, meek and humble of our heart ,make our hearts like unto thine.*"

40) The Fifteenth Sunday

Scripture Readings: Is. 55: 10-11; Ro. 8: 18-23; Mt. 13: 1-23

Everyone has probably heard the story, but it bears telling again, about the father who had twin sons, one an incurable optimist, the other a confirmed pessimist. He wanted them each to achieve better balance and on their twelfth birthday he hit upon the perfect solution. He called them to himself and gave quite different gifts to each.

To his pessimist son he gave a beautiful, young vibrant pony and invited him to go and take a ride on his new horse. No boy could withstand the wonders of such a gift.

To his optimist son he gave a barn entirely full of horse manure. This must dampen even the most positive spirit.

An hour later the father came back to see how his sons were faring. He found his pessimist son sitting dejected on the hillside watching the horse run and prance about a lovely field. He asked him why he was not riding, not enjoying the horse. The boy replied that if he got on it he'd probably fall off, or the horse would trip and break a leg and need to be shot. No sense getting into it; everything would turn out awful.

Next the father went to the barn where he heard shouts of joy, and singing. He entered and found his optimist son throwing the manure right and left, laughing in glee, enjoying a romp in the distasteful gift. "What are you doing?" the father asked, amazed. The boy replied, "With all this manure, there must be a pony in here somewhere."

I want to hear the readings today, especially the Gospel, from the vantage point of this second son.

We can be tempted to hear today's' gospel as an invitation to examine ourselves with fierce scrutiny to discover what kind of field we are and how the soil of our spirit welcomes the seed of God's word ... are we fertile, or shallow, short-term or long-lasting in our response?

If we listen to the gospel against the background of the other two readings, and even of the historical development of the parable itself, we are more likely to "find a pony."

The first reading, from Isaiah, promises that the word of God spoken in our midst will not return empty ... it will accomplish its purpose, no matter what kind of soil we are.

The marvelous reading from Romans invites us, with Paul, to view every human struggle, every pain, as birth pains in a world "groaning in one great act of giving birth." Suffering now need not be compared to the glory that is on its way. What a positive view of the manure that may seem to be overwhelming us in life!

I find it most exciting to read the Gospel from this positive stance. It helps to think of the reality of farm life. Any reasonable farmer would likely prepare the soil, dig it up, turn it over, and then carefully put the seeds down in careful rows. But the surprise of the parable, the twist if you will, is that this farmer (apparently an image of God) just throws the seeds everywhere. God is wildly abundant, crazy in the enthusiasm and lack of discipline of his planting. He throws seed of his word, his love on the rocks, on the hillsides, even in the midst of thorns. Some of it will grow everywhere. And every bit of growth may be good. Some of it will flourish abundantly and that will be even better.

It is perhaps only later, as the gospel is written down, that the writer is forced to do what Jesus apparently didn't do at first, explain each part of the sowing in an allegorical, rather than parabolic fashion.

I listen to the hope in these readings, the conscious decision to interpret the world hopefully. I hear it encouraging me and all of us to a similar stance in our world. I celebrate the Jesuit congregation that speaks so eloquently about "the salvific work of God's revelation present in every culture," before we do anything.

The seed is already thrown everywhere.

In a small paragraph of presupposition to the Spiritual Exercises, St. Ignatius suggests that the relationship between the one making a retreat and the one directing it ought to be founded on each trying to put the best possible interpretation on whatever the other says, or does. Not a bad presupposition for any relationship.

I want to be part of a Church, a faith and hope-filled people, who keep whistling and singing while we look for the pony that may well lie hidden in anything.

There must something to this music our kids listen to . . . how can we find it?

Underneath the quest for material comforts there must be some hidden human value, some hunger or thirst that Jesus can satisfy.

This desire for painless death, and the passage in several states of laws allowing assisted suicide must have some human yearning not to be abused by medical science, some longing to retain human dignity that we can appreciate and build on.

Even those holding onto traditional marriage views ought to appreciate that gay couples want as the right to visit a life-long companion dying in the hospital, or to pass on an inheritance, or a home to someone with whom one has shared one's life.

Even those who elected an undisciplined and uneducated president can be seen yearning for a strong nation, a level playing field, a chance for a good job.

There is something in me that wants to at least try to look at everything that makes me uncomfortable, everything that confuses my value systems, everything that threatens my complacency as a member of the Church, or a citizen of this country or the world . . . . I want to look at everything and try to see what good might be in it that we can work with to help build the reign of God, rather than simply attacking.

I want to believe that the word of God is spoken in Jesus in our world and cannot return empty back to God, that every struggle or difficulty is, or can be Jesus coming to birth, that God is alive and present and throwing the seeds of life everywhere.

We turn now to Eucharist, letting God feed us with the word that is Jesus, trusting this planting will bring forth fruit.

41) The Sixteenth Sunday

Scripture Readings: Wis. 12:13, 16-9; Ro. 8: 26-8; Mt. 13:24-43

"Be careful about getting rid of your demons, or you may lose your angels too!"

The renowned psychologist, Rollo May, offered this warning. It's true. It is also the point of today's gospel. As you struggle to rid yourself of your worst faults, you may discover them to have been but the other side of your nicest and best traits.

Let me back up for a moment.

As with last week, the gospel today offers a parable, a story "thrown out" to be "thrown around" to see what it says. Parables are not allegories in which every point has a direct literal parallel. Both in last week's Gospel and today's the early church managed to turn the original parables into allegories, but scholars suggest Jesus original was just the parable. Certainly, because they are scriptural, the explanations are valid and part of revelation, but, it is illuminating to look first at the parable as parable.

The first reading from Wisdom today suggests that the theme holding the readings together is something about mercy, compassion, forgiveness, openness.

Look simply at the parable in the gospel asking the question: "What is the reign of God like?" The answer comes back, the reign of God is like a person sowing good wheat in a field. An enemy comes and puts weeds into the same field. These weeds are not wanted or desired, but, by golly, there they are, and since they are there we have to work with what is, not what might be.

The servants want to rush out and cut out the weeds. Weeds are messy; they disturb order, frustrating the initial plan. The uninformed first plan is to get rid of what is messy, unwieldy, unwanted.

In the Kingdom, the wise farmer says:

"No! Let the weeds live; we will try to work with them, and draw good out of their presence."

In the parable, as in life, it is sometimes very difficult to tell the difference between weeds and wheat. We do not want to wreck the whole wheat field trying to get rid of the weeds. Better to let them grow up together, and try to find some use for the weeds.

(Parenthetically, I was helped to understand this parable during a year I spent in Lesotho, in southern Africa, where there is no wood. People they needed the weeds to burn for fuel it they wanted to cook the wheat. The wheat was all but useless without the weeds with which to cook them ... a bit of a parallel parable, itself!)

A parable about the importance of holding on to the weeds feels quite true to me.

I spent a lot of time in my life lamenting my quick, smart-aleck tongue. I can so easily say things that hurt people, just for a laugh. When I began to realize this fault I wanted to get rid of it, but I could only do so by quitting talking. My glibness, quick wit, easy jibe is a gift; I can bring lightness and laughter to situations. My comments don't always, or even usually hurt. Rather than kill the fault and risk destroying the gift I need to work to integrate, to bring life out of both. Over the years I have needed to work at supporting people, speaking compliments, building up ... so that if I say something too quickly it has a context of love and support within which to exist.

We could all give our own examples of this. Every fault, (every Sufi number if you are so inclined), has a compensating virtue to balance it.

The compulsive helper really does help and needs to become non-compulsive, not quit helping.

The (Jesuit) or scholar who can be reclusive holding all he or she learns to oneself needs to learn to share the wisdom, not quit being a scholar.

The person who over does everything -- gives you ten books when you ask for one, or a five course meal when all you want is a sandwich -- that big hearted soul can't risk rooting out the exaggeration without losing a lot of life and laughter and charm.

Thomas Green's wonderful timeless book, *Weeds Among the Wheat*, suggests that a central task for Christians involves the life-long project of prayerfully discerning what is wheat, what is weed, seeing how what looks good might be bad, and what looks bad may be good. The role of the Spirit is to help us know the difference and live and work with both.

A further level of this wonderful parable suggests the need to learn to live with the essential messiness of the world. I remember years ago listening to the testimony of Oliver North on his illegal aid to the Contras in Nicaragua. What scared me was not so much that this responsibly placed man could break international law, but that he lived with such a neat and tidy division of the world into good guys and bad guys, communists and anti-communists. He was willing not just to break the law, but to do anything he could to further the cause of right as he saw it . . . no matter what anyone else said.

How insufficient to say that there are *two* sides to every issue. In reality there are many sides, many nuances, many shades of gray to almost anything.

The Republican compulsion to overthrow anything that has Obama's name on it, seems the same kind of total good-bad, black-white dilemma. Obamacare, refugees, migrants, dreamers, taxes, minimum wages, and every other significant political, *indeed human*, issue has many, many sides.

We only get rid of too early or too easily named weeds by killing an awful lot of wheat in the process.

Finally, as this parable bounces around in my head and heart, I wonder if weeds aren't an absolutely necessary part of reality. I wonder whether there is, in fact, truly an enemy who sows these things, or are they simply there. We don't need to blame anyone. We just need to work with reality, with the world the way it is, messy, unclear, not always digestible, but real and human and ours to exploit, enjoy, or build to a better place.

As we move now, with all the weeds that each of us bear within us, towards eating the wheat-become-bread-become-body we might ponder personally what are our worst faults . . . and what angels might live on their other side, waiting to be harvested.

42) The Seventeenth Sunday

Scripture Readings: I Kings 3:5-12; Ro. 8:28-30; Mt. 13:44-52

Since my name is Pat Carroll it is all right for me to tell ethnic jokes about Irishmen.

There was an Irishman who found an old bottle of beer in a dust bin. As he scraped the dust off a genie appeared out of the bottle and told him that since he had set her free he could have any three wishes he wanted. What did his heart most desire?

The Irishman thought for a moment or two then asked for a big cold beer in a glass that would never become empty. Suddenly the glass was in his hand, ice cold and brimming over. He drained the glass in a single gulp; the glass immediately re-filled. He was overwhelmed with wonder and awe. The genie asked: "What else does your heart desire, what other wishes do you have?" Without batting an eye the Irishman said, "This is so great I'll have two more of these!"

What does my heart desire? What do I most want? What is the deepest, most true longing that I experience? The readings today invite us to consider such desires. Hopefully ours are deeper, less basic, than my countryman's

The First reading from Kings tells the wonderful story of Solomon who was granted by God anything he wanted. Like the genie, God told Solomon he could have anything asked for. Translations vary but my favorite rendition of Solomon's request is his desire for a "smart heart." Out of infinite possibilities, what Solomon most desired was a wise and discerning heart that could help him know good and evil, help him to know how best to lead the Israelite community as their King. God not only granted Solomon this wish but also praised him highly for what he sought . . not eternal life, not the death of his enemies. Solomon wanted the "right stuff."

As I listen to these readings today I am brought to the foundations of what is Jesuit life. For Ignatius of Loyola all spirituality is about having "great desires." To be holy is to want the very best, deepest, truest things. All prayer begins, for Loyola, with "asking for what I want."

This is important!

I suspect that many, like myself, grew up believing in a kind of spiritual dualism. I pitted what God wanted for me and what I wanted for myself against each other in a kind of cosmic battle. I prayed to know and do God's will, believing that I would have to sacrifice my own desires in the process.

I no longer believe in this God.

I have come to believe that what God wants for me is exactly what I want for myself at my best and truest self. That is the catch, *my best and truest self.* I am so often trapped in my petty desires, my little hopes, my superficial dreams. I could have **The Kingdom** and all I think to ask for is a never ending glass of cold beer.

We all have various levels of desires . . . security, peace (perhaps at any price) in my family, or place of work, . . . fame, . . . fortune. I want to win the lottery. I want to look like Dr. McDreamy, or a Kardashian or, god forbid, have yellow hair.

Our task as believers searching for the life that Jesus wants to offer is to get beneath the surface and see what I really want. When I get beneath the surface, beneath all the cultural messages that deafen my best and truest ear, I want to love, to be loved. I want this love to grow in ever wider circles; that would bring me joy, satisfaction, fulfillment. I want to help bring about justice, love, peace. I want the kingdom, the reign of God to come and I want to be part of the process of bringing it about.

I honestly do, and I suspect you do too, or you would not be here today.

There is a part of us that at our best and truest self desperately wants to change the world, to live in Christ, to be a saint! That's what today's Gospel tells us.

The reign of God is like a treasure hidden in a field. I will sell everything all I have to buy that field.

The reign of God is like a fine pearl; I will sacrifice everything to own that pearl.

I believe God wants to reign in my life, to give me fulfillment, happiness, joy, everything that is wonderful in human existence. I want that too ... and the gospel today invites me to ask and be able to answer clearly what I desire, so that I am willing to go after that deepest, truest desire at any cost.

The final of the three short parables takes us back to Solomon. The reign of God is like a net thrown into the sea catching every kind of fish. We gather up the catch and then sort out, from everything, what is good and life giving and what is not. We need to be able to tell the difference. We need a "smart heart." We need to be able to know what helps us find that pearl, unbury that treasure.

I spent a number of sessions once with a wonderful man going through his mid-life transition, the movement from wanting to be what everyone else wanted him to be, to wanting to be himself. Jeff had struggled all his life against a wonderful dimension of himself, namely his incredibly affective nature. He *felt* everything; and for years he felt silly doing so! Unless he consciously repressed the tears, he cried at the drop of a hat.

Sadly he never had this gift of tears and compassion affirmed. His boyhood message from parents and teachers was clearly, "big boys don't cry." His compassion led him to try a seminary after high school, believing his deep caring would work well for the church, but the message again was not to get involved in feelings, in other people's problems, in caring too much for too many. Later, as a counselor he learned the tools needed to clinically help people, but rarely let his clients know how deeply, intensely he felt their pain.

At mid-life this man came to own and relish his tears. To cry easily and often publicly and privately. He came to pray to "have a heart" trusting that this feeling heart would be wise in its tears and in its laughter. For the first time he was able to use the gift God had given him as gift, a pearl of great price, a treasure hidden in the field of his various other gifts.

This man struggled to ask for what he wanted, to know and name the gift he desired. What he most wanted, finally was to be the unique, precious individual person God had made him to be. I think of his story as living out everything that is important and true in the message of scripture we hear today.

I have prayed to know what my deepest and truest desire might be. To discover that deepest desire demands "a smart heart." I discover what I really want, at this stage of my life, is to be a good and loving husband, to have my wife know to her deepest core how treasured and loved she is, to acknowledge her many her gifts, her wisdom, her generosity and know I know and love that in her. That's all I really want right now . . .that treasure. which I do believe, at my best, is exactly what God wants for me.

As we turn to Eucharist today, we pray to be set free from all the superficial desires that keep us from fulfilling what God is constantly desiring for us.

43) The Eighteenth Sunday

Scripture Readings: Is. 55:1-3; Ro. 8: 35-39; Mt. 14: 13-21

*"Nothing can separate us from the love of Christ ....
death can't, life won't; nothing in the past, nothing still
to come, nothing, nothing, nothing, can separate us
from Christ Jesus."*

In the face of whatever persecution, darkness, confusion comes, I
hear Paul inviting me to believe with him. Nothing can separate us
from Christ. We move to the gospel today asking who is this Jesus
with whom we are so inextricably bound, in whom we so desperately hope, on whom we so lovingly depend? We enter again into
the story of Jesus as we gather for Eucharist today.

Often in the story of Jesus, events become parables. Something
which began as a factual event has, by the time it is written down
in gospel form, has taken on the character of archetype, a cosmic
story, with ramification for all of human life. As the story today,
the multiplication of loaves, becomes a metaphor for life and the

miraculous power of Jesus to feed us with life . . . **no matter what!**

I have come to this story in past years returning from vacation. I vividly recall one year in which I left the parish for the month of July overwhelmed with the experience of death. In the final weeks of June I had buried seven parishioners, several of them very close friends, and said good-bye to two long time staff people, a kind of metaphorical death. I had been on vacation for only two days when death came again, this time a close Jesuit friend, elderly and done with life, but still beloved. I was invited to go and preach at the funeral of this beloved mentor and guide of many years. I needed time alone, needed to be with the mystery of his life, the reality of his death to see how it felt inside me.

After a time away though I needed to be with others, to tell the story of my friend . . . with another friend, or two, and finally with a community of those who shared my love for him, people who could nourish one another in this loss.

This personal but very common human experience of wrestling with the mystery of death, doing so both alone and in community, provides the central backdrop for my listening to today's gospel.

This gospel story begins with Jesus overwhelmed by death, both real and metaphorical. Jesus has just heard about the death of John the baptizer. He retreats to a desert place to be alone. John is his cousin, his friend. Like any of us, Jesus needs to be alone and to mourn.

John was also a prophet, one who had believed fiercely, passionately in God, who had the courage to live out, speak out, his divine convictions. For this passion John has been killed. Jesus knows all this. He cannot help but see in John's death the immanent expectation of his own. So Jesus needs not just to mourn, but to weigh again, in quiet, the implications of the passionately, faithfully lived life to which he also is committed.

But Jesus is not allowed to be alone for long. Those who need him search him out, discover him. When he sees the crowd he is moved by pity at their plight for they are like sheep without a shepherd.

Jesus is called away from nursing his own wounds to respond to the wounds of others. He teaches them, touches them, heals them, and, finally, in what is the central parabolic dimension of this passage, he feeds them. He fulfills the prophet's word of Isaiah by giving them the bread of life. In a passage that uses all the later language of Eucharist, the plentiful, abundant banquet bread of life, Jesus *takes, blesses, breaks, gives* . . . more than enough for all.

This wondrous, familiar story is replete with implications, hints for our reflection, things to throw around in our minds, our hearts. Let me break open just two related ones.

First, this passage raises for me the whole question of prayer and spirituality. We of the Roman church have had for centuries a bias to a kind of monastic spirituality, to prayer done apart in a deserted place. Prayer must mean going apart, filling up our own tank so that we have something to give to others. Such spirituality implies that God is best found apart from life rather than within it.

There is an alternate kind of prayer, of spirituality, an apostolic piety that finds God in the midst of the world, in its joys and pains, its sorrows and struggles, its laughter and hope. Such spirituality is nourished by compassionate attentiveness to what is before our eyes.

Where do we meet God? Where does God meet us?

Does Jesus recover from the pain and doubt occasioned by John's death in his quiet time alone, or is he relieved of his own pain as he responds to the pain of others? I suspect the answer is "Yes!" Both! My central point about our Christian lives, our lives of following Jesus is that we are as likely to meet and be nourished by God, to be pulled out of ourselves and made whole by God, in our interaction with people, needy and broken, . . . with people like ourselves.

I had a life-long friend who always maintained that when he was really low, really down and hurting, what he required was not solitude and quiet prayer which tended to drive him further into himself. He needed then to spend time with someone who was hurting worse than himself.

Moved with pity at the sight of others, Jesus himself is healed.

The second parabolic dimension of this passage, something we can fruitfully throw around, is the entire theological concept of hunger, of food. The metaphor and reality of our longing for food in the midst of scarcity pervades human life. The messianic expectation is centrally about abundant food and fine wine. This is the deep symbolism of Eucharist.

Curiously, John the Baptizer is killed at a meal, a banquet of the rich and powerful that lead to his tragic beheading. The passage moves from John's death at this sumptuous, sinful banquet to the simple miraculous picnic, a hint of the messianic banquet we so long for.

One cannot help but notice the symbolic line of Jesus to his followers who lament the hunger of the crowd:

"Go and Feed them yourselves."

That is, you have enough in you, among you. You have the resources to take care of this hunger. Don't turn to me. Don't turn to God to fix the problem of hunger (again, real or metaphorical). Trust yourselves. Act yourselves. Know that you <u>are</u> and you <u>have</u> enough.

In a world of rich and abundant resources, we live with a scandalous amount of hunger, again, both real and metaphorical, and Jesus tells us over and over, to feed them ourselves. Mother Theresa was fond of saying, "Let the people eat you up!" We have the resources to feed that world. What is missing is the will to do so, and perhaps the trust that we do, indeed, have the power.

The gospel today ends with that strange line, "5000 people not counting women and children." Today as we deal with hunger we still don't do well at counting the women and children. Jesus fed them even if the evangelist didn't count them, and Jesus has always counted them. I find myself praying for us, our nation, our world, our church to be able to look with the same compassion as Jesus at the numerous hungry women and children in our midst.

To see, and be moved with pity at the sight of the hungry in our midst is constitutive of Christian spirituality. Any prayer that does not lead to that vision is not the spirituality, not the prayer of Jesus, or his followers. And when we are able to see with the eyes of Jesus, we can trust whatever spirituality is ours.

As we celebrate Eucharist, if the bread we receive here truly feeds us with the life of Jesus then we will see the hungry, perhaps especially the women and the children, with his eyes.

44) The Eighteenth Sunday
A Creative Alternate

Once, As I sat in my office praying over the scriptures pondering how to talk about the miraculous multiplication of bread, how to relate it to the celebration of this Eucharist, and our consistent need to be fed by Jesus, to share in his life so we can live his life, a marvelous thing happened to me. You may not believe the story I'm going to tell; indeed perhaps you should not!

As happens so often a knock came to the parish office door, and when I answered it I met a woman, smiling with a bag in her hand, asking to come in. She wanted to talk to "the Priest."

I brought her into my office, sure that she wanted some kind of help but before I could ask what, she sat herself down and said to me, "I would like to give you something, . . . in fact there are two things I would like to give you." It felt backwards; I mean, I'm the one who is supposed to give stuff to people who come to our door.

"First," she said, "I would like to give you a story. It is a story that goes back many, many years, long before you or I were born. Long before our parents were born. In fact, so long ago I don't even remember when.

"In a land far away from here there was a tiny village. In the center of the village was a small table, and on that table was, always, a loaf of bread.

No one ever ate of the bread, no one ever took the bread, no one touched the bread.

Many stories about the bread circulated in the village.

There were stories of people who had taken and eaten the bread and had become slaves. So no one now ever touched or ate the bread for fear of becoming enslaved.

There were stories of people who had taken the bread and had disappeared. So no one now took the bread for fear of being seen no more.

Still other stories were told of people who had taken the bread and had died. So no one ever took the bread for fear that they would die.

No one remembered who it was who had taken the bread and been enslaved, or disappeared, or died . . .but they remembered the stories and that was all that mattered.

Now there grew up in the village over the years a kind of puberty rite, a rite of passage for young boys and girls as they reached 12 years of age. Each child on his or her 12th birthday would be brought before the table in the center of the village. The elders of the village would gather before them on the other side of the table with the bread, and the rest of the villagers would gather around them.

The elders would ask the young boy or girl 'Do you wish to eat the bread'?

And always, out of fear of becoming a slave, or disappearing, or being killed the young boy or girl would say, 'No!'

Three times the elders would ask the question. Three times the young person would say 'No!' "

I found myself thinking as the apparent bag lady continued, "What a strange story, and why is she telling it to me?" But she went on.

"Then one day a young boy turned 12. As usual he was brought to the center of the town, before the elders and all the people. The elders asked the boy 'Do you wish to eat the bread?'

This time the boy said "Yes!' The people all gasped; no one had ever said 'Yes' before.

The elder inquired again, to make sure. 'Do you wish to take and eat the bread?' The boy said, again, 'Yes!'

Once more, in order to make sure the boy understood what he was doing they explained to him the stories about slavery, and disappearance, and death, and asked again, 'do you wish to eat the bread?' Again, the boy said 'Yes.'

Everyone in the village stepped back; the boy walked forward, he took the bread in his hands and began to eat. He left the village square chewing on the bread.

In the days that followed, the boy did not become a slave. But as he grew into manhood, he did begin to go about the village doing all kinds of good deeds, caring for people in ways that no one else did, visiting the sick, fixing meals for some elderly people, sitting by the bed side of the dying. He became each day more and more of a servant, for anything anyone asked he would do.

And when he was about 30 he did disappear, at first, only for awhile, for about forty days. Then for a longer time as rumors reached the village that he had gone to other villages telling people about God, and the joy of serving. He promised that God loved them no matter what, for always and forever.

One day the boy returned to the village.

Because he was so loving and serving,
and because he told people about a God who cared for them,
and because he invited people to live with a generosity and joy that they did not think they had. . .
because they could not be what he invited them to be,
they did indeed kill him.

The bag lady paused, seemed to have ended her story, looked me in the eye and said a final line, "But the word spread among the people that he still lived among them."

Then my visitor got up from her chair, and walked out the door, leaving me in my office. I was stunned for a moment . . . then got up to pursue her but she was out the door. I came back to my office and realized she had left her bag, this bag *(hold up bag)*. I picked it up, ran out the office door, looking for her everywhere, but she was gone. I could not understand how she could have disappeared so quickly, but she had.

I walked back to my office holding the bag. I entered my office thinking about her story, and the boy who once took the bread. Hardly thinking I reached into the bag and discovered a loaf of bread (take out the bread and hold it up).

I was frightened, for I realized that I had now taken the bread. Would I become a slave? Would I disappear to be seen no more? Would I die? Somehow I knew this bread was the lady's second gift.

I wondered if perhaps she and that young boy were not the same?

I am glad I took the bread, but am still afraid. Perhaps I need to seriously decide whether I want to take and eat this bread each time I come here.

Do I want to take the risk of becoming a slave, a servant of others, of all?

Do I want to take the risk of having my very self disappear, of becoming someone very different from who I have been so far?

Do I want to risk this death, receiving this bread that has been multiplied for us?

We all need to pray about this now, and then decide. Do we want to take this bread?

(Obviously, offering this story at Eucharist, one then would actually consecrate the very loaf used in the story and offer it to the assembly at communion…..)

45) The Nineteenth Sunday

Scripture Readings: I Kings 19:9, 11-13; Ro. 9: 1-5,; Mt.. 14:22-33

Martin Luther's wife told a story about her husband. She said he often fought with fear, depression and bouts of discouragement. When he was at his lowest point he used to go into his room and, in prayer, "grab God by the beard and shout: 'You promised!'"

We've all been there; we may be there now, invited to trust no matter what in the God who promised to be with us. Everything depends on our having met God, and our ability to trust that God is with us.

The wonderful Elijah story we just heard speaks about such a meeting with God not in the thunderstorm, not in the big flashy, knock your socks off experience, but in "the still, small voice." Such a meeting is the link between the readings today. and the basis of our Christian life. Holiness is all about meeting God, and then having the courage to trust in that relationship, risking our lives on whatever experience of God is ours.

The Gospel story today is perhaps the finest paradigm in the entire Jesus story for what our experience of meeting God is like. This story is so carefully constructed that the primary concern is not whether or not it happened, but that it happens all the time, continually, everywhere, to everyone. All of us have lived out of that story or we would not be here today. We live in it still.

Let me go slowly back over this gospel, inviting you to feel the story, to feel where it fits you, touches on your life, helps you tell your own story.

We all at times know what it is to feel abandoned by God, by Jesus, to be, 'at sea," in a storm, unsure where Jesus is, afraid he does not care. We have all felt abandoned by our perhaps God.

And most of us have at times experienced looking off in the distance, thinking we see something, . . . an answer, an approach, a solution presenting itself; it may an illusion, a ghost, a phantom. If I could just talk to Joe, or get to Wyoming, or get rid of this illness, or win the lottery. . . .

Perhaps the vision is no mirage, but Jesus, walking on the waters, in the midst of the storm, coming to help us.

In various ways we yell out to that dimly grasped vision, "If it really is you, let me come to be with you . . .call me out onto those waters."

Sometimes, perhaps to a new job, a new location, a new relationship, a significant risk, something that can change our entire lives, in one way or another, in small or incredibly risky ways, Jesus has invited us to "Come" and we have tried to respond. We have stepped out on unfamiliar waters; we have moved towards that haunting, life-giving voice.

If you are like me and others I have known so well, so often, you have also known what it is like to enter into a new venture, initially sure it was God's desire for us, only to discover that it doesn't seem to work, that I'm not the right person for this job, or I never should have married this person, or this is not a city where I can live. Three times in my life I have undertaken major new directions in my life only to, within weeks be convinced that I could not possibly survive where I had been led.

We have all begun something in hope and moved quickly to panic, all but forgetting how we got out there, and who it was we thought invited us to risk. We have been "in over our heads," and we have begun to sink . . . going down beneath the waves of life, even a third time.

Our presence here this day suggests that, even then, something, someone reached into the waves and rescued us, brought us safely to shore when we could not get there on our own.

We have all been in this story. Perhaps we are in the midst of it, right now! We have all in very ordinary ways met Jesus and his God -- that is enough. Everything else will follow. Before I conclude, I want to pause for a moment to let you make this real for you. Consider, Where has this story been true for you in the past? Where might it be going on right now?

(pause for a few moments reflection)

When someone asks "Is the Gospel true?" I maintain that the real question is not did it happen, but does it matter. The question is not, Did Jesus ever walk on water and Peter with him? No the question is, if I am sinking will anyone lift me up?

Cardinal Newman is reported to have said: "To be good is to change, to be perfect is to change often." I recall a child psychologist once saying that "Maturity is the ability to give up what you have for what you don't yet have, on the word of someone who loves you."

More colloquially, life is like riding a trapeze. Just when we get comfortable on one bar, we have to let go and wait for the other to come, with our feet firmly planted in mid-air. We can only do this with a sense that Jesus is out there in the future, on the other side of whatever risk, saying "Come."

46) The Assumption of Mary Aug. 15

Scripture Readings: Rev. 11; 12; 1 Cor. 15:20-16; Lk. 1:39-56

It is difficult to preach about a dogma.

It is particularly difficult to preach about a dogma that seems at first glance to depend upon:

Weird cosmology (earth down; heaven up, so Assumption)

Questionable dualism (like body and soul-- as if everyone else's body goes to earth, while the soul goes to heaven; But Mary's body went too! Mary's body is in heaven now, ours will come later!. Is there a later in eternity?)

The first challenge of preaching a dogmatic feast is to get behind the simplistic images. Let me start with three pre-notes:

1. Any dogma is only as important as it helps us live our lives more fully; The sign that we are saved is not what we think or believe, but the way we live.
2. The Second Vatican Council placed Mary within the context of the Church by putting all they had to say about her in the final chapter of the document on the church. The Council fathers asserted that Mary was the first and best of the redeemed. Consequently, whatever we say about Mary can be said of all the rest of us, all those saved by Christ.
3. In the bull of proclamation of Mary Assumption in 1950 Pius the Twelfth asserted the hope that belief in Mary's Assumption will make belief in our own resurrection stronger.

In the light of these somewhat abstract statements let me share personal example related to today's gospel that helps me discover something here to truly celebrate.

In 1968 I had been ordained for one year. Already in the confusion of the Church of those days three of my classmates had left active ministry. *Humanae Vitae*, the Encyclical on birth control had just been issued and I, along with many others, found it very difficult to assent to this teaching. I was between jobs, unsure what my personal future held, discouraged with the Church, with myself, with everything. In this context I began the Thirty Day Retreat that was to conclude the formal part of my training as a Jesuit.

I was several days into the retreat and nothing much was happening. My head was only slightly above water. The retreat director suggested I pay over the gospel passage we heard today, the story we have come to call *The Visitation*.

I prayed, or tried to pray my four hours that day, using this passage but nothing much came of it. I could recite it, I believed, by memory, but nothing touched me. I told my director that things were pretty dry. He suggested I pray over the same passage again tomorrow. That day's prayer was the same. Again he suggested I stay with this passage. It began to feel like water torture, very slowly boring me to death.

On the fourth day I looked at the passage again and words flew at me off the page, words not heard before, words spoken about Mary, but directly to me. Words I had somehow not noticed before.

Elizabeth says of Mary: "Blessed is she who trusted that the Lord's words to her would be fulfilled." That is, you are happy, Mary, because you believed that God will do what God says God will do. By implication:

"Pat, you will finally be happy when you are able to trust that God can do what God says!"

I cannot adequately describe the feeling, but an enormous weight came off my shoulders, a very deep pervading joy entered my heart. It was not up to me to figure out how I was going to continue to minister in the Church while I was so confused and the Church appeared so messed up. It was up to God to work it out and bear some fruit in me, despite the church, despite myself.

The concepts I can express now were not as clear then, but the feeling was.

I do not think this is a truth just for me. I think this gets at the heart of the feast. We celebrate that a woman, Mary, accepted her invitation from God to give birth without grasping all the implications. Mary trusted that if God invited her to be the unwed mother of one who would become our savior then God could work it out. Her happiness lay in her initial, and her heroically lived out act of trust.

The first movement, first moment of Incarnation, as this great mythical story is told to us, is not Mary sitting in her home in Galilee trying to understand what happened. No, this moment finds Mary getting up and going to her cousin, aged and pregnant, and ministering to her. Luke presents Mary singing a wondrous compilation of the great hymns of Hebrew Scriptures to a God who is faithful. Then the entire Gospel of Luke speaks of trust and fulfillment, on the most personal level, on the level of the Hebraic people, and on the cosmic level of universal salvation.

God will turn things upside down, the lowly will be raised up. The powerful will brought down. The hungry will be fed good things. The promised made to our ancestors will be fulfilled, finally.

At the very beginning of her mission as the mother of Jesus, mother of the Messiah, mother of the one ushering in God's reign, Luke presents Mary singing a hymn proclaiming the beginning of God's reign, the fulfillment of all the messianic promises, not just to her, but through her, to the entire world, the universe.

Some years ago I came across a wonderful Easter poem by a Jesuit priest friend, Fr. Bill Bichsel, in which he described the Risen Jesus coming out of the tomb on Easter Sunday Morning laughing and singing, dancing naked in sunlight of dawn, rejoicing that "He was right!' God is faithful. God had raised him up. The feast we celebrate today says "She was right." Mary shares fully in the triumph of Jesus, the Resurrection.

This feast says if we act on the same trust, if we do our part to give birth to Jesus, if we trust that God will be faithful, we will share fully in that Resurrection too! I do not think we should spend our lives waiting for or getting ready to go to heaven. I had a friend who asserted frequently: "I'm not trying to get to heaven; I'm just trying to get down to earth!"

Still, as we struggle to learn and to love while we live, we celebrate today that however frustrating things may be as we go along, finally all the promises will be fulfilled!

47) The Twentieth Sunday

Scripture Readings: Is. 56:1, 6-7; Ro. 11:13-15; Mt. 15:21-28

The Gospel today leads to reflections on our experiences of alienation.

Once, in the turbulent 70's I went going into the gym of school made up entirely of African American students. I hoped to arrange an exchange program between students from our Catholic school and some Junior high students from this school. The room hushed as I entered. The eyes of a hundred black faces stared at me with something less than welcome. I was clearly on other's turf, unwanted, unwelcomed in those stormy, racially tense days.

I recall also going to do a workshop with a community of sisters in 1982. I was supposed to be working with another religious woman who was not able to make it because of an illness in her family, so I showed up alone. This community had recently had one of their sisters expelled from their community by the Pope, and their mother general had gone to Rome to speak with the

Pope about it. He had refused to see her (ironically the same week he met with a man who had tried to kill him.) These sisters were filled with real and fairly understandable rage against the patriarchal, hierarchical dimension of the church and I felt like their primary target, a priest unwanted, unwelcome in their wounded midst.

When I was pastor of an inner city parish we had a very large feeding program. Up to 500 people a day ate lunch in our old high school gym. Frequently I would need to go in there for something when I was dressed professionally. Though otherwise comfortable there, every time I entered that dining room in a suit I could feel the tension. I was "the enemy." Unwanted, unwelcomed in this poor people's single place of safety.

More recently, for 8 years I have been an "older man," working in my 80's with folks mostly in their 30's, young, vibrant, tech savvy, friendly, but distant. I am a stranger in their milieu to whom they know not how to relate!

A peculiar feeling being an outsider, not wanted, not welcomed on someone else's turf! We have all been there; we need to touch that experience if we are to be sensitive to what we also know--the other side. How often I have been on the flip side of that experience, one who belongs, making others feel unwanted, unwelcomed as I kept others away.

I turn, then, to the Gospel reading this week.

There was a painful history between Jesus' Jewish people and the Canaanites from which this woman came. They had struggled for the land, had warred with one another for 500 years. At the time of Matthew's Gospel a very real struggle was occurring regarding to whom the Good News was to be preached, Jews or Gentiles. The message was spreading rapidly outside of synagogues though the disciples were still firmly rooted in their Jewish roots.

The first big battle within the early community of Jesus' followers, The Council of Jerusalem, took place shortly before this Gospel was written. It dealt with whether and how to incorporate non-Jewish converts into the emerging Community Matthew presents Jesus struggling with a question that still haunts his followers as the gospel is written down: *Who belongs?*

Against such a psychological backdrop this story of Jesus is told, crashing into all our pre-existing categories and prejudices. The peculiar heart of this story, unlike any other in the Gospels, is that Jesus himself had to be converted, had to discover in a particular context the universal love of God, had to meet this specific woman, know her in her unique individual need, and in her faith, and then to let himself be changed. She hangs on, hangs in there, accepts his initial rebuke without walking away, trusts that this good man can be led to new light.

The wondrous point of the story becomes, *if Jesus can recognize a new truth so can we!*

I treasure this little vignette of a woman who believed that she belonged, and who trusted the possible openness of this Jewish man.

The disciples complain, want to throw this foreigner out, want to send her away. Jesus talks with her and meets her, as a person not a type. She is not "a Caananite woman," finally, but "Suzy, or Sally, or Mary." Out of this interchange is realized the reality of the prophetic word from Isaiah we heard in the first reading: God's call to everyone, Jew or Gentile alike.

All of which leads to a terribly important gospel-based reflection: Who excludes me; where do I desire to be known as a person, not a type? Where do I need to experience myself not just as white, not just male, not just comfortably middle-class, but as I am, as Pat Carroll?

And more importantly, who do I exclude from my family, my church, other communities of which I am a part? So often we have family members to whom we no longer speak, or people of our parish who have drifted away feeling unwanted, unwelcome. We speak of our differences of values, life-styles, conviction, race, sexual orientation, or gender and these differences often become reasons for distance or alienation.

And our political, cultural world is torn again and anew by white nationalist demanding "their country" back, by flag waving, torch carrying young men refusing to share their world with "Jews."

The Kingdom of God wants to break into our lives on every level and say: We are all one body, there is no Jew or Greek, no slave or free, no male or female. All are one.

Three brief, final thoughts.

If this realization were easy to live out it would not be so prevalent in the Gospel stories, and the writing of the New Testament. This unity of all into a single body seems a central, challenging, radical demand of our faith. It speaks directly to perhaps the least attractive dimension of our human existence, our tendency to war, to separate, to define as "other."

Secondly, it is often most difficult to remain open to differences not with those totally other but with those most close to us. How difficult to see the personhood of the one next to us at work, in church, at the dinner table, or an office meeting. We are so often most closed to those most close!

Finally, perhaps central to our call as Christians is not the invitation to do great things, but the more subtle and even more difficult invitation to witness to a new reality--that people can indeed be One! No message is more badly needed than what Jesus prayed for his followers at their final meal, "That they may be one, that they can be so completely one that the world can believe!"

We turn now to Eucharist where we share, and hopefully become, one bread, one body.

48) The Twenty First Sunday

Scripture Readings: Is. 22:15, 19-23; Ro. 11:33-36; Mt. 16: 13-20

(Pre-note: Suggestion. Before reading the Gospel, perhaps invite Assembly to listen to this story as if for the first time, despite its familiarity, despite its institutional implications. As with other recent Gospels this is as much a parable, a metaphor, as an historical event. Peter stands as "everyman/ everywoman" as he speaks for each follower of Jesus. We stand in his shoes in this story.)

Who do you say I am?

Obviously this is the central question for Christians. Who is this Jesus we follow, for us?

I remember years ago in the controversial days of the early seventies when someone at a Jesuit meeting said, "After all, we are all trying to follow Christ; we ought to be able to get along." It struck me at the time (and still does) that the Jesus whom we followed sometimes divided us as much as he united. At that meeting I shared an image from an Episcopalian priest in what he called "Western Theology" that made this quite serious divisive point clearly and playfully.

In Western Theology we are divided by whether we see ourselves as *pioneers, or settlers.* Everything changes depending on whether we view the world and ourselves as part of an <u>encamped city</u>, surrounded by hostile forces, or as on a <u>wagon train</u>, forging new paths to places unknown.

For example: To a settler, God is the mayor, making the town's laws. To a pioneer God is the trail boss, who gets the team together for the challenging task ahead.

To a settler sin is breaking one of the town's rules. To a pioneer, sin is turning back, abandoning the trail and the others pioneers who depend on you.

I love the implications for the Holy Spirit!

To a settler the Holy Spirit is the barmaid who tickles the settlers under the chin and assures them everything is OK.

To a pioneer the Holy Spirit is a mad-buffalo hunter who is always playing tricks, always surprising; the only thing the buffalo hunter does regularly is sneak into the town on Saturday nights and throw bombs into the bar to upset the settlers!

Well obviously the image of Jesus, the Christ, is different in each mentality. Both respond differently to the question, "Who do you say I am?"

To a settler, Jesus is the sheriff, the one who works for the Mayor and enforces the town's laws.

To a pioneer, Jesus is the scout, the one who rides out in front of the wagon train, checks out the trails, sees the dangers, and never asks the pioneers to go anywhere he hasn't already gone!

Who do you say that I am?

Looking more carefully at the gospel, we need to let go of how the church has come to use this text as a proof text for the primacy of Peter, and the development of the Papacy. There is certainly grounds for that development, but first this is a faith testimony central to the Gospels. Peter is every one of us, a spokesperson for all believers.

Jesus says, "Who do you say I am?" Peter says "You are the Christ." Jesus says to Peter, to all of us, "Because you recognize this, You are Rock." Peter's affirmation is the foundation, the basis, the starting block of his Church.

We have been in danger of focusing more on Jesus commission to Peter, than on Peter's profession of faith; the two need to be held together. Put simply, The Rock foundation of the Christian Church is the faith that Peter manifest in calling Jesus Messiah.

Put another way, if we ask whether Jesus says he will build the Church on Peter, or on Peter's faith, the answer is probably "Yes!" Our Church is rooted in Peter's personal faith as presented in this story.

At any rate, Jesus himself then switches the image from "rock" to "Key!" Because Peter knows that Jesus is the Christ, Peter is told he has the keys Great image! If Jesus is a sheriff, then the key lets people in and out of jail, but if Jesus is the scout then the key is the clue, the hint, the secret, the answer, the path. The key is the way, the truth, the life!

As I pray these days about who Jesus is for me, I know, despite all my stumbling, my wanderings, my infidelities, I want to answer this question whole-heartedly. I want to say with my lips and with my life, "Jesus, you are the Christ!"

I want to stake my life on your words.
I want to trust in you and in your God.
I want to live and invite others to live by your values.
I want you to be key.

As I say this I think of various "key" words of Jesus

"... blessed are the poor, the sorrowing, those who hunger and thirst for justice.

I was hungry and you gave me to eat.

The grain of wheat must die.

Seek to save your life and lose it, to lose it and save it.

I tell you this so that my joy may be in you, and your joy complete.

I come so you have life and have it more abundantly,"

and on and on and on, saving, life-giving words.

I hear such words in a world filled with other words, other keys. A world where we are ready to risk a million lives to preserve our access to oil, where we perform sophisticated surgeries at great expense for those who can afford them, while children go without medical care at all. A world where 50 million people live in poverty, hunger. A world where life is ended prematurely in the womb, or on death row, where little care is given to the widows, the orphans, the aliens in our midst. A world where refugees are abandoned and immigrants are demonized.

"Who do you say I am?"

If I get the answer right I have the key, to happiness for myself, for others, for all.

Peter got the answer right, and, at least for a moment, Jesus told him he had the key to eternal life.

As we move to celebrate Eucharist again, we hold the key, and Jesus asks us again, over and over, "Who do you say I am?"

49) The Twenty Second Sunday

Scripture Readings: Jer. 20:7-9; Ro. 12: 1-2; Mt. 16: 21-27

The readings today are so rich; there are so many avenues to walk down, so many themes that could be explored. I want to hint, first, at several homilies I might have given (Perhaps should give) then take a moment to expand the possibility that most strikes me.

I am fascinated by Jeremiah's lament at the pain of being prophet. Though he laments his prophet call, he cannot give it up. Some translations say "you have duped me Lord, I let myself be duped." Stronger ones imply "You have seduced me, or even raped me... violated me, taken away my freedom, overwhelmed me." Jeremiah with legitimacy complains to God that he feels overcome with a vision, a word that no one wants to hear. He has become a laughing stock, the butt of jokes, the prey of everyone. Jeremiah knows first hand what we would like to forget, that the word of God has a crunch to it, has teeth, has tension.

I am also fascinated by and could talk of Paul's invitation to "let our bodies become living sacrifices for Christ." Paul encourages us not to buy into easy conformity with the age in which we live, but, rather, to be transformed by Christ. Again, much like the Jeremiah theme, this avenue invites reflection on our cultural blindness to the piercing word of God, challenging our propensity to be co-opted by the world. A recent New York Times magazine section spoke at length about the Catholic Church in America, with its tendency to close or abandon inner-city parishes and follow its people's move toward the suburbs, into the middle and upper middle class, taking on an almost wholesale acceptance of the American Dream. I have been appalled by the American Bishops' lack of support for a health care program that helps millions of people but might allow some payment for birth control... not to mention the so-strong support for A trumpian presidency by many nominal Christian leaders. We are far more likely to be taken over by our culture than to transform it. But I prefer not to think about that either, so will let it go.

I am also fascinated by that strange aspect of the Gospel in which Peter, who has just proclaimed Jesus as Messiah and has himself been proclaimed Rock, is but a few short lines later called "Satan." How quickly the leader of our church falls from grace. How fragile is the line between exalted insight, and cowardly betrayal. How consoling for us in our fragile bouncing from grace to groveling, from heroism to cowardice, from insight to blindness, that Peter is onetime saint and instant Satan, How grateful we can be that Peter and all of us are called and commissioned not because of our greatness, but because we are undeservedly loved by Jesus.

And how fruitful it might be to pursue the theme of fragility in ecclesial leadership from Peter to today, including myself, but I will let that go.

I do want to expand for a few moments on what most fascinates me about the readings today, the relationship between Jesus and Peter. Let me retell the story a bit, in its vivid detail.

Jesus and Peter have walked together for some time. Peter has gotten to know Jesus, to understand him, to become not just follower, but friend. He has some insight, now, into what Jesus is about, so, faced with Jesus question about his identity, as the story is told, Peter proclaimed in the name of all the followers, "You are the Christ!" You are the messiah, the one all our people have awaited, the fulfillment of our dreams. This proclamation of faith is appreciated by Jesus. This faith Peter has proclaimed will be the foundation of the community of faith, the Church Jesus will establish. "On this rock I will build . . ."

Perhaps emboldened by Peter's growing recognition of his identity and mission, Jesus begins to speak about the implications of his messianic call. It will not be easy. Jesus recalls the plight of the prophets of old, like Jeremiah. He recalls the "Suffering Servant" theme of Isaiah. He recognizes the realities surrounding him and begins to predict his passion.

Peter doesn't want to hear that part of the story, doesn't want to think about the shadow side of the Messianic mission. He says in effect "No, Jesus, not like that; you don't have to do it that way. The path need not be so difficult. Look, we're winning, everyone loves you. It will all be fine. We will find an easier way."

And Jesus loses it! He becomes angry at his friend, let down when he most needed support. He turns in an almost teary rage, "Get behind me, you Satan." You my friend who should understand, you whose support I need, you try to talk me out of who I have to be. How can you do that? Get back. You are talking out of your weakest, worst self, out of a too human perspective. Stand with me, Peter. Look with God's eyes, and help me to endure what must come. Don't you know that the path to real life is love, sacrifice?"

I love this passage because, though painful, it is so, so true. Which of us has not stood with Peter and tried to talk someone we love out of a painful decision they had to make? Which of us has not let down a child, a parent, a friend struggling for authenticity and courage and faith in following God's call to them into darkness?

--I think of the many Jesuit Volunteers I have known who are asked by parents or others "when are you going to get a real job," rather than being supported in the Gospel choice they are making.

-- I suffered with a Jesuit friend often in Prison for his protests as some of his best friends tried to talk him out of his action.

Love at its weakest is always tempted to protect, to warn, to insulate. How difficult it is for one who loves to set free, to push, to encourage the very best in the beloved despite the cost.

This gospel invites me to wonder how well I love, to pause and ponder whether I really tease the very best out of those I befriend. I want to support my wife in a challenging program she wants to build, knowing it will take much time, enormous energy and much hardship.

The other side is also true. Which of us has not stood with Jesus, seeing a new place to which we feel called, a new word we must voice, a new stance we must take, knowing the suffering that will come from our decision? We look (sometimes desperately) for friends who will understand, support, encourage, walk with us this rocky road. It is so much more painful to have a friend insist "Don't go!" than would be the same words from someone we never expected to understand.

To feel the hurt and rage of Jesus at Peter we need only recall our disappointment when friends have thus hurt us, and also the joy when friends come through.

We have listened again to the word of God, the story of Jesus, and tried to let it speak to us in our lives. Today, a powerful, a disturbing word. As we move to Eucharist, we move together, uniting ourselves with Jesus, invited both to support each other and to count on the support of others as we try to walk with Jesus.

Could we pause for a few moments, joining hands in quiet prayer, before we go on.

50 The Twenty-Third Sunday

Scripture Readings: Ez. 33; Ro. 13:8-1; Mt. 18: 15-20

We are all in this Together.

I have often reflected that since we are all "recovering Catholics, recovering Christians," we can learn much from the various twelve step programs for recovery from various addictions: AA, NA, Over Eaters Anonymous, and others. We can especially learn about conversion, about how to facilitate change, how to get someone into or back into the program. AA and other recovery programs have developed a very Gospel based method of intervention. People whose lives are connected with an addict approach in love and honesty, confronting the person with the effects of behavior that is hurting both the addict and the community, family, or work place to which he or she belongs. Those intervening speak clearly about the consequences if their loved one refuses to get help.

How well this approach acknowledging that we are all in it together, mirrors the Gospel teaching today. What an excellent model for any Church community.

But how different is the frequent reality in our families, our church, all our various communities. How difficult it is for us to deal with reality head on.

I recall in horror a story of a Jesuit called in by his provincial to be told all kinds of things three men he lived with had reported about him. None of the things were true. None of the men he lived with had spoken to him personally about their concerns. The provincial erred terribly by not inviting the other Jesuits to go and talk to their brother before coming to him.

I was once co-pastor of a parish in which the other pastor and I were sued by twelve parishioners over a high rise apartment building for elderly that we, with the parish leadership, had decided to build on church property. None of the twelve families came to speak with either of us directly to hear our side before the suit.

Acting as a priest, I had people write letters to the bishop complaining about something I have said or done without the courtesy, the charity of speaking first to me!

How often do we say things *about* someone that we have not had the courage, or the love *to* say to them. Sadly lacking the maturity to which the Gospel calls us we are all tempted to remain in the childish posture of a child yelling to a parent that our brother or sister "broke our favorite toy," or "took our candy!"

The Gospel today invites us to be adult, to talk to each other, individually and together whenever there are problems among us. We are not to go to someone else. Go to the one with whom we have a problem ... our brother, our sister.

How this Gospel clashes with our American rugged individualism. We are not all on our own. And this Gospel wars with American moral indifferentism: "Well, maybe it's OK for him, for her; who am I to judge?" "You do your thing, I'll do mine." No, we are our brother and our sister's keeper. We are appointed by God to be watchman, watchwoman for one another, with love.

We are all in this together.

"Go to your brother, your sister, talk with him or her, invite them to conversion. If that doesn't work bring a few friends. If that fails bring the whole church community with you and intervene."

The final suggestion of the Gospel can sound quite harsh. It isn't. Quite the opposite. If all of the above approaches fail, we are told, and the offender still does not listen, "treat them like a pagan, or a tax collector."

For many years I thought this meant "cast them out," or as some churches practice, "shun them." In context the Gospel suggests just the opposite. In fact, Matthew's Gospel purports to be written by a tax collector who had been specially loved by Jesus. In the approach of Jesus, to treat one as a tax collector or a sinner must mean *to love even more*, to overwhelm with love, to keep trying desperately, looking for the one lost sheep, turning the house upside down for a single coin, welcoming, no matter when, the lost son.

This wondrous Gospel passage about how we are to treat each other in our fragility within the Christian community reminds me of a story.

Once upon a time . . . .

In a diocese far away, in a time quite different from our own, there was a parish. It had once been a good a vibrant parish but it felt now like it as in danger of dying.

Elderly people who had shaped the community's past were feeling neglected.

Children felt estranged, unwelcome.

Many who had experienced loss or hurt, the widowed, the divorced, sometimes the lonely single, straight or gay, felt unaccepted, not part of whatever community was left.

People had taken to back biting. Some formed into small tight cliques, no longer communities.

(Aside: the difference between a community and a clique is that in a community "Anyone is welcome who can stand us!")

The parish had ministries to be sure, but mostly to itself, and only a few shared in them, and these few felt resentful that they had to do all the work. The parish outreach beyond itself had dwindled to almost nothing and only a few, resentfully, took part.

Liturgies had become routine, lifeless, uncelebrated, unsung. People sat ever further towards the rear, present only as spectators at something someone else did, while they watched.

The staff of the parish was at its wits end, knowing they must be part of the problem.

Luckily in this parish far away, and in time past, their bishop was a wonderful and wise man. So the staff went to see him with their concerns. And the end of their long lament about their dying parish the Bishop simply said:

"Go back and tell your parish this truth.

'The Messiah is in your community;
When Christ comes again,
he will come from your parish!'

Tell them this, for it is true, and your parish will change."

Not quite understanding the parish staff went back to tell the parish this most unlikely news. When it was announced at Mass that "The Messiah is in this community; when Christ comes again, he will come from your parish," most of the people laughed. The message, repeated, was neither understood nor believed.

But, slowly, surely, the parishioners thought about what they had heard. They thought at first it must be the priest or one of the staff; those professional church people. They began to see the gifts of those who served them, appreciating for the first time their service to the community.

Then some thought it must be from the elderly, with their years of service and wisdom that the Messiah will come, and they began to look with different eyes into the eyes and hearts of older people

Then some were sure it must be one of the children who would grow into the presence of Christ in their midst. Then, instead of childish noise and irresponsibility, they began to see much life and energy and hope.

Then some began to suspect that the Messiah might come in one of those they did not usually notice, so they sought out those whose names they did not know, whose faces were not familiar . . . and began to discover amazing gifts in those on the edges of their community.

Some eventually began to suspect it must from one of those well known, but not liked in the community . . . the marginal, or messy, or manipulative; perhaps just one an individual could not abide. They began to look at those they thought they knew too well again, anew. All throughout the parish each looked at others differently, and slowly came to love, respect and even cherish gifts unrealized before.

And the parish came to life. People served each other with love and tenderness. Together they reached outside themselves with care for the Messiah that may wander at any moment into their midst alone, hungry, a refugee, an immigrant, perhaps illegally here, a gay couple seeking acceptance.

When they gathered for Eucharist the parish celebrated with great joy and song and laughter, believing the Messiah was really present at their gatherings. They mourned each death with the greatest sense of loss, mingled with the deepest hope. They came together in groups large and small to pray, to plan, to dream, to hope, to share their ever growing faith in the promise given to them.

Slowly, surely, the Messiah was found alive and well in their midst. Christ *had* come again.

"Where two or three are gathered in my name, I am in the midst of them."

We are all in this together.

When Christ comes again, he will be found here, in this parish, or he will not be found anywhere.

51) The Twenty-Fourth Sunday

Scripture Readings: Sir. 27:30-28:7; Ro. 14: 7-9; Mt. 18:21-35

The parable we heard today is not difficult to understand. What is challenging is to understand that it is about me. Little need to explain a very clear story:

> A man with an enormous debt is forgiven; he turns around and refuses to forgive

someone who owes him a little bit. Isn't that awful?

What I would rather hope to do is to convince myself and all of us that this story is ours that it is about us.

I love the story of Dorothy Day. One day she was upset at the quality of the meal being served to the poor at the Catholic Worker Kitchen in New York. One of the people serving the meal said: "Well, it's better than they deserve." Dorothy Day replied, forcefully:

"God help any of us if we get what we deserve!"

It is so difficult for any of us to acknowledge "I am a sinner." Although we Catholics are supposed to be guilt ridden, when we get beyond the false consciences some of us have and the piddly little faults we are supposed to feel terrible about, we find it most difficult to admit our true failures, our sin. It takes a mature person to say "I am a sinner." I screwed up. I failed. No one else. Me. I did it. Pogo was right, "I met the enemy and its us!"

For most of our lives, perhaps most of the time, it's my parent's fault, or the teacher's, or the boss', or almost anyone else's but me. What goes wrong is seldom the results of my actions, or, if it is, doubtless it is so for a very good reason.

I deeply believe the reason it is so difficult to own our failures is that we cannot believe that we will be *loved anyway!* Yet the beginning of Christian life depends on the assertion, "*I am a sinner, but I am a loved, called, chosen and redeemed sinner.*"

Today's parable only makes sense to those who are able to acknowledge the reality of sin – don't like the word sin, OK. Use -- failure, stumbling, hurting people we love, unable to live up to my ideals, not being my best a truest self. However we phrase it, *The Good News is about God loving us anyway!*

So what does it mean to say I am a sinner?
and what does it mean to be forgiven?

To be a sinner does not mean to be a bad person, a malicious person, a vicious person. It does not mean I have broken a rule, or failed to uphold a law.

Early in his presidential campaign Donald Trump was asked if ever asked God for forgiveness. He replied that he hadn't done anything wrong! I find that astounding.

To be a sinner means not to love as I would like to love, to endure family relationships that are not all that I want them to be, to be one who causes, or continues conflicts, tensions, disagreements, even hostilities in relationships -- at home, in workplace, communities of which I am a part. To be a sinner means not to be able to love, relate, interact as I would like

To be a sinner means being unable to fix all the brokenness in and around me, or to sometimes even fail to see, much less respond to such suffering.

To be a sinner is to be caught up into all the systemic structures that oppress, injure, kill people, and to experience a powerlessness to alleviate the curse of such structures. I am not solving global warming, or sexism, or racism, but adding to them.

To be a sinner is to be a human being in a broken world, in every way that I contribute to that very brokenness.

So it is impossible to be honest and not to say: "*I am a sinner. I apologize and ask for mercy.*"

What does it mean to forgive, to have God forgive me, to ask others for forgiveness?

We too easily equate forgiveness with forgetting, as if we could say "It didn't happen," or "it doesn't matter." But real forgiveness means remembering, naming, owning the evil done, the harm caused, the hurt received, and then being able to say, "This hurt is not the whole, the only truth."

To love someone, to forgive someone means to have unending hope in them! What I have seen so far is not the whole story; there is more, better, deeper in you than I have seen so far.

When I have really failed, hurt someone I love, disappointed myself and another, when I have truly been dishonest, or selfish, I get up in the morning and the sun still shines! Someone is still nice to me, even though I don't deserve it, haven't earned it in any way. God is saying I still love you, no matter what. There is more to you than this failure. I want to love you out of the hole you are in, the rut you've carved for yourself.

And when I forgive myself (often the most difficult task of all) I am saying, "Yes, the harm is real, the hurt is true, but that is not the entire truth about me." When I forgive another I am saying, "The debt is real, but there is more to you than that."

I had a wonderful priest friend who always talked about forgiveness, always went to people to seek their forgiveness or to give his own. One time he went to parishioner who worked at Costco and knelt down in the middle of the aisle seeking his forgiveness for a small way he had hurt the man earlier that week. I asked him why he was so "hung up" on forgiveness all the time and he told me "Because we don't do it very well." I think if we knew how to do it better Jesus may not have talked about it so much!

I could go on, but what I want to suggest today is that we are all debtors to God. We are all people who in one way or another have failed to make this world, God's universe, all that it could be.

And God has written off our debt and loved us, not because we deserve it, but because **we are**, and God has boundless hope in us.

Here in this parish, or in any community when we are invited to share our time, our energy, our talent, our financial offerings with the parish it is because this parable is true, and it about us.

We are invited to serve and share our gifts,
not to earn God's love;
not to look good in other people's eyes,
but to give back because we have been given so much.

God has canceled all our debt, freed us from any prison, invited us out into the light where we can shout for joy, and jump, and sing and dance. We cannot wait to give back something of what we have first, so freely received.

52) The Twenty Fifth Sunday

Scripture Readings: Is. 55:6-9; Ph. 1:20-24,27; Mt. 20:1-10

I want to start today with what will be my final point, then surround it and return to it.

The point: the conversion hoped for, in this parable of the various workers in a field, comes from where we choose to stand in the story. Through whose ears do we hear it?

If we are the hard workers who have born the heat of the day, the story sounds, and is, unfair, unjust, bizarre.

If we are the Eleventh hour people, the lucky ones, those who got so much more than they expected or deserved -- if we are the people surprised by grace -- then the story is pure gift. And that is the point! That's what the story is about!

Let me back up a bit.

It helps to reflect on why it is so difficult for us to stand where we need to stand to hear and love this parable.

On one side the story feeds into something pernicious in our culture. I remember hearing the marvelous Franciscan preacher Richard Rohr speak once about our cultural addictions, ways of being that keep us from being able to hear the Gospel. He remarked that he had never heard a homily on the tenth commandment ("Thou shalt not covet thy neighbors goods.") He suspected the reason to be that our capitalist bias runs too deep. Advertising in every medium hopes to convince us to covet, to need and hence want whatever anyone else has, and we don't. Far from being a *sin* coveting is the basis of our entire economy, our way of life. When we go "Malling," we want -- and do not easily admit how much we want -- to get a better deal than the other guy!

Our free trade, free market place mentality is built upon getting a better deal than the other guy. We even think it is a virtue to save money. I think we will be astounded when we die and discover that clipping coupons to save a quarter is not a virtuous act. We are so thrilled when we make a bargain -- "I got this shirt marked down from 42.00 to 17.00 dollars?" I may not have needed the shirt, but I think I saved money! There is no particular virtue unless we want to give the savings away.

On the other hand, paradoxically, besides our deep desire to get a good deal, we also have, deep in our collective American psyche tapes that tell us:

You get what you work for;
There's no such thing as a free lunch;
A guaranteed annual income would take away motivation, destroy initiative, create a

Welfare state of lazy bums;
We cannot afford to get medical coverage for everyone;
We can't just let everyone into our country; they don't all deserve to be here;
People only value what they work for, and earn.

I hear again Dorothy Day's famous, penetrating statement, contradicting all the above:

"God help any of us, if we get what we deserve."

All of which leads to the Gospel story, so difficult to hear, so inequitable, so un-American. Imagine working a ten hour shift, and then only getting the same pay as those that worked only the last hour . . . and having to stand in line to get it! There is no sense in working harder. How can you pay the late comer the same pay as me?

In this parable, as so often, Jesus turns our images upside down. Jesus is not afraid of offending us with "cheap grace." Jesus is utterly convinced that everything is grace, is gift, is cheap, is free! Nothing is earned. God's grace comes first, before we earn anything. The God that Jesus believes in has a special love for the late comer the last chosen, the most needy, the left out, the marginal.

To see the ramifications, the "so what" dimension of this, I am reminded of James Carroll's story from many years ago, about *The Barge People,* from *Wonder and Worship.*

One day a barge arrives in a city on its way to the sea. People from the barge go into the back alleys, the hospitals, the nursing homes of the city and invite wounded people to come and journey with them towards the sea. Some join them and discover that the people who sought them out and brought them to the barge leave and stay in the city. In several cities on the way to the sea, this story is repeated. Barge people go into the most forlorn areas of the town and gather the most lost and needy, giving to them a vision of the sea. In each city those that got new people to come on board the barge leave the barge themselves and remain in the city.

Finally, one day the sea becomes visible, the mighty, beautiful, freeing ocean. The people stand on the deck to see the sea, the destination to which this journey has led them. Slowly it dawns on the city people that there are no more barge people left; no one is steering the boat. As Carroll writes:

> No one spoke. All thought of the sea, of their city of before, of the barge person in whose place they slept . . . . At that moment, all the back-street people moved slowly and together to the left side of the barge. Such a delicate shifting of weight was it that the strange vessel turned slightly to the left. Not much of a turn. Just enough to turn the barge inland again to the cities instead of to the sea. Not much of a turn. Just enough to turn the back-street crowd into barge people."

Without the awareness of life as gift today's parable makes no sense.

We would all like to see ourselves as hard working, full hearted, totally worn out Christians, earning God's love by all we are and do . . . just like the scribes and Pharisees, the religious folks to whom Jesus told this story. But, in fact, we cannot, do not earn the gift of life. All of us are more honestly those hired at the last minute, those who do nothing to earn our reward, whether life, or life eternal. The love we have been given is *given* ... given freely, before we do anything.

If the parable and life itself is about Justice we would all be in danger. But both are about Mercy and we are all last chosen, richly, deeply, undeservedly blessed. The story only makes sense depending on where we stand! We can be bitter because others get as much as we, or unbelievably grateful that we are so richly rewarded.

Jesus tells this parable to his listeners, and to us so that all that we do flows out of the gratitude we have because of this freely given opportunity. Our ministry in our parish, to ourselves in Liturgy, or education, or serving on various committees; our outreach as a people to those in need around us, the love we share in our families, our fairness at work, our participation in our neighborhood, our city, our world ... all flow out of the gift of life and love and laughter given to us freely in the first place.

We turn now to feed again on the meal we do not earn and cannot deserve, the life of Jesus who tells us such amazing stories about God.

53) The Twenty Sixth Sunday

Scripture Readings: Ez 18:25-28; Ph. 2:1-11; Mt. 21:28-32

I used to enjoy preparing couples for marriage. Often these young people were estranged or distant from the Church, apparently from God. Then they fell in love and *covenant, commitment, sacrifice, gratitude* . . .all those religious terms perhaps make sense because for the first time they've had the experience . . they are able to be present with their heart!

I have delighted watching people who are joining the Church get "turned on," have their hearts touched for the first time. I have worked with people recovering from alcoholism, or drug addiction, with those who have survived a number of broken marriages, or the trauma of an abortion, who may have suffered the most painful of life experiences before they show up at a church door. Now they come before God with hearts touched. They sit close, they sing, they respond with their whole being. They don't just go to Mass; they celebrate it. They don't just receive communion, they become it.

I loved guiding people in retreats as Jesus touches them deeply in their hearts. I recall a single parent, divorced woman who had led a fairly promiscuous life, had been on welfare. Despite a lifelong if sporadic practice of religion she never "got it." In the midst of a retreat, out of prayer, for the first time, she knew she was loved; her heart was touched. And she changed ...not by force but by choice. Now she is a lawyer working almost exclusively with those who cannot afford to hire legal help. Her "Yes," is deep and meaningful.

In today's Gospel, Jesus tells the religious folks that prostitutes and tax collectors, sinners can get into the kingdom because they heard the call to conversion and responded. They said "Yes," perhaps belatedly, but with their whole hearts. Somehow those who have said "No," can change to "Yes" and have it really mean something.

When we listen to the parable today we need to hear, with old Paul Harvey ears, *the rest of the story!* It is very easy to answer the question Jesus asks; "Which son did the father's will?" Well, obviously, one kid went into the vineyard after he said he wouldn't, the other said he would and didn't. Any idiot can tell you which son did something!

Though easy to answer Jesus' question it is more difficult to grasp his point, and to let it speak to me, be about me!

<u>Everybody needs conversion, a change of heart!</u>

And it is more difficult for religious folks to let that happen.

The <u>crunch</u> of the very small story Jesus tells about the two sons, as with the later longer version Luke tells us about two sons and their loving father, comes with the application -- John the Baptist came preaching to everyone the need to change, to renew our hearts, to prepare for the messianic coming. Sinners got it; religious folks didn't. Sinners, broken people, outcasts can be part of the reign of God. Some religious folks can't. They have the right ideas, say the right words. But their hearts aren't there!

Matthew's Gospel, written down around the year 70, is concerned in part with trying to explain why so few Jewish people accepted Jesus as Messiah, while many other, non-Jewish people, did. What happened to the chosen people? Why are the chosen people so often outside the fold now as the church begins to grow? What happened? This is one of three parables that deal with religious people having become complacent, not letting conversion happen.

We mustn't trivialize this passage. We do not have here a simple little invitation to walk our talk, though that is part of it. This is a warning to never think we have it made. At the beginning of the Second Vatican Council John XXIII reminded us that the Church and every member of it is "*semper reformanda*," always in need of conversion, reform. Pope Francis, since the day of his installation has echoed that conviction. We Catholics have had as much difficulty listening to John or Francis as did the religious folks of Jesus day did to that other John, the Baptizer. I often reflect on the big conversions that Council asked of us:

- conversion from private spirituality to communal, especially in our liturgical and sacramental life -- we are all in this together and our lives, our prayer are communal,
- the call to ecumenical conversion, to see Christ present in other churches, other cultures, other ways of being before God,

- and, from The Church in the World , conversion to a deep concern for the sorrows, sufferings, pains of people throughout the globe, the Church's mission is not to itself, but to the world.

So, often people we would not consider terribly religious folks have heard that call; others of us have been comfortable in the faith we'd always known, and missed it.

In a way this homily is finished, but it would be shame to quit without looking at the wonderful hymn from Philipians that was our second reading today. In that hymn, Jesus is the model for our deeply human, full hearted "yes," to the Father. Jesus is the son who says and does "Yes!"

I know for me, right now, the call to conversion, to change involves leaving all that was familiar to me for a life, a new way of being a follower of Jesus. I do not know what conversion your "Yes" to God might entail. . . where you individually, or we together need to reform our lives, but I believe God's invitation, God calls to us not just to "Yes," but to an ever deeper "Yes!"!"

Letting go of the religious language in which the hymn is couched, this hymn tells us that Jesus loved; he faced the suffering love brought. When challenged he kept loving, kept speaking the truth, kept acting with integrity, and even though that led to enormous suffering, and finally death, he didn't turn back, didn't say no, didn't change his heart's direction.

So God lifts him up before us and says "Look at Jesus," That's the way to go, that's the way to live. That's what I had in mind when I turned out this human model. You can all be like that . . You can all be that full hearted, that loving, that courageous.

When we proclaim that Jesus lived and died for us, that "for us" doesn't mean "so that we don't have to," but "so that we will be able to." His "Yes" to God's invitation to go into the vineyard enables us to say, and to live out our own.

Finally we live out this gospel in our lives every time we celebrate Eucharist. God invites us to go into his vineyard and labor. He offers us the example, the story of Jesus, offers us the very life of Jesus to help us. Our presence here is a way of beginning, of *saying* "Yes," but when we leave we have not yet done anything. We will discover the depth of our "yes," as we leave.

54) The Twenty Seventh Sunday

Scripture Readings: Is. 5:1-7; Phil. 4:6-9; Mt. 21: 33-43

This is the third week in a row that we city dwellers, are invited to understand our faith in terms of vine, vineyards, vine growers, workers, . . . good grapes and sour grapes. Today even the first reading spells out a famous song of the vine grower from Isaiah.

In this touching poem, God, through the prophet laments about Israel in a dark time in their collective history. God speaks of spading, clearing, planting, manuring his vineyard...doing everything he can to make it fruitful, but all he got back was "Sour Grapes." The poor vine grower. What more could he do that he has not done?

Jesus picks up the vine image in the parable today. . . the third week in a row that God's reign is understood in terms of a vine- yard. Today a most peculiar parable. Like many parables, this is not a story that makes immediate sense; the sense is achieved by gross exaggeration.

The parable is rooted in two different sets of unbelievable behavior.

What tenant farmers could be so stupid as to think they'd get away with what they are doing? Could they really totally forget that they are renters and believe that by maiming the servants and then killing the owner's son that they will own everything themselves?

It would seem obvious that the exact opposite would happen. Because they don't give even minimal respect to the owner they will certainly lose everything. Shouldn't they have expected that?

And the owner is even more nutso! His servants are beat up, so instead of sending the police, he sends more servants, who are treated even worse. Then instead of sending in the INS he sends his son, as if he believed his son's presence would solve everything! Stupid! They kill the son.

Even Hollywood couldn't make a movie out of this unbelievable story. What's even worse, the story offers a terrible image of God who besides initially being almost incredibly naive, is then awesomely vindictive.

The story at first glance seems too simple: Those whom God entrusted with producing good fruit foolishly betray God's trust. God responds in kind by wiping out the fools.

We have two major problems: An unbelievable parable, peopled by idiots, and a very negative image of God.

Can we redeem either of them? I believe we can! First, we need to consider the parable as written in italics. We are initially struck with the apparent absurdity: who could be so silly as to think they own the field given them in trust? Who, *we might be forced into asking*, could imagine that they own this world, which really belongs to God?

And even as we ask, we become aware that we manage to line our highways with McDonald wrappers, insist on driving large cars all alone while we destroy the Ozone layer, build high-rise condos along waterfronts likely to flood, cut down trees on hillsides that used to hold back water while we build big houses below, destroy whole species of eagles, or put Atlantic fish in the pacific, and do almost anything to support our abundant life-style?

What kind of tenant would maim the owner's servants, or children? And we find ourselves forsaking Syrian or Iraqi refugees left with nowhere to escape to, young 'dreamers – immigrants -- in danger of being cast out of the only nation they've known, 12 million people in the richest nation in the world, with no guarantee of health care and a federal law to protect children's health care disappearing without a vote. And 300 million guns gradually kill our sons and daughters.

The frightening truth is that if we take the parable seriously it becomes too terribly real.

Are we not in very real danger of being those foolish servants who thought the gift was our own possession? How do we differ from the foolish servants who beat and killed the servants and even the children of the owner? We might quite rightly be afraid that the wrath of the Owner/ God will be wreaked on us who have so carelessly used the earth and its people that we hold in trust.

Which leads us back to the image of God. Does God in fact wreak vengeance on those who have disrespected his fields, and killed his servants and his son? Actually a more careful reading suggests this conclusion is not the one presented by Jesus. Those who heard the parable, the religious folks supply that ending.

The actual ending is more enigmatic; Jesus responds with a koan, a kind of open ended reflection: "The stone rejected becomes the corner stone."

Jesus ending suggests that this foolish farmer trusted and loved beyond reason. He trusted the tenants with all of his servants, and finally with his son. When even this son is killed, the farmer, rather than wreaking vengeance makes sure that this son becomes the cornerstone, the foundation of whatever will happen to the field next!

The slaughtered son becomes the heart of the message.

To say the same thing from another direction, The vine image of the past few weeks has a wonderful later New Testament use. In this week's reading Isaiah asks: What is God to do? What more can God do that God has not done?

Centuries later, John's gospel provides a response, a cornerstone response. The son, rejected, becomes the vine. Jesus says "I am the vine, you are the branches" God is not longer outside pruning, manuring, loving the vineyard; it is as if God says:

> I unite totally with you, and work in you, work through
> you, so this silliness can finally stop. I will no longer
> try to fix things from outside the vine, outside the
> work. I will become totally untied with you, as the Vine
> itself.

You may have the same trouble I do relating to these rural images, of vines, and vine dressers, and vine growers, and field hands. We are city folk. But we city folk continue to try to unite with the vine and offer our gifts to make the field fruitful.

We try not to hold onto the gifts we have, as if they were indeed our own, as if we were owners of the field.

We try to offer food to the children hungry because the goods of the earth are not well distributed, try to help build homes for those who would otherwise sleep in the fields.

We sing and celebrate the centrality of the Vineyard owner's son in our midst, in our vision, in our dreams.

We look at the needs immediately around us for ministry to ourselves, and to our neighborhood, and to our world. We share our gifts within our own families, our work place, our neighborhoods. Each of us tries to be a faithful tenant.

Today, in Eucharist, we offer again our gifts, our lives (in the form of the fruit of the vine) for the task. And we know, that to live out what we promise we need to receive this Eucharist that again unites us with the vine who lives in us.

55) The Twenty Eighth Sunday

Scripture Readings: Is. 25:6-10; Phil. 4: 10-14,19-20; Mt. 22: 1-14

You may not have noticed that we celebrated Groucho Marx 's birthday this week! Groucho was a master of the *insult*, a trait I admire. One of his classic insults helps me frame my reflections on the Gospel today.

A priest came up to Groucho one day and said: "Mr. Marx, I want to thank you for bringing so much joy into the world." Groucho replied, "And, Father, I want to thank you for taking so much joy out of it!"

That is the perception often voiced of our Church, our faith. How ironical that the dominant image of God's reign is that of a colossal wedding feast to which everyone is invited. We don't have to deserve or earn it; in fact those that thought it was earned didn't go, and missed the party.

The Gospel today says two very important things: everyone can come to the party, but we cannot take the gift for granted. *Grace if free.* But *it is not cheap.*

For the past several weeks we have heard a series of parables about the Reign of God. Every parable invites us to reflect both on the gift of God's love but also the cost of being loved by God.

In God's reign all our debts are written off; but we have to be willing to write off the debts of others.

In God's reign we all get more than we deserve; but we have to be willing to see those that who come late and broken to God's love be loved as much or more as those who have worked hard all their lives.

In God's reign tax collectors and prostitutes experience conversion and share the joy of the kingdom, but some who thought they were part of the family miss the point. Those that might think they own the land, own the world, will be replaced by those who own nothing, have nothing but their need and dependence on God's mercy.

Matthew's Gospel explains to the first generation of Christians what happened to those chosen people who miss the messianic presence, while others, gentiles, heard the message and responded. When we read the message today we transpose it and wonder if we religious folks are in danger of missing the wonder of Jesus presence and message, while those outside the fold hear it and celebrate the gifts of the kingdom.

The parable today suggests that if we do not and will not celebrate, sing, dance, rejoice in the gift of life and love then we are not the Church, the family of God; we don't live in the kingdom, *and* we are also not the Church of Jesus. We cannot continue to celebrate if we do not come to the party with a sense of gratitude and responsibility.

Grace is Free, but it is not cheap!

I find myself asking, as I have the past few weeks, where am I, where are we in this parable? The Gospel is supposed to be Good News, but it can only be good news for those who appreciate that the Messiah has come, the party has started, the wine is flowing, the joy is here. Grace is Free.

I am haunted by the poor guy who doesn't have the right clothes on and gets treated terribly because of it. He just came in to see what was going. He thought maybe he'd grab a bite to eat, and leave. He wasn't there for the evening; he didn't know the bride and groom. He thought he would just be a bit of a spectator. But grace is not cheap.

The parable suggests that we have to really join the party. Give our lives to it. The wedding garment is a metaphor for the Baptismal garment. Baptism is not one truth among many, not just one part of the truth about the followers of Jesus. We are Democrats, or Republicans, Irish, or German, or Vietnamese, Elks, or Moose, or Knights of Columbus, bankers, or homemakers, or teachers, gay or straight, young or old, we live in city or on a farm…, and, by the way, we are Catholics!

No!

The followers of Jesus put on a garment, and join fully in the celebration. Our Baptismal garment, the sign that we join the celebration with the bridegroom, is constant, complete, total; this identity permeates everything we do, everything we are.

Grace is free; we don't have to do anything to earn God's love. But grace is not cheap. We have to respond to it with our whole lives.

This parable suggests something about how we gather here for Eucharist and something about how we live when we leave.

We receive the wonderful gift of Eucharist. Without earning or meriting it at all, we get to come to this feast, hear the stories of God's love, share at the banquet of the very life of Jesus. It's free. But we have to be here, have to join in the songs, listen to the stories, be actively part of the celebration. People that don't even pick up a book to sing, fail to put on the wedding garment. People half-heartedly responding to the prayers or passively present to a feast they do not enjoy, live in the middle of this parable. We can be here over and over and over again, and never really meet, never celebrate the presence of the bridegroom, Jesus.

Sometimes that is the fault of the presider and those leading us in prayer who don't let it feel like any kind of real celebration .. is the homily carefully prepared? Is the music well done and inviting? Do the readers read like what they are saying matters?

And we can leave this Eucharistic celebration, and not wear the wedding garment, our baptismal garment out the door. The feast doesn't go with us. We vote just like our neighbors, we work for the same material ends as our culture, we live the values, or lack of them and are not changed because we have been told Good News!

We are perhaps unmoved that too many are still excluded from the feast for us to simply party and rejoice without concern. Too many have still not experienced the Good News. Faith, and food, and freedom do not flow for too many, for the rest of us to totally enjoy the feast ourselves.

There is a cost to Christianity. The cost is primarily extending the invitation to everyone, to all,

> to refugees from Syria, Iraq, Somalia

> to immigrants, even those here illegally

> to a rural parish in Zambia with 616 Catechumens, or a new school in Malawi, or reservation Indians in South Dakota

> To earthquake victims in Mexico, and flood victims in Texas and Florida and Puerto Rico, and fire victims in California

We are not just invited to a banquet from out of the highways and byways of the world. We are invited to be so present at the banquet that we cannot help but extend to others, cannot keep from inviting everyone in to share the wine, to taste the earth's abundance, to know of God's exorbitant love.

So the feast is going on and we are present at it. But the feast is not yet full, and so we do not simply celebrate and rejoice. We cannot, until all share the celebration.

Grace is, indeed, free, but it is never cheap!

56) The Twenty Ninth Sunday

Scripture Readings: Is. 45:1, 4-6; I Thes. 1:1-5; Mt. 22:15-21

Two avenues of reflection help me to hear today's gospel about what belongs to Caesar and what to God.

Frequently at this Eucharist, we celebrate Baptisms of young members of our community. Each of us renews our own Baptisms at the same time, and try to re-capture the all-pervasive spirit of that continuing event. We stand with these parents and respond to questions:

Do you renounce Satan, and all his works, and all his empty promises?

Do you believe in God, in Jesus, in their Spirit, in this community of saints and sinners?

These questions really ask: To what do I pledge allegiance?
To whom do I pledge Allegiance?

This is the same question asked of Jesus in Today's Gospel!

Secondly, a recent poll of Catholics. One thing in particular caught my eye -- something like 16% of Catholics said their church was the most important part of their lives. Another 35 or 40 percent said it was among the most important. So 50-55% of Catholics rank their Church as a pretty important part of their lives. And I find myself asking whether it makes any sense to say my Church is important, my family is important, my job is important, my country is important, my golf game is important, as if all were ranked side by side. (Note: When I say Church, I do not mean the institution, but the people of God, the companions of Jesus, into which we are baptized!!)

In terms of today's gospel, does some stuff belong to Caesar and some to God? It seems to me that religion, faith, the Church, Jesus, Baptism either matter totally, completely, or do not matter at all. Either my religion, Church, faith -- better, my relationship with God in Jesus -- totally encompasses every other aspect of my life, or it has no meaning at all.

Let me turn to the gospel, to help me talk about both these things.

First, we realize that the question asked Jesus was asked precisely to trap him. What was the trap? The Pharisees, religious folks who claimed complete separation from the Roman invaders, want to trap Jesus. In order to set the trap they asked the Herodians to join them...the Herodians would be the party of Herod, a Jewish political folks who had accommodated to the hated Roman presence in their midst.

The Pharisees and their friends would like to pretend to have nothing to do with Caesar. The Herodians had learned to make common cause with Caesar. This was the trap.

If Jesus said "don't pay the tax," the Herodians would be offended, would tell the Roman officials and Jesus would be in trouble, perhaps killed.

If Jesus said "pay the tax," the righteous religious Jews would call him a traitor. All under the pretense of seeking truth. "Come on, Jesus, you can trust us, tell us how much you resent the Roman intrusion into our land and our lives!"

Jesus does a wonderful thing by asking the Pharisees for a coin, so that they had to reach into their Jewish pockets for the coin he did not have in his. To possess the coin at all is already to be a part of the political system in question. Jesus didn't have the coin; they did. So they may as well take part in the entire system the coin represents.

Jesus response, though ambiguous, means the exact opposite of what some have tried to have it say over the centuries. Jesus certainly does not say we owe a little allegiance to God, a little to Caesar, so keep them separate. His response and the entire passage that follows implies:

> "Go ahead and give to Caesar the piddly little bit that
> may be his, but, By God, give to God what is God's
> and that is everything!"

Shortly after these lines Jesus will reiterate the Jewish injunction to love God "With your whole heart, whole soul, whole mind."

Jesus entire life was a giving of his very self to God...with nothing held back nothing given elsewhere that was not in line with that central gift. The gist of the passage says most simply our entire life, all our energy and effort, all our dedication, all our allegiance is to God, and God alone.

To return to my second introductory point: Our faith in Jesus isn't one part of our life, like many others. This faith is what gives underpinning, backdrop, color, tone to everything. I'm not sometimes a Christian and sometimes a Citizen. I don't leave my baptismal robe outside the voting booth. I can't vote for a state ballot measure that saves me money, but hurts the poorest most fragile among us. I don't get a job, buy a house, marry a wife, select a whole series of hobbies, and then figure out how to fit my religion into the pattern. What I do, where I live who I marry, how I recreate, are all part of who I am, a member of Christ's body, one who has put on Christ. to believe is literally to "give my heart" my whole heart to another. To believe is to become one who "lives now not I but Christ lives in me."

Simply put, our faith either pervades everything or it touches nothing.

Baptism speaks and reinforces that single-hearted allegiance!

We used to talk about Baptism taking away Original Sin; we didn't understand it, but we said it. Even though our experience tells us plainly that sin still has some power over us. I, at least, have had a temptation or two since Baptism.

What we mean, more carefully, is that Baptism aligns us with a community that, in everything we do, tries to stand with Jesus, over and against the power that sin has. . . . We stand against the origins of sin; we say "no" to sexism, racism, ageism, materialism, consumerism, legalism, militarism, and every other *ism* that can kill the human spirit.

We say "Yes" to Jesus, to his values, pledge allegiance to his God. Then we plunge into the waters of death and we die to those *isms,* we die to sin, we put them behind us, and stand with the community of the followers of Jesus, striking at the roots, the origins of sin. We deliberately choose to live allegiance to Jesus, as best we can, with all our faults, in everything we do.

What we do in Baptism, put most simply, is say we want to initiate our children into such a community; a people that will help them to give everything to God. And what is given to Caesar or anyone else is done in keeping with what God would ask of us.

To whom, to what do I give allegiance?

And is it only part time, only partial, only when convenient?

or do I give to God what is God's.... **Everything?**

57) The Twenty Ninth Sunday

(An Alternate, especially for Rite of Welcoming Catechumens)

Often during this season our parish and many others celebrate the Rite of Becoming Catechumens or Rite of Welcoming, the first formal step for those who say they want to become Catholic Christians, want to be, with us, as followers of Jesus.

The Gospel today invites us to wonder out loud: Does it matter? Does anything change for them or for us when we become Christians? Specifically today's Gospel raises the question about our relationship with our civil society, our culture. Does our discipleship support, inhibit, challenge our citizenship in any way?

Some images to flesh out the Question:

- Some Churches have American flags in the Sanctuary. Should they? If this parish is like most Catholic Churches. I suspect they used to have one here and removing it caused some uproar.

- John Kennedy was able to be elected president because he was able to say clearly that his political life would not be guided by his allegiance to the Catholic Church. Was that good, bad, true?
- Should a Catholic politician necessarily speak with the same voice as a local bishop on matters like Abortion, or the Death penalty, or immigration, or gay marriage?
- I have a friend, a Jesuit priest, was often in the Federal Penitentiary for protesting the School of the Americas where our government trains military forces for Latin America, forces that have been involved in the death of Jesuits, and many others in El Salvador and elsewhere. Should he be there? Why are we not there?
- Before his election as president, the First George Bush gave a major presentation at Seattle University; the University's Jesuit president sat next to him; another Jesuit was arrested for demonstrating at that event against what he felt were Bush's policies towards the poor, and towards Latin America? Which was right? Could both of them be?
- A Jesuit was a speechwriter for Richard Nixon. Another Jesuit at the same time was a congressman who led the fight for Nixon's impeachment. My beloved local bishop refused to pay taxes that supported building nuclear weapons. Are such actions good or bad, or what?
- Should we register voters in Church? Support specific candidates? Specific causes? A recent Trumpian suggestion is to let churches speak on political matters without threat to their tax exemption; is this good or bad?
- And when we vote does the Gospel, the voice of the American Bishops, or the teaching of the Church necessarily influence our choice?

The question that was asked of Jesus today about paying taxes to Caesar raises every question about our relationship with civil society, our culture, our world. How should we stand? Where should we stand?

A variety of forces tugged at Jesus as they do at us.

Pharisees, like the Amish, said "Separate yourselves, have nothing to do with the Roman conquerors, with Caesar."

Zealots, like radicals today, said: "Throw the rascals out, fight them, resist them."

Saducees, like most of us, said "compromise, work stuff out."

Herodians, perhaps like Marco Rubio or Paul Ryan, of Nancy Pelosi are part of the system, hold office, work alongside the Roman ruler, said "We can build the Kingdom by making this kingdom work."

Where did Jesus stand in the midst of all this. That was the question asked him.

I, for one, wish Jesus was less Irish. Why must he always answer a question with another question? But then, he was in a trap.

If he says "Pay the tax," the Pharisees and Zealots are offended; religious powers will gather against him.

If he says, "Don't pay the tax," the Saducees and Herodians are offended; Political powers will gather against him?

So, rather than answering, Jesus asks another question. "What's on the coin? Whose face? What inscription?" For besides Caesar's

face/ a forbidden image, the coin declared Caesar to be Divine ...
a blasphemy to the Jewish faith.

It is fascinating that when Jesus asks for a coin, the Pharisee, the
one who apparently did not traffic with Caesar at all, had one in
his pocket. So before Jesus answers the Pharisee's righteousness
is already undermined.

What does Jesus enigmatic answer mean? "Give to Caesar what
is Caesar's; Give to God what is God's!"

What it clearly does not mean what only the first half says; Many
civil religionists, contemporary Herodians seem to wish it did.
How often have we heard only the first half quoted, "Render to
Caesar what is Caesar's!" This clearly is not Jesus intention. He
clearly does not say:

> *"Give the State whatever it asks. Always pay taxes.*
> *Always obey civil laws, even Hitler's. Always do*
> *what civil leaders demand, and keep what is religious*
> *only in the religious sphere."*

Jesus may be saying something closer to:

> *"If you are going to carry Caesar's coin, enjoy*
> *Caesar's world, benefit from Caesar's power, then*
> *probably you ought to give something back to Caesar.*
> *But do not give to Caesar what belongs to God alone!"*

In the context of the entire Gospel it seems to me what Jesus
says is even stronger. His answer seems to me to imply as the
entire Gospel bears out:

Finally, nothing is Caesar's; it's all borrowed from God,
with a high interest loan. Everything ultimately is God's.

So, what is our relationship with Civil Society? What are the implications of Jesus invitation to give everything to God?

Ignatius of Loyola helps me here. He invites us to a radical indifference towards everything of the world in relationship to our call to build God's reign. The followers of Jesus do not separate ourselves from the world, nor do we immerse ourselves totally in it. We stand able to pay or not, to use or not, to attack or to agree. We stand neither as *unloving critics* nor as *uncritical lovers*. any political system, or nation-state. Rather, with Jesus, we are *critical lovers* of every thing that is from God but is not God!

To be a follower of Jesus implies that I want to make every decision, cast every vote, take every stance, pay or not pay every tax in so far as it helps to build God's kingdom, helps produce Justice, Love and Peace, helps bring liberty to captives, helps bring Good News to the Poor.

The issue of taxes or any other Church-State question invites us into a prudential decision about whether this promotes or diminishes God's reign in my heart, in my community, or in my world. Our answers may vary, but our questions ought to be the same.

Perhaps the real question is: "Whose face is on the coin of my heart?"

58) The Thirtieth Sunday

Scripture Readings: Ex. 22:21-27; I Thes. 1:5-10; Mt. 22:34-40

Which rule matters the most? It used to be so simple. In my long-ago youth, you often heard people say: "He's a good Catholic, he goes to Mass every Sunday." Or "He's a good Catholic; he still doesn't eat meat on Friday." Or, "She's a faithful Catholic; great devotion to the rosary, to Mary. She spends hours saying her prayers every day."

Have we ever heard someone say "He's a great Catholic banker; he spends lots of time working out loans so poor people can to get into their own homes?" Or "She's a wonderful Catholic lawyer; she does half of her work *pro bono* for Native Americans." Or, "He's a great Catholic teacher; always has time for the student who is not succeeding in class." Or "It's a great Catholic parish; they have a special ministry to the elders among them; and they give a proportion of their budget to help settle immigrants in their city."

If we listen to today's Gospel it becomes more complicated to say what makes a good Catholic., a good Christian.

On the other hand maybe we have always made things _too_ complicated. In Jesus times, when he was asked the question about which is the most important law there were 613 Jewish Laws that the religious person was expected to observe. By comparison, our Canon law has 1752 Canons.

The context of today's Gospel and the question posed to Jesus about the most important law is a section in Matthew with a number of conflict stories:

> Those who want Jesus to deny the Resurrection ask: "If you get married a number of times in this life, to whom are you married in heaven?"

> Those who believe in the need for Jews to be separatists from the Roman world they live in ask: "What should you give to Caesar?"

> This story offers Jesus another dilemma. He is challenged by those who believed that failure to observe any one of the Laws was to break them all; every jot and tittle was important. Others felt with equal passion that there must be a gradation of laws and the injunction to love God with one's whole heart, soul and mind, was prior and weightier than all the others. Which side was Jesus on?

So what does Jesus say: He affirms the centrality of the _Shema_, the great Jewish prayer: "Hear, Oh Israel, that your God is one God . . . " This affirmation that we are to love God with entire mind heart and spirit was on every door knob of a Jewish home, was contained in a wrist band on every observant Jew's wrist. They all knew what was important.

But Jesus does not just "side" with one party of this dispute. He adds a nuance that is fresh and surprising. He says the second is *like* it, *similar* to it. Language fails us here. In English we use *like* and *similar* in two quite different ways. An apple is kind of like an orange; is similar to an orange. But we also say "like two peas in a pod," or "my view is similar to yours," meaning exactly the same as. Hebrew scholars affirm that, Jesus words would have been understood to say, "This is the first, and greatest commandment and the second is exactly the same thing, the second is identical to it."

Love God . . . love your neighbor. The same commandment. Two statements exactly alike!

Again we make religion too complicated. It all boils down to: "Love God; love each other." How simple to say; how difficult to live. In religious practice laws and rules, those 613 laws, or 1572 canons keeps bumping into love and make it difficult.

"Bless me Father, I missed Mass on Sunday. I had some visitors come over and they stayed through the final Mass." And I reply, "So, you stayed home and loved your visitors and you missed Mass . . . Isn't that a virtue? To love our neighbor?"

Or more complicated: When marriage is killing people and damaging kids can divorce be responsible?

Can we give large doses of addictive drugs to ease pain when someone is dying?

Do we insist that parents be going to Church before we baptize a child? Should we marry a couple who are not now, but someday may again be Catholics because we want to honor the person more than the various laws of the Church?

Can a Catholic vote for a politician who supports legislation he personally disagrees with on, say, abortion or capital punishment because in other ways he or she seems to honestly care about people?

Can I give communion to someone who deeply believes in Jesus and the Eucharist, though the law says they are of another faith and can't receive or have divorced and re-married?

And on and on and on -- the laws and rules seem to come into conflict with the real needs of real people.

Although the matters can be very complicated, Jesus seems clear; we love God by loving our sisters and brothers. To love God is to love our neighbor.

The perhaps best contemporary book on moral theology is aptly titled "Just Love,"

I cannot leave the Readings today without two final comments.

First I am grateful for the first reading today, that fleshes out the Gospel. Problems arise in trying to figure out what love means. The passage from Exodus today is so helpful. It invites us to focus on those God apparently focuses on . . .the alien, the poor, the widow, the orphan. Love needs especially to be given to those without power, without voice, without support systems to care for them. The neighbor we love as ourselves ideally is the one who most needs that love, not just *our* family, *our* friends, or, *our* *individual* neighbor. Providence Health & Services from whom I have worked the past 18 years aim to serve all people "especially the poor and vulnerable."

Love of God is the same as, identical to, our love for the fragile . . . how we care for the widow, the orphan, the immigrants, or foreigners in our midst,

How we treat children in our society, the unborn, and the born poor,

how we treat the aged and the infirm.

Secondly and finally, this story needs to be read always in the light of a similar one. In another place in Matthew's gospel a rich young man comes to Jesus. The man knows this interpretation. He knows that loving God and neighbor constitute one, all-encompassing law, but he has kept this law from his youth, and asks Jesus what else he needs to do. And Jesus suggests that his perfection and perhaps our own lies not in following laws at all, but in following Jesus. "Leave everything," he says, and "come, and follow me."

This gospel passage suggests that the fulfillment of Jewish faith is in loving God and neighbor. The fulfillment of our *Christian* faith lies in following Jesus and finding out the enfleshed meaning of these laws in relationship with him.

59) The Feast of All Saints: Nov I

Scripture Readings: Rev. 7; I Jn. 3; Mt. 5:1-12

Three images have danced in my head all week as I listened to the Beatitudes yet again: First, I had a bizarre picture of the floor at the stock exchange on Wall Street on a day the stock market went crazy . All kinds of investors, financiers, power brokers alarmed, disturbed, panic stricken, rushed around on the floor of the stock exchange as suddenly, over the loud-speaker, came a voice saying: "Remember, Blessed are the poor in Spirit, theirs is the kingdom of God."

The second image was the picture of a marvelous elderly woman parishioner in her late 80's whom I greeted coming into Mass one morning. I said "Hi, Irene, how are you?" She responded without batting an eye: "I'm just perfect!" Despite the loss of a son-in-law the previous week, despite the frailties of old age, despite the worries that could come, she was perfect, happy, blessed!

Third, I have been imagining Jesus coming to preach a homily to us today on these beatitudes. I wonder what he would say to us; more specifically I wondered what he would say to me, that I can pass on to you.

I think he would remind me that he didn't make these sayings up out of thin air. *They are not true because he said them, but he said them because they are true.* These beatitudes describe reality as Jesus experienced it. If I pay attention I may experience reality this way also!

Then he would remind me that we hear these word today on the Feast of all the Saints, all those who are, in that wonderful image from Revelations, "washed clean in the blood of the lamb," all who are living and have lived in the Reign of God. This is the feast of those "Happy" folks who have gone before us, and who live in our midst still.

And I suspect that Jesus would remind me that these beatitudes are not rules, laws, something to be lived up to, worked hard at, and around which I will be punished if I fail. Though they parallel the ten commandments in their structure and their setting, in the scripture story they are significantly different. True, Jesus is seen as a new Moses, coming down from a Mountain and speaking on behalf of God, but he is speaking a different way of life, a way of happiness, a way of living blessedly because the Reign of God has already broken into life.

As in the original ten commandments, Jesus tells me that the first one says it all: There is one God before whom I stand with open hands, needy heart. If I stand dependent, longing, poor in Spirit, then the Reign of God can break in. If I get that one right everything else will follow! Being Blessed means recognizing the simple truth that God is God and I'm not!

Paradoxically, the reign of God can break in when I am feeling most powerless, most poor in my spirit. I'm at my best and most honest, I live closest to the reign of God when:

- I talk to a family whose son has died and don't try to comfort them with meaningful words, but simply stay with them, love them, listen to them, help them celebrate the gift of life they had for eighteen years. No easy answers, just a sharing of pain, mourning, holding on to hope!
- I am at my best when I feel overwhelmed by a project that seems to be going nowhere and I let myself feel helpless, powerless, unable to "make it happen," feeling very needy, very dependent, forcing myself to trust that it will work out how and when and if God wants it to.
- I am at my best when I let myself feel a deep concern over our nation's foreign policy, when I hunger and thirst for justice in Afghanistan or peace with North Korea; when I let my heart cry out in pain at the plight of people I/we are oppressing, killing, and I cannot see clearly how to end it all.
- I am at my best and living in the Reign of God, even, when I feel torn by some breakdown of love in the wonderful wounded community of our parish and I need to depend on God's power not mine to fix it.

I believe Jesus would remind me that often I cannot see, feel, or conjure up my own happiness, blessedness, awareness of God's reign. I need to remember Jesus not as one who merely spoke these words of blessing, but lived them. I need to know that I, like him, often won't feel or understand. I need to see him on a cross, at that extreme moment of poverty of spirit, mourning, persecution, neither knowing, nor experiencing God's reign, but trusting in it, hoping for it.

Finally, it is trusting in Resurrection, both the big one at the end and all the little ones along the way, that assures me the promised beatitudes are true.

And Jesus would remind me to look at him to see the truth of all of this. To see Jesus as the one without sin, the one most Blessed, the one who enfleshed the Reign of God. Jesus who was free! Free from anxiety over success, anxiety over survival, anxiety about relationships.

Something in me, something not the Reign of God, wants to avoid these anxieties, wants to hold them back, protect myself from them, not let them get at me.

- I want to get enough power over my world so that I can be on top of things.
- I want to get enough security from sickness and pain to insure that I will always feel OlK.
- I want to get enough control in relationships so that I cannot be hurt by them.

And Jesus tells me again that these beatitudes are not rules to be lived up to but rather a freedom to be gained. He holds out the hope that if I let the real God into my life I can be freed from the anxiety that makes me hold onto all these little gods, the anxiety that keeps me from forgiving injuries, turning my cheek yet one more time, sharing my goods, time, talent, money, love.

Let me end with a final image, a final picture of myself listening to Jesus talk about the beatitudes.

I see myself standing before God, before life, before you. One hand is stretched out open, trusting, inviting. The other hand is up, protecting myself, holding back, anxious. In everything Jesus says to me he invites me to let the other hand down, to be open, to trust, to take the risk of truly being blessed, happy ... living in the Reign of God!

As I rush about my life, frantic about many things, I hear the voice of Jesus over the loudspeaker of my life saying, "Blessed are the poor in Spirit." How I long for the day when you ask me how I am, and (now finally dependent on God, now finally "poor in spirit,") I am able to say with Irene, "I'm just perfect!"

60) The Thirty First Sunday

Scripture Readings: Mal. 1:14-2:2, 8-10; 1 Thes. 2:7-9, 13; Mt. 23:1-12

Someone asked a marvelously talented Jesuit brother why he didn't go the whole way and become a Priest, a Father. His response was to wonder quietly aloud why so many priests didn't 'go the whole way' and become brothers! For a follower of Jesus to "go the whole way" is to become a *brother, a sister.*

Perhaps the most exciting, most life-changing assertion of the Second Vatican Council was the "Universal Call to Holiness" in the first document on the Church. Vatican II insisted that there are not "special people" in the Church, some who take the gospel seriously so others don't have to, some who are supposed to be sacred, separate, holy, while others don't. We do not set aside some people -- priests, sisters, church workers -- while everyone else just has jobs! All our jobs, all our lives are holy and challenged to become more so.

Despite all the evidence to the contrary we are not meant to b a church with a caste system.

We are all invited to full hearted following of Jesus. When we welcome new members into our community of faith, we renew the faith each of us began at our own Baptismal font. We consider what it means to be "Church" together. The readings today are helpful in that reflection, especially as they deal with the role of leadership in the Church.

In the first reading, from the prophet Malachi, leaders are excoriated, -- indeed *screamed at* -- by the prophet for taking advantage of the people, for not treating them as equals, for using their position of prominence to oppress people "Do we not all have one Father?" asks the prophet. Are we not all in this together?

In the very early letter to the Thessalonians -- the first book written in the Christian scriptures, twenty years before the first Gospel, Paul reminds the community that he did not come in power, in fancy robes, asking to be treated royally, but rather he worked among them as his "sisters and brothers," supporting himself so as not to be a burden to them. Though he comes as teacher, he is not more important than the least of them. They are all in this together.

In the section of Matthew's Gospel from which today's reading is taken the Evangelist presents a Jesus truly frustrated with the leadership of the Jewish community of his day. Over and over again he calls the scribes and Pharisees hypocrites, blind guides, people who dare to use roles of authority in the community for their own aggrandizement. He does not want his community to be like that. In the community of Jesus everyone is equal, no one is special, everyone is called to the same holiness. We are all in this together.

Though I think we need to keep examining our use of "Father," even "Holy Father," or "Your Lordship," any titles of honor, it is not the title that matters but the spirit behind the title. Jesus forbids titles because all are equals. If I were a priest, whatever you call me, I am not father, rabbi, teacher, but brother. We are all learners. We are all called to the same holiness. We are all in this together.

So back to Baptism. Since most of us are baptized as infants we don't think about it nearly enough as we go on. Baptism is a profound, and profoundly equalizing event. We plunge into the waters, we die to who and whatever we have been, and we come back to life, arise out of the waters re-born into one body in Jesus.

The sign and symbol of Baptism is not a few drops sprinkled on our heads, not a little washing away of some black mark. Baptism is serious, even dangerous. We are hopefully immersed, buried, put to death; we go into the tomb with Jesus. And we are lifted back up alive. Resurrected with our leader.

And though our primary concern when I was young was to have original sin blotted out, I believe now that baptism only begins that journey from sin to grace. In baptism we join a community standing over and against sin, the community of Jesus. We join a community that says "Yes" to life, to love, to hope, to grace. We pull ourselves away from a community of sin, those trapped in evil, the origins of sin. We say "No" to abuse of power, to sexism, militarism, racism . . . no to anything that puts some people over, above, better than others, anything that separates people one from the other by reason of position, or gender, or age, or race, or even religious affiliation.

Again we are all called to the same holiness; we are all in this together.

Some years ago I heard a wonderful baptismal image that, for me, ties all this together. A Lutheran, woman minister preached on Church Unity Sunday in our Catholic church. She told the story of growing up on a farm in Iowa. When she was very young the farm had limited water, and no running water at all. For her, her sister and two brothers, Saturday night was "bath night." A tub of warm water was drawn and one after the other the children bathed in the same water. This minister spoke of the union between her siblings because of this common bath every week. Then she looked at us, her baptized Catholic sisters and brothers. She smiled at us, held out her hands to our community and said , "You are my sisters and brothers; we have washed in the same tub." Her words are true.

We have washed in the same tub. We are sisters and brothers. To go the whole way *is* to become sisters and brothers. To be no longer Greek or Jew, Irish or Polish, or African American, or Asian, or Hispanic; to be no longer priest or pope, sisters or lay person, to be no longer man or woman, child or elderly, to be no longer anything that separates us one from the other. It is such divisions that kill us as a people.

We are all in this together.

61) Thirty Second Sunday

Scripture Readings: Wis. 6:12-16; I Thes.: 4: 13-18; Mt. 15: 1-13

Ray Chandler has a very moving poem about the day he hears from the doctor that he has inoperable cancer. As he and his wife arrive home after this news he says "This is it!" Their time together is short. They no longer need any veils between them. Nothing is in the way of complete honesty; there is simply nothing left to lose. "This is it!"

The immediacy, the intensity of that revelation coupled with my own experience of near, and imminent death help me approach the readings this weekend. In fact, the readings for the next three weeks invite us to look at "the last things."

We do this so that we will live with the sense that "This is It!"

Immediacy is demanded when the bridegroom is about to come!

"Be ready, drop the veils, light the lamps, . . . the trumpet sounds, the search is over, the bridegroom is at hand, the party is about to start. This is it, that great 'gettin' up morning.'"

Some context for both the second reading and the Gospel parable today helps our understanding. After Jesus' Resurrection the early Christians believed the second coming would follow shortly. They firmly believed in what we call an *imminent parousia*. As the first generation of Christians began to die Paul had to wrestle with what that meant. In the letter to the Thessalonians he shares his conviction that neither those already dead, nor those "still awake," would have any advantage when the end comes.

By the time the Gospel is written down most of the whole first generation has died. That is partially why the gospels are written down . . . to preserve the story. So in today's parable Matthew uses a story of Jesus to explain the importance of being ready for a long, long time. . . through the night, perhaps through many nights. Keep vigilant, keep the baptismal flame alive for the long haul. Who expects a wedding to start on time anyway?

At first glance this parable unnerves me. I do not like its negative aspects. I want God to love us and <u>let us in</u> no matter what. I don't like the foolish virgins being sent away because the bridegroom didn't know who they were. I am initially confused by the unchristian and selfish attitude of the "wise" virgins who refuse to share their oil with the more careless sisters.

This story helps me make sense out of their refusal to help.

A few years ago a retired priest in Portland, a bit of a curmudgeon, fell into the habit of making sandwiches and coffee every Saturday for some street folks that hung out on the corner near the apartment where he lived. He made up about thirty sand-wiches and a couple thermoses of coffee, took them out around noon, and shared them with the men on the corner. Eventually the newspapers heard this story and did a feature article on the kindness of this retired priest. As a result of the story some other priests of the diocese sent him money to "further his work with the street people." Stubbornly the elder priest sent the money back to each priest with a note saying: "Make your own damn sandwiches!"

There are some things we just have to do for ourselves. Nobody can light all our lamps for us. If there is a rift in the relationships in my family, no one else can make the peace I need to make. No one else can determine for me how to share my gifts, my time, my treasures with others. If I don't share anything, no one else can light my lamp for me.

No one else can bring the light of Christ into my family, my neigh-borhood, my work place as I can.

Also, in a very true way, no one else can take my place is speaking out against the lack of health care for the poor, or nourishment for children underfed and under loved in our country. No one else can do what I do to protect the unborn, or fragile elderly of our land, or refugees from Syria, or folks who live in our midst without legal documentation. It's my oil, my lamp! Each of us must make our own sandwiches.

I am reminded of that terribly sad Harry Chapin song about a father and a son, "Cat's in the Cradle."

> The Boy asks: "When you comin' home, dad?"
> The Father responds: "I don't know when, . . .

> But we'll get together then,
> You know we'll have a good time then, . . . "

Finally the son now grown trades roles: the Father, now lonely asks,

> "When you comin' home, son,"
> and the son replies: "I don't know when . . .
> But we'll get together then,
> You know we'll have a good time then.

They never met; they didn't have time. There was no immediacy, and no one could do it for them. There was no oil in their lamps , no way to celebrate together.

The readings today invite us to pray for and to have the kind of immediacy, the kind of intensity in our expecting, our preparing for Christ's coming about which Chandler wrote: "This is it!"

This sense of urgency is not just for some coming in death, or at the end of the world, but every moment, all along, for every appearance of Christ in our midst. This presence is right here! Right now!

I remember consulting with a doctor for some time about back surgery that I may or may not need. Finally the doctor said, "OIK., It's shoot, Luke, or drop the gun!" Well we want to live always like, now it's time – "shoot, Luke, or drop the gun!"

The very real trick of living out today's gospel is to keep the flame alive over a long, long time. Keep the faith when God seems absent or distant. Keep alert when no one seems to care, or notice.

Hang in there when the bridegroom is a long, long time coming. Be faithful when the benefit seems slim, the reward remote.

I love the old spiritual sung by a slave on the plantations a couple hundred years ago:

> There's a man they thrust aside,
> Who was tortured till he died,
> And he'll find me hoeing cotton when he comes.
> He was hated and rejected,
> He was scorned and crucified,
> And he'll find me hoeing cotton when he comes.
>
> When he comes, when he comes,
> He'll be crowned by saints and angels when he comes,
> They'll be shoutin' out 'Hosannas'
> To the man that men denied,
> And I'll kneel among my cotton when he comes!

We are people waiting for an enormous celebration, a wedding feast. And we are all invited; we can all come if we are ready . . .

hoeing' our cotton,
our lamps lit,
makin' our own damn sandwiches
no veils,
saying, . . .
living,
"This is it!"

62) The Thirty Third Sunday

Scripture Readings: Prov. 31; I Thes. 5: 1-6; Mt. 24:36, 25: 14-30

Let me begin by pointing out, perhaps to your chagrin, that I will not suggest that this Gospel parable of the talents given to each of us is a biblical apology for unbridled capitalism, encouragement to take risks so that we can get "our piece of the rock."

What the Gospel is really about can best be summarized by a line from my Ethics teacher fifty years ago, "The greatest enemy of the good is the perfect." Afraid something won't turn out perfectly, we often never let it turn out at all! So the thesis never gets finished, the book never gets written, the marriage is never celebrated, the move is never made, the risk is never taken!

Or, the Gospel might be captured by recalling a poem by the novelist, my namesake, James Carroll. He shares the experience of being in a plane that nearly crashes. The pilot keeps everyone calm as gasoline flows out of the wing. The stewardess smiles calmly. The poet is bothered both by her smiling at the prospect of his death, and his lascivious thoughts about her as that death seems imminent. When the plane lands safely he descends and says, too politely, to the still calmly smiling stewardess:

"It's all extra from now on, Miss."

She replies, with no effort to be polite:

"It was all extra to begin with, sir!"

It is all extra to begin with! My own experience of a cardiac arrest, and resuscitation tells me the same thing. It is all extra from now on, but it truly is all extra to begin with! We don't deserve anything we get -- no single day of life, no smile, no laughter, no joy. It's all extra. Risk it.

These thoughts frame today's gospel.

Let me step back a moment for context. Last week, this week, next week, we listen to the twenty-fifth chapter of Matthew's gospel, three parables about the need to be prepared for the coming of Jesus, that final coming and all the smaller comings along the way. Each parable stresses the need to respond, and accept our individual responsibility for our lives. The emphasis is on what we do with God's gifts, rather than on what God does for us first. All may be gift, but we *are* held accountable. The parable presumes the prior *Good News* that God's gifts come first.

This parable of the talents given to each person is based on the conviction that "It's all extra to begin with." None of the recipients of the landowner's largess had done anything to earn the gift. Although the third party got less than the others, a thousand silver pieces was still a sizable portion of money.

Each of them had won the lottery without even buying a ticket! We cannot understand the parable unless we begin with the realization that *each got a huge, free, unearned, undeserved gift.* If it is all extra to begin with; we haven't got anything to lose!

To understand the parable I also need to know where I stand within it.

I was inclined to invite us all to prepare to hear this parable by taking a few moments to write down our five best gifts, the five most desirable traits of our personality. The five things people justly praise us for. We usually have difficulty doing this.

The point of such an exercise would be to suggest that most of us identify with the third party in the story. We all think we don't have much. We all see that others received more and so are able to risk more.

I know lots of people who seem to me very wealthy, but I have never met anyone who thinks himself rich. People who think about money much never seem to have enough. But I've also never meant anyone who was truly proud, who had a too lofty sense of his or her own goodness or importance, (though admittedly, I have never met Donald Trump.)

Most of us think far less of our importance than others do. We fear to try, to go out on a limb, to risk showing our limitations. If we are honest, we all worry: "What will I do if they find out about me?" My favorite bumper sticker says: "They'll never know you're swimming naked, unless the tide goes out."

We all feel under-gifted; we enter life faking it.

Consequently we show, we share, we risk very little of ourselves. Since we can't be perfect we may not even show that we are good.

On the other hand there is a better, more true, more grace-filled part of us that trusts the gifts we've been given, a part that knows, "It's all extra . . ." There is part of each of us that appreciates God's love for us, and the love we receive from others. We want to show our appreciation by trying to use our gifts, to contribute back, to risk even looking foolish. We all live trying not to let the notion of the *perfect* get in the way of the *good*. We want to risk the possibility of making a mistake

The Gospel point about "those who have getting more," and "those who have little losing even the little they have," is not the whim of some cruel divine decree, but an obvious psychological truth. If we risk we can get rewarded and thrive. If we hold on tight, even what we have does us no good!

Think of any moment of risk in your own life and see if this does not ring true.

Any example is perhaps too specific, but just within the past few weeks I have been with people who have taken enormous risks in their lives:

A political action with the possibility of jail as a consequence.

The decision to retire to preserve one's health, despite clear lack of financial resources to do so.

An effort at some great personal risk of time and money to help form a program to help young people in gangs

Whatever the outcome, the risk itself enlivened the person.

I have also heard people say, "I can't start all over now," or "I just can't see how to get out of the mess I'm stuck in." I have been saddened by the prospect of talents buried, lives buried, people dead long before their funerals.

The gospel invites us to prepare for God's bursting into the world, into our lives, into our deaths. It invites us to prepare for this "coming" by being risk-takers, gamblers. We have nothing really to lose because "it's all extra to begin with."

The most interesting detail in the parable is perhaps one not even mentioned. What would have happened if one of those who risked losing the silver pieces did lose? The one who buried the treasure and gave back only what he had received is treated with such anger. We cannot help but wonder how would the landowner react if he got back no coins at all?

The absence of such a "loser" is the point! We *can't* lose! Since it was all freely given in the first place, it's OK to attack life and fail. It's not OK to do nothing at all.

Finally, in a parable about taking risks, about being a gambler, it is critical to acknowledge who really takes the risk. Who really is the gambler? Isn't God the primary most "bodacious" gambler, risking everything on mediocre chances, like you and me ... or at least, me?

The least we can do ... and isn't this the point... is to share in the adventure!

63) The Feast of Christ the King

Scripture Readings: Ez. 34:11-12,15-7; 1 Cor. 15:20-26,28; Mt. 25: 31-46

Once upon a time there was a man,
We call him "Christ," and "King," but he
Was simply Jesus then, a man, like us.
His tribe was small, despised, his town among
That nation smaller still, unknown and unloved.
He worked with wood when young, then left to walk
and wander telling of a Kingdom come,
So "Change your hearts," he cried to all who'd hear.

He'd knew his people's books, the poems and prayers
And Prophets of the clan.
The first and greatest King they had, had shepherd been,
King David was his name -- first shepherd king.
So Jesus spoke of sheep, and shepherds who
Were called to care for them.
These sheep were used as heroes of his tales

For rumor had it that at Jesus' birth
Was only shepherds noticed and rejoiced.

He had, this wan and wandering Jew, of God
An image strange, derived in major part
From poets of the clan, that God like good
And gentle shepherd was, who rounded up
And cared for lost or helpless of his fold,
That "fresh and green" were gardens for their rest,
And "nothing could his people want" for he
Provided pasture, sought the strays,
And lugged the lost and lonely
On his loving back to home.

And when this Jesus spoke of God this way
A wondrous thing began to build in him,
This wandering poetic, vibrant man.
He spoke about himself as he of God
Had spoken, called himself a shepherd too,
A shepherd good, a shepherd somewhat strange,
Who'd leave the ninety-nine and go to find
A single lost and lonely one astray.

Then, strangest thing of all, his word became
His way, the way he said his God to be.
He shepherd was!
He searched for those who'd lost their way, and found
A prostitute who'd lost her sense of life,
Some fisherman unsatisfied by fish,
A tax collector faithless to himself
And to his tribe,
A Pharisee who made the law a God,
A priest who prayed for years but without heart.

He bound up wounds
Of paralytics lying on a mat,
A widow's only son who'd seemed so dead.
A blind man saw, a deaf man heard, and all
Who'd been afraid were helped to hope.

To all in darkest valley he brought light,
To lepers cast outside the town, the tribe,
To woman found in bed with no wife's name,
To one who came at night, afraid of day.

And then, perhaps the most amazing thing,
This shepherd changed,
Became himself the lamb, was slaughtered by --
Was sacrificed and eaten up by those
To whom he'd spoken of His God's great love.
This carpenter became the Lamb of God
(Of God who was, recall, a shepherd too).
He bent his neck to ax, he poured his blood
To bathe his scattered sheep; he lost his life
That all of them might live in him.

Then, just as initial king of all
His people had a shepherd been, this slain
Shepherd-sheep was seen as King, as Christ
The King, the first, most richly-honored of
The flock of shepherd God.

His people honored him around the high
And distant altars, often gold. They trumpeted
His name with pomp and circumstance. They sang
In sacred song their savior King, and bowed
Around his memory at altars now

Nice marbled and no longer blood-bedecked.
Hosannas rang, and rang, and tymbals played
To praise his name, not Jesus now, but Christ;
Not shepherd now, but Christ -the-distant-King.
The people -- proud to honor such a King.
The King -- suspected sad remembered so.
For they remembered King while he recalled
His shepherd shape. They honored Him and He
Their imitation hoped, and laid-down-love.
Had they forgotten now, or set aside
The tale he'd told about the final day
When shepherd came, as caring King, in faith
To face his flock, to judge, in love, his friends?

He deeply wanted them as shepherds too,
To search, to find, to bind each other's wounds,
To be the kind of lamb of sacrifice
That he had been for them. He hoped for them
To find him here, not throned on altars high
Or even simple songs of God-like praise,
But in the hurt and needy ones among
His fumbling flock.

"I'm hungry will you feed me, will you come
To give my thirsting lips a simple drink.
I'm prisoned here in fear and failure fast,
Come visit me, and clothe my nakedness.
I, shepherd-King, will be your broken lamb,
In need of care. You find and honor me
In finding those among you in their pain."

If this tale be true, so true it shapes
The substance of our lives, then may we pray

The honor, pomp, and music sung today
Becomes the honest homage due our King,
Reminding of his shepherd role and ours,
His sacrifice as lamb, his presence still
In any lost or wounded ones we meet,
Reminding us our common call to be
Not subjects of a King, but in his place
As shepherds too, to all who need his love,
His caring still!

Book Two
The B Cycle

1) The First Sunday of Advent

Scripture Readings: Is. 63: 16-7,64: 1, 3-8,; I Cor. 1: 3-9; Mk. 13:31-37

I recall walking from my home to my office one day, just before Advent began. On a bitingly cold day about a hundred people were waiting in line to get some food from the parish Food Bank. The sight was tragic, depressing, overwhelming. At the same time I peeked inside the door and saw twenty-five people, people who did not have to be there in this cold, cold weather, working on their behalf, preparing to give them food for their families -- a truly hopeful sight!

This simple experience captures for me the point of our Advent prayer this year, and perhaps every year. The Gospel today on this first Sunday of Advent, and our Liturgical year, urges us to be awake, to be watchful, to look -- not to miss the master when he comes, at dusk, at midnight, or at dawn. We are challenged to be constantly on the watch.

Advent is a time to grow in our attentiveness, our ability not just to see, but to adjust how and what we see, to train ourselves, to make conscious choices about what we see and how we choose to look at reality.

We can see the hungry people and miss the caring helpers.

Let me back up for a moment and say a word about the whole of Advent. The season used to invite a kind of "Let's pretend" stance towards our faith and our world. "Let's pretend" that Jesus has not come, and let's go back in the history of the Jewish people as they looked forward to the Messiah's coming. "Let's pretend" that we are without a savior and focus on John the Baptist and the preparation for the savior. Then on Christmas when we tell the story of a baby's birth, "let's pretend" that Jesus comes as an infant into our world for the very first time.

But this has all already happened; it is either already true, or it never will be.

Advent is not "Let's Pretend!", but "Let's get real!"

Jesus has come; he is in our midst. And there is never a time in our lives when we cannot challenge ourselves to a deeper internalizing, a deeper realization, a deeper belief, a deeper ability to see the reality of this Incarnation. There is never a time that we do not need to look more carefully, to discern, celebrate and believe more deeply in this presence. There is never a time that we do not need to be more awake, more watchful, more willing to focus our vision on the hope, the possibility, the love already present in our world. We are urged to see in a way that will not allow the long lines of needy people, the pains that surround us, to overwhelm us.

Advent is so very difficult to do. Everything in our culture wars against us. Everything in our culture is bent on shopping, partying, staying busy, and spending not one single moment reflectively preparing for Christmas. Everything in our culture invites us to fill up our emptiness before we have even begun to experience it.

And we can be overwhelmed by the larger, more painful realities of our lives: Refugees, mostly children, from Iraq, Syria, Somalia; thousands devastated by Earthquake or hurricane, a drive by shooting in our neighborhood; our best friends going through Divorce,

It so easy, so tempting today to see only the terrible dysfunction in our nation and our world, the prejudice towards immigrants or refugees, the pervading we- versus them mentality, the glorification of power, the ugliness of sexual exploitation….and miss the thousands working for justice, promoting peace, serving the poor.

Hunger, violence, misery abound while the populace shops to distract itself.

We can feel the misery of the First reading today:

"Why do you let us wander, Lord, from your ways?
Why are our hearts so hard?"

We can be overcome by the absence of God from our midst even as we try to push it from our minds by staying busier than ever. We need Advent. We need to be able to look again, to look more carefully.

Advent invites us not to pretend, not to imagine, but to be real. And part of our reality is to focus on, to watch, to be attentive to, to see the seeds of hope. We can spend this season prayerfully scanning our newspapers, magazine and the particular events of our lives for things that give us hope. We will chose not to look primarily at the messiness of our political world but see those finally speaking out for honesty, integrity, humility in our leadership.

As we look attentively at ourselves this Advent season we might see, most vividly our failures (as I and most of us are wont to do). We can be aware of people we have hurt, mistakes we've made, things than have not gotten done; aware of love gone awry. As the first reading says:

> "We have all withered like leaves,
> Our guilt carries us away like the wind."

We can, indeed, look at the ugliness in ourselves, in the world around us, and be fixated on that sight, overwhelmed. We can see only the long lines of the hungry waiting in the cold.

Advent invites each week to light one more small candle, to gradually brighten up our world, helping us to look more carefully at the same sights, and see the successes.

We want to see the essential Advent-Christmas truth that even in our messiness "God loves us to much to leave us alone."

That love of God for us is our Advent hope.

Our prayer this season, this year invites us metaphorically to walk into a cosmic optometrists office, put on a new pair of glasses, and try to see everything in us and around us with the eyes of hope,

- to see the seeds beneath the sin,
- to see the hope beneath the despair,
- to see the promise beneath the pain.

So we enter into this season prayerfully and together. We help each other to look, and then look again, to watch in hope.

We are not pretending. Finally, when Christmas comes, Christ will not be born anew unless he is born new in us.

The world, at Christmas, will not be different, but we may be!

2) The Second Sunday of Advent

Scripture Readings: Is. 40: 1-5, 9-11; 2 Peter 3:8-15; Mk 1:1-8

Today's readings both from Isaiah and the Gospel offer us two prayerful images for our Advent preparation.

First, in the days of Isaiah as a ruler, a Lord, traveled from one place to another servants went before him to "Prepare the Way." Where roads did not exist their task was to create one, to level out the hills, to lift up the deep valleys, to "make straight the path." When John the Baptizer surfaces proclaiming that the reign of God is at hand he picks up this image and invites his listeners to prepare the way of the Lord by getting rid of the mountains that seemed so difficult to climb, and to level out the deep crevices into which they had already fallen or were in danger of falling. The Gospel of Mark begins with this image as John invites people -- as we are invited -- to turn around, confess our sins, be baptized into that faithful messianic community waiting, making straight the path for the coming of the Lord.

The second image is that of Baptism -- plunging into the waters as a sign of repentance and forgiveness of sins. John takes the ritual that his people used for gentile converts to Judaism. How does someone not a Jew become a Jew? Well the Jewish people became a nation by passing through the waters of the Red Sea, as they went from slavery in Egypt to freedom in the Promised Land. Now, even for his fellow Jewish people, John says: "My fellow Israelites, as a sign of repentance and re-dedication to our covenant life with God, come forward and signify your fresh start by sharing in the rite we use for Gentile converts."

The Gospel hearers would also identify John's ritual with the messianic promise of Ezekiel:

"I will sprinkle clean water upon you to cleanse you from your impurities . . . I will give you a new heart and new spirit, taking away your stony hearts. . . ."

John invites the people to confess their sins and be baptized into a community waiting together for that incredible Messianic coming.

So here we are the Second Sunday of Advent, preparing for the coming of Jesus. We are not preparing for the first coming, not the birth of a baby, the initial entrance of God into our history. That's already happened. We are not even preparing exactly for the second coming in some distant time, unknown. We are preparing to let Jesus be born in us and through us, right now, this year, this Christmas, preparing to live more fully the mystery to which we have already given our lives. We hope this will help to usher in that second coming.

We do that today by doing what John invited his followers to do . . . going through a ritual of re-commitment, conversion, re-dedication to the covenant we have with God. Before we take some time for ritual confession of our sins I suggest a brief time of reflection in the light of the images I've mentioned. You may want to close your eyes and be honestly within yourself as I offer these reflections:

1. What are the mountains in my life that need to be brought low?

What relationships seem overwhelming where love seems totally blocked? Where do I just get paralyzed by fear or inactivity at the mountains of problems?

And on the larger level, what are the world problems that just seem too overwhelming to face or deal with effectively . . . unbalanced inane leadership in our nation, endless actions against the common good for immigrants, and precarious actions regarding peace in the Middle East or Korean peninsula, unimaginable homelessness in our own city, the incredible numbers of refugees wandering different parts of the earth . . . so big we don't know where to begin so we do nothing.

2. What are the valleys that need to be raised up?

Where do I experience the depths, depression, discouragement, cynicism? Is there anyone I find myself constantly criticizing to myself or others? Does the Church, large, or even in this parish sometimes become a source of depression more than life either because it changes too much, or not enough. Is there a child, or a spouse, or a parent in whom I have lost hope and need to renew it, raise it up, this Advent season.

And finally,

3. Where am I enslaved, and need to come into a promised land of freedom this Christmas?

Can I look honestly at my use of alcohol, or tobacco and admit my dependency? Do I use food to insulate myself from life? Have I lost my freedom to love as I would like. Is my marriage stuck in routine, boring, even painful because our freedom is gone? Am I enslaved to sexual activity that is not an expression of love and commitment?

Am I enslaved to the American dependence on things for my happiness, to getting more, bigger, better things thinking this will bring me happiness?

Be still for a few moments with these images:

Where are the mountains overwhelming?

Where are the valleys, the depths apparently impassable? Where am I unfree?

If Christmas is to come for me, in me, from me this year I need to be healed.

We take the time to pray for that healing now . . . for ourselves and for each other.

3) The Third Sunday of Advent

Scripture Readings: Is. 61: 1-2,10-11; 1 Thes. 5: 16-24; Jn. 1: 6-8, 19-28

The World is divided into two kinds of people, those that think there are two kinds of people, and those that don't!

Actually there are two kinds of Christians, or at least two approaches of Christians to our ultimate destiny, and our approach to Advent. Some believe the Second Coming of Jesus will come from the outside, in an act of God on us, when some will be caught up into the rapture, and others will be cast into hell.

Other Christians believe that Jesus is already here, and the Second Coming will be realized from the inside out. The Spirit will work in us until we achieve God's design; the fullness of God's plan will be accomplished in us, by us under the influence of that Spirit.

I firmly believe that Jesus is already here and our task is to let him live, love, act, re-create the world through us and in us. When we finally have it all together, through the Spirit working in us, the Second Coming will have happened.

So, our Advent prayer focuses on preparing ourselves to let Him who is already here come fully alive in us.

An image might help! One Advent, we invited a potter to work on a wheel at the entrance to our Church as we began each Advent Eucharist. We sang about our potter God "molding and fashioning" us into the "image of Jesus the son." The first Sunday a young woman preached about how God had fashioned her life in that God. I heard people, life-long-believers, remark that year that for the first time they "got it!" They understood Advent. For the first time Advent made sense . . . a sense of the heart, more than the mind, a sense of God doing something in us as we prepare for Christmas.

Meister Eckhardt asked five centuries ago what difference does it make if Jesus was born 2000 years ago if he is not born again, here and now, in our time and place, in us?

The readings today help us define what it is that God might be doing in us, fashioning in us in this or any Advent. Isaiah writes:

> "The Spirit of the Lord is upon me, sending me to
> bring good news to the poor, to proclaim liberty
> to captives, sight to the blind, to bind up the
> brokenhearted."

More than any other passage this section of Isaiah seems to have framed the messianic mission of Jesus. Luke uses this passage as the first words spoken in Jesus public ministry. These words frame our mission too, define how it is that God wants to mold and fashion us. Put most simply: During Advent God desires to shape us into the image of Jesus reaching out to the most needy in our world. Christmas comes when we come to the poor.

I heard recently about a priest new to a parish in an inner city in on the East coast. Over the first few months almost every day as he came out of his residence to go the few blocks to Church he came across a homeless person sleeping in his doorway, or under tree. Early in December on a cold winter morning he got into his car to discover someone sleeping in his car. He scrapped his planned homily that morning and talked with the parish about using the basement of the Church for a shelter for homeless people ... How God might be shaping us for the mission of Jesus is perhaps more subtle, but no less real ... where are our eyes being opened to the cry of the poor as we move towards Christmas this year?

The Gospel also helps to define our Advent challenge. It reminds us that what is being fashioned does not depend solely on us In the Gospel of John, Jesus uses the Expression "I am" many times to exclaim who he is. This "I am" is the name God gave to Moses when Moses asked who he should say sent him to the Israelites. Jesus says: I am the bread of Life, the Good Shepherd, the Way, the truth and the life. I am the Resurrection and the Life.

In today's Gospel passage, John the Baptizer is equally clear: "I am not the Messiah." I am one preparing the path to him. Part of our Advent task is to acknowledge that we are being molded into the image of Jesus. We are not Jesus. We are not the Messiah. We are more messy, more broken, more stumbling. Everything does not depend on us, is not on our shoulders. We are invited, shaped, formed to be the Image, reflection, sign, symbol, the sacrament of God's presence:

- by our commitment to justice,
- by our hands reached out to prisoners,
- by our good news to the poor.

We point to God, witness to God's presence. But we are not nor need we be, ourselves, God. However much God will come again into this world through us, God will not come because of us, because of what we do. But "God's power working in us can do infinitely more than we can ask or imagine."

I do not know what all of this means for you in your Advent prayer. I know that God is trying to shape something new in me. I find myself trying to "feel" the prisoners, the captives, the blind, the brokenhearted in our midst -- to notice the homeless person sleeping "in my car." Where in our community, and in the larger city does the messiah need to come through me, through us? Is it among the large number of elderly, shut in, aging lonely people in our neighborhood? Is it in the midst of the many people with various handicapping conditions that make up our community? Is it with the so tragically large number of homeless that seem to surround us in our city? Am I being invited to help some link between our parish community and the people of the downtown streets not so very far away?

I am still wrestling with the questions. What I am sure is that Jesus is struggling to be born again this Advent and wants to come where he is most absent, most needed and if there is to be a Christmas for me I need to discover some aspect of that molding, shaping, fashioning going on in me.

What it means for you, I do not know, but before we go on with Eucharist, let us be still with the question: (speak slowly, prayerfully, perhaps with a music background)

God is shaping Jesus in us. What does that mean?

What is God doing in me this season?

During this Advent how am I . . .

--being dressed in the wedding garment of justice,

--blossoming to fullness,

--proclaiming good news to the poor,

--liberty to captives,

--sight to the blind,

How am I being called to point to God, to Jesus in my ways and words?

4) The Fourth Sunday of Advent

Scripture Readings: 2 Sam. 7:1-5, 8b-12, 14a, 16; Ro. 16:25-27; Lk. 1:26-38

Prenote: Before Reading of the gospel this weekend take some time to invite the Assembly to enter into the scene they are about to hear. Be quiet, attentive to breathing, perhaps close our eyes, as we listen to this Annunciation scene as if for the first time. See the scene, . . . see Mary, . . . visualize the angel.

Listen to the word. Try to "feel" the scene, not just think about it.

Read the Gospel deliberately.

After the Gospel begin the homily in the same mood.

I invite you to stay in the same reflective mood in which you listened to the Gospel. Keep your eyes closed if that helps; stay with the same scene, but now, on this fourth Sunday of Advent I invite you to put yourself in the scene.

What we say about Mary, we say about all of us.

Mary leads us through Advent; we let her do that in a very intimate way today as we share her story.

I invite each of you to imagine yourself somewhere in your own home where you can be quiet, alone.

Get a sense of being in touch with yourself. In touch with God.

What happened to Mary a long time ago happens to each of us today.

You hear a voice, a message from God saying:

> "Rejoice, highly favored son or daughter. God is with
> you. You are very blessed in the midst of this people"

I suspect you are troubled by these words. God would not speak them to you. You are not important enough to be told such a thing . . . it isn't even true. What could such a greeting mean?

The message continues:

> "Don't be afraid. You are very special to God. In fact
> God wants to come to life in you, through you. This
> Christmas, Jesus wants to put on flesh through you, live
> through you, love through you."

You respond by wondering how this can be . . . Mary was a Virgin, Isaiah couldn't speak in public, Moses was wanted for murder in Egypt, Jeremiah was too young. What is the reason why this can't be true for me. I am too young, too old, too much of a sinner, too wild, too introverted, too loud, too quiet . . . what are my excuses not to help Jesus be born, not to be quite central to this process?

The message goes on:

> "You don't have to do this all alone. The Holy Spirit, the Spirit of God will come to you; God's power will over-shadow you, if you let it. You won't be alone.
> Just promise to cooperate."

And you try to say:

> "OIK. I will be God's servant. Let whatever is to be done to me, through me, happen."

Stay with this prayer, this imagining, which is not imagination at all, but terribly, terribly true. Talk to God, listen to God for a moment or two. (Pause for time for individuals to pray as they wish.)

This prayer that we have done this morning invited us to use our imaginations, but what we did is not fantasy at all. This is the point of Advent. We do not celebrate Christmas just to remember the past event, but to let it happen, to help it happen again, more deeply in our day, in us.

If we are not afraid in Advent, if we are not overwhelmed and challenged when invited to share in the process of Christ's birth then the season has passed us by untouched and not much will happen at Christmas to make it different from any other time.

So we go on and we pray, "Come, Lord Jesus," but we do so with more awe, more quiet as we realize this coming is in part dependent on us.

5) Christmas Family Mass

Scripture Readings: Is. 9:2-4,6; Lk. 2: 1-16

(This homily is intended for a Christmas Eve liturgy with many children present.)

For years I have had trouble thinking of something new or fresh or original at Christmas. I would love to come up with something that really helps people understand and appreciate the gift that this feast is. In all honesty it was the same this year. What can I say? What should I say?

As I was stewing and worrying, fretting and fidgeting finally I went for a walk along the waterfront. I wanted to think and pray. Well, I walked and thought and thought and walked and walked and thought, . . . and nothing happened. Nothing at all. Finally I sat down on a bench. now you may not believe what happened then, but I know with all my heart that it is true, so it must have happened.

Day was passing into night when it happened. A voice called out "Hello" and there on the bench beside me was a tiny little man. He hoped onto my knee, looked me in the eye and said:

> "Pat I have a Christmas message for you!"
> "How do you know I'm looking for a Christmas message, and how do you know my name and who are you?"

I asked. Pretty normal questions for such a strange situation.

> "My name is Gabe," he said. "And the reason I know your name and what you desire is that I am an angel. In fact I am the best big time angel of Christmas. I am the one who gave the message to Mary. I am the one who told the Shepherds about this baby. I am the one who led the singing you just read about in that story of yours."
> "You are an angel?" I asked.
> "So you don't believe me?": said Gabe.
> "Well," I said, "you are awfully short and I expect an angel to be tall and young and beautiful. And you're not dressed in white. Everyone knows angels should be dressed in white and you've just got shorts and tee shirt on."
> "Who told you angels were dressed in White?" He asked.

He waited in silence for an answer.

I waited too, then blurted out with incredible stupidity.

> "And you don't have any wings either, and everyone knows angels have wings. It's in all the pictures!

Gabe replied:

> "So who said Angels needs wings? Really, we're just messengers, and I have a Christmas message. It's a secret though. Do you want it or don't you?"
> "Oh I do,"

I said, but suddenly realized I'm not very good and keeping secrets and besides I was looking for a message I can share.

> "But why does it have to be a secret? I need something

good to tell the people, especially the children on Christmas Eve! What good is a secret message. I can't keep a secret!"

> "That's OK," said Gabe. "This is a different kind of secret (He got very excited and talked very fast) In fact I can only tell you if you promise to tell someone else and then they have to promise to tell the secret to someone else, and on and on and on, until everyone knows. OIK.? Is it a deal? Do you promise? Do you want to know the secret?"

He was so excited he fell off my knee to the ground and I had to pick him up and put him back in my lap.

> "Yes I do, and I promise to tell someone else, too"

Then Gabe climbed up in my arm, got on my shoulder, and whispered into my ear and told me the secret. And a grand secret it is too, well worth the price of agreeing to pass in on to others. As he told me I had to turn my head so my ear could get close enough to hear him and by the time I turned back to say "Thank you," he was gone. He simply wasn't there, leaving as quickly and as mysteriously as he had arrived.

I sat there on the bench, holding a new secret in my heart, excited and thrilled by the privilege . . . and so it is that I want to tell you this Christmas secret. I want to keep my promise and to share the secret of Christmas that he gave me.

Now there is only one condition . . . and you can easily figure it out, if I am to tell you this secret. What is it? That's right. You have to pass it on so that the message of Christmas does not die. So any of you that want to know the secret come close and I'll tell you and then you must go out and tell all the big people out in the Church. Come close and I'll tell you.

(Kids come up close; whisper in a loud voice.)

This is the secret you must pass on; the Christmas secret:

"GOD LOVED US TOO MUCH TO LEAVE US ALONE;
THAT'S WHY JESUS CAME TO BE WITH US.
GOD LOVED US TOO MUCH TO LEAVE US ALONE!

(Tell this to several groups of children at a time, then send them out to spread the message to the grownups.)

6) Christmas Day

Scripture Readings: Is. 52:7-10; Heb. 1:1-6; Jn. 1:1-18

Impressions of Christmas

Let me share with you some images of this day, this season. You may identify with them, live in one or more of them, with me.

During Advent I was reminded of the image of a multi-sports marathon in which athletes swam two miles, bicycled for 26 then ran a final 26. As the few who finish come to the end they are almost (or literally) on all fours, just barely making it, crawling across the finish line. Some of us get to Christmas like that, just barely making it to the end... limping in, victorious but too tired to enjoy it. If you come that way today, let yourself go limp, listen to the songs and for an hour or so, let the God who joins his life with ours love you back to life.

A second image: My grand-nephews and nieces love to play "Where's Waldo," looking at a picture with hundreds, even thousands, of people, animals, do-dads of various kinds, and hidden in the midst, somewhere, is Waldo. It takes lots of practice, a trained and eye, and even a little luck to spot Waldo in the picture.

Sometimes Christmas strikes me as a "Where's Jesus" kind of game. In the midst of parties, songs, cards, letters presents given and received, travels here and there, deadlines met and meals served, somewhere there is, perhaps, Jesus. I wonder how difficult it is to find Jesus in the midst of my Christmas picture? Waldo is never central, obvious, never the hub around which the entire picture flows, but Jesus can be and for many of us is. I play a Christmas game with my self: Where's Jesus?

A third image: It is a delight to go to the airport at holiday times to see people getting off airplanes with excitement, meeting with family and loved ones, embracing, rejoicing. How good to be reunited, to be together. Occasionally one sees a traveler get off the plane with great buoyancy, excitedly exiting, looking for loved ones and then not seeing anyone, looking around calmly at first, then a bit frantically, then a face turns from delight to sadness almost without missing a beat.

Jesus arrives into our hearts, our lives; he has come from a long ways to be with us. Some of us are truly present to meet him, to embrace him, to take him home for a warm family day and a hearty dinner. Some of us aren't there, or even though here aren't here. How do we meet the plane? What is Jesus experience getting off the plane hoping to meet us, his deeply and forever loved ones?

A fourth image. I have had years in my life where I only saw my family, those I loved the most, at Christmas. This year will be like that for me. Some people are only able to get together at

Christmas. A brother and a sister unite, spend a few days catching up, remembering, planning future times together, then separate for many months. Some write, some don't; some phone, some don't... nowadays some E-mail, some don't.

I have a sense at Christmas that the deepest love relationship of our lives, our relationship with God is just like all our other relationships. Sometimes we only meet at Christmas. Or other holidays: a word of "Thanks: at thanksgiving; a quick visit over Easter. And sometimes Christmas renews the friendship, opens the relationship up again so that the meetings continue, the relationship restores and deepens at many opportunities throughout the year. I pray our meeting here even if we haven't met for a long time, is the first of many, many get-togethers this year.

A final image. I recently read a touching story about twin girls born prematurely and whisked to separate incubators. The larger girl slept peacefully, but the smaller one had trouble breathing and a very unstable heart rate. They feared for the life of the smaller twin until a nurse tried a technique called 'double bedding' and put the sisters in the same bed for the first time since they shared the womb. The stronger sister immediately cuddled up to her more fragile sister, even throwing an arm over her shoulder, and, with her sister near, the more fragile twin began to thrive. A loving touch, the closeness of an intimate love, brought life. Sooner than expected the girls went home where they share a single bed.

And we hear again today, in the face of images like these and so many, many more: "The Word became Flesh and dwelt amongst us," more literally, he "pitched his tent next to ours." God breaks into our lives, our arms our hearts.

He visits us from afar,
    enters into our picture,
    invites us, again into a close and intimate relationship,
    wraps his strong arm about us.

We celebrate the fact today.

We live, or do not live it out tomorrow.

For now, "Come let us adore him."

7) January 1 The Feast of Mary, the Mother of God

Scripture Readings: Num. 6: 22-27; Gal. 4:4-7; Luke 2:15-21

This feast is a celebration looking for an identity . . . an identity it has finally found. Over the years January first has had offered a variety of reasons for us to be at Eucharist today:

- For centuries this was called the Feast of the Circumcision, an event difficult for us non-Semitic people to celebrate.
- Also because I have been around Sisters of the Holy Names all my life I know this is a feast day for them, for it is the day Jesus is given his Holy Name.
- Most of us are at Church today because it is New Year's Day, a day for starting over, for making resolutions, (perhaps for recovering from last night's revels), and a day quite fitting to begin in Church, both thanking God for the past year and beginning anew.

- Some twenty-plus years ago Paul VI also declared this feast a day to pray for World Peace.

And perhaps lost in the midst of all these other themes, since 1969 the First Day of the year, the octave of Christmas, is on the Church Calendar as the Feast of Mary the Mother of God. We are invited to celebrate Christmas all over again, invited to view the wondrous ministry of Incarnation through Mary's eyes.

The preacher on this day can easily get stymied by this variety of directions. Personally, I am glad the Church most underlines the Marian theme. Way back in the early 5th century (431 to be exact) at the council of Ephesus the Church gave Mary the title "Theotokos" (Christ-bearer) because in giving birth to Jesus, Mary did indeed birth our very God into the world. Since the 7th century Catholic Christians have celebrated Mary's role in giving birth to God in our world.

Throughout Advent I found myself reflecting the deep belief that Mary helps us know what this Christmas feast is all about. Each of us in our own way celebrate Christmas most authentically by doing what Mary does, that is, by saying our own "yes", our "be it done." and giving birth to Jesus in our own time and place.

So, put simply, it is good to celebrate Christmas again with Mary. It is good to begin this new year viewing the Incarnation through Mary's eyes, at Mary's side. It is good to join her in "treasuring all these words, and pondering all these things in our hearts."

How interesting that about the only thing Luke has to say about Mary is that she kept pondering, kept turning these things over, kept trying to prayerfully figure out what everything she is experiencing means.

I read a wonderful article once that called Mary as "The Original Perplexed Catholic." Mary is the model of all of us, disciples of Jesus, who do not have all the answers, all of us who have to take what we know and try to see how to bring it into the future. Everyone confused by the entrance of God into history in general, or our own individual history can imitate Mary by praying over the meaning of it all. Mary wonders, perhaps:

- what does it mean that I am pregnant and unmarried, needing to trust that Joseph will understand? If this is such a great event why is it so painful?
- what does it mean that we go to Joseph's home town, the village of all his relatives, and no one welcomes us into their home? If this child is so special why are we outcasts?
- what does it mean that only shepherds, poor outcasts, come to watch this child? Where are the religious leaders, the people who have so long claimed to await this birth? If this is really the messiah, how come no one notices?

When God breaks into history, Mary's or ours, it is not light and easy and always pleasant. It is confusing, perplexing, troubling. This entrance demands reflection, prayer, understanding.

So as we come, you and I, to this New Year Mary's feast invites us to be aware of the questions we bring with us. I am not sure New Year's is a good day for resolutions. I believe it is a day for pondering. For looking at what is, and wondering what it means. A day for praying, inviting God to help us to keep giving birth to Jesus in a new time and place.

I know that since coming so close to death in 1995, I keep thinking that life should be clear to me. I should know why I am alive and what it is I should be doing, and how I should be doing it. If all is gift, why isn't the gift unwrapped more than it is? I am still not sure why I am in this place, or what I am supposed to offer here. I need to ponder this mystery in my heart.

What does this mean for you today? What questions do you bring to this New Year, this Eucharist?

Are there trials, troubles, tensions, difficulties in your family or community? Ponder them in your heart!

Is it difficult to love someone who is close to you? Ponder that challenge in your heart?

Are you disturbed or upset because some aspect or your life which you thought your faith would help you bear is more confusing than ever? Ponder it in your heart!

Let me end by praying over us the blessing given in the first reading today . . . a blessing given to Mary from the beginning, a blessing given to each of us as we begin a new Year, pondering everything in our hearts:
May the Lord bless you and keep you;
The Lord let his face to shine upon you,
and be gracious to you,
The Lord look upon you kindly and give you peace.

8) The Feast of the Epiphany

Scripture Readings: Is. 60:1-6; Eph.3: 2-3, 5-6; Mt. 2:1-12

One of the finest poems in the English language is a meditation on the meaning of this feast, and its relevance for all of us as we come to the end of the Christmas season. Partly because I love to read this poem but mostly because I know no better way to celebrate this feast, let me share the poem with you, The Journey of the Magi, by T.S. Eliot, then briefly meditate on his meditation.

(See Epiphany homily, Year A, p. 41, for whole poem)

The heart of the feast of Epiphany for Matthew is the revelation of this new born Christ to "The Nations," the non Jewish world. As Jewish leaders (Herod) reject the birth, the larger gentile world begins to receive this child.

Most of us are not Jewish. We come as did these men from the East to discover something, someone wonderful. Every year at Christmas we are the outsiders being gifted with the Christ.

What Eliot's poem says, really quite simply, is that if we really see the gift, it (in perhaps the greatest understatement in English literature) will be, "(you may say) satisfactory." We will not ever need anything else again. But thinking we do we may try to return to our previous lives, our places. But if we have seen the Christ we will be no longer at home there.

Christmas is about birth . . . but just as Eliot subtly puts in the poem intimations of Christ's death (three trees on the sky line, hands dicing for silver), so Christmas contains within it Christ's passion – the self-offering of God, completely to us. If we "get it," if we ever fully see the implications of God becoming one with us, of Jesus sharing life with us and telling us how to live, if we ever glimpse how deeply, irrevocably loved we are, after Christmas nothing will ever be the same. Did that happen this year? Is it happening now?

9) The Baptism of Jesus

Scripture Readings: Is. 42:1-4,6-7; Acts. 10:34-38; Mk. 1: 7-11

Although for most of us, the Christmas ornaments have long been put away and the music dimmed today is actually the final weekend of the Christmas season, or, more properly, the Epiphany, the manifestation of the Word made Flesh in our midst. This child born into our human condition is revealed to us, gradually over the weeks and months ahead.

I am aware that our Gospel today is the very first scene in the first of our Gospel stories. Mark's Gospel begins with the baptism of Jesus by John. This baptism scene is the prelude toe Mark's Gospel, setting up every theme of the Gospel itself. The presence of God in our midst. The challenge of discipleship. The centrality of the cross. Mark's gospel invites us to celebrate not the birth of a child, but the Incarnation of God, the infleshment of God in our midst.

To get a sense of the importance of this scene as the beginning of the gospel: Imagine that all our crib scenes, all our mangers, our stars, our beds of straw, our songs of "silent night" were all changed. What if we had no angels, no shepherds, no Anna, no Simeon, no "finding in the Temple;" no dream of Joseph, no magi, no slaughter of the innocents, no flight into Egypt.

What if the Gospel began not with a baby, but where Mark begins it, with a fully grown adult young man, clad in a rustic robe, standing knee deep in the River, wringing wet with a glowing face. The young man is overwhelmed by an intense, personal experience of knowing he is loved by God, is special to God, is called by God both into relationship and into service. All of this happens in a flash, in an instant.

What if our dominant image/story of the word made flesh, of God with us was the story of this young man from a small and insignificant town on the periphery of the world's power, who comes into adulthood after years of prayer, study, community with his people. He is impelled by something (we call it God's mysterious grace) to go out to a river where another young man, apparently his cousin, is calling people to conversion, to fidelity to the ancient covenant they had with God. The Baptist is preparing the people for the coming of God and then from the edges, the least likely of places, way out in Galilee, comes this man, Jesus

The young man takes a risk, steps into to join with this people, to share in their ritual washing. Where others were baptized, cleansed in the waters, Mark says Jesus went into, under . . . in fact the word means "drowned" by the waters. He is buried and comes out alive, changed, different; he comes out Son of God, beloved. He is overpowered by a most profound experience of God. The experience is so profound that he will withdraw for 40 days and nights, a kind of personal Exodus in the desert, to assimilate what has happened to him here at the River. And he will spend the rest of his short life responding to the implications of this profound experience of God. And he will be faithful to this experience no matter what! Even to death!

This is the Christmas story in Mark. This is the first moment of Incarnation as Mark tells it.

In some ways Christmas, Incarnation is better located here at the river than in the crib. The Church is wise in ending the Christmas season here.

This scene invites more than wonder, or awe or admiration. This scene calls for imitation. We are invited to hear, as Jesus does, God's voice in our lives, to trust that voice, to leap into the fleshy fray of relationship with God and service to God's people.

When I was young I remember hearing this baptismal scene normally treated like "Let's pretend." Jesus apparently went out to the river and to John pretending that he, a sinless one, needed to be baptized, though obviously he didn't. Nothing in this story suggests that. What is suggested is that someone greater than John is coming, and now does come. He comes to be part of a people faithful to God and he is singled out by God and told how loved he is ... something he very much needed to know if he is to carry on the mission given to him.

The Christmas season ends today:
It is about God coming from the edges, from the least likely places.
It is about Jesus being fully human.
It is about Jesus symbolically being buried and coming back to life as he will at the conclusion of the story.

It is about Jesus, like us, seeking for direction and meaning in his life. And in this search he is touched and called by God, and is sent to save the world.

And this season is about us, who share the name of Jesus being fully human, becoming disciples,
searching for meaning and direction in our lives,
being touched and called by God,
and being sent to save the world.

We end the Christmas season realizing that we are not just praying before the crib of a child, but entering into discipleship, becoming followers of Jesus. If we really do this everything in our lives will change. We too will be drowned and come back out alive as sons, daughters of God ... beloved children on a mission.

So I wish you a final time what is a wondrous, but frightening greeting: Merry Christmas!

10) The Second Sunday of the Year

Scripture Readings: I Sam. 3: 3b-10, 19; I Cor. 6:13-5,17-20; Jn. I: 35-42

Introduction: I simply want to remind us that we celebrate this week the birthday of Dr. Martin Luther King, Jr. This is the only national holiday in honor of a professed follower of Jesus. I just want to plant his image, his marvelous voice, his vision in your hearts before I begin today. Martin encompasses almost perfectly everything we can say about the Gospel today.

What do you want?
What are you looking for?

How I answer such questions in my life determines what I will find, determines who I am.

Stay with the questions for a moment:
What do you want out of life?

What do you look for when you come here to Church?
What do you want for your family, your community, your loved ones?
What are you looking for?

I can imagine a variety of answers for myself, for you:
I want peace of mind, peace in the world, harmony with those with whom I work or worship.
I want security. I would like not to worry about everything.
I want to know if I'm going to live with God forever in heaven.
I want to know how to love, how to give love, how to receive love.
Perhaps deepest down in me, I want to know I am loved, that I'm cared about, that I am special to someone, somewhere.

Let us take a moment now to go back and walk through this gospel, to see what it says that might help me answer these questions. What do I want?

This Gospel passage is the very first scene in John's Gospel, immediately after the prologue. At Christmas we heard that prologue: "In the beginning was the Word, the Word was with God, . . . The Word became flesh and dwelt among us. The light shines in the darkness and the darkness cannot blot it out. We have all received from this fullness."

This passage, indeed every passage in John's gospel fleshes out this prologue, develops these themes. Every story puts flesh on the same themes. Unlike the Gospel of Mark that we listen to most of this year, John's Gospel has the divinity of Christ shinning through every passage and everything we know or can say about Jesus is present from the first scene on.

John's Gospel has no Baptism scene, but it does begin, as we did last week in Mark, here at the river as John passes on the mantle to Jesus. Like Eli in today's Hebrew scripture story, John, the prophet, helps his followers see and hear the word.

> "There he is! Go for it! It's not me you want to come to, come you! Listen for the word of God, enfleshed among you!"

The whole Gospel is in this passage. They see him, follow him, recognize him as Messiah. They have seen already through the darkness to the light. When Peter recognizes Jesus and calls him Messiah, Jesus calls him Rock. Right here at the beginning. It takes half the story in Mark and even then Peter doesn't really know what he is saying.

It's more that seeing. They ask Jesus "Where do you stay?" The word is much more than stay. It's the same word we hear in John 15 in "I am the vine, you are the branches, stay in me, abide in me, remain in me." The question is more "Where do you live, really, . . . deep . . . inside? What is your secret? What is deepest in you? How do we catch it?"

Jesus says to them: "Come and See!"

And they go to follow Jesus, to see where he finds life, where he abides, with God!

As in the Samuel story, disciples are invited to learn, starting now, to hear God's voice, to recognize the ways and words of God, to experience God in an ever changing, ever shifting reality of life.

What do you want?

What are you looking for?

Ignatius of Loyola invites us all during the second part oft the Spiritual Exercises to "ask for what we want," as we consider the mysteries of the life of Jesus? His prayer was purloined by the musical Godspell and turned into a song:

> Oh dear Lord, three things I pray,
> To know thee more clearly,
> Love thee more dearly,
> Follow thee more nearly,
> Day by Day!

Our presence here Sunday after Sunday suggests we long for the same thing way down deep. What we want is to know, to love, to follow Jesus. We believe he is the way to life?

Here at the beginning of the Gospel story, this first Sunday of Ordinary Time, we want to walk through the entire Gospel story again and hear the words, see the deeds, feel the love of Jesus. We want to wonder at the miracles, stand in awe at the wisdom, be dumb struck before the suffering, and share in the Resurrection of Jesus. We want to see where, how he lives and abide with him.

And he says to us, "Come and See."

We do not just see Jesus looking at the old story, but we discover Him where he said he would be . . . in His Body, in His Church, in two or three gathered in his name. Let me end this reflection about coming and looking for Jesus, about abiding with Jesus with a story that may seem far afield, but actually gets the point perfectly.

One upon a time an Abbott from a crumbling monastery went to see a wise man who lived in the forest. He came because his once flourishing religious community was now filled with cynicism, pettiness, languishing in a loss of faith and hope and love. He asked the wise man how to get the numbers of monks to soar again, how to revive spirits, restore hope and laughter to those ancient halls.

The wise man said, simply: "The Messiah abides with you!'

The Abbott didn't understand but he went back and told the monks what the wise man said: "The Messiah lives with us."

From that day on every monk kept looking to see the messiah – they looked in the face of the old, the novices, the scholars in the library, the cook in the kitchen. Every monk kept looking to see the face of the Messiah in every other monk. And the monastery flourished again.

What do we want. To Find Jesus, to know him, to love him, to follow him.

The Messiah is in our parish. Come and See!

11) Third Sunday of Ordinary Time

Scripture Readings: Jonah 3:1-11; 1 Cor. 7: 29-31; Mk. 1:14-20

For a moment I want to do an unusual experiment. I want you to imagine that I am Jesus standing here before you.

I know you have just come from breakfast, or from watching a ball game on TV, or reading the Sunday paper. You've just been fighting with the kids to get here on time. You have a million other distractions. Perhaps you are hardly settled here, Perhaps you have a major hurt you wrestle with this morning, a deep concern, an enormous pain in your family. You hope for some words, some help, some answer today at Mass. Or perhaps you come with great joy, you celebrate some recent good news ... a pregnancy, a new job, a loan for that home you've wanted, some excitement as you walk in today.

Wherever you are as you come this morning, Jesus is here before you today, as truly as I am and he says:

"This is the Time of fulfillment; The Reign of God is at hand. Reform your lives. Believe in the Good News!"

I mean Jesus believes it! He almost yells at you:

"Now is the time! The Reign of God is right here, right now! Turn your life around; believe it! God loves you, is present to you, and everything changes now!"

What is your reaction to that "in your face" message? (Perhaps invite people to take a minute and share their reaction with someone near them at church.)

Ho Hum?
I hope so?
Maybe it can be?
You've got to show me?
What is the act this preacher is putting on?

Whatever your reaction, what we have been pretending is true. Jesus is here, is saying this to us, is saying it all the time. What difference does it make?

I want to suggest for a few moments that the truth of this message of Jesus effects the way we worship and the way we live.

This immediacy touches the way we Worship

Let me tell you about two experiences within a single week, the very week, one year, when we listened to these same readings.

I went to a noon Mass on Sunday in Calgary, Alberta. The Cantor was O.K. She did the songs. The people joined in a little bit. The music was obvious, but all right. The readers were O.K. They didn't miss any words. the readings more or less made sense. But there was no passion about them. The homily was trite, but true, as far as I remember. In honesty, I fell a little bit asleep. The assembly did what they were supposed to do. They had a brief missioning ceremony for lay ministers in the diocese. (I was at the service because a friend was being missioned).

They said a prayer, shook hands a little. Nobody ever shouted; nobody really sang out like they meant what the songs said. Nobody woke me up. It was all done correctly, according to the best rubrical tradition. But there was no soul, no immediacy, no sense of a Kingdom of God at hand about to break into our lives. There was certainly no need to change anything, no time, no fulfillment, no conversion.

And finally, no Good News!

On the other hand, on that Monday I went to an ecumenical prayer service at a local "Black" Church to celebrate the Birthday of Dr. Martin Luther King, Jr. We listened to the singing of two Gospel choirs, with a vibrant congregation. What I love about the predominantly black churches is that the assembly is there "Amening" and "Yessing" and crying out "Tell it to 'em preacher man" at everything that strikes them.

A visiting Lutheran pastor spoke, a Caucasian. He spoke mainly about the life and deeds of Dr. King. He believed what he said and he had lived out this belief for many years in the "hood" in which he spoke. He had been touched deeply by King; he shared how and why he was touched. Not great preacher, but a believer with some deep immediacy to his words. He ended up reciting (not reading) a large portion of Kings' "I have a dream" speech.

"In every corner of our land, let freedom ring,
let freedom ring."

As he ended the speech he carried it over to the city in which he spoke, with the congregation flowing along with him like a river, "amening," and "Yes sir-ing".

"In the Blue Bird Inn and Smiley's Tavern, let freedom ring; up and down K Street, let freedom ring.

"In the hiring halls of this city, where young black men cannot now find work, let freedom ring.

"In the court house and the city-county building, let freedom ring.

"In our hearts, our lives, the lines of hungry people at food banks, in our schools, our shops, and on every street corner of our city, let freedom ring ...."

I think my point is clear. There is a difference between a two thousand year old message that we've heard before and more or less believe and a Christ who is alive, here, with us now, inviting us to conversion right now. The reign of God must be always constantly at hand, or it will never come!

When we as a community gather to worship it is partially my task, but equally ours, to make it new, alive, fresh, life-changing by the way we pray and sing and reflect and celebrate.

More important than how we pray, obviously, is the immediacy, the dynamism, with which we live all of our lives. The Gospel scene today contains more than this sense of immediacy about

Jesus message. It goes on to present Mark's version of the first movement of Jesus into the lives of those he calls to follow him.

Jesus has had a profound experience of himself as beloved Son of God in his baptism. He has gone into the desert and wrestled with his various demons. Now he begins his ministry. As he walks along a sea shore he calls men from their nets and they drop everything, immediately and go with him.

What kind of personal dynamism does this Jesus have? What moves these men to give up what they have done all their lives to go and wander off after a stranger?

What is it in his voice, his eyes, his words that pulls them out?

Immediately they abandon their nets and follow him. That word, immediately, is used nineteen times by Mark in the first two chapters of his Gospel. Paul in the second reading today invites us to that same immediacy--"Live in this passing world knowing that the end is near".

Paul and the writer of Mark's gospel apparently believed in an imminent parousia, that is, that the second coming of Christ would come shortly. This whole things is almost over, so get on with it. Shape up, get up, full time, whole-hearted, full speed, right now!

We, now, no longer believe necessarily in an imminent end to everything, but do believe in immediacy. The reign of God is happening Now! It is at hand! This is the time of fulfillment, so we cannot wait
-- to get this relationship straightened out,
-- to make peace with our family member or friend,
-- to renew harmony in our community.

It is too important to let it slide any longer!

We can't wait to get food to the hungry,
to correct the structures that leave people starving.

We can't wait to end abortion,
to have immigrants feel safe
or refugees find a home with us,
to bring justice to Porto Rico, or Haiti,

People are dying!

We can't wait to build community,
to love our kids,
to encourage our neighbor.

The reign of God is at hand. It's just about to break into our lives.
It's here now Get on with it!

As I've become an old man, I fear becoming bored, or boring .
.. .The Gospel, the celebration of Mass, nothing about our faith
need ever be boring. What we hear in Mark's Gospel and will
hear over and over again this year is that we are about a terribly
important task.
It is big,
it is important,
it is serious, and
it is very, very Good News!

The reign of God is at hand.
The time is now.

We hope to reflect that in the way we worship, and the way we live.

12) The Fourth Sunday of Ordinary Time

Scripture Readings: Deut. 18: 15-20; 1 Cor. 7:32-35; Mk. 1:21-28

Something is seriously broken.

Something about us is tragically out of whack. Something is twisted in our human psyche and it is not easily fixed. Traditionally we have called this "original sin." Chesterton once said that if we did not have a doctrine of original sin, we would need to make up something to explain the way things are.

Something is seriously broken.

What a strange, messed up kind of creature we human beings are. We have learned to spill millions of gallons of oil into our environment, fouling waters, destroying entire species of life.

We are able to create fantastic weapons, capable of striking incredibly swift missiles in mid-flight to protect ourselves but we do not provide minimum health care large swaths of our country. We can keep people alive for ten or more years than we were able to 20 years ago, but we have not improved the quality of their life so now many are howling for 'the right to die," and we have destroyed some twenty-eight million fetuses before they had the opportunity to be born.

We destroy our planet, on which some 20 million refugees find nowhere to go.

Something is broken in us; we are obviously all in danger of being caught in the grip of something demonic. We are the victims of massive sin.

When I was young I was offended that I had to suffer for what some people called Adam and Eve did thousands of years ago. As I've gotten older I know less about Adam and Eve but it is pretty clear to me that we are all impacted by the evil that other folks do. Forget about thousands of years ago. If you choose to drink and drive today, my life is at stake. If I lie to your friend, her ability to trust you is damaged. It seems obvious to me that we all suffer because of what others do. So the leader of a nation, like North Korea does something incredibly stupid and the leader of our nation refuses to negotiate with him, and innocent people in both nations might die by the thousands . . .

We are all in this together. We are all touched by the cumulative effect of the world history of millions of years. And we continue to add to that misery day, by day, by day. We do not seem to be able to get out of it all by ourselves, not by trying harder, not by prayer, not by learning even from our mistakes. We keep making new ones.

The first miracle story in Mark's Gospel that we listened to today is radically about primordial combat between Jesus and the demonic powers that threaten to destroy us. Jesus ultimate power over evil is the point of this story, and much of Mark's story of Jesus. Here Jesus comes into the synagogue, into the seat of religious power. The hoi polloi, the folks come with him. He teaches them in a way that has "authority," a way that frees and excites them. Not like the (oppressive, dictatorial, paternalistic) way of the scribes.

After Jesus spoke, "immediately" a possessed man, one in the grip of demons, is brought before him. In his very first miracle, Jesus silences, and sets free this possessed man. By extension, Jesus begins his ministry of setting people free of the demons that possess them. The story of baptism, of discipleship begins.

The demon tries to name Jesus: "I know who you are, the Holy One of God." Jesus says, quite literally, "Shut Up. You cannot name me; you do not have power over me. I overpower you. Come out of that man!"

Jesus initiates his public ministry asserting his power over the demonic, over evil. He comes into our midst to correct and heal what is broken in us. He comes to overpower the cumulative effect of sin in us and in our world so that, as Paul says, "Where sin abounds, grace does more abound!"

In Baptism each of us experienced being anointed, "exorcised," protected against the power of evil that seeks to destroy us. We made, or our parents on our behalf, made promises to renounce Satan, and all his empty works, and all his promises. We said "No" to the demonic in our lives -- not necessarily no to some little red-suited guy with a pitchfork, but "no" to the evil that permeates our world, no to the cumulative, powerful, environmental evil that so clearly tries to overwhelm us in our world. Each of us, figuratively at least, was plunged into the waters with Jesus who has put evil to death by his own death. We drowned sin!

Like many, I suspect, I grew up with a simplistic theology of Original Sin. I was told baptism took away original sin. But somehow I have always still been infected by the demonic afoot in the world. Such "taking away" may have started at baptism, but it wasn't finished. My dad used to say that I was able to do everything wrong I could think of, at least once. Perhaps you share with me the sense that, despite your baptism, sin still has some, at least minor, foothold over you. Apparently putting on Christ, becoming really baptized, is a life-long project. Letting Jesus cast the demons out of us, ridding our world of the cumulative demons, takes a long, long time.

What happens in our baptism, it seems to me, is like choosing sides. It is like declaring, loudly and lovingly where we are, whose we are! In Baptism we say we are with Jesus, we are the community of the followers of Jesus. We are not with the Satanic, the demonic, the selfish, the unloving.

We choose Jesus and we want a community to help us, to stand with us against the forces that can crush and break the human spirit. We choose, we want a community to help us to not be fooled into thinking that violence is the proper response to violence.

We the baptized members of Jesus body out of whom he has cast demons want to say no to those isms that kill us: racism, ageism, consumerism, militarism, sexism . . .

Such healing of demons is so necessary in our lives, individually and together. We stand always on the verge, it seems to me, of collective madness. The demons are everywhere.

They speak about acceptable levels of unemployment,

of maximum extensions of benefits to the poor, even the poor with conditions handicapping their possible productivity.

The demons talk about reducing the welfare rolls, as if those lists were not people, families, mostly children. The demons name as enemy whole nations like El Salvador, or Haiti, then punish entire populations already at home and thriving in our nation.

Three more school shootings occur and we scarcely blink an eye.

Every year, in every way we must keep bringing our demons to this story to be touched by Jesus. We need Jesus to stand near us and say to those evil forces: "Shut up! Get out." We need still to be gradually, ineluctably healed so that we ourselves can be, with Jesus, healers of our world.

13) The Presentation of the Lord

Feb. 2 (When this feast occurs on a Sunday it supplants the Sunday Readings)

Scripture Readings: Mal. 3:1-4; Heb. 2: 14-18; Lk. 2:22-40

I had a friend who taught a high school religion class he entitled, "Revelation is a dirty trick." His point was, somewhat facetiously, that if we didn't know how loved we were we wouldn't be so responsible. Good News has a payback! That seems to me to be the sum and substance of this feast. But let me step back to consider the feast and this scripture, then return to this point.

This feast of the Presentation of Jesus used to be the end of the Christmas-Epiphany Season . . . just the magical forty days after Christmas. Now we celebrate it formally only on the rare occasions that it occurs on Sunday. The feast uses the same gospel as the Feast of the Holy Family but here the focus is clearly on Jesus, rather than the parents. The prophecy from Malachi foretells the great gift this Messenger of the Covenant will be when he comes to the temple. Malachi also stresses the great judgment this messenger will bring, and will himself be!

It is that dual note of both gift and challenge that seems to focus of the Gospel also. Simeon is ecstatic at the fulfillment of his and Israel's hopes and dreams, such that he can now "die in peace." This child will be a light to the Nations, as well as the Glory of Israel. Simeon is equally clear that this child will be a source of the rise and fall of many, a sign that will be opposed. Thus the cross and suffering continue to be a part of the Christmas message. Again the Good news has a shadow side!

At the end of the passage this child goes back home with his family to grow and become strong in wisdom, to prepare for this mission of light and struggle.

So this feast that presents Jesus in the temple presents Jesus, in germ also into our lives. He comes as Good News of God's love; He comes also as a challenge, as a disturbing presence into our world and our individual lives.

And isn't that the truth of it? Does not Jesus both provide the deepest, richest, most meaningful reality of my life? And isn't He at one and the same time the source of my deepest most enduring challenge? Jesus tells me of a God who loves me, of a forgiveness that is always available, of a unity with God and all God's people that is life giving now and forever. The presence of Jesus in my life is light shinning in darkness, is God pitching a tent next to mine, is love unable to be overpowered.

At the same time the presence of Jesus in my life challenges me to respond to the gift given. I cannot refuse to love those that I would rather not like, who oppose, or irritate, or even despise me. I cannot quit caring about the fifty million people in the world who are constantly hungry while I eat three meals a day. I cannot forget the twenty-five percent of our population, mostly children who live in relative poverty, with little or no health care. As I work in this parish I am unable to see only the wonderful things around us and not notice the absence for the most part of any people of color, the sad neglect of some of our elderly parishioners, the sometime lack of passion in our liturgies and compassion in our lives.

Jesus is both gift and challenge. Jesus is good news, but revelation is also a kind of dirty trick that makes me instantly uneasy with the "not yet" dimension of the coming Kingdom of God.

This feast of the Presentation of Jesus invites us to serious reflection on the mystery of God-with-us. How does it play out in our lives? It would be most sad if we do not appreciate the wondrous gift of love born in our midst. But it would be equally tragic if we did not experience this love given as an incentive to love in return, to proclaim liberty to captives, sight to the blind, freedom to prisoners and all the things that this Jesus will say he came to accomplish.

Take a moment to rest in the wonder of the gift of God's love we have received because of Jesus? Then pause for a moment to see how that same gift impels us into dynamic, active involvement to bring the light of this love to the world.

14) The Fifth Sunday of Ordinary Time

Scripture Readings: Job 7:1-4, 6-7; I Cor. 9:16-19, 22-23; Mk. 1:29-39

Not long ago I saw movie on television that really bothered me. I slept fitfully and only in the morning did I name what was troubling me. The move was typical TV. fare; a woman innocently, accidentally gets involved in a murder, sees a series of violent deaths, barely escapes being herself a victim. Finally she is re-united with a handsome man she met during the adventure and, presumably lives happily ever after.

I realized what bothers me in this and so many similar stories, whether fictional or real, is the completely false appearance that any person can go on after being touched by enormous gobs of violence, death, pain, fear, and not be traumatized by them. I doubt that the woman in this story would ever return to "normal" again. In reality a large part of the tragedy of war is that it never really ends for the survivors. Women who have been victimized in sexual or physical abuse never seem to get over the abuse. A person who has been mugged never again is comfortable coming into their house alone at night. The witness to a murder is forever somewhat uneasy. We all live with the cumulative effect of sin in and around us. It piles up, often overwhelms us. We cannot easily dismiss the evil that touches our lives.

So different from this TV. fantasy is the reality that something deep in human beings needs to name, own, grieve, mourn, acknowledge the overwhelming pain of human existence if we are ever to rise, even partially, out of that pain to new and truly miraculous life. That possibility of passing through pain to new life is at the heart of today's readings.

First the Book of Job. The most inappropriate phrase in the English language might well be "The patience of Job." Job is anything but patient, nor should he be. Job has lost almost everything that mattered in his life. His wife is gone, his children dead, his property depleted, his health broken, his reputation destroyed. And Job complains about it all for forty chapters.

Job is the italicized symbol of "everyman," "everywoman," worn out by the successive violence and tragedy of life. Every misfortune has had its impact on Job. He cannot just walk away, start over, ignore the effect of all that tragedy. Job laments:

> "Life is a warfare . . . a series of miseries;
> at night I cannot wait for morning;
> all day long I eagerly await night.
> Life is the pits. I'll never see happiness again."

At the end of the book of Job we are given no answer to this "problem of evil," no rational solution to the question why we must suffer so much. God asks Job only "Where were you when I made the whales?" That is, "What do you know about anything, especially about being God? I am God and you are not!" It is as if God says to Job, "Shut up, and trust me. Face Reality!"

Not a very satisfying answer, but all we had to go with for hundreds of years until Jesus.

Jesus when he comes, as we see in Mark's Gospel, does not solve the problem of evil, does not take it away. Rather he enters into the depth of human suffering with us, is apparently victimized by it, only to, finally, triumph over it.

The gospel today is the story of one day in the life of Jesus ministry: a whirlwind of healing, helping, holding the world's pain and suffering. At the end of the day, Jesus withdraws for a bit to pray. His followers come after him and call him out again, now to go attack the demons in an even broader sphere in the surrounding towns and villages.

Two readings, both deepening our awareness of the cumulative effect of suffering. The presence of Jesus touching, and helping us to endure, survive and overcome this suffering.

Soon we celebrate Ash Wednesday, we begin the long season of Lent-Easter. We begin forty days getting ready for Easter. We will spend three days celebrating Easter, then fifty days getting over it. We cannot have Easter without Lent, and that is my central point today.

There are, I have heard, four ways to approach life:

Some people never get involved in the pain, the darkness, the demons – their own or anyone else's – or at least they try not to. They drink beer and watch ball games on TV., or else they shop!

Other get close to Jesus, get involved, then get scared, run away. They find like-minded friends with whom they can form a little safe sanitary community in which they can pray and sing and avoid reality.

Some get involved, see the pain, get angry, pick up a club or a rock and begin to add to the violence.

The faithful followers of Jesus, we call them Christians, get involved in life, feel the pain, see the demons, get overwhelmed, withdraw to a quiet place to get recharged, and then are able to stay in the pain and help to heal it and to celebrate the hope that is there.

Easter cannot come to us if we deny the overwhelming accumulation of dust and ashes, of pain and death, of violence and destruction and the toll they take on us.

Unless we sit for awhile with Job on our dung heap, taste the ashes in our mouths, experience the depth of our thirst, no Easter will come.

Lent will say to us: Go ahead, touch the ashes, put them on your forehead, go into the desert, wrestle with your demons, your frustrations, your fears, for any cure can only come out of knowing and naming the disease.

We must not overlook that detail in the Gospel that tells us that Jesus Prays! He stops his work to withdraw, to enter again into the relationship with his God, to restore his faith, his hope and his power to touch and love and heal. Nothing so points out the fragile humanity of Jesus as this need to pray. Nothing so underlines our identity with him as this need to pray.

We will approach Lent as a time of prayer, but not just prayer for healing of ourselves, but so that we can re-enter the very violence of our world and struggle with Jesus to over come it. Our prayer, like the prayer of Jesus, empowers us to be part of the healing of those around us, our mother-in-law, our neighbor, our war-weary world.

I have come a long way from the T.V. program with which I began. But I am glad for my reaction to it. We cannot deny the awful effect that human tragedy has on us and everyone around us. But we can enter into it in faith, face it with Jesus who shares the mess with us, and emerge able to offer hope that out of suffering and death endured, Easter can indeed come!

15) The Sixth Sunday of Ordinary Time

Scripture Readings: Lev. 13:1-2,44-46; 1 Cor. 10:31-11:1; Mk. 1:40-45

What does it mean to be a disciple of Jesus? Everything in Mark's Gospel responds to that question, forces that question on the hearer. The Gospel of today asks that question with power. What does it mean for me to be a follower of Jesus?

Before I look at the Gospel, let me look carefully for a moment at the first reading from Leviticus. This passage spells out how a leper is to be treated in the Hebraic community. We hear no word of compassion for the victim; there seems a presumed suspicion, as with every disaster, that the victim deserves the plague received. Perhaps every illness or tragedy is a punishment for one's sins. There is here, as in society in general, a terrible propensity to blame the victim.

So the leper is unceremoniously thrown out of the temple. Can I feel what the leper would experience?

> Told to leave the community, home, family, friends.
> Told to dishevel clothes and beard, so that even before anyone can see the sores one's identification with an afflicted group would be obvious.
> Told to cover mouths and cry out "Unclean, Unclean" to every passerby.

Only if we know, and beyond knowing, feel, the reality of the leper do we capture this gospel passage which, perhaps more than any other, reveals the personality of Jesus to us, lets us know who and how he is, tells us what it might mean to walk with him.

In the story today this leper breaks the Leviticus code:

> He does not stand apart.
> He does not cry out "Unclean!"
> He approaches Jesus in some trust.

Something in this itinerant preacher, this healer, invites the outcast to come closer, to trust in this him as he can in no other. He comes close to Jesus, kneels at his feet and makes his acclamation of faith: "If you want to you can heal me!"

I love the Jerusalem Bible translation of Jesus response: "Of course I want to!" Every translation falters in conveying the pity of Jesus who is "moved to the very core of his being," "touched to the heart," "overwhelmed with deep sadness and compassion." Jesus does not stay distant. He touches the leper. He makes himself unclean, takes on himself the risk of the disease, shares the fate of this outcast – for to touch the leper is to join with him in his alienation from the community.

This passage offers one avenue to understanding the entire second half of Mark's Gospel. Now Jesus has touched the leper, has broken a taboo. He shares the lot of this marginalized man. Jesus too must now go apart. He must stay in desert places. He must, like the one he has touched, live on the edges of society.

Jesus, living already on the spiritual, psychological edge, now must live physically outside the community. Jesus says in his own way: "If this man is unclean, unwanted, unaccepted, then, for him, I will be too!"

But a strange thing happens. Even though Jesus goes apart, shares the lot of the "kicked out," the alienated, the unclean, people are still drawn to him, drawn to the edges with him. They continue to seek him out. In breaking the tradition himself, Jesus invites everyone to do the same. To come to Jesus is to come to one who is apart, counter-cultural, different, unclean by acceptable standards. The authentic followers of Jesus know this somewhere deep in their hearts.

As we listen to these readings what do they tells us about discipleship? How do they flesh out an answer to our initial question: *What does it mean to follow Jesus?*

First, a word about discipleship, about the following of Christ. We are not concerned with simply the "Imitation of Christ," if that means acting as he did. We are not speaking about wearing sandals, growing a beard, doing this or saying that because Jesus did. (I think of the New Yorker cartoon with the wealthy man in his sky scraper office looking out over Manhattan and saying, "Whenever

I'm in a tight spot I ask myself, 'What would John Wayne do?' "It's not like that. We are talking about more than wearing a bracelet that says "What would Jesus do?") We are talking about putting on the mind and heart of Christ, talking about seeing with the eyes of Christ Jesus, talking not about imitation, but assimilation. We are talking about letting the same spirit that animated Jesus animate us.

So what does it mean to follow Jesus?

First, it means to somehow see the outcast as the center-piece! The follower of Jesus knows that those who appear afflicted are the most favored, most loved.

As I reflect on this scripture I have been thinking as I suspect you have, about persons with AIDS. People shunned by society, doomed to be set apart, unclean, often presumed to be the source of their own illness, with little compassion, little understanding.

People with AIDS are not the only outcasts of our society, our church.

Once I was on a radio talk show. Two people who had left the church called. They had left because as divorced women they literally said they "felt like lepers" unwanted, unaccepted in their communities of faith. Despite the enormous pain divorce always causes to the couple and to those who share life with them -- if we convey to them that they are shunned, cast out, we are not terribly good followers of Jesus.

In three parishes I have served I spent much time with elderly people who often speak painfully of the sense of being extra, un-wanted, a burden in their understaffed nursing homes. If they are not feeling that now, they live with the fear of one day being so set aside from life.

I once noticed in the paper the most painful column. I wanted to turn away my eyes and not know the story. An Oregon Judge sentenced a known child molester to put a sign on his door that said, "Dangerous child-molester lives here; children stay away."

This bothered me so much because I hate what the man has done. I have no sympathy for him. I want children to be safe. I think people should be warned. I thought the judge had a great idea.

At the same time, I was overwhelmed with the sense that Jesus would have knocked on this man's door, would have gone beyond the sign to share a meal with him, would have done all in his power to love the man back to life, would have risked public condemnation by befriending him, loving him, sharing in his expulsion.

I thought further: isn't it to be a follower of Jesus to recognize that each of us, in honesty, has our own sign? Each of us knows deep down where we are "unclean." I could wear a sign that says, "Look out for him; he talks too much and sometimes he hurts people." "He doesn't measure up to his words; watch out!" I could have many signs.

I know mine; you know yours. But Jesus reaches beyond our signs, beyond our faults, beyond our fears, and says "Of course I want to heal you!"

Jesus freely choose to share the brokenness of the leper.

Each of us are that leper in our own way. Discipleship is a question of admitting it, and loving *from* this recognition, so that in our lives, in our families, in our communities, and more and more in our world, the followers of Jesus see with his eyes, see everything, knowing that despite whatever may seem unclean about us we can all say to each other:

You are my brother; you are my sister.

You are like me and I will be with you.

We pray that grace of discipleship today!

16) Ash Wednesday

Scripture Readings: Joel 2: 12-18; 2 Cor. 5:20-6:2; Mt. 6: 1-6, 16-18

When I was young it was relatively easy to define a good Catholic. The definition was primarily negative, but measurable. A Good Catholic didn't eat meat on Friday, never missed Mass on Sunday, and probably didn't eat candy or go to movies during Lent. It is more difficult to define ourselves as good Catholics now and certainly our understanding of Lent has dramatically changed the past forty years.

In the light of the Gospel and our other readings, let me reflect for a few moments on Lent.

Lent now is the beginning --and only the beginning-- of the most dynamic and dramatic period of our Christian year. For Forty days we will prepare for Easter. We will take three days to celebrate Easter when it comes, and we will spend fifty days getting over it, as we celebrate Easter over and over and over again up to Pentecost.

In Lent, we enter into the desert for forty days with Jesus, so that like him we can prepare for our part of his messianic mission. During Lent the Good Catholic goes on retreat, we move more deeply into prayer and reflection; we become more intentional about our faith in Jesus. We renew and rediscover all that this faith means to us.

Lent was, in its origin, the final period of preparation for Baptism. People had been preparing for years for the experience of entering into this community of faith. Now this final six weeks instructs them in the awesome meaning of that initiation. Every reading, every ritual, every gesture, every prayer of Lent is geared to lead them to the Baptismal font.

Throughout Lent we tell ourselves again all our best and most dramatic stories, stories that build up our faith, deepen our hope, support our awareness of God's love for us that empowers us to love in God's way. We tell these stories to prepare new people in our midst for Baptism, and to help us renew the baptismal life we have already.

Again, every story is in some way about Baptism, and the life lead by the Baptized.

The ashes we receive today remind us of our mortality – that each of us will die. We can begin to ward off the fear and power of that death by dying already with Christ, and rising with him As we enter into the baptismal waters and rise up new born with Jesus that death has no more power over us.

During Lent we remember: In the traditional formula for distributing ashes we remember our mortality, that all of us are dust, that we will die.

In the formula recommended now, we remember that we are loved. As the Ashes are put on our foreheads we are invited to "Repent and Believe the Gospel," that is, to turn our lives around because we remember God's love for us and we believe that great good News.

So, in Lent the catechumens and all of us will be "called," elected as God's chosen people.

In Lent catechumens and all of us will be smeared with oil to ward off the demonic powers waiting to crush us.

During Lent the catechumens and all of us will let the word of God penetrate our hearts and scrutinize us, searing into our very souls and moving us to conversion.

During Lent the catechumens and all of us will prepare to die and rise with Christ.

The Gospel today presumes the means to this conversion. In this section of the Sermon on the Mount we notice that Jesus tells us how to fast, how to pray, how to give alms . . . that is, without calling a great deal of attention to ourselves, but rather so we and God will know it is going on. In telling us how, Jesus seems to presume already that we are in fact doing these things. The characteristics of the Good Catholic during Lent, then, are that we pray, we fast, and we take money saved from that fasting and share it with those in need.

Parenthetically, the Rice Bowl program is a wonderful help. I suggest that we not leave it on the periphery of Lent, but let those Bowls which you can get after Mass be a central reminder of what we are about, a way for us to set aside some money throughout the season to give to the needs of hungry people at the End of Lent. If we all fill those bowls with the fruits of our fasting during Lent and bring them back to the Church on Holy Thursday to help feed hungry people in our city and throughout the world, we will have accomplished a large part of the Lenten task –to know God's love for us and share that love with others.

Together then we turn to the Ashes that help us enter into this Lent-Easter Season. To go back to where I began: It is perhaps much less precise, but far more challenging to say today:

> The Good Catholic is an Easter Person who lives fully
> the life of the Risen Christ.

Lent, every year, is a necessary preparation for such a life. We enter into this season, fully, together!

17) The First Sunday of Lent

Scripture Readings: Gen. 9: 8-15; 1 Pet. 3:18-22; Mk. 1:12-15

I am a Catechumen; you are a catechumen.

Unless you and I can imagine, pretend, or, better, really experience that we are walking through Lent as Catechumens, moving towards Baptism, we cannot hear the readings today (and throughout Lent) as intended.

The readings during Lent are prepared to be the final instructions to those who will be baptized at the Easter Vigil. Everything in Lent moves towards that Vigil, towards the font, towards Easter.

The readings we hear from the Hebrew Scriptures will all be reprised again at that Vigil. So we begin with the Flood, one of the great stories of our tradition. The flood becomes an image of the baptismal waters, as the baptismal rite says "an end to sin and a new beginning of holiness." In what scholars call a "pre-covenant" even before history, before recorded time, God promises to be faithful to people, never again to destroy us. The rainbow, the sign of having passed through the waters, becomes an enduring sign of God's fidelity.

The catechumen, the one waiting for the waters, is poetically invited to long for that water that will end sin, begin holiness, is invited to trust in that sign.

More centrally, on the first Sunday of Lent, we go out into the desert with Jesus. We go out, sent by the Spirit. We watch Jesus very closely because we are making our final discernment about whether we want to be his followers. Just as Jesus went apart for forty days of prayer before he began his public ministry, we catechumens, we go out with him for our own prayer before we undertake our Christian life.

Out in the desert Jesus does warfare with the devil, with the demonic, with the forces of evil and denial and death. Before we plunge into the baptismal waters we go out into the desert warfare with Jesus, to wrestle with our own demons, all those forces that want to kill us, to crush our spirit. This is part of our preparation for the waters of life.

All of us today, this first Sunday of Lent, are here to renew the grace of our own Baptism, to start over as it were. We need to stand with Jesus, to stand with the catechumens.

How was Jesus tempted? Mark doesn't really tell us. He remains silent. Just, "Jesus was tempted."

The central temptation is hinted at in the first line, "After John was arrested ..." If the prophet that precedes him is arrested and surely will be killed, Jesus can easily imagine his fate if he is faithful to God's invitation, if he speaks an even louder and a more radical voice than John to the civil and religious powers of the day.

And we, today, we go into the Lenten desert, after John's death, and after Jesus' death too. If misunderstanding, rejection death happened to John, happened to Jesus, we must pause and ask: Do we really want to enter those baptismal waters? Maybe we want to stay in the dry, barren, violent, tempting, but safe desert. Many in our world stay out here in the barren desert. We ourselves have perhaps lived there for a long, long time. We don't have to come out. We don't we share in Jesus mission.

Matthew and Luke's Gospels will spell out the temptations, suggesting what Jesus might have wrestled with out here. At bottom the temptations are about power, about being number one, about not being fully human – turn stones into bread, leap off high buildings, adore the demon and get all kinds of power. Perhaps we share that temptation and we need, this Lent to settle down our egos, our need to be significant, important.

More likely our temptation is in the opposite direction. More likely out here in the desert we don't think much of ourselves. most of us believe we have no importance, no relevance, no power, no pizzazz. Most of us think too little of ourselves, believe we do not count, do not matter. Perhaps during these forty days as we prepare to follow Jesus, our real temptation is to give in to this sense of powerlessness.

Whether the demon inside encourages us to assume more power and try to run the universe, or tells us with an insidious voice that we do not count for much, the root temptation is the same. We are tempted to listen to the voice of the demonic in us or in our world, rather than the baptismal voice of God's love that says "You are beloved sons, beloved daughters."

Jesus will come out of the desert saying only that we need to follow him, to be faithful to who we are, and how we are, faithful to the deep precious unique truth in each of us.

At some point in the process we always ask those preparing for Baptism what they ask of God's Church. I remember vividly a woman who joined the Church a few years ago. She came back with some hesitance. What she asked of God's Church was to know that it was all right to be here "as herself?" She had made mistakes in life. She had made some tough but honest personal choices. Her life had been fairly messy. She needed to know it was all right to be here as she was.

Her desire finally is the desire of all of us, we catechumens out here in the desert. We wrestle with our deepest temptation to be someone else, something else. During Lent we are invited to become the beloved son or daughter God tells us we are!

I love the image of this temptation scene in the movie "The Last Temptation of Christ." Jesus sits in the sand, with a circle drawn around him. Wild beasts outside the circle snarl, bark, hiss at him. They threaten him. But Jesus decides to sit there until he is ready to come out, as he is. When God lets him know who he is and how he is supposed to be, then he can come out and act on that self-understanding. For being faithful to that self-understanding is what will save him, and save the world.

We begin our journey with the catechumens today. This journey will lead to all of us gathered here at this font saying:

"We reject Satan, and all his works, and all his empty promises.
We believe in Jesus, we choose Jesus, we stand with Jesus and his followers."

May our prayer together, our lives together this Lent lead us all, old and new catechumens, to or back to this font!

In the Spirit of this prayer we will invite our Catechumens and candidates to come forward now so that we can send them to the Cathedral, to our Bishop, where they will be elected, called, chosen for the Easter Sacraments this year. They help all of us to know that we have all been called by God, chosen as we are to be God's Beloved Sons, beloved daughters.

18) The Second Sunday of Lent

Scripture Readings: Gen. 22:1-2, 9-13, 15-18; Ro. 8:31b-35, 37; Mk. 9:2-10

During an Easter Vigil a few years ago this first reading we heard tonight about Abraham and Isaac truly came alive for me. We had asked a family to do the reading for us any way they choose. That dark night as we gathered, after we lit the fire and sang our song of praise around it, after we heard the wonderful poetic story of creation, the family came forward, outside, behind the fire on top of a garage roof to tell this Abraham story. The stark near tragedy of it totally captivated me, and I believe the entire assembly.

The wife and mother read the story, while the family acted it out. In asking them we had forgotten that their youngest child a boy of 8 or 9 was named Isaac. As the mother read, the father and son acted out the story, while the other children, a boy and 2 girls reacted in horror and pain. They watched as their father bound up the child, placed him on an altar/table and prepared to slaughter the boy. The Father had honest tears in his eyes as he held a make-believe sword over his son. The other children turned their eyes in fear as just before the blow was dealt. At the final moment God's voice comes: "Do not lay your hand on the boy!" The relief was palatable, . . . for the family, and the entire assembly breathed a collective sigh of relief.

For the first time the incredibly radical challenge of God that this story encompasses touched me to the bones. If I were a catechumen, (which I must pretend to be this Lenten season) I would be afraid to put myself into the hands of such a God. The mythic story makes no sense unless one knows, as Abraham is presumed to do, that absolutely everything about this boy, everything about his life was totally a gift from God in the first place. In the legend, Isaac was not born until Abraham was over 80; his wife well beyond menopause. The promise to Abraham's entire line depended on this child and obviously could not be fulfilled if the child was dead. Abraham was asked to sacrifice everything he had, but everything he had was so obviously dependent on God's gift in the first place. He knew that. Abraham knew that this God loved him, loved Isaac, loved his entire family then and forever. This God deserved to be trusted.

It is this deep, unwavering trust in God's love, God's call that connects this reading with the Gospel, and connects them both with us, with the Elect in our midst. Those who are preparing for Baptism, Confirmation, Eucharist at Easter and all of us preparing to renew that Easter life have to hear the readings in the light of our entire experience of God.

The Transfiguration experience is for Jesus a renewal of his baptismal experience. Before he goes down from this mountain and begins to go towards Jerusalem where the prophets are all killed, before this final stage of his journey to death, Jesus is reminded of God's great love for him, reminded that he is indeed God's beloved son. He is given what he needs to go on with his mission.

I find myself constantly wondering whether this transfiguration scene is primarily for Jesus or for his three closest friends. The answer is "Yes"! The focus here in Mark is on the religious experience that the friends have. They get a glimpse of the glory of Jesus that is to come. They are prepared, though they cannot know it now, to see beyond the passion and death that are imminent to the glory that is to come afterwards. This Jesus they are following is part of the great company of the very best of their heroes, is special child of God. They can trust their lives with him.

Again, as the Elect prepare for baptism, and as each of us prepare to renew the spirit of our being God's beloved sons and daughters, we are invited to trust our experience of God.

We must have the courage of Abraham, so that knowing God's love we can do whatever God asks, no matter how outrageous.

We must have the faith of Jesus, to trust that we are beloved, and can enter into whatever suffering love brings as we follow Him.

We must be like the three closest friends then, and close friends of Jesus ever since, trusting what we have seen and heard, and having the courage to build our lives on those experiences.

Like Peter we are tempted to want to build a tent or two, tempted to enjoy the experience, even the experience of this Lenten journey. But we have to know that God really does love us, that we really have experienced God's love, that we can go down from this mountain top, go forth in trust from our experience and live the Christ-life before us. It is this trust we deepen that during Lent.

I know that personally this means remembering the very special times when God was very close. I need to remember a moment early in my priesthood when I was terrified by a job I did not know how to do. I experienced God's love for a moment telling me

"You can not cause any permanent damage!"

-- telling me that I was loved by that God and nothing I did could stop that from being true. I need to remember that experience, trust it, build my life on it.

I need to believe that when I suffered a cardiac arrest 20 years ago and did not stay dead that God was involved in that resuscitation, that God wants me alive, continuing to do the Kingdom's work It was not chance, it was not accident, it was neither a dream, an illusion, nor something I ate. God is with me. I have to trust that, and live it out.

I do not know what experiences of God you have had, only that you have had them or would not be here today. During this Lenten season if we are to walk with Jesus, we, like Abraham, like Peter, James and John, like Jesus himself, and like the Elect in our midst, need to (Perhaps sing here)

"Remember how you loved us to your death,
and so we celebrate that you are with us still,
and we believe that we will see you
when you come,
in your glory Lord.
We remember, we celebrate, we believe."

19) The Third Sunday of Lent

Note: Since most parishes celebrate the Rite of Christian Initiation of Adults the readings for the Third, Fourth, and Fifth Sundays of Lent are the same each year. See Year A for these three reflections.

20) The Fourth Sunday of Lent

Again, See Year A

21) The Fifth Sunday of Lent

Again, See year A.

22) Passion /Palm Sunday

Scripture Readings: Is. 50:4-7; Phil. 2:6-11; Mk. 14;1-15:47

One is inclined to be silent. The appropriate response to the story of the Death of Jesus is, perhaps, silence. My words will brief, but speak I must for this narration of the Passion by Mark deserves attention. We only hear this Markan account once every three years. It is so very different from the others, so stark, so relentless, so pain filled.

As we watch and listen to the story this day it is so terribly clear that the *only* words Jesus speaks from the cross are his last, and they color the entire story.:

> "My God, My God, why have you abandoned me?"

Abandonment is central to this telling. The passion begins with Jesus asking his best friends, his closest followers,

> "Could you not stay awake and watch one hour with me,"

and ends with this sense of being left alone even by God.

Mark tells this story with none of the supports the other Gospels offer; no one gives comfort to Jesus in his trials:

--No women stand along the way weeping for him,

--no "good thief" believes in him,

--No Mary or John stand by the cross at the end,

Nobody, nothing supports him except his radical trust in God, his faith. He goes to his death, goes through his death alone!

This abandonment is heightened by a wonderful small detail found only in Mark when that young man in the garden runs off leaving behind his white garment. This garment, a symbol of baptism, suggests to the hearers of Mark in that first generation of Christians, that faced with the scandal of the cross we are all tempted to leave behind our baptismal garment and abandon Jesus.

Mark's Jesus is stripped of everything.

There is no hint of divinity, no power, no glory, only emptiness and loss. Jesus is indeed the Suffering Servant of the Isaiah passage we heard in the first reading.

This telling of the passion invites us to acknowledge how difficult it is for any of us to be authentically who we are, to say what we believe, to act on our words no matter what the cost. How difficult it is to go to suffering, even to death, for what we believe. It is even more difficult to do so when we have to do so alone, without human support, without even the felt support that God is with us.

And this is the story of the Passion in Mark!

We need to feel this abandonment today. More than any of the other Gospels this passion telling invites us to be with Jesus:

(sing) "Stay with me, Remain here with me, Watch and pray, Watch and Pray."

Can we offer to Jesus now the compassion missing then?

Ironically, it seems to me, this account of Christ's passion can also be the most consoling to us. When we are alone, feeling abandoned, then we are most like Jesus; Jesus has been there before us. Jesus knows this deepest of human pain from the inside, from our side!

Although the divinity of Jesus shines through consistently in the Passion account of John that we will hear on Good Friday, it is almost totally absent from Mark. Only finally at the end of the story does someone other than a demon acknowledge Jesus as God's son. The centurion looks at the dead, limp, beaten, bruised body. He sees something of the love of God in this man on a cross.

I am reminded of the wonderful story from Elie Weisel. The great Jewish narrator of the holocaust tells of a scene in a Nazi death camp. Prisoners are forced to watch the slow death of three men who tried to escape. The men are hung as the people watch. One young man, stronger than the others keep clutching at the rope, pulling himself up, prolonging both the agony of his death and the horror of the spectators. A bitter young man in the crowd turned to the rabbi next to him scoffing,

"Where is your God; where is your God?"

The rabbi spoke softly,

"He's hanging there on that rope!"

Our God does not take away human suffering. God does not ease our agony, answer all our questions, alleviate all our fears, fill up the gaps of our loneliness. Rather our God shares in these deepest moments of human suffering with us.

We have heard many words. We pause for a few moments of silence to feel the power of this passion narrative, to let it penetrate our weary hearts, and in the great depths of the sadness of this story, we prepare for Easter!

23) Holy Thursday

Scripture Readings: Ex. 12:1-8, 11-14; 1 Cor. 11:23-26; Jn. 13:1-15

Note: The homily tonight occurs after the ritual action of washing of feet. This homily presumes that after the Gospel the Elect, both those preparing for Full Communion and those preparing for Baptism have come forward. They first have had their feet washed, then have gone out into the assembly and washed the feet of others.

This Triduum we celebrate is more about imitation than admiration. Though we remember and celebrate what happened to Jesus, our concern is more with what happens to us because of Jesus.

"I have set you an example, that you also should do as I have done."

Tonight, as throughout the Lenten season, the Elect lead us. They have their feet washed and then join the community of those who wash feet, the community of Jesus, the servant of Yahweh. Those who are preparing to join us at this Eucharistic table, those who are going to be baptized at the Easter Vigil pick up the towel, the bowl, the pitcher and imitate Jesus in serving their sisters and brothers. They remind all of us that such service is the very heart of our baptismal call.

For years I recall going to Holy Thursday services in which the homily focused on the Eucharist. This is, after all, The Mass of the Lord's Supper. But, strangely, the gospel on Holy Thursday is not immediately about Eucharist. How ironical that on this Feast of the Lord's Supper the Gospel is not about the supper at all. In fact in John's gospel their is no institution narrative, no focus on the Eucharist at this last supper. Unlike the synoptic Gospels John's supper revolves around servant-hood.

> "You call me master and Lord, and so I am...
> If I, your Lord and teacher have washed your feet, so you
> ought also to wash one anther's feet."

I think of all the times I've heard someone say to me "I didn't want to bother you." "I know how busy you are." So I am not invited to do something for them, when doing something for them is the entire point of my life... and really the lives of all of us.

I learned something important about this "doing something for others" once during a retreat in everyday life. I was directing a middle-aged woman. She was at a turning point in her life and seeking direction to life's second half. In the midst of the retreat I had her pray about this passage from John.

The woman came back a few days later and said she couldn't get into this passage so she prayed over something else. I was curious, so suggested that she take the same passage again for a few days. She came back the next time, threw the bible on my desk and said,

"I hate that passage. All my life I've washed people's feet. If there was a foot around I washed it. I've spent my life taking care of everyone else, and I think I've lost my own identity in the process."

With great caution I suggested she pray over this passage for a few more days. When she returned she was much more mellow. She spoke softly. She said:

"I have decided that it makes an enormous difference whether we wash feet because we have to, because we think we should, or whether we wash the feet we have chosen to wash. I think I need to choose where and when to wash, where and when to serve, where and when to share my gifts, entrust myself to others. I can do that."

Some months later, as we met the final time during this retreat this woman got up and came over to me. She took ointment out of her purse, knelt at my feet, took off my socks and began to massage my feet. I was embarrassed and wanted her to stop. But she was choosing to serve me as her way of saying thanks.

This symbolic act, like the foot washing we have experienced to-night was just a gesture, a sign, a sacrament if you will. But these ritual acts of service point to the larger invitation of Jesus to come from some deep center of identification with him, laying down our lives for our brothers and sisters.

Here the washing of feet and the sacred meal we share come together. In a few moments some of those who became foot washers tonight, and all of us will share in the body and blood of Jesus. Again, this sharing of a sacramental meal is about assimilating ourselves into Jesus, his vision, his values, his life.

It is about imitation more than admiration.

We are celebrating not only what happened to Jesus but what happens to us because of Jesus.

And so we will take this bread which we believe to be the Body of Christ. And we will invite Jesus to live in us, and let his flesh be on our bones. We will sip this cup, and drink this wine, which we believe to be his blood, and let his blood flow in our veins. We invite Jesus to live in us so that we can be, as he was, as he is, servants of one another.

We begin our sacred Triduum remembering Jesus final meal with those he most loved. We remember the commission he gave them, and gives us, to be servants with him. We acknowledge that we cannot do that on our own, but need him to live in us, live through us. We eat, we drink, and we go forth from here to serve.

Now let us invite up around the table those who wish to enter into full communion with us.

23) Good Friday

For a Homily on John's Passion account, see Year A

24) Easter Vigil/ Easter Sunday

Scripture Readings: Various, but rooted in Mk. 16:1-8

I am held captive by the story we celebrate tonight/ today. I am captivated by the story of women who witnessed something awesome and in fear and trembling "said nothing to anyone." I am captivated by a story that is too wondrous to believe:

"Jesus is risen from the dead!"

and we with him.

And I am led to ask myself and us, "How/ Why do we believe in Resurrection?"

I must wrestle with that Resurrection question before I go on – before we baptize new people into it, before we renew it in ourselves again. Why do I, why do we believe?

I remember vividly a ten year old boy named Gordon who hung around a parish where I worked. He had no sense of religion, no experience of church, but he used to come around on Sunday morning while his mother slept, just to visit, and watch, perhaps to score a doughnut or two. Shortly after Easter one year Gordon asked our Religious Education director about the cross he saw in the center of our church, with a white drape all around it. She stopped and told him, for the first time in his life, the story of Jesus -- about his life, his death, his rising from the dead.

Gordon heard the story for the first time. He was amazed, awe-struck, thrilled. "Wow!," he cried. For the rest of the morning Gordon rushed around the church telling anyone who would listen the amazing story he had just heard.

I think about an article I recently read by a high school religion teacher who wished he could get the only response the story of Jesus deserves from his students . . . "Holy Bleep!"

This is an amazing story. It can seem like nonsense. Why do I believe? Why do we believe?

We live in a world of much death. Death surrounds us. Death pervades us. Two people died in our parish last week. Everyone I know and love will die. Almost all my longest and best friends are now deceased. I myself have died three times, and I will die again finally and forever.

In the face of so much death I must go like those women, or like Peter to look, to hope that the tomb will be empty.

Everything in me cries out that this death of everyone, everything cannot be, must not be the final word.

Death squads that kill an Archbishop in El Salvador cannot be the last word. Fifty years ago, Martin Luther King was shot; that cannot be the end of his story. Another black kid shot in Sacramento. Syrian civilians killed by the thousands for no purpose. Thousands of children dying of hunger, and the slow death of my friend with cancer – these cannot be the last word.

Even broken relationships, the little deaths that make up human life cannot be the final word!

Why do I believe? Why do we believe?

I recall the year before I was ordained a priest I tried not to believe. Before I could give my life to preaching a message of Resurrection I had to read Albert Camus, had to try on the clothes of unbelief.

I could not wear them and stay warm.

I discovered that I could not, not believe!

Believing, I discovered what felt and wore like truth. I discovered, looking through the lens of faith, that life indeed comes out of death. I discovered that the most painful moments of my past become the seeds of whatever peace is present now.

I have loved those whose minds or hearts were so big, whose creativity was so vast, that in their death I knew that death could not be final or futile. I knew and know they live. I have had friends whose love was so deep, whose compassion was so all embrassive that death could not possibly end that love. I knew and know they live.

Tonight/today as I ponder the question of belief I picture in my mind the ancient Easter Vigils of which I have read, the Spirit of which we try to capture here this Easter

All night long people listened to their best and deepest stories.,
remembered God's presence to them in Creation,
in Exile,
in Bondage,
in beauty.

All night long they prayed and sang,
while in another building, a baptistery across the square,
people gathered.
Over hours deacons and deaconesses took new Christ-followers,
reckless new believers
and plunged them naked as the day of their birth,
into the re-birth of baptismal waters.
They pulled them from the watery tomb,
covered them with oil from head to foot,
and garbed them in white.

Then just at dawn,
after the stories, the songs, the prayers,
just at dawn,
after the baptism, the oil the robes,
These neophytes came into the Church,
ringing wet,
covered with oil,
stunned and starry eyed,
looking for all the world like ghosts – like those risen from the dead.

They came down the aisle into the midst of those who asked as we do "Why believe in Resurrection?" These people came back from the dead to witness to them the truth of what they were celebrating that night.

Again this Easter in our very midst people come back from various kinds of death to be reborn in our mist.

We believe because throughout our past people have witnessed to us by their lips, and by their lives the truth of this story. We can believe because at times, like Gordon, each of us has rushed around to tell the story. We have in our own ways, at moments cried out "Holy Bleep," trusting this story to be true. We can believe because we see tonight, today these sisters and brothers (*names would be good here*) live out this story for us again..

And we are here again surrounded by the people and the symbols that make the story true:

- A community gathered in that faith helping each other to believe,
- Stories of God's fidelity, all through our messy history,
- Light breaking into darkness,
- The candle of Easter, the light of Christ, come into the World plunging into the water's womb, making it pregnant with Christ's new life.
- This touch of hands, of oil, of love, Confirming the Baptized in their share in this Risen-Christ-life,
- The bread and wine of life, poured out, given for me.

We do not look for Jesus among the dead, for we believe he is risen and goes before us.

Despite the cynics voices constantly crying in me that this may all be nonsense, I/ we come to the tomb together and find it empty. Death does not have the final word!

I can end no better way than to remind us what we have sung so faithfully together all through Lent:

> We remember how you loved us to your death,
> And still we celebrate that you are with us here,
> And we believe that we will see you when you come
> In your glory, Lord.
> We remember, we celebrate, we believe.

Let the heart of our celebration begin!

25) For Daily Eucharist or Other Celebration during the Easter Season

In The Spiritual Exercises St. Ignatius suggests that the grace we pray for during the fourth week (the period in which we consider the Resurrection of Jesus) is "to share in the joy of the risen Christ." What an amazing thing to ask. I want to be as filled with joy as Jesus was when God raised him up! I want to know that kind of excitement, fulfillment, joy . . . when Jesus knew "I was right! God is faithful! Yes!!!"

A friend shared with me an original poem that captures the "feel" of this joy better than anything else I know. The poem is unpublished before this and deserves to be read, prayed over . . . enjoyed! I offer the poem as an excellent way to get at the grace of this Easter season. It seems a perfect reflection for any number of occasions around this time:

An Easter Poem

Bill Bichsel, S.J.

Earth-filled man.
You were dead.
You were supposed to stay dead,
 as all the broken do.
But, earth-filled man,
 in the dark and dank of Joseph's cave,
 far away from Bethlehem,
You began to quicken,
 like a potato bud in a root cellar.

Life began oozing in your veins,
 and your toes and brain began to feel the trickle of energy.
The pace stepped up.
Laughing life surged like a river
 rushing through a broken dam
 into every artery and synapse of yourself.
You felt joy, and laughed.

Your wrapped hand pressed against your clothed thigh;
You began to unwrap the prison clothes that bound you.
You rose naked from your stone slab and felt your open
wounds,
 which did not smart;
You ran your hands through your bloody matted hair.
The laugh of cascading spring water
 broke out of your mouth
 and you raised your arms and sang
 your joyful alleluia song
 to your delighted God.

With hands and shoulder against the boulder
   and feet braced against the stone slab
   and power racing in your sinews
You pushed mightily against the rock and moved it aside.

You strode naked and singing through the crypt entrance
out into early sunlight and blossoming time.

26) Second Sunday of Easter

Scripture Readings: Acts. 4:32-35; 1 Jn. 5: 1-6; Jn. 20: 19-31

First note that this is "the second Sunday of Easter, not after Easter. This is the 2nd Sunday we celebrate Easter and we will do so 5 more times....Easter is what we celebrate again and anew today!

I am convinced that the Triduum, Easter, the entire Lent-Pentecost cycle is not primarily about what happened to Jesus. What we celebrate is about Jesus certainly, but on the deepest level it is about what happens to us because of Jesus. What most matters is that we have died and come back to life with the Risen Christ and everything is changed because of that.

Easter one year was colored by a particular challenge, the irony of the death of thirty-nine people in San Diego. Part of a cult called "Heaven's Gate" these people committed mass suicide, trusting that they would go to some "higher plane," some heaven. If Easter and the promise of our share in Resurrection is simply that we get "to go to heaven," then these prematurely dead believers are on to something. If Easter primarily affirms that we don't need to bother much with this world because "There will be a pie in the sky when we die by and by," then we all ought, logically, to long for the earliest possible death. Put on your Nike's, lie down and die.

In fact, the readings today and throughout the Easter season suggest over and over that this celebration is about life going on right now, about how we live in this world, about our relationships with one another on this so earthy plane. That first community of believers described in Acts were transformed. They shared everything in common; they became a community of love that led others to believe. They were not mere recipients of a promise but witnesses to it for the sake of all.

Easter is not just about going to heaven; The appearance of Jesus in the upper room on Easter Sunday night speaks about how his followers are to live with one another in this world.

The risen Christ shows his wounds, suggesting that what we become in any eventual heaven has something to do with what we pass through in this life. What will be transformed are the scars of love that we have passed through – we cannot avoid or walk around the cross. We have to pass through it, with Jesus if we hope to enter into His glory.

This display of his wounds that both begins and ends this passage is critical. The defibrillator I wear to keep my heart from stopping will still be with me in any eventual after life. The courage or lack of it I show will be a mark I carry forever. Our physical ailments, our job losses, our failed marriages, our or tears at the death of a loved one -- our broken lives and broken hearts – every suffering we pass through in this life, every cross we bear, we will bring with us to eternity. And these sufferings make us into who we will be forever. With Jesus we are what we have passed through!

We are not encouraged to skip steps. We cannot just decide to die now and avoid the hassle. To do so would be to risk bringing nothing with us when we go. There may be "no U-Haul behind a hearse." We do not get to bring our "stuff" with us. But we do and will bring our love –- every bit of love, every single wound incurred as we pass through life in God's time, not our own.

"Peace be with you," says the Risen Christ, over and over, and over again, not a peace that takes us out of this world, but one that allows us to live in it with equanimity.

Central to today's gospel is the gift of the Spirit of Jesus, given to the Church. Jesus breathes his spirit on his followers and this Spirit will help us to live in community, in this world. The Spirit of forgiveness, the gift of "letting go" not "holding on," is at the heart of the community of the followers of Jesus as we believers live and love through the ages. If we forgive each other then we can know we are forgiven. If we hold on to each other's faults and foibles then it will be so difficult for us to believe that God does not likewise hold on to them. We become the sprit-filled signs of God's love right here, in this life.

This life matters. What we do with and in this life matters. At the same time I wrestled with the tragic insanity of Heaven's Gate, I found myself celebrating the return to Church, really the re-turn to life of a person who discovered Jesus and God's love this Easter. For the first time he is ready to live. After numerous mistakes, several failed marriages, a nearly life-long inability to love well those who have loved him, life begins. In the face of moral failure and physical disability, for the first time in his life, this Easter he has discovered that he is lovable and loved by God, and can be by others. Before he knew this he was most willing to die. He could have been part of this next-life-cult. Now he is ready to live, for the first time.

Easter is about choosing life, believing in Spring, trusting in love.

Jesus is risen. The newly baptized are risen with him. All of us are renewed in hope. Life, with all its challenges has never looked better. In that Spirit, "Happy Easter!"

27) The Third Sunday of Easter

Scripture Readings: Acts 3:13-15, 17-19; 1 Jn. 2; 1-5; Lk. 24: 35-48

This is the third Time we celebrate Easter. We celebrate Easter over and over because the reality of the Risen Christ, the presence of this Christ in our midst, is the corner stone for everything we believe, everything we live as disciples of Jesus.

The Gospel today concretizes my theoretical framework about Easter. I offer two convictions. First, the Risen Christ is the one we meet now. Second, these early stories of the Risen Christ help us to know where to look for Jesus now. We break open these stories not primarily to understand what happened two thousand years ago, but to understand what is happening to us now!

In that spirit, consider today's Gospel.

We begin in the middle of a longer story. To understand we must recall the wonderful preceding story of the two disciples on the road to Emmaus and how they met Jesus along the road. That story ends as Jesus disappears from their sight; they run back to Jerusalem to tell the others what they saw. In the verses just before today's Gospel the two from Emmaus don't get to tell their story; first they have to listen to the folks who stayed in Jerusalem tell how Jesus came to them. Then the disciples returned from Emmaus tell

> "... what happened on the road and how they came
> to know Jesus in the breaking of the bread."

Then and now the Church is made up of people who have had some experience of the Risen Christ. This experienced is shared with others who have had a similar experience and all are built up in their belief. You come from your life to gather here with me. I tell you what I have seen and heard. You celebrate your own experience and we all leave ready to trust that Christ is truly alive in us.

And, today, still, we do this around the "breaking of the bread."

Our Church tells us Jesus is not just present in the broken bread but is present already in the Community of faith gathered, before we do anything. In today's story, as the Emmaus travelers tell their story, and listen to the story of the Jerusalem disciples, Jesus manifests himself to them again. He is there where two or three are gathered in his name. He is here where we gather in his name.

As in the gospel today, Jesus is also present when the word is broken open. Jesus talks about Moses and the prophets and the psalms. We still meet Jesus when we break open God's word, struggle to make sense of our lives in the light of it. I am struck over and over how Jesus explains the mystery of suffering, insists that "... this had to happen." We still need over and over again to turn to the scripture story, to rub it up against our own stories, to understand why there is so much struggle, hardship, pain in our lives and our world. We need Jesus to help us see how much love costs, how, integrity brings misunderstanding, how virtue is killed. The necessity of suffering in a badly broken world is still true; whenever we grasp this truth, and are able to live with it, we have indeed met the risen Christ.

Parenthetically I am reminded of Scott Peck's inarguable insight with which he begins still relevant treatise: The Road Less Traveled. "Life is Difficult." It is not difficult just for me, not difficult just for today. Life in this fragile world is difficult. Jesus grasped, lived, loved through this truth for our sake a long time ago.

The Resurrection stories present this illusive truth in another way, also. In the story today, as in the Gospel last week, the Risen Christ identifies himself by showing his wounds. These signs of suffering are no longer, brutal, hideous, agonizing. They have become the marks of glory. How dramatic that the Risen Christ still carries the signs of his suffering with him into whatever life is next. They then, we now, know who Jesus is by what he has passed through. We still meet the Risen Christ whenever what were impossible tragedies, painful episodes, destructive relationships, unimaginable losses have been passed through and become part of who we are and will be forever, but are no longer tragic.

The sign of the presence of the Risen Christ frequently involves passion and death passed through and become transformed.

I have a crooked neck from Polio at age eight. I have this sense that in whatever heaven is my neck will still be crooked. People will look at me and say, "He went through live, bravely, with a crooked neck!" On a deeper level I am convinced that I carry with me all the collective pain of my life from sin done by me, and toward me . . . as do we all. When we are able out of faith and hope to overcome the past and move into a light-filled present it is because the Risen Christ is in our midst:

- that divorce we thought we never live through,
- that financial failure,
- that totally unfair damage to our reputation, or our ego, or our credit,
- that life-threatening illness,
- the untimely death of a loved one,

Every possible human pain out of which we stand alive, and still able to risk loving reminds us of the presence of Christ, Risen, alive, and showing his wounds, explaining suffering to us, inviting us to "pass through" our own.

Finally in this reflection on the Risen Christ as the one we still meet today, consider the closing words of the today's Gospel.

"You are witnesses to this!"

We gather here to share our Easter faith, but the most important moment of our gathering is the last. This Eucharist is not something we go to, so much as what we go from, to witness to the truth our world needs to hear. Our experience of the Risen Christ is partially for us, and mostly for others. We have a message to proclaim to all the world once we have again recognized Jesus here in this breaking of the bread.

We need to go from here showing, not just with words, but with lives made whole and holy, that suffering and death do not have the last word, that failure is not final. We live believing that life comes out of death, darkness cannot overcome light, the victory is assured and we have the glorified wounds to prove it. We have a community of faith that keeps reminding us of this truth. We are nourished by this sacred meal where week after week after Easter week we recognize the Risen Christ in this breaking of the bread.

It is to this we witness.

28) The Fourth Sunday of Easter

Scripture Readings: Acts. 4:7-12; I. 3: 1-2; Jn. 10:11-18

Again today we celebrate Easter. For the Fourth Sunday in a row we celebrate Christ risen from the dead. Though today's readings seem to move away from the Easter story, we can let that remind us what is the most important fact about this continuing celebration of Easter. Namely, our concern is not primarily with what happened to Jesus two thousand years ago, but more, what happens to us, now, because of Jesus. What we celebrate through these days till Pentecost is the birth of the Church, of us, in the image of Jesus.

In the reading from Acts Peter and John continue the healing ministry of Jesus and inherit all the conflict that ministry brought Jesus. Our reading from the letter of John reminds us that we are God's children now; baptized into Jesus we continue the life and work and love of his family. In that same Spirit we hear Jesus speak of himself as Good Shepherd in part to remember what Jesus revealed, but more to tell us something about ourselves, his children, his people, his church.

What does this wonderful gospel say about Jesus? What, then does it tell us about ourselves?

First, I love to remember that Jesus comes precisely to give God a face. Paul calls him "The image of the unseen God!" We get to know what God is like by looking at, listening to Jesus. The Good Shepherd is one of the most precious pictures of God. You've seen the pictures.

Jesus, tall, bronzed, bearded, handsome, with a staff in his hand, a single sheep wrapped around his shoulders. Jesus smiles, and so, it seems, does the sheep. This strong, but gentle, caring Jesus is a picture of God, an image of God.

I imagine this shepherd sitting down at the end of the day, checking the feet of each sheep for bruises, looking carefully at their wool for a cut from a fence or a tree. This gentle shepherd binds up wounds, soothes spirits. Once all are settled, the shepherd stands guard so that no thief comes to steal them, no wolf comes to eat them. A picture of God, an image of God.

This shepherd is no hired hand, just doing a job. He's not just making a living, staying busy until something better comes along. These are his sheep. He knows them each by name. He loves them, each one. What a marvelous picture of God – like a perfect mom, a perfect dad. Why he would even give his life for any one of these sheep!

Personally I found this image particularly challenging, frustrating. The word pastor is the same as shepherd. I was for years fascinated by the job description implied for a pastor – knowing each member of the flock personally, by name, caring for them individually as deeply as possible, willing to give up his life for anyone of the flock. What a challenge! As one ages and memory fails. The sheer inability to remember names hints at the larger difficulty of the task ... but what an attractive task it is to be as loving towards the flock of God's people as Jesus was.

I am deeply moved by the image of Jesus being here in this Church, in this community, looking out at us and saying, "I love you, Pat." "I love you, Don." "I love you Ann, or Tina or Dave ..."

I am moved by the image of myself, or any of us, looking at this community with love and saying the same words as we call one another by name.

This love and care that the shepherd has does not mean that nothing bad will ever happen. It doesn't mean that a kid won't fall down the stairs, or another won't be hit by a baseball, or another won't have a problem with his heart. Some really bad stuff happened to Jesus even though God looked out for him. It does mean that God will touch us tenderly, care for us, soothe our wounds, love us in our pain, kiss our various bruises.

The psalmist says:

> "Near restful waters he leads me,
> (the Shepherd) revives my drooping spirit ..."

He does not take away our pain, but is with us in the midst of it. As we remembered in Holy Week, Jesus doesn't suffer and die so that we won't have to, but so that we will be able to.

We have already begun, then, to reflect that this passage is not just about how Jesus is for us. We are Easter people and we become the Shepherd as we let the Risen Christ live in us. This image of how Jesus is, how God is towards us is also the image of how we are invited to be for each other.

Once I presided at a family wedding, a huge affair with several hundred people. Many were of different faiths, or no religious conviction at all. After the wedding I had many, many people almost in awe remark on how personal the wedding was, how warm. It was, after all, my nephew getting married. I called the couple by name, and I do love them. I was struck by what these compliments said about most wedding these guests must have attended. Their general experience in church was so distant, so ritualistic, so formal. Where was the Shepherd? This image of the Shepherd invites us to make our Church services warm, personal, loving, caring?

This image of Jesus the Good Shepherd challenges us to surround the neophytes in our midst, those who celebrated the Easter Sacraments, with this individual, called-by-name love, to welcome them warmly deeply into our midst.

This image of Jesus the Good Shepherd challenges us to notice and care for the sick, shut-in, home-bound in our midst – to visit them, to pray for them, to keep reminding them that they are loved.

This image of Jesus the Good Shepherd challenges us to treat any sick child as, in some very real sense, our own – "Holding them tenderly, close to our hearts, leading them home."

This image of the Good Shepherd is why a parish has a homeless shelter, or a tent city, or n evening of feeding at Matt Talbott Center, or St. Vincent de Paul group of parishioners vising hurting neighbors in our name.

As a people, a church, our challenge is to become like Jesus for each other and for all. We try to take care of one another, to make sure there is for everyone a place to sleep, something to each, a heart to hold onto. When one of our family gets hurt, we hurt. When someone dies, we grieve.

We don't do this perfectly, but this is what we who are baptized, we who today again share in communion with Jesus at this altar say we must try to do.

Today, then we celebrate two things as we celebrate Easter again.

First, we celebrate that our God is like a wonderful shepherd, a perfect mom or dad, or like Jesus who loves us deeply and personally and calls us each by name.

Secondly, we celebrate that all of us are invited, challenged, helped together to be the body of Christ, to be Jesus, to be a collective shepherd to the hurts of each other.

It is a scary thing to say but it is at the heart of today's Gospel message:

God looks like Jesus! And Jesus looks like us!

29) The Fifth Sunday of Easter

Scripture Readings: Acts. 9:26-31; 1 Jn. 3:18-24; Jn. 15: 1-8

What happens to us because of Easter. It's so simple, so terribly simple. Nowhere in the New Testament is the summary more straightforward, more clear than in John's letter today. This is the commandment, this is what matters.

"Believe in the Lord Jesus Christ; love one another!"

We are invited not just to talk about this but to act on it . . . "in deed, not just in words." If we were able to do this – to believe in Jesus, and love each other – everything would change. That's what we are about, that's the point of Easter as we celebrate it over, and over, and over again. We are people who try to believe in Jesus and love one another. Everything else is a relatively unimportant footnote!

Some years ago I was with a group of high school students as a young African American man spoke to them about being Christian.

He told them of his conversion from being in a gang. He had hesitated a long time because, as he said,

"I thought if I believed in Jesus I could never do any of the things I wanted,

but then, when I fell in love with Jesus, from that moment on I could do exactly what I wanted all the time. But all my "'want-to's changed!"

"All my want-to's changed!" If I fall in love with Jesus, all my want-to's change! That's the Easter message we hear today. All we want to do is to love one another.

That's what happened to Paul. Paul had been a Pharisee, a perfect student and keeper of the law. He knew every jot and tittle. He was willing to persecute those that were following this new "Way" of Jesus. The story today tells how after he was knocked off his high horse Paul changed. All his commandments, all his 'want-to's", changed.

From that moment of conversion on what mattered to Paul was believing in Jesus Christ, and loving people: He was willing to be himself persecuted. He envisioned a community where every part of the body depended on every other part, where there were many gifts, but the greatest was not fidelity to the law, but love, where there was neither Jew nor Greek, nor male or female, but all were one body in Christ, and no part of the body could say to any other part "I do not need you."

Paul's entire understanding of what mattered religiously changed. And so can mine. Let me tell you about a similar personal image.

For several years after I was ordained the thing that most bugged me was the infighting in the church:

- between liberals and conservatives, those that wanted way more change and those that didn't want any,
- between those that wanted a Catholic School and those that didn't want to spend the money that way,
- between people that wanted to spend money renovating the Church and those that wanted to care for the poor,
- between those that longed for more inclusive language that those that shuttered at any change in traditional prayers,
- between those that wanted desperately to sing, and those that only wanted to listen.

We fought about renovating churches,
about moving tabernacles,
about teaching of religion,
about building a senior retirement home and blocking out stained class windows,
about when to do Confirmation,
who whether women may preach,
about encouraging gay members to fully participate
and on and on and on.

I couldn't imagine why I used up so much of my energy getting along with the people I was supposed to be working with to change the world.

Finally I "got it." Getting along with each other was not an unnecessary struggle in the midst of everything else we were doing. *Getting along with each other is what we are doing.* What we do "out there," is far less important than doing it together, loving each other, struggling together to be the body of Christ. If we fall in love with Jesus our very deepest "want to" is to get along with each other. The only commandment that matters is to believe in Jesus Christ and love one another!

Believe in Jesus, and love each other.

The Gospel today ties this truth together. We are bound together like branches of a single vine. The same life flows in us, keeps us alive, makes us one with and dependent on each other whether we want to be or not. We cannot live apart from the vine and the vine has all these other messy branches. Jesus lives in us together, and we find our life in him and without him living in us we can do nothing.

A final word about the gospel that really challenges me. If we listen carefully to the Gospel today Jesus suggests that we will suffer. We will suffer if we stay with him. We will suffer if we don't. The gospel puts it this way:

"He prunes away every barren branch."

"The fruitful ones he trims to increase the yield."

If I don't live in Jesus, don't try to love, I will suffer, by being pruned away. If I do live in Jesus and try to love I will suffer by being trimmed. How do I tell the difference? This trimming can feel a lot like pruning.

The point is that even though I do what I want to as a disciple of Jesus even though I live freely and with hope, to love means to suffer. Paul, like Jesus was killed for what he believed. But the suffering was fruitful, it yielded rich harvest ... and that is the only kind of suffering that should be endured. Now the central point is to try to love each other, to live through our disagreements, our arguments, our differences, to make our relationships with each other more important than the things we argue about is very, very, very painful.

All those struggles, arguments, contentions among the followers of Jesus today are born and worked through, loved through, because finally to so will bear fruit. It is really difficult today to work through all the things that can divide us in the Church, in civil society, in our own parish or family. It can be really painful not to!

What I want to do – and as a follower of Jesus I can always do what I want to – is to face all the issues that are problematic, be open about where we stand on them, wrestle our way through them, and keep loving each other as we do so. There the Spirit of Jesus lies.

So, we turn now to drink, in Eucharist, the fruit of the vine, the one life uniting us all together. We believe in Jesus; we love, not just in words but in deeds, our brothers and sisters who share this one bread this one fruit of the vine with us.

30) The Sixth Sunday of Easter

Scripture Readings: Acts. 10:25-26, 34-35, 44-48; 1 Jn. 4:7-10; Jn. 15:9-17

I begin my reflections today with the sad realization of how many people I have known deeply committed to Jesus who began their adult lives trying to live and love and serve in his image and then made a mess of it. I begin saddened at the people who choose to spend their lives with the poor but burned out, those who gave themselves to every cause, every burning issue, every Gospel mandate and had their marriages fail, or their children tragically fall apart, or found their lives buried in alcoholism or premature death, real or psychological.

I begin conscious of my own youthful desire to love God and God's people and all my well-intentioned failures along the path.

The second reading from last week invited us to reflect on the central reality that God's command to us is

"To Believe in the Lord Jesus, and to Love each other.

That's it, that's all. Everything else, I had the temerity to suggest, can be considered "a relatively unimportant footnote." Today's readings re-inforce and underline the centrality of that command but with a terribly important caution.

Even though the Gospel today repeats the simple statement:

"This is the command I give you, That you love one another,"

we are at the same time reminded that this love starts and continues with God, not with us. We are urged to "Live in God's love."

Today I want to suggest how terribly important is this caution.

I was for many years inspired and challenged by the presence of Jesuit volunteers in the midst of wherever I was serving. Every year these young, intelligent, idealistic young people come, leave everything they are familiar with behind, take a job serving the poor, live simply in community on about $60.00 a month . . . and have a great time doing so! Very often I was personally challenged by their simple life-style, their ability to do without a lot of stuff. I looked at their life style compared with my own, or the Jesuits I lived with and wondered who is authentic. I have heard the same question from them. But over the years I have come to realize two very connected, very important truths.

First, they are living this way for one, maybe two years;; others are in it for the long haul. Second, the call to simplicity of life is a vocation that has to start with God to be endured with joy and laughter. It is not something someone decides to do, on his or her own.

This realization helps me look at the scripture today. The readings are rooted in God's initiative necessarily before our response..

The amazing first reading from Acts tells the story of Peter and the apostles being surprised and converted. They thought their message was only for Jewish people, not Gentiles. They believed that if they were to invite non-Jews into this new "Way," such converts would necessarily need to follow the entire Jewish law. Then God acts and gives this entire Gentile household the gift of the Holy Spirit before the Apostles had even decided to baptize them. Before they get their act together, God acts. they respond to what God has already done in their midst. It is always so, or should be!

The letter to John suggests, even as it reminds us that the one important invitation is to love each other, that love consists in this:

"Not that we have loved God but that God has first loved us."

The simple reality is this. If we try to live a life of love, if we try to love everyone as God loves us, if we take seriously this first commandment without stopping long enough to let ourselves be loved first, we will fail.

The first movement of a Christian person is not service. It's prayer.

The first activity of a follower of Jesus is not to do something for another, but to let God do something for us. The first significant thing I do is to do nothing!

I think the holiest people I know are people who started on the wrong track, fell apart, then got the idea. I think of a priest friend who spends his life living with and serving the poor. When

I knew him he came home every day exhausted, worn out with the tiredness of compassion. And he ended that day with an hour or more of quiet reflection, writing in a journal, debriefing the day to see where God has been present. And he started the next day with quiet time, prayer, letting God love him to the place where he can pour himself out in love again. He had enough burn out, enough failure, enough wasted years to know that he has to let God love him first ... or he has nothing to give, and he cannot continue to try.

All God asks us to do is to love one another. All God asks us to do is to lay down our lives for our friends. All God asks us to do is to give to all our brothers and sisters the love God has for them. But God asks us to let love be given to us First!

How does a parent keep trying to love the child that continues to be rebellious, continues to push the edges, stretch the truth, test every possible limit? Only if that parent is first filled with God's love for him, for her?

How does a spouse continue to love and hope in the alcoholic, or unfaithful husband or wife? Only if he or she has first know the awesome fidelity of God's love.

How does a teacher hang in there when the administration is not supportive and the students are not responsive, and the system is broken, but Joe and Suzy and Skeeter and Natalie and Pedro need her to be in that classroom? Only when she has first known to her toes the love God has for her. And on and on and on.

We can only love with love of God when God's love fills us up.

So here we are at this Eucharist. Are we fulfilling an obligation? Are we doing something to please God by our presence here? Is Sunday Mass something we do for God or for ourselves? Personally I come here week after week, I listen to this word, I share this body and blood because I need to know God loves me and nowhere is this more clear than around this altar, when the life of Jesus is given to me . . . not because I have earned or deserved or somehow become worthy of it, but because I need it so badly.

This is what love is all about; not that I/ we have loved God, but that God has first loved us. I need to abide in that love. Join me!

31) The Feast of the Ascension

Scripture Readings: Acts. 1:1-11; Eph. 4:1-13; Mk. 16:15-20

The context for today's liturgy is huge. There are a lot of things going on:

It's Mother's Day, school is winding down, some graduations already have happened, and we have had lots of post Easter Baptisms. We celebrate, today, The Feast of the Ascension, and It's Spring — all related somehow in one line from the Gospel. In the New Revised Standard Version the line is translated like this::

> (Jesus) was taken up into heaven and sat down at the right hand of God; They went out and proclaimed the Good News everywhere!

Jesus sat down; they went out.

Jesus was finished with his work on earth and now he works in and through his followers as they

give birth, and raise their children,
go to school,
enter into the community of believers,
become the Church,
and relish the lives they have been given in this world.

I had a priest friend who regularly said:

"I'm not trying to get to heaven;
I'm just trying to get down to earth."

This is the culmination of the Easter season. For fifty days we pay attention not just to what happened to Jesus but what happens to us because of Jesus. This feast of the Ascension begins a 10 day celebration of the beginning of that Church that will conclude next week at Pentecost. Ascension and Pentecost together are our birthday as a Church, a people; We are trying to get "down to earth." As Jesus enters back into the fullness of the life of God he leaves behind his followers, living in his spirit, to continue his work.

The Spirit of the Risen Jesus lives in the Church, lives in us.

He sits down; we take up the mission.

The first reading from Acts tells of an Angel rebuking the disciples, asking "Why are you looking up to Heaven?" Get about your lives. Spread the message.

And we celebrate today what that might mean.

We are to give birth to life in our world. As Mothers, some cooperate with God in the continual process of new birth, new life. We reverence the gift of life; we nurture and support and encourage others as they grow into adulthood.

Like the prototypical mother of Jesus we proclaim the greatness of God who does wonderful things in us. We invite our loved ones to use their gifts for the good of others. They have no more wine, we say, and our children bring forth more than they knew they could. We stand by and support those we have loved in the midst of their sufferings.

All of us, the followers of Jesus are invited to mother life and love in our world and we are grateful today for those who do that so literally, our mothers.

We baptize; we invite new members into our community, invite them to die and rise with Jesus as we have done. We promise to support them in their life of faith, and to see them called to the same one body, one spirit as our selves. We keep becoming an ever wider, ever deeper body of Christ.

We go to school, literally and figuratively; we keep learning about our faith, ourselves, our world. We pursue and never turn away from knowledge. We read and study and think and pray for everything tells us a little more about our God, and the world whose betterment our God has charged us with. Sometimes, at stages measured or not, we graduate, and move to new challenges, new questions.

This feast of the Ascension is the beginning of our birth as people, a Church, a community that embraces and loves this world and its people as passionately as Jesus did, does.

If this feast truly occurs; if it transforms us and gives us new birth, then we are changed; something happens to us.

I Imagine myself walking down the street. I see a naked, crying child, shivering in the cold and am deeply moved. Later I hear the cry of violence in an apartment above me in the street. I see in the headlines of a Newspaper on the corner headlines featuring yet another battle in yet another war.

When I return home I kneel and pray, a little angry at God.

"Why do you permit such pain? Why don't you do something?"

I wait for an answer and for a long time, God is silent. In the middle of the night I hear the voice, finally, saying: "I did do something; I created you, all of you."

"Why are you looking up to Heaven?"

Jesus sat down; "The disciples went out and proclaimed the Good News everywhere."

32) Pentecost

Scripture Readings: Acts 2:1-11; Gal. 5: 16-25; Jn. 20: 19-23

We human beings are wonderfully complex and terribly predictable. We come into life needing to be gently slapped to begin to breathe new air. We leave life reluctantly, often the spirit hanging on staying alive after every system of the body seems to be finished. At every moment of life we resist new birth, resist change, resist giving up the familiar for the new.

I have heard human life described as a movement from one trapeze bar to the other. Just as we get comfortable on one, swinging back and forth, we have to let go and wait for the other to come with our feet firmly planted in mid-air.

My wife and I moved this weekend from one apartment/condo to another, just across the street. I can't find anything, especially in the kitchen. Where are my socks. Small change, but difficult as one ages.

I am aware of endings and new beginnings today, at Pentecost – the finale to the long season of Lent and Easter. For the past three months we have celebrated who we are as Christians, remembered the story of Jesus who died and rose again, remembered why this story matters to us. We have celebrated what happens to us because of Jesus. Today we are, in a sense, cut loose and invited to live out what we have declared and celebrated.

Jesus gives his spirit to us and sends us out into the world – the world that killed him. His mission and perhaps his fate become ours.

Quite naturally we are reluctant to go.

I remember a new Catholic from a few years ago, a lobbyist in Olympia. His job was to urge lawmakers to legislate and act on behalf of the poor. He spent his work days cajoling, arguing, compromising. He spoke often of how difficult he found it to bring his faith life, its vision and energy, to work with him. He loved Sundays in the parish. He loved our mid-week gatherings on Wednesday. But in between he found it easy to forget.

Pentecost is about living our Faith on Monday. It's about being a disciple of Jesus while we raise four kids alone,
or while acting as City attorney
or labor as a nurse,
or teach small children.
Pentecost is about proclaiming the good news in a legal office,
or while selling stuff,
or driving a truck,
or hanging up pictures
or moving into a new home
or singing with the sweet Adelines.

How do we carry Lent and Easter with us into ordinary time? How do we act as believers on Monday and Friday? The invitation to do so touches every part of our Pentecost readings.

On Pentecost, in Acts, the disciples have a profound experience of the presence of the Spirit of Jesus. They see tongues like fire. They speak in strange languages. They are on Fire. They cannot just stay in that upper room having a "good time with Jesus." They must go into the market place, the square where all the people were gathered. They must find a way, inspired by God, to speak in languages everyone could understand, sharing their profound experience with others, with all.

In the second reading to the Galatians, we were reminded that whatever gifts we have, whatever we receive is not for us alone. Gifts are given not for the individual but for the community. We are not blessed by God and loved by Jesus so that we feel all good and cuddly with them, but so that we can go and give whatever we have to the building up of the body, the Kingdom.

It is in the gospel that we especially see our invitation to Monday, to ordinary time, to the market place. We are called and challenged to be a very different presence in our world. Jesus shows up in the midst of the disciples, the church (note it is not the "twelve", not just apostles) on Easter Sunday night. He breathes on all his followers, saying:

> "Receive the holy Spirit ... as the Father has sent me
> so I send you ..."

We are given the Spirit of Jesus to disperse it to the world. and spirit is precisely a spirit of forgiveness. This gift of forgiveness is not, in the first instance, given primarily to those in charge, but to the Church. We are to be a spirit of forgiveness pervading our world, spreading the forgiving mission of Jesus, himself.

Many of us were gathered together at the Easter Vigil. We lit a new fire against the darkness; we lit our own candles and held them against the night as we sang the song of Jesus victory over death. After the readings and the water and the oil we asked the Elect (and ourselves with them):

Do you want to plunge into the baptismal waters?

Do you want to die with Christ?

And Rise again to new and more abundant life?

They said "Yes," and were baptized. We said "Yes" with them.

We spread out the gifts liturgically, but Easter and Pentecost are, in a deep sense the same event. Here we ask the neophytes and ourselves:

Are you ready to be empowered by the Spirit to go forth from here, to move from Sunday to Monday?

From liturgical celebration of our faith, to the living out of that faith in the market place?

In the schools where you work, the buildings you build, the songs you sing, the laws you enforce, the mail you deliver, the families you are part of?

Are you ready to go with Jesus from the mountains of Transfigured vision to the hillside of suffering?

To speak the truth to those who need but may not want to hear it?

Are you willing to forgive and not hold onto hurts, to set others free?

As the Father has sent me so I am sending you!
The gifts you have are for the Common Good!
Go, and speak my love in language all can understand!

33) The Feast of the Holy Trinity

Scripture Readings: Deut. 4:32-34, 39-40; Ro. 8:14-17; Mt. 28: 16-20

As we begin I invite you to be still and close your eyes. As I mention a word, form a picture of that word in your mind. I will go slowly; just form and relish for a moment whatever picture comes:

Tree,
Sunshine,
My friend,
My mother,
Guns
Happiness,

God.

I am tempted to invite you to tell the person next to you what you pictured at the word "God." (Perhaps do so)

If you are like most people you went temporarily blank, had no picture at all. Amazingly, many will still get a picture of an old man with a gray beard. I guess I wish more people (especially after our long, Lent-Easter-Pentecost time)came up with some picture of Jesus, (who is "the image of the invisible God") or perhaps of a community, like this, gathered in Jesus' name.

The point of this simple exercise is that this feast of the Holy Trinity is a feast of "God," a celebration of God, our multiple images, the variety of ways that we try to explain our relationship with this God. As we celebrate the classic names given to different dimensions of our relationship with God we enter into both danger and wonder

The danger of the Feast is that by God as Father, Son and Spirit we may think w even come close to knowing, or defining God. It is dangerous to believe that we can pin God down.

The wonder of this feast is that our church helps us to know that our God comes with many faces: Father, Mother, Son, brother, friend, companion, Spirit, love, community of love.

The readings we heard today tease out the images of our tradition.

Deuteronomy insists that our God is not a long ways away. God speaks, God is very near, gives us direction, helps us on our journey. The Jewish people, u and we who inherit their tradition, knew that nobody else has ever had a God like this. God is close, is overseer of our fate, is our friend, our good guide.

The reading from Romans suggests that when Christ comes we really are God's adopted children, part of God's family, co-heirs with Christ. We can speak to this God with terms of endearment.

Unlike Paul's Jewish tradition where people skipped over God's name when they came to it in scripture, we become a people who speak tenderly, intimately to our God. We call our God Abba, not Father really, but Daddy, or Pop.

And at the end of Matthew's gospel which we listen to this day we hear Jesus, who has been given the fullest authority of God, pass that authority on to his followers, to us. In the name of this God who is like a Father, like a Son, like a Spirit that is Holy, we are to go out to all the earth and invite people from all the world into relationship with God . . . a God who will be with us until the end of the world.

So today we close our eyes and try to image God. And every image fails, every image is partial, incomplete, to some extent untrue. But we trust the direction of those images that tell us we are loved, those images that invite us to love.

I find myself on this feast wondering about my own God-Images, the ones that I really employ, that work for me, that help me pray.

Paul Tillich's "Ground of Being" has always made sense to me. God is the place where we stand, that on which, on whom, everything is built. Perhaps for me God is more a backdrop, in front of which or whom everything is played out, enacted. At my best I see absolutely everything against the backdrop of God . . .

One of my most powerful personal images of God arises out of an experience shortly after I was ordained a priest. I went with one of my theology professors to visit a hospital where the child of a friend of his was critically ill. I stood slightly outside the room as he entered. His friend was beside herself, distraught, in deep pain. She began to berate him yelling:

"Where is your God now? My child is dying, so painfully! Where is that God of yours. Tell me about your God!"

This priest was a large bear of a man, somewhat awkward socially but with a heart as large as his amazing brain. I watched in awe as this brilliant theologian went across the room, took the woman in his arms and said:

"I can't explain anything to you, but I can hold onto you!"

As he embraced her I felt God's presence, and so did she. That image has stayed with me for a long time as a powerful picture of the only God we know.

A former co-worker of mine, a recovering alcoholic himself, captured something of this same idea when he explained the enormous compassion with which he often met a "drunk" in the neighborhood, or at the door of our parish offices,

"I may be the only 'Big Book' this person ever reads!"

As we celebrate this feast of God, under our hallowed images of Father, Son and Spirit, our personal image is important. What do the words mean and how is our relationship transformed by them? Every image is, indeed, imperfect. But God is revealed to us,

Very near to us,
who are like adopted children.
This God sends us to the whole world telling the story of unimaginable love.

What does this love look like, feel like, seem like to you and how can you proclaim it?

34) The Feast of the Body and Blood of Christ

Scripture Readings: Ex. 24:3-8; Heb. 9: 11-18; Mk. 14:12-16, 22-26

(Note: Because, historically, this feast has been thought of as Corpus Christ, The Body of Christ, it is important this year to indicate at the outset that in cycle "B" the focus is much more on The Blood of Christ than on the Body.)

One of the most difficult human tasks is understanding a culture different from our own. As a Caucasian Priest I make some incredible gaffs dealing with people of different backgrounds, worlds with which I am insufficiently familiar. I recall often my first effort to plan a funeral for a Native American family. As usual I met with the family and tried to elicit remembrances about the deceased. The family sat in almost total, stoic silence. I did not yet have their trust and I was either unable, or unwilling to take the time needed to be with them in such an intimate way. I didn't serve them very well.

I lived this year with two seminarians from Nigeria and heard them tell a "horror" story about the first Jesuit community they lived in when they came to this country. Once they got settled they purchased food with which they were familiar. After they prepared a single meal they returned home the next day to discover the Jesuit minister of the house had thrown all he food out because "it smelled funny" to him. All they could see was years ahead of them eating foods that smelled and looked funny to them.

More pertinent to our subject of Christ's blood today, I recently heard about two showings of a typical "slasher movie" of our era. At one a teenage audience met the spectacle of much blood, mayhem, and gore with laughter and clapping throughout. The same movie shown to their parents was greeted with uncomfortable silence and gasps of horror. The reaction to the rampantly bloody was quite different. I'll return to this observation later.

First, let me recall that the very feast we celebrate today, originally called Corpus Christi, was established by Roman Catholics in opposition to what we thought was the Lutheran denial of the real presence of Christ in the Eucharist. On this Sunday we asserted with great pomp and celebration our deep seated belief. 400 years later we began to talk to Lutherans and discover for the most part that their belief is quite similar to our own, but uses different language to explain that belief.

In so many ways we make assumptions, usually false, about cultures with which we do not communicate.

I begin with these cultural reflections today because our appreciation of the readings for the feast of the Body and Blood of Christ this year depends on our ability to totally immerse ourselves in a foreign culture. Our readings, our insights today are buried in Jewish culture, Jewish concepts, Jewish faith that will shed light on our own faith and practice only if we first take the time to understand theirs.

To celebrate the Eucharistic symbols we hear about today, we need to see those symbols buried in a culture. Then we can begin to realize that blood is a sign of life -- when blood drains from a body, the body is dead; where there is blood flowing there is still life. Immersed in Judaism we would realize that blood splattered first on an altar and then on a people seals the life of God shared with those people. We would become aware of a sacred meal in which the eldest present explains to all present the symbolic meaning of every particle of food taken, each sip of wine drunk. When Jesus speaks over the bread and wine calling them his body, his blood, he continues, then transforms a 2000 year old tradition.

Young and old in our own culture vary in our approach to blood; imagine the difference if, truly acting out of our Jewish roots, we did our Eucharist quite differently. Imagine ourselves at the entrance rite of Mass not sprinkling just a few drops of water, or at communion just taking a sip of wine. Imagine ourselves rather gathering around an altar literally soaked in blood, and that blood in profuse abundance being sprinkled over us. Imagine if instead of drinking from a cup of wine that the cup was, indeed, filled with blood and that blood was poured over us each in turn as we approached the table.

We may think this was bizarre, but we would also realize it was something terribly important. We would doubtless hesitate before getting involved in something so truly messy. We would be wary of performing a ritual that would certainly change us.

Beneath any authentic cultural symbols lies an abundance of meanings. Let me reflect for a moment on two things we might catch in this symbol of a cup shared, blood drunk if we approach them from our Jewish roots:

First, our sharing in this cup at every Eucharist would invite us to share in the very life of Jesus.

Jesus says: "This is the blood of the covenant to be poured out on behalf of many." The blood of Jesus is shed and poured out on this altar; then taken and sprinkled on us, shared by us. We are united in a new bond of love with God We say we can drink the cup that Jesus drank. We who share in the life of Jesus enter into a covenant promise to share his blood, his life, and then his mission. We are promising to pour our blood out for others as he does.

- We may find ourselves disturbing the civil or religious peace as Jesus did, risking everything on God. We may sprinkle blood on a nuclear weapon, or trespass at the School of the Americas – taking a risky stance because we share the values of Jesus, and must stop or prevent the shedding of others' blood.
- We may sit by the bed of a dying loved one when others who should be there aren't but we pour out our lives for our loved one.
- We may take a brand new stance in the middle of our lives in ways that appear foolish to those around us as did the death of Jesus even to his best friends.
- To share in the cup of this blood is to share in the life, the mission, and perhaps even the fate of Jesus.

Secondly, wherever blood is poured out and people suffer, Jesus still suffers and invites our compassion. The blood of Christ splattered on a people, poured out on a community like ours suggests that this people shares in the very life of Jesus. So, when or wherever the blood of any of us is taken, our lives are threatened, our sacrifice is asked, it is, again, Christ suffering.

When any human person for whom Christ shed his blood is forced to suffer, Jesus suffers again, suffers still. The same compassion, sympathy, concern that we might give to Jesus, we would want to give to them. This splattered blood is the symbolic source for our deep, but often ignored belief that all of us are not only Christ-risen; we are also Christ-suffering. The hungry, naked, imprisoned are Christ. His blood is their blood, his life their life, his suffering, their suffering.

To return to where I began, when the power of this blood symbol from another culture gets inside of us, takes over our consciousness, then this Eucharist can change everything we think, everything we are.

We call ourselves to share over and over in the mission of Jesus because we are splattered with the blood of Jesus.

We bring compassion to all in our world who suffer because they are splattered with the blood of Jesus.

Perhaps today at this Eucharist our drinking from this cup will have a power and a challenge it has never had before.

35) The Tenth Sunday of the Year

Scripture Readings: Gen. 3:8-15; 2 Cor. 4:13-5:1; Mk. 3: 20-35

Throughout the Gospel of Mark the story of Jesus is the story of the struggle of the forces of good versus the forces of evil. The story of the Church, the followers of Jesus, is the story of the struggle between good and evil. This struggle is the focus of an outstanding book, the title of which – "Binding the Strong Man" – arises from the Gospel passage we listened to today.

This struggle between good and evil is the human story, a story that has not changed much in 2000 years. Really it hasn't changed much from the beginning. The first reading today from the Book of Genesis is part of a story poem that hints at the origins of sin, the origins of evil. Sadly the version we heard today leaves out the final verses which promise that God will work with us and goodness will eventually triumph. What we hear today is the division between people who are under stress from their selfish choices.

The man blames the woman, the woman blames the serpent. Men and women are at odds with each other, and with nature as the sad story of sin and evil begins.

Jesus enters into this world of sin and separation. Our God does not stay apart from the fray. That is the point of today's gospel. Let me take a few moments to break open that story.

Today's gospel is a very tight, very dense, rather difficult selection. It is a kind of "sandwich passage" beginning and ending with vignette about Jesus and his family, surrounding an accusation against Jesus that he is in cahoots with the devil. Jesus' relationship with and reflections on his family are related to the struggle against the forces of evil. Rather than try to unveil every aspect of the passage, I want to focus on just two points.

First, in Mark's Gospel, though Satan is strong, Jesus is "the strong one." John the baptizer had foretold that one would come who was greater/ stronger than he. This strong one is Jesus. In this passage Jesus talks about entering the strong one's house and binding the strong one, overpowering the strong one. He assets that he is not working with the demonic, but is rather the one who is stronger than the power of evil. He binds up the strong one as God's Kingdom bursts into history.

Secondly, consider the saying about blaspheming against the Holy Spirit. There are various explanations of this passage; no one seems exactly sure what it means. But in the context it appears clearly to mean "refusing to acknowledge that the work of Jesus is the work of God's own power." That is, to deny the Jesus is to deny the Holy Spirit, to call the Divine Demonic.

It is not that God makes up a rule saying "This sin is so awful that it is the only one God can't forgive." Rather Jesus simply asserts the fact that if someone obstinately refuses to see the good in him, then God's Spirit cannot get at them.

Let me say this more simply, in everyday language that relates to us. If someone thinks that Jesus is crazy, or that the values of Jesus are crazy or demonic; if someone thinks that caring for the poor, or laying down life for a friend is crazy or demonic then there is simply no way that the Spirit can get at them. God's hands are tied.

In the passage today Jesus own family comes out to bring him home. When he entered into the struggle of Good versus Evil, his relatives were embarrassed by him. They want him to be quiet and quit making waves. Some of those closest to him do not realize the power that has come into the world through him.

Many times I have heard a parent's strange concern about a son or daughter who has taken on the values of Jesus by joining the Jesuit Volunteer Corps, or some other kind of low or non-paying social service work. I have heard such parents say, in effect,

"That's crazy; he's got a college education. Why doesn't he get a real job?" Why fight against poverty or injustice when you can be making money, getting some security, building a reputation.

This small example is dangerously compounded when we experience those who struggle to help the poor, or to effect the structures that create poverty dismissed as "radical" or "leftists," or "commies". But it happens too frequently. I have had good friends jailed and known Jesuits killed because they took on the values of Jesus and spoke or acted on behalf of the poor. People said about them as they did about Jesus, "He seems crazy," or "He's got a demon," or "he works with demons."

The point most simply is that today's Gospel invites us to stand with Jesus and his unlikely values, his world changing vision. Jesus invites us to go with his vision against the forces of evil that abound in our everyday life.

We know two things; In a world where evil is rampant the values of Jesus will be challenged. But these values will, ultimately, triumph.

We can stand with the values of Jesus on a couple of different levels.

First, on the Familial level:

Mark suggests that Jesus family had some trouble with his way of life. That is still too often the case. But we can respect and honor and encourage the choices our loved ones make to stand against the "strong one," the dominant values of our culture. We can love and set free our children, our friends who choose to live simply. We can encourage those who consciously work at bringing people together rather than dividing them by gender, religion, age, race, nationality, or sexual orientation. We can lend support to those who try in various ways to be peacemakers.

And, with Jesus encouragement we can expand our notion of family beyond those related by blood. We can extend our understanding of brother and sister to all who share in building God's Kingdom. Jesus says, as he spreads his arm all over this church,

> "These are my mother, sister, brother;
> These are brother, sister, mother father, family to one
> another."

We are invited with Jesus to extend our sense of family to everyone who lives out the vision and the values of Jesus.

We can also stand with Jesus on the world-social level:

There is constantly a cosmic struggle going on between the forces of good and evil, the forces that separate and those that unite. Wherever we work, or live, or love, we are always involved in activities that touch human values.

We stand with or against Jesus by:our reaction to a sexist or racist joke, our attitude towards the poor, the homeless, anyone different from ourselves, our discussion, actions, attitudes towards other religions, cultures, nations, our more or less seamless garment regarding life issues from the Death Penalty, to care for the unborn, to compassionate care to the end for the undying perhaps especially these days by our pleading on behalf of refugees and immigrants so harshly treated by our own authorities as as asylum seekers are jailed and children are separated from their parents.

All of these are ways for us to stand with Jesus in "binding the strong one," working with him to overcome the diabolic forces that pervade our world.

I am reminded as I reflect on the scriptures today of a meditation in The Spiritual Exercises of St. Ignatius. Ignatius invites us to imagine the world as a great battle field. At each end of the field a general gathers an army under a banner, a standard. Satan invites his minions to gather under a standard of riches, honor, the pride of a great name on earth. Conversely, Jesus invites his followers to gather with him in poverty, humility, the cross. The point of the meditation is not to ask whose side we are on, but rather to be honest about the values we espouse: Which values do we live, pass on to others. What do we label as foolish, crazy, demonic?

Today, At Eucharist, can we unite ourselves again, no matter the cost, with the values of Jesus? Can we join him in his fragility in his efforts to bind up the strong one?

36) The Eleventh Sunday of the Year

Scripture Readings: Ez. 17:22-23; 2 Cor. 5:6-10; Mk. 4: 26-34

I enjoy preaching and generally feel that I do it well, but whenever I begin to get proud about my skill or artistry I try to recall a most humbling experience.

One morning after Mass a man came to me with tears in his eyes thanking me profusely for how much my words helped him that day. Something prompted me to ask, for future reference, what in particular of the many profound things I had said touched him. He replied that when I said at the very beginning "The Lord is with you," he was overwhelmed by the realization of the truth of that simple statement. He admitted he didn't hear much of anything I said after that greeting; still the awareness of God's presence with him was wonderful and he was deeply grateful.

That this simple ritual greeting moved him far more than my carefully prepared words strikes me again as we listen to the readings today.

Even while we are asleep, the first parable suggests, stuff grows, and life happens and joy in abundance comes. We plant a tiny seed, the second parable suggests, and the biggest imaginable tree can grow.

Both parables remind us that the kingdom of God comes and grows by God's power rather than by ours.

Once, at a party for our eighth grade graduates I heard a parent say about a particularly insightful comment from their daughter, "Sometimes I wonder where she came from." Haven't we all stood in awe that our children learn things, we never knew, have insight we never had, compassion we've never felt. We may plant and water, but God gives the increase.

Obviously, on the most basic level, this word of God encourages us to let God be God, let God be in charge. Everything we care so much about from raising our children, to changing the world, to building the Kingdom of God depends more on God than on us. That is a good thing to remember.

But I find the most consoling and challenging implication of this Gospel comes into play when I experience not the successes, but the pain of world. Sometimes life is awfully fragile, even ugly. Things today seem bad and getting worse. "Things fall apart, the center cannot hold." No matter how hard we try, we cannot improve the world very much.

The Eighth grade graduate continues to make mistakes than can be very costly. Our family finances spiral down hill with no apparent course correction. The numbers of hungry or homeless or hapless increase steadily. Good people continue to leave our Church both because it resists change and because it changes too much.

We listen to Jesus; he stands with us as he did with his followers centuries ago. He assures us that the growth of God's kingdom in our midst is the work of God, the result of God's power, not ours.

He will speak other words encouraging us to keep working, keep plugging away,

keep being "light to the world and salt for the earth,"

keep "loving one another, so that the world can believe,"

keep "feeding the hungry, clothing the naked, hungering and thirsting for justice."

But today, at this Eucharist he balances that word of action with a word of receptivity. He reminds us today that no matter how hard we try, the fruitfulness depends on a framework and a God far bigger than we see.

Ignatius of Loyola is reputed to have said:

> "Work as if everything depended on you,
> and pray as if everything depended on God."

This encouragement urges us to much harder work.

I have heard more lately that what Ignatius said was actually the opposite, and to me it makes much more sense:

"Pray as if everything depended on you,
and work as if everything depended on God."

Should I learn to do this I would be much more fervent in my prayer, and much more relaxed in my work; not a bad combination, and faithful to the Gospel this morning.

37) The Twelfth Sunday in Ordinary Time

Scripture Readings: Job. 38:1-4, 8-11; 2 Cor. 5:14-17; Mk. 4: 35-41

I remember preaching on this Gospel some years ago at a time when I must have personally been in some serious funk. I recall being deeply caught up in the line yelled out by the disciples in the boat as Jesus slept, a line that seems to be the cry of all of us, at least at some stages of our lives. There they were, in the midst of the storm, crying out: "Don't you Care?"

Who of us has not been there, feeling to our toes that we are not sure anyone, even Jesus, cares about our storms, our sorrows, the whirlwinds that overwhelm us?

Don't you care that my family is falling apart?

Don't you care that my wife is drinking herself to death? Or that my child has lost his faith?

Don't you care about the growing numbers of poor and homeless all over our country, especially little children?

Don't you care that your church is crumbling, splitting apart, that women are alienated and priests are almost non-existent?

Don't you care about children at or borders being ripped from their mother's arms.

Don't you care about my illness, my loneliness, my pain, whatever it may be?

Don't you care, don't you care, don't you care?

Although I remember lamenting in this fashion I cannot honestly recall how I recovered, how I answered my own question. I know it must have been along the lines that the Jesus who cares is only shown through the caring of people who bear his name, the caring of people like ourselves, the Body of Christ.

This year I hear the same Gospel with some of the same sense of that question being part of the human experience of everyone of us. But I was more struck this year by the juxtaposition of this Gospel story with the Book of Job.

In our first reading today Job has suffered, cried out, asked where the heck God is for thirty-seven chapters. Anyone who talks about the "Patience of Job" has never read the book. Job is a constant complainer, and he has every right to be! Job had everything, and everything has been taken away: wife, children, fortune, health, reputation . . . everything but Hope.

After these thirty-seven chapters of Job's lamenting, in the reading we hear today, God begins to respond to Job. God asks Job, in effect: "So where were you when I made the sea lions, or what do you know about whirlwinds?"

The essence of God's response is simply, "I'm God, You're not!" God is ultimately in charge and Job may not understand, but he is presumptuous to question. It is not a very satisfying response. What strikes me most, however, is the deep, universal, utterly real framing of God's answer: The passage begins" God answered Job out of the storm!"

"Out of the Storm."

Doesn't God always meet us "out of the storm?"

Perhaps my largest single insight this year has been that we frequently (if not always) meet God in the storm, meet God in creation still coming to be, meet God in the not yet.

I wish it were not so but my life-long experience --from the Polio I had when I was eight to the cardiac arrest I suffered two at 58-- has been that I meet God most in the storm, in the darkest and most confusing times.

This may be true because I'm Irish, but I believe it matches the human experience more broadly.

If it were not for the polio from which I almost died at eight years old I'm not sure I would have paid as much attention to God. My life always felt like a gift that I could easily not have had so I have lived from the earliest age with a sense of needing to say "Thanks" for that gift of life.

I keep wishing it were not the case but I live now with some heart disease, with a machine to keep me alive, with fatigue, and a certain sense of detachment from life that could so easily be over. I wish I felt better. I wish I had more energy, wish I could be more dynamically engaged with life. But I cannot. I must meet God in this storm, not in some other more peaceful reality of my choosing. God is God, I am not.

I suspect this is true not just for me. God has always been closest, felt most present, when I am most in confusion, most struggling to believe anything, most uncertain of myself, my world, my relationships, my Church. When I was most in doubt about my ability to be a priest, God worked most dramatically through me. Now, unsure how to be retired, or how to be husband to a wife when she's in pain, it is in the midst of the storm, when I am most inclined to cry out "Don't you care," that I must honestly look and acknowledge the caring that surrounds me.

I have spoken about my own experience. I do not know your experience but I suspect it is not so very different. I suspect we all are tempted to cry out "Don't you care?" I suspect God speaks to all of us "in the midst of the storm."

As we move towards Eucharist, take a few moments to name for yourself, in the very real fabric of your lives:

> Where today is the storm in your life . . . in home, work, community, world, church? Where are you tempted to cry out "Don't you care?"

> How does God/Jesus seem absent, or uncaring, or asleep in the boat?

Hopefully, at some deep level, what word of God is spoken to you "out of the storm?"

After a moment of quiet let us gather for Eucharist; let us be grateful for the storm.

38) The Thirteenth Sunday in Ordinary Time

Scripture Readings: Wis. 1:13-15, 2:23-24; 2 Cor. 8:7,9,13-15; Mk. 5:21-43

Two weeks ago we reflected on a passage in Mark's Gospel that was a "Sandwich" passage – a typical literary device of Mark. Today we have another, more obvious sandwich. Our story starts with a man asking Jesus to come and cure his daughter. This story is quickly interrupted by the story of a woman in the crowd who touches Jesus and is cured. Eventually we return to the first story, and Jesus cure, from a distance, of the little girl.

The sandwich is important. We are tempted to cut the Gospel up into little pieces, taking one story or the other. The lectionary even encourages such barbarous behavior by putting the middle story in brackets to be skipped if you so desire. But we cannot understand either story without the other. Besides who likes a bread sandwich?

We have another enduring temptation – to read the Gospel stories as if they were written yesterday in Toledo, rather than in a culture very different from our own, for a very different audience, with an almost entirely different set of premises. If we read these two stories in a fundamentalist way we have only two tales of wonder, miracles, signs that the messianic age is here in Jesus. That surely is part of the story. But if we step back and into the culture in which these stories are written they become the basis of a religious, political statement of enormous impact. These stories reveal a disturbing social relevance that gets at the very foundation of Jesus' message and ministry.

I want to retell these stories as a first century Jewish community might have heard them. First, we must recall that in Mark's Gospel the message of Jesus comes, for the most part, through action, rather than through sermon or parable, as in Luke or Matthew. What is the message contained in the action of these juxtaposed stories?

A large crowd gathers around Jesus. The word for the crowd is hoi polloi , that is "the folks," the ordinary people, the poor, the lowly – not the rich and powerful. These "little people" listen for a message and the message comes through action.

As Jesus speaks another man comes up, one not of the hoi polloi, but an official, a significant personage in the synagogue. This man even has a name, Jairus. Jairus comes and kneels before Jesus asking for a favor. He requests that Jesus come to his house and lay hands on his daughter who is deathly ill. She is a twelve year old--twelve being the fullest of numbers, the same number as the tribes of Israel.

Jesus, of course, loves everyone so he is willing and he begins to go off with the man; there is need of hurry for the girl is close to death.

Seeing that Jesus is leaving a woman in the crowd is impelled to touch Jesus – a woman with no name, a woman who is ritually unclean, an outcast from the synagogue, a woman who has been cheated by doctors, treated, with no cure for twelve years (notice, the same number of years as the little girl has been alive, again the fullest of numbers). This woman represents everything the synagogue leader is not. She knows she deserves no attention, but she trusts in Jesus power. She is cured instantly and anonymously.

This true physician has cured her instantly, and for free.

Now Jesus could have gone on to the house of the important Jairus; this woman has been cured. But he stops his hasty journey for he knows someone has touched him differently, touched him with reverence, touched him with faith.

It is by no accident that Jesus cuts through the objection of his disciples who urge him on to the house of the powerful. He stops and pays attention instead to his woman. He chooses to pay very close attention to the "inappropriate" touch of the woman, more than to the appropriate, proper approach of the synagogue leader. In fact, Jesus calls the woman "my daughter," and thus the story becomes a tale of two beloved daughters.

While Jesus is engaged with this poor woman, the news arrives that the official's child has died. But Jesus goes on with the official, urging him to the same faith as the unclean woman, despite this apparent bad news. Jesus' confidence is ridiculed, not by the crowd, the hoi polloi, but by the people of the official's house. But the official himself, having seen the power of Jesus at work, believes, and his daughter, too, is cured.

Heard through the ears of a first century Jew, the story reaches far beyond that of a mere miracle story. In a perhaps too simple summary, the story says:

> Israel in all its tribes is bleeding.
> Israel in all its tribes seems dead.

To be saved the people of Israel must embrace a new social order, more faithful to their covenant, in which all people are equal, in which there is as much concern for the crowd, the hoi polloi, as there is for the powerful, for those with names, for the rich.

If we hear the story through the ears of a twenty-first century American the message is not significantly different. Certainly this story invites a response that is deeper than "Wow, what a neat miracle. Look what Jesus did!'

This story invites, challenges us to believe in the miracle that Jesus is as he levels the distance between God and humankind, as he challenges the distance we put between one human being and another. The last are indeed first.

This gospel invites us in every arena of our lives to notice to whom we pay attention, whose voice we hear, whose touch is noticed, and heeded -- in our families, work place, and in our own church community!

Let us take a moment to see how these powerful stories play out in our lives before we turn to Eucharist.

39) The Fourteenth Sunday of Ordinary Time

Scripture Readings: Ez. 2:2-5; 2 Cor. 12:7-10; Mk. 6: 1-6

Shortly after I was ordained a priest I was assigned to the parish where I grew up. I remember the first time I preached from the old high pulpit in my home parish. I stood there looking down from the same pulpit to which I had so often looked up. Immediately below me sat a couple with whom I had frequently double dated and other various life-time friends and acquaintances. Today's gospel is the same one I read that day. It was easy to convey the feeling that no one is a prophet in one's own country, among one's own people.

Many years later I lived for a summer with a young seminarian from Chicago who studied at the seminary where one of my Theological heroes, John Shea, taught. He hadn't taken a class from Shea who was, to him, just another teacher.

I am not in John Shea's league but I have given missions, or retreats in places like Calgary, Alberta, or Dodge City, Kansas, or
Hamilton, Montana and there are people there who think I'm
famous; they even ask people in the Spokane, or Seattle, Tacoma
or Portland area if they know me. Usually they don't.

I mention these experiences because they give me a slant on the
gospel today. We know that Jesus was rejected by many of the
very people he came to serve and save. He has been rejected in
our time and our inclination is to imagine the reasons are the
same for both. Surely Jesus was rejected because what he says is
difficult, challenging, upsetting to the existing order of things.

The Gospel today suggests that Jesus is not heard, is ineffective
in his home town, among his relatives and friends not because
he was so challenging, but simply because he is too familiar, too
ordinary. He is just the kid down the street, just the son of Mary,
whom everyone knows. He's the carpenter's kid. Why, his compa-
triots ask, should we pay attention to him; he's always been a little
strange? Jesus rather than being too dramatic to follow is apparently not important enough to warrant attention.

As I listen to the gospel this week I find myself following a train
of thought I had not before considered. I am struck by the ways
we fail to listen to the voices we hear every day, see every day,
especially if they are the voices of those that seem little, or unimportant, or insignificant. We miss the prophetic dimension of the
poor, the children, the lowly, the little ones with whom Jesus so
often identifies.

This reflection seems especially relevant around the fourth of July
as we celebrate our national birthday for it is so difficult for our

nation to hear the prophetic voices of what we in the church call the anawhim, the little ones.

I once heard Helen Caldicott, the founder of Physicians for Social Responsibility, tell a story that dramatizes this. She told of visiting a fourth grade classroom and talking with children in the mid 1980's, at the height of the real possibility of accidental or intentional nuclear war. After a short while she invited the children to share their concerns, their fears, eventually asking them how many in this fourth grade class were fearful about a nuclear war, and their world being blown up. All but one child raised their hands. She asked the one exception, a little girl, why she was not afraid. The girl was not afraid because her "mom and dad go to lots of meetings trying to keep it from happening."

We could focus on the need for us to be involved in significant issues precisely to support and alleviate the fears of our children, but my point is to suggest that these parents, unlike the others, heard the voice of their child which most ignored, which most of our society ignores. The child is too small, too familiar, too insignificant to be listened to. Besides if we hear the child's fears we may be forced to hear our own. Today, our children are crying out, among other things, for an end to gun violence, and reasonable restrictions on the ownership of weapons of destruction.

Children are often the prophets whose voices we would rather not hear. I recently heard a child psychologist maintain he had never met a child seriously involved with drugs or alcohol who did not need to be! He meant that in the sense that these destructive behaviors were, perhaps, better than suicide. The kids he dealt with, without exception, needed a buffer between them and the overwhelming pain of living; they were crying out for help, using something to block pain that was usually not heard.

We as a nation engage in a major war against drugs, especially among children, and rightly so. But a "Just say No!" stance that refuses to look at the social realities that lead the young to say "yes" is to not hear the prophetic voice in our midst that is too poor, too black, to weak to warrant our attention. How much of the proliferation of drugs is more a prophetic cry against inadequate housing, continued hunger, poor health care, weak job opportunities, sub-standard educational development?

I have heard therapists say repeatedly that the member of a family who comes to a counselor with a problem, often a major problem – serious crime, sexual deviancy, an attempted suicide – is often the healthiest member of the family. The one "in trouble" can be the one who on some level feels what is wrong with the entire family system and so cries out for help. The whole family needs to be worked with not just the one with the presenting problem, who is perhaps the prophet in the midst, sometimes not heard because too close.

As Jesus was unheeded by those who were closest to him, we often miss the voices we need to hear around us.

I recall once experiencing physical pain as I watched endless lines of people waiting for food outside the old school building in a parish where I served. I was surprised; I thought I'd grown used to the sight. But I found myself that day thinking: How we can miss hearing, not just the need for food, but the cry they were making on behalf of all of our society who have fallen through the cracks, the "safety net" – those lines of women with children, young families, the elderly poor. Early in July as we recall our nation's birth, such pictures speak to me more than any flag of the challenges to our great nation.

Let me call to mind one final way we may fail to hear the cry of the too familiar, unheard prophet in our midst. I admire those who fight against abortion but in that very serious struggle we may not hear the message in the voices of women who need, or think they need to pursue that (admittedly tragic) option.

The voices are myriad; they can't afford doctor bills, or child care, or endure the embarrassment that society still heaps upon the unmarried pregnant woman abandoned by yet another irresponsible man. Often they speak eloquently if only we did not take for granted the violence in our society against women, against the poor, against children. If we truly heard these voices perhaps we'd spend more time working in those areas that would make abortion an unnecessary option than in trying to change the law, or in picketing clinics that provide the option, or trying to get a Supreme Court Justice appointed or a president elected on this single isolated issue.

To put a single point simply. As I listen to this gospel about hearing the cry of the prophets in our midst I wonder if we as a nation, as a people do not need to listen to the voices that seem too poor, too familiar, too close.

Jesus was not able to work any miracles among those who knew him too well, those who had grown accustomed to his face, those for whom he had become insignificant.

That voice of Jesus still speaks in our midst,
    speaks in a child afraid to face the future,

a teenager turning away from a too painful world to drugs
or suicide,
in a woman afraid to bear a child,
in an aged person waiting in a long line for food,
Speaks in so many other voices become perhaps too
familiar.

They speak to us, in Jesus, of our radical interdependence on one
another.

40) The Fifteenth Sunday

Scripture Readings: Amos 7:12-15; Eph. 1: 3-14; Mk. 6: 7-13

As a Jesuit I always appreciated my sense of being "missioned" sent by the province to whatever work I was doing. I still have that sense of being sent. I like this notion. I helps me remember important truths. Like, the work I'm doing is not just my idea. Or, finally, I am not in charge of my life. Success and failure are not up to me but are the responsibility, in part at least, of the community I'm part of, and even of God who we believe works through this missioning process.

Although Jesuits may "name" it, I think this sense of being sent, missioned, called . . . this sense of vocation is central to any Christian vocation. Being sent is central to the readings we have heard today.

The first reading from Amos is a bit terse, perhaps difficult to follow but actually quite easy to identify with. Amos has gone where God sent him and the people, the priests of Bethel are not pleased with his presence; they try to send him away. But Amos maintains: "I have to stay here because God sent me here. I was just a shepherd and God told me to go prophesy to this people. It's not my fault, I have to be here!"

Then the Gospel tells of Jesus sending out the Twelve, later called, literally "Apostles," (those who are sent.). They are told to preach the good news and to have power over evil spirits. So they go out to do what they never would have thought of on their own. They are sent, missioned, called into this ministry shared with Jesus.

The truth underneath my reflections so far is that all of us have a Christian vocation; all of us are called; all of us are sent. It can help us enormously to know that this is so. All of us, in fact, have this same vocation, with incredible variety among us. We are to speak the "Good News," and be a healing presence in our world, our church, our neighborhoods, our families and communities. Through this message and this presence together we build God's Reign.

Every sacrament is a sacrament of sending. Baptism and Confirmation are not just for us, but they send us in God's spirit as "the body of Christ" into our various missions. Marriage is not just something given to a couple for themselves; it is a call to two people to let their love become a sign of God's faithful, loving presence in the world. When I witnessed a marriage I watch a couple assume a vocation, take on a mission, be "sent," by Jesus as a sacred sign of his presence.

Every parent is given the mission, is sent to be a sign of God's love to his or her children, instilling hope and laughter and love into each child.

Every friendship, every job, every volunteer position is a vocation, a call. It can help enormously to know that if I am a teacher, I am "sent" by God to this classroom. If I am a carpenter, a plumber, a hygienist, a doctor, lawyer, a day care worker, or sanitary engineer, each task can be a mission, if I choose to see it with such eyes.

I love the language of people in the twelve step programs. They go to help a fellow addict with the belief that they may be "the only 'big book' this person ever reads." Clearly a sense of being sent.

We pray so frequently for vocations and we used to think those were for priests and sisters, perhaps deacons in the Church. But every Christian has a vocation; Vatican II tells us we are all called to the same holiness, each in our unique way. All of us are sent out to preach good news and be a source of healing.

This sense of being missioned, sent, called to wherever it is life finds us can reach into every aspect of life. I remember a few years ago when one of our Jesuit parishes had a healing service. They invited a parishioner who was dying of AIDS to preach. Thankfully the service was taped. In one of the most moving homilies I have ever heard this very sick man spoke of his present vocation--to be sick, and to die well. He talked of other jobs, tasks, vocations he had along the way, some of which he had obviously not done very well. But not he had a new and very important call, If he responded prayerfully, lovingly, with integrity and hope to this new vocation he would be a very important part of building the kingdom of Jesus. He had to be sick now and let other people care for him, care about him, love him through the final stages of his life. Such a being sick is a very difficult thing to do. And he had to die, quite soon, with dignity and grace. He had a very healthy sense of being missioned, sent to his life as it was right then.

May all of us see our lives, in faith, in such a light--each in our own way telling good news, and bringing healing to our world.

41) The Sixteenth Sunday

Scripture Readings: Jer. 23:1-6; Eph. 2:13-18; Mk. 6:30-34

How often even the most simple of Gospel stories play themselves out in the everyday lives of the followers of Jesus. Today's gospel may be the least remarkable event recorded in the dramatic stories of Jesus, but a few moments reflection makes it as real, vivid, and challenging as any story. Every human being has experienced *plans disrupted*. How we react, even to this apparently commonplace human experience, says something about the quality of our discipleship.

There is something terribly fitting that we hear today's Gospel story in mid-summer when people are taking — or trying to take - -vacations.

Some years ago left the parish to get away for awhile. I went to another city, a place in which I had previously ministered. I settled in only to discover that I had five telephone messages awaiting me when I arrived. Shortly after that I read this gospel passage and laughed!

The gospel tells us that the Apostles – note that last week, when they first set out, they were called disciples but now are called Apostles, literally "those who are sent" -- have returned from their first mission. They are excited about all that they have done and taught.

Jesus invites them to take a small vacation with him.

"Come away to a deserted place and rest awhile."

So they go away, but like many a planned escapes this one doesn't work. People see them leaving, guess were they are headed and run to the place arriving there even before Jesus and his apostles disembark.

Now the heart of the Gospel today concerns *how Jesus reacted when his plans were disrupted*, his vacation scuttled, his desire for a small respite ruined. We presume his apostles were with him in this instantaneous change of plans

I had a friend, a very productive Jesuit, who was often heard to say:

"I couldn't get a thing done today, people kept interrupting me."

His sentiments are not that unfamiliar to us all. Life is indeed what happens while we are planning something else, and the best laid plans of mice and men do regularly run amuck.

But: "Jesus saw the vast crowd.

He pitied them for they were like sheep without a shepherd;
and he began to teach them at great length."

Jesus adjusts his plans to the needs of the people who sought him out. He spent time with them; he talked with them. He loved them.

We Christians stress, and rightly so, the saving death of Jesus. We dwell on his enormous sufferings. We talk about his cross and our sharing in that cross. I suspect most of us feel inadequate in the face the mystery of the suffering and death of Jesus. This simple Gospel story reminds us that the way Jesus finished his life was exactly as he lived its entirety. He "laid down his life for his friends," not just at the end, but all the way along. If we feel inadequate to follow Jesus to the height of the cross, we can perhaps find solace here, in the seemly commonplace.

We will not likely be asked to climb any very real Calvary's hill. We will not likely have nails pierce our literal hands and feet. We will not likely be denounced by the religious and political leaders of our day and sentenced to death because of our teaching or our actions.

But everyone of us will be inconvenienced by the needs of others. Everyone of us will have our vacation plans turned upside down because someone gets sick, or dies, or asks our help in smaller ways.
Everyone of us will experience the suffering that love ineluctably brings.

Just as I was originally writing these words, my phone rang with a crisis I had to deal with, only coming back to his hours late. . . .

The very human reality I was reflecting on and seeking to express to you burst into my preparation. A mother told me of the sudden death of her son by drowning. This homily needed to wait; I would prepare it later. The memorial service for her son was obviously going to clash with the plans I had for Friday morning. I had hoped to stay the night in a resort area about 90 miles away where I was to do a wedding Friday evening. These plans would need to change because of this tragic and untimely death.

This need to change plans is not an occasional reality for me or any of us. This challenge presents itself almost every day, almost every moment. And each time our response says something about our very real, very concrete, very specific desire to follow Jesus.

I do not do it consistently or well; you may not either. But we want to look on the "crowds" with the eyes of Jesus, with eyes of compassion, with eyes that see their needs more clearly than we see our own.

42) The Seventeenth Sunday

Scripture Readings: 2 Kings 4:42-44; Eph. 4: 1-6; Jn. 6:1-15

In this season of vacations it is perhaps appropriate to step back from the Gospel of Mark we hear through most of this year. Because Mark's Gospel is the shortest we interrupt its narrative for four weeks and listen to the Gospel of John. We listen to just one chapter of John, the sixth, devoted entirely to the mystery of Eucharist. We step back, pause, and enter deeply into one event.

Right away we notice how different are these two gospel stories. Mark never would write "Jesus knew what he was going to do ... "Where Mark tells us of a Jesus who is very, very human, trusting in the power of God, John's story is more of the divine power of Jesus himself, manifest in our midst.

Still whether we listen to Mark or John our task is the same – to let this story become our story, to let Jesus penetrate our lives, to connect what we hear, the stories from this book, with the stories of our lives. The Sixth chapter begins today with the miracle of

Jesus feeding five thousand people starting with nothing or next to nothing. This is the only miracle that is told in all four gospels. Clearly John adds some details to this story that pre-dated his telling of it. Also he uses the story as a lead in, an introduction to an entire chapter about feeding.

After this miracle Jesus will speak about himself as "the bread of life," as new manna, as the bread we need for our journey. So only John mentions that the miracle takes place at Passover, when the Jewish people celebrate that sacred meal reminding them of being brought from slavery to freedom, of being saved from death by manna when they were starving in the dessert. All of this is the backdrop for John's story.

I am most struck by and want to develop the notion, that John tells this story as a "liturgical text" to a community that would have already been celebrating the Eucharist for almost a century. His telling has Gathering rite, Offertory, Fraction rite - all after Jesus has spoken a liturgy of the word for a long, long time. John incorporates the community's already existing liturgical awareness into his story.

I empathize with the gathering rite, as Jesus "looks up and sees the multitudes." The first thing a priest does at Eucharist is look out and see the multitudes, hungry faces. After some time in a parish the faces take on names, and stories, identities. These faces are people who are known and loved. Each time I looked out I was aware of stories of people, joys, sorrows, hopes, dreams, tears, laughter. I looked out and saw Joe whose wife we just buried, or Susie and Bill whose wedding we recently celebrated, or Elsie recovering from surgery.

These stories, these faces, are present through the week as we plan our liturgy. How can these people be fed? How can we nourish this community? How can we help them to hope, or deepen their awareness of how much they are loved? The question is bigger even than this community, this multitude gathered here? How can we look out at the multitudes of the world and feed them? How take this meal to the hungry, and the manifold hungers of our world?

We begin, with Jesus. . . and all of us, seeing the multitudes and wondering how we will feed them.

Then the offertory, the presentation of gifts. Only John's gospel we has the detail of a small boy offering to share some stuff he has brought with him, a little bread, a few fish. When the community gathers and the need is great, the fulfillment of that need begins with each one offering what he or she has, what he or she is. If we all give what we can, even the little we think we have, then the miraculous power of God can transform this offering into more than enough for all.

In that gathering with Jesus, it was critical that a small boy be willing to share the little he had. Without that offering Jesus had nothing to work with; no miracle could happen. In our gathering today what we bring matters; we need to be here. God's ability to feed us and feed all begins with our being present here willing to offer what we have, . . . our prayers, our financial offering, our lives. Without such generosity with the little we have the miracle cannot take place.

The third liturgical moment in the Gospel story is the fraction rite. The language of the story prefigures the language we use here again today, the language of Eucharist – again words the community would have been using for a generation before the story is written down.

Jesus "took, and blessed and broke and gave."

And there was more than enough for everyone. The Passover is renewed, the feeding goes on, the freedom increases. Hungers are fed.

Throughout these weeks of ordinary time we struggle to connect what we do here at Church with our lives away from here, throughout the week. How do we live out our Sunday faith in the marketplace of real lives? If I rehearse this gospel the answer seems obvious, but with the clarity of poetry, more than prose:

Perhaps the central human question is:
How will we feed this multitude?
How will we get what we need?
How will we be able to give to others what they need?
Where will there ever be enough for everyone?
Enough love in my family?
Enough patience in my office?
Enough peace in my neighborhood, in Syria, along our borders ...

We come here and enter into prayer. In response to God's words we again try to offer ourselves, all we have and are, all we can be or do; we bring a little wine, a few pieces of bread, a little money.

Then in the central mystery of all we imitate what we offer and **we let ourselves be taken,** blessed, broken and given in whatever way God wants to satisfy those needs.

What we do here is a poem, a preface of how we live out there!

43) The Eighteenth Sunday

Scripture Readings: Ex. 16:2-4,12-15, 31a; Eph. 4:17-20; Jn. 6:24-35

It is difficult to give a sermon on a sermon. But that's my task today – to give a sermon on the first part of a sermon Jesus gave first, and doubtless better.

We continue this Sunday to listen to the gospel of John. The readings today build on the readings from last week. I suggested that the story of the feeding of five thousand last weekend was presented in a liturgical form – a gathering rite as Jesus looked out and saw the multitudes, an offering of gifts as a small boy presented his loaves and fishes, a fraction rite as Jesus took and blessed and broke and gave away the gifts given. Today we listened to the first part of the homily, as it were, the reflections of Jesus on the deeper meaning of last week's event.

Today's Gospel builds upon one of the greatest of the people's stories, from their Exodus experience. As they passed from slavery to freedom, from Egypt to the land God promised, the people were marvelously, wondrously fed. They had been hungry, and grumbling – scripture says "murmuring" against God and Moses. "Why have you brought us out here to die? At least in Egypt we had enough to eat." Then, miracle of miracles, they discover each morning bread enough to sustain them through the day.

John has Jesus reminding his hearers of that story, even comparing his listeners to the original Israelites. He relates this ancient story to their present reality. They want to know what "sign" he will do. Jesus even uses the same word "murmuring." He is a trifle angry because they come to him not out of faith, but because they had received some food and wanted more.

Here is the challenge of the sermon Jesus gives. Jesus reaches down into their deepest experience – into our deepest experience. What will sustain us on the journey when the food isn't there? When we don't have stuff, or health, what will keep us going? How difficult to keep going with just a couple crusts of bread?

The questions are enduring, human questions: How keep from murmuring when my hunger is deep, desperate, continuous? When my family is falling apart? When I'm sick with a cancer, real or metaphorical, that is incurable?

Jesus will tie all this in with Eucharist in the next part of his sermon – a section more familiar to us. But the words today are prior and in some ways more important. They speak the reality towards which the Eucharist points. Jesus says "I am the bread of Life!" Here not "going to communion," but entering into a relationship with Jesus is finally what alone will feed our hungers. Not bread, not food, not answers, not ease. What finally matters is your love for me; your knowledge of my love for you!

The heart of Jesus homily is the heart of our Christian lives. The only thing that matters is a personal love relationship with Jesus as the Christ – the bread of life.

The Evangelicals get at this with the expression about "Taking Jesus as our personal savior." I'm not fond of this language because it is never merely personal. This acceptance is always as "our" savior, always within, and from and for a community. But this language points to something very central.

I need to know I am loved by Jesus. This is the bread of Life that alone will sustain me.

Personally I need frequently to return to an event some years ago. I was totally discouraged about myself, my shortcomings, my job . . but also the Church, the people I worked with and for. I was engaging in some very destructive behavior, running away at nearly break-neck speed.

Early one morning I stood in my office looking out the window -- at the bottom of the well of life. Then the sun rose just behind Mt. Rainier. It shone into my office directly on me. I felt something way down deep in my bones (though I saw no vision, heard no voice). I knew Jesus/God was saying to me "I love you Pat; there is nothing you can do to stop me loving you!"

Nothing changed in me or in my circumstances, but I was deeply fed.

Finally experiences like this are what sustains us.

I don't tell you this so you can write my autobiography but so that you will trust your own. Each of us, in our own way, way deep down, in small or large ways has felt, has heard that voice, has known that touch, the love of God in Jesus, telling us we are loved – that he is the bread of our lives.

We may be sinners, but we are sinners whom God has touched and loved and called and sent. There isn't any other kind of folks.

Maybe this knowledge comes through the eyes and voice of a spouse,
or through a sunset,
or an ocean wave,
or through the pages of a book read,
a song heard.

I don't know where you've felt or heard it, but somewhere for all of this to make any sense at all we must know Jesus as "bread of life," as incarnation of God's love that finally alone will feed us.

It is very difficult to hear or to remember that we have heard this word when we are truly hungry, when life is falling apart, or when we face illness or death, our own or that of a loved one.

And Jesus refuses steadfastly to be "God of the gaps," taking away human suffering, or pretending it doesn't matter. Jesus never seems to feed us with easy, or temporary food. Finally in the face of all the trials life can offer we are sustained only because way deep down we know that we are loved.

The entire Christian "thing," really the entire human life "thing"" only makes sense, only fits together, only is livable because Jesus is the bread of life – the love relationship that sustains me on the journey.

We celebrated this week the feast of St. Ignatius Loyola, founder of the Jesuits. Each year I recall once going to Cataldo Mission in Northern Idaho on the feast of St. Ignatius. Cataldo is the original Jesuit mission in the West. I remember honoring Ignatius as we sat in this one-hundred-fifty year old Church, high on a hillside above a plush, luxurious valley. About 30 Jesuits gathered, sitting on wooden floors, as one of our number took the role of Ignatius. He told us his story of being a companion of Jesus, and reminded us of our own stories, each unique. We remembered times of discouragement, disillusionment, our "murmurings." And we remembered being fed. He connected our stories with those of Ignatius and those first heroic brothers of ours to come into this area. What we did that day I need to do often. We all do.

Before we go on with Eucharist today, we all need to reclaim in our hearts, to go deep down and remember our deepest source of belief in Jesus and his love for us.

And when we remember that we can celebrate at this table because he has first been present to each of us as bread of our lives!.

44) The Nineteenth Sunday

Scripture Readings; I Kings 19-4-8; Eph. 4:30-5:2; n. 6: 41-51

The scripture readings this week provided me with wonderful grounds for reflection on my experiences of the summer. Perhaps my summer was not unlike your own. Often in the summer when we take some time, stop, rest, we may find ourselves, initially, feeling like Elijah, sitting under that tree longing for death. Once we stop and look at our year we may want to say,

> "Take my life, Oh Lord, I am no better than those
> who have messed up before me.!

We may not even know what it is that bothers us. I know I used to go away and worry vaguely about all the sick people I didn't visit often enough, all the names of people I should know and can't remember, the people whose marriages or lives are falling apart in the parish and I don't know how to "fix it." I still worry about the Gospel call to struggle for justice, to care for the materially poor and how little I and the rest of this parish seem to really care about that arena. I worry how to keep myself together in the process of worrying about all these other things.

When my health is bad, I worry about why I am still alive and sort of wish it were all over.

I easily identify with Elijah, himself weary, under a tree, wishing it were all over.

I love the fact that Elijah kept falling asleep. In these few short verses he takes two naps. I like that. Bone weary and willing to quit.

I love, also, the first verse of the 2nd reading from Ephesians:

"Do not sadden the Holy Spirit."

I think I, Elijah, and all of us have that deep down weary feeling that we have saddened the Holy Spirit, that God, like ourselves, is vaguely disappointed in our performance in life.

In the reading from Kings God provides Elijah with miraculous nourishment, food and drink for the journey of life. A voice tells him:

"Here, take and eat, drink lest the journey of life be too long for you."

Elijah eats, and drinks, and then gets up and goes on to the mountain of God. He keeps on keeping on, nourished by God

This summer again, after the weariness, I am nourished by God. Gradually I feel things differently, and the forces preying on me become not just a burden, but grace. I began to see the life, the laughter, the hope, begin to see things a little more, with the eyes of God. With time, and space and quite a few naps life becomes gift and grace again.

I hope something in summer does this for us all.

It is with this experience behind me, perhaps behind all of us, that we can listen all this month to the Gospel of John, and hear again that promise of nourishment-- Jesus is the bread of our lives!

The gospel today begins with the backdrop of the Jewish people's weariness, their murmuring. Jesus recalls the murmuring of their ancestors in the desert during the Exodus when things got difficult, and the people grew weary. They said, in effect, to God "What have you done for us lately," forgetting the escape from Egypt, the parting waters, the food they ate on the journey. Here, as in the story of Elijah, we murmur and God feeds.

In the light of this movement from weariness to nourishment, let me offer three personal beliefs about this "bread of life, this Eucharist, really, this Jesus.

First, we have heard and perhaps even shared the thought that many people who go to church are hypocrites. I mean, people go to church, share in communion, then go on living their messy lives. Isn't that phony? And I say a resounding "NO!"

We eat the bread, we tell the story of Jesus, we keep feeding ourselves under our various weary trees because that's who we really are at our best. During the week we may forget and lapse into our oldest and weakest patterns, but here, around this altar, if only for an hour or so, we celebrate who we really are. We remind ourselves of that wondrous identity. We let ourselves be nourished in that belief. We strengthen ourselves to go on.

Here we eat and become the Body of Christ. Here for awhile we are brothers and sisters in Christ. Here we are a community, God's people. Later we may forget, grow weary, take a nap. But we never apologize for coming over and over in our weariness to be fed, and to keep being fed so we can try again to be faithful on the journey!

Secondly, just as Elijah had a vision of God feeding him for the journey, each Eucharist, each feeding on this bread is an exercise of "vision" – an invitation to see differently.

If we can see the presence of Jesus, of God/love in this bread and wine we can look at everything else differently. We can see the stresses of life not just as pressure but as grace, not just as burden but as opportunity. Sometimes I picture life as a series of forces preying upon me, overwhelming me, wearing me down and out. I know I can just as well see the exact same realities as grace, gift, the very real presence of Jesus. To look with the eyes of faith and see beyond the signs of this bread and wine, to see Jesus present here, feeding me, invites me to see Jesus everywhere, in every relationship, every pressure, every failure, and indeed in every joy and gift too!

Thirdly, the image of "bread:" the word bread in contemporary American slang means money, security. As a slightly crude bumper sticker reminds us:

"Life is a (manure) sandwich;
the more bread you have, the less (manure) you eat."

Bread, we are tempted to believe, can protect us against the forces of the world that would overwhelm us. Gathered here we affirm that Jesus is the bread, the only real security. It is as if Jesus says, quite clearly:

> "I am not a fly-by-night, fast-food, not a religion
> concerned only with blessing your consumption.
> I am a different kind of nourishment that will stick
> to your deepest ribs, and satisfy your most authentic
> longings."

Jesus as the bread of our lives is not just a food we eat but an entire life we take on, a way of living and seeing, a way of overcoming weariness or discouragement, knowing that we will be raised up from under our trees, we will live, and live forever, knowing that life can come out of every kind of death.

Jesus is a nourishment that lasts forever.

Like Elijah, at the end of our rope, we can and do meet God.

45) The Twentieth Sunday

Scripture Readings: Prov. 9:1-6; Eph. 5:15-20; Jn. 6: 51-58

For the Fourth Week in a row we listen to Jesus discourse on the Eucharist from John's sixth chapter. This must be important. I know it is and has been important to me all my life. I find myself stepping away from the text as such and reflecting on my life-time love-affair with Eucharist, with this mystery of the flesh and blood of Jesus.

I remember as a young boy going to Mass almost every day with my dad. He would come in and shake my toe before he went to the garage; I had about 20 seconds to jump up and run to catch him as he drove to Church. My dad loved the Mass. I loved my dad.

I remember fondly Sr. Agnes Cecilia in the 7th grade who taught us to us a daily missal. I was so proud, finally, to know what was going on.

I remember in seminary I prided myself on daily Eucharist. From age 18-30 I never missed a day.

My theology through all those days was fairly simple. The bread and wine became the body and blood of Christ. We receive God. My focus was almost exclusively on the Real Presence.

Mass was an act of adoration, worship, reverence; something I did for God to show my love. I felt good going to Mass regularly, even if I messed up or forgot about it the rest of the day, this early morning exercise grounded me.

Then came Vatican II and in its wake and in the light of the first document of that council, on The Sacred Liturgy, I was invited to re-think the Eucharist almost entirely . My understanding changed and expanded dramatically. I still believe what I have all my life but the picture became so much larger, fuller.

I had to re-think what I meant by Real Presence because that document insisted that Jesus was really present in the Eucharist in at least four ways —in the community gathered, in the word proclaimed, in the sacrament celebrated, and even in the minister.

I was told that the Table of the Word was as important as the Table of the bread and wine and that building up of the community was as important at both of these, and the reason for each.

In fact the entire Vatican II theology with its emphasis on scripture study and our entire tradition opened up whole new avenues of reflection. Jesus is indeed really present in the Eucharist, but Jesus is really present everywhere – for example, "In the joys, hopes, struggles of the people of our age," as the final document of Vatican II insists. The Eucharist is meant to call my attention to this presence everywhere.

I began to understand that our dogmas, what we believe, are important not for what they put in our heads, but because of how they change our hearts; each dogma, each teaching calls us to conversion. To believe that Jesus is present in the Eucharist, that when I receive he is present in me, invites me to let my life be transformed. It is wonderful that the bread and wine change into the body and blood of Christ but it is so much more important that I/ we do – that we become what we receive.

Because Vatican II invited us to revisit our sacred scripture and our entire tradition back behind Trent, back to our gospel roots we looked at texts like today's Gospel and discovered amazing things.

I began to realize that this sixth chapter of John is more about Life than about Eucharist. The entire text is about Jesus as living bread, of which the Eucharist is a sign and symbol. The word Life is used eleven times in the passage. Jesus is living bread. Jesus draws life from his father. We draw life from Jesus. This life is life right now. This life will be forever, creates something in us that cannot die. We receive the life of Jesus and are transformed by it. We put on Jesus; we live no longer ourselves but Christ lives in us.

Even the words we use are about life. Eating the flesh and drinking the blood of Jesus are not words of Cannibalism . . . not like arms and legs and eyeballs. To be alive, for Jesus' Jewish listeners is to have flesh on your bones; when we die the flesh falls away and only bones are left. To be alive is to have blood flowing through out veins; when we die the blood coagulates. We are invited to let Jesus live in us, be flesh on our bones, blood in our veins.

Finally as my understanding of this text and Eucharist expanded I became aware of the implications of this mystery beyond a pious "me and Jesus" union. Eating the flesh and drinking the blood of Jesus invites me into the ministry of Jesus, the preaching, the example, the "work" of Jesus. We who share in the bread and wine take on the commission of Jesus to build the reign of God. We cannot eat the bread and drink the wine without concern for the banquet to which God invites everyone. We cannot celebrate this banquet and remain oblivious to those who have no food, no drink, no banquet. If Jesus lives in me I have a passion for justice, a thirst for holiness, a taste for ever expanding love especially for those who are left out.

So I am grateful for my father, my childhood faith, the sister who taught me to use a missal in the 7th grade. But I am far more grateful for the fuller, more biblical, more adult understanding of these past years. I believe more deeply than I did then. I can say with more conviction what I heard Fulton Sheen say 60 years ago:

"My life will either be a Mass or a Mess."

46) The Twenty First Sunday

Scripture Readings: Joshua 24:1-2, 15-18; Eph. 4:32-5:2, 21-32; Jn. 6:53, 60-69

(N.B. It seems important to add the introductory lines to the reading from Ephesians, especially the line "Be subject to one another out of reverence for Christ." to balance the oft quoted "Wives be subject to your husbands." Otherwise listeners may be too distracted to hear any reflections on the sixth chapter of John!)

I like the story about a young priest who frequently went blank when he preached. He asked the advice of an older priest who suggested that whenever this happened he simply close his eyes, get very quiet, and then say the first scripture verse that comes to his mind. The younger priest tried this technique for the first time in *a wedding homily*. He went completely blank, prayed, waited, then said: "Father forgive them, they don't know what they are doing!"

I like this joke, but use it more today because it helps tie the scripture readings together and becomes the foundation of my reflections. When it comes right down to it, in any love relationship we, indeed, don't know what we are doing, but we trust and love anyway!

I don't want to spend a lot of time on the reading from Ephesians today, but it is impossible to simply skip over it. The line, "Wives be submissive to your husbands" is too provocative to simply ignore. It invites far more reflection than this, but I do urge you to note that the context of that line includes Paul insisting in an earlier verse that both husband and wife should be subject to each other out of reverence for Christ. Also, this line is followed by the direction to husbands to love their wives. The entire passage holds up the love of husband and wife as a sign of the presence of Christ's love for the Church. Spouses are to love and reverence each other, "in good times and bad, in sickness and health," just as Christ loves us, faithfully and forever. Without developing this, let me simply assert the enormous trust, the leap of faith, the decision to go beyond what "we know we are doing" that marriage involves; this trust filled love unites the second reading with the gospel today.

For five weeks we have listened to the sixth chapter of John's Gospel. The bulk of this chapter presents Jesus discourse on himself as "bread of Life," and the Eucharist, our eating the flesh and drinking the blood of Jesus, as the sign of our acceptance of that bread that lives forever. The chapter concludes in today's passage with an emphasis on faith, deep faith, life-transforming faith. The relationship into which Jesus invites Peter and all of us is based on acting not on what we know, what we can prove, but on trust. Every human endeavor that matters at all is based on something that cannot be proven, something that leaps beyond the evidence given. In any important matter, we do not know what we are doing!

This is the heart of the gospel passage today as many of the followers of Jesus walk away. They do not understand and cannot accept what Jesus has proclaimed. Peter speaks for the faithful followers.

Jesus asks: "Will you also go away?"

Peter replies: "Where should we go; you have the words of eternal life."

If I were to paraphrase Peter's response it would be as if he said:

> **"Jesus, I'm not really sure what you are talking about.**
> **I do not understand everything you are saying, about eating flesh and drinking blood. I am not sure where it all will lead. I am not staying with you because I understand all your words. I'm staying because I have come to trust you. I'll hang around until I find out. My head doesn't get it all, but I give my heart to you!"**

We have cheapened the notion of faith in recent times. We talk about faith as if it were notional assent, something only in our heads. Faith does not respond to the question, "What do you think?" I believe, in its Latin roots, Credo, really means "do", "cor", "I give my heart," to something, someone.

Faith, for Peter or for any of us, means precisely not knowing what we are doing, but trusting fully, completely anyway.

Sometimes people misunderstand this passage about the followers of Jesus walking away. Some think they walked away because Jesus' teaching – this talk of eating flesh and drinking blood -- sounded like cannibalism and was unacceptable. But, clearly, to the Jewish audience the passage was not about cannibalism. Jesus doesn't ask them to eat arms and legs. No. the passage is about life. Jesus as life. The word life is used more than twenty-five times.

A more accurate understanding of this passage depends on a simple physiology. Flesh is about life; when one dies there is no flesh on the bones. Blood is about life; when one dies, the blood coagulates and is no more. To eat flesh, to drink blood is to take on the life of Jesus and let him live in me, be flesh on my bones, blood in my veins. Flesh also implies life in all its weakness, its vulnerability as in "The word became flesh." Jesus invites us to take into ourselves his mortality, his vulnerability, his frailty. "Trust me," he says, "let me take over your eyes, your ears, your heart!"

Again, I don't know what all this means precisely. I don't assent to it because I understand it. I believe because I can't make sense out of my life without Jesus, without a relationship with this Jesus. I do not know what I am doing, but I trust in Him.

The year before I was ordained I temporarily lost my faith. It happened pretty dramatically. I was at St. Aloysius Church at the ordination of the class ahead of me. In the middle of the ceremony I was struck with the fear that I did not believe any of this. I left the Church and wandered alone around the Gonzaga University campus. I was overwhelmed with the reality that next year I would be in a similar ceremony. Right now I wasn't sure about the truth of any of the things I had believed all my life, any of the things I had been studying for years. I felt unsure whether there was a God, and if there was whether I wanted to give my life to that mystery. Over the next months I found myself wrestling with the mystery of faith. I tried a stance of unbelief, tried going without the Eucharist for awhile. Finally, I recall, in some agony but with a kind of freedom, coming to a place where I knew that Faith was a choice, a decision to surrender to mystery, a kind of leap into the unknown, into darkness, into trust, into love.

I knew that I, Pat Carroll – maybe not anyone else, but I – could not live with any kind of integrity or peace without Jesus, as the Christ, them model, the example, the vision of my life.

I did not **know** more; I **trusted** more!

I have not lived out that moment of faith perfectly by any means, but I am grateful to be able to go back to that experience and affirm the truth of the Gospel today. I believe that finally, at some crunch point for all of us, Jesus looks us in the eye and says:

> **"Will you also go away? You can, you know.**
> **You are free. I will not force you to follow me,**
> **to walk with me. But I cannot make all the impli-**
> **cations clear.**
> **If you find some other way to make sense out of**
> **your life, to live a full and**
> **happy human life, to make some sense of what**
> **happens beyond this life, OK!**
> **Do you want to go away?**

Finally, all of us have to say, way deep down: "I have no where else to go. You have the words of life."

Today we come to the end of our reading of this chapter of John's Gospel. We celebrate this sacred meal, this mystery of faith. We eat flesh, drink blood. We take into ourselves that life. We decide again to walk with Jesus, to let him live in and through us.

We do not really know what we are doing. We give our hearts, our trust to him who has, for us, the words of life.

47) The Twenty Second Sunday

Scripture Readings: Deut. 4:1-2,6-8; James 1:17-8, 21-22, 27; Mk. 7:1-8, 14-5, 21-3

A somewhat feisty pastor was preaching on today's Gospel. He gave a very short homily; it consisted of only three short statements.

First: Fifty million people are hungry every day on this planet, many of them in our midst.

Second: Most of us don't give a damn.

Third: More of you are upset that I said "Damn" in Church than that fifty million people are starving!

And he sat down.

Well, I'm not as disciplined as that pastor, so I won't just stop here. I also do not think the story is true of this community, but it certainly raises the question that the Gospel today seeks to raise: In our practice of religion what really matters, what really is important?

We return this Sunday to Mark's Gospel. We move into the center of this first Gospel, the center of the mission of Jesus, the center of his teaching Good News, a fresh religious word to the world.

A few years ago I read a wonderful small book, Jesus: A New Vision, by Marcus Borg. In one section Borg speaks of Jesus as a SAGE, in the tradition of the teachers of wisdom. Borg uses today's gospel passage to heighten what Jesus added to the wisdom of his day. He suggests that Jesus teaching was not that of a new religion (Christianity) to supplant and old religion (Judaism).

Rather **Jesus consistently took one side in the tension between two ways of being religious that run through every religious movement.**

Every religion eventually becomes torn between external observation and inner transformation. Jesus as sage, as wisdom teacher, continually invites us to a transformed heart.

It is important to acknowledge that Jesus also comes out of the tradition so beautifully captured in today's first reading from Deuteronomy. This tradition celebrates the reality of law, celebrates the fact that God is so close, so dear to us that this God gives us a law, gives us precepts to help us guide our lives. These laws and precepts far from being a burden are a great gift, a joy, a sign of God's deep and so personal concern for us. Still, over time, and through interpretations, any law or rule can become merely external and unhelpful.

Law can be gift, or trap:

This struggle between our laws, precepts, rules and the trans-formed heart never seems to go away. That line in the gospel in which Jesus criticizes the strict adherence to washing one's hands before eating (even if one is out in the desert) captures an enduring tension between what are important values and what is simply conventional wisdom. What really matters? What is really important?

Reflecting on this Gospel today I decided to just think out loud about some stories, real stories, the kinds of situations that come up almost every week. Each of these stories raises questions about what is important? What really matters? Without much comment, I share them with you.

I was working on a homily when someone knocked on my win-dow and asked me to go over to church and get them some holy water. I was busy and told them;" No, you can come and get the holy Water tomorrow." Holy water is not very important to me. The person began to curse and swear at me, mostly convincing me that Holy Water was very important to him.

A transient family came to the parish and asked to have a baptism for their child on a specific day in August. The last time we had seen the family was at a previous baptism two years before. At that time they assured us they would be at church frequently. I still thought baptism had something to do with entering a community of faith. I explained to them our policy on baptism. They got angry and left. What's important?

A young woman came to me and wanted to be married in our church. She hadn't been to church for several years but wanted to be married in a building familiar to her and her family. Being Catholic had been part of her past, and may be part of her future. We Catholics believe that marriage is a commitment not just to each other, but a promise to be a sacramental presence in the Church, a sign of God's love in the midst of our community. How can she witness to something if she is never present? Should we celebrate that wedding in our church or not? What's important?

And if we do that wedding should we insist on good liturgy, a singing assembly, a celebration that captures Christian values and does not just ape expensive secular celebrations? What's important?

A year after I left active ministry, I wanted to marry a woman I loved. I had a short life expectancy. I had not yet received permission from Rome to marry, but wanted to do so in a Catholic ceremony. I asked a priest friend/relative to help us with the wedding which, according to church law, was not yet "legal." What should he have responded? Should I have even asked?

A wonderful elderly couple has been in the parish for many years. One day I notice that they never go to communion. One day I summon the courage to ask them why and they explain that they had both been married before, many, many years ago. They were told they could not receive communion if they married. They separated for a time, then came back together, deciding to do the best they could with the situation. Probably they could get an annulment but they struggle with what that means. In the meantime can they receive communion? Should they? What is best for them and for other married people? What's important?

A woman who has fallen away from the Church tells me she tried to go to a church in the fairly small city to which she moved. The only Church available to her has made no effort to adjust its language and be even modestly inclusive. She finds it extremely difficult to be prayerfully present in a place where God is exclusively male, and nothing ever implies that "brothers," or "all men" may not include everyone. It feels to her that women do not exist. She has spoken to the pastor, but he says he cannot adapt the ritual or lectionary until the Church approves. She, and a million like her cease going to Church. What's important?

Your child is being married in a civil ceremony. You are very Catholic and this marriage troubles you. Do you attend the wedding?

Some years ago two middle-aged women came to my parish office. They live together and have for some time. They had been attending our Church for a year and wanted to register in our parish, but only if they could do so as a family unit. They asked my permission.

I could go on and on. I do not have answers to all these individual issues and many, many more like them. Some seem more clear than others. All involve not just the individual but the entire community. Each invites transformed hearts, mine, theirs or both.

As we reflect on today's gospel it is clear that the conflict between a religion of external observation of customs and laws and a religious faith that comes from deep, personal heart conviction has neither gone away nor become more simple.

If it were not so difficult to know what really is the loving thing to do in any given situation I do not think Jesus would have talked about it so frequently. Jesus asks us to honor God in our hearts. The only thing that we can say for sure, it seems to me, is that whenever our customs, laws, rules, regulations, practices get in the way of honoring God with our hearts then they come, not from God but, as in the Gospel today, from mere human precepts.

We continue to pray that we as individuals and as a community can share in the wisdom of Jesus, God's Sage.

48) The Twenty-Third Sunday

Scripture Readings: Is. 35:4-7; James 2:1-5; Mk. 7:31-37

Over and over again we tell the story of Jesus. Each time we tell it differently because we continually change. Our context shifts, our ears are opened in a new way. In today's Gospel, this marvelous tale of a man who begins to hear, I hear three things I had never before noticed.

First, the man who cannot hear or speak needs to be brought to Jesus. He would have no way of knowing Jesus, of knowing Jesus was around, unless others who knew him and who trusted Jesus managed to bring the two of them together. The inability to hear includes the inability to know about the one who can heal the problem. Isn't it always thus? I listen to this gospel and ponder who it is that brings me to Jesus, brings me back to Jesus, when my heart is empty, my ears deaf, my mouth dry.

The second thing I heard in a new way is how appropriate it is that only Mark's Gospel tells this miracle story. Only Mark would have the vivid messy details of spittle, fingers in the ear, hands in another's mouth. We used to preserve this story in our Baptismal rite. We were instructed to touch the ears of the baptized child with spittle as we prayed for this child to see, taste, hear the splendor of God's world. I remember discreetly kissing my fingers and barely touching the ears, eyes, and mouth of infants. I wish this gesture were still part of the rite. I think now we should have huge messy gestures, spread mud all over the child, bury her or him with kisses and hugs. Our sacred signs would do well to capture the essential truth that human life is messy. Christianity is truly messy. Jesus liked mud, spittle, water, wine, food, laughter, tears, blood, flesh; he still does. We come to Jesus in a messy world, in messy relationships, an imperfect muddy people needing to be opened up to new sounds, sights, tastes and love.

The third thing that struck me for the first time in this wondrous passage is the ambiguity about where, or to whom Jesus words are addressed. His "Ephphatha--Be Opened" could have been spoken either to the heavens, or to the man's ears, or to both. Jesus seems to demand that the man's ears open. But equally clear in the text, Jesus could be demanding God to open up. There is something amazingly fitting about seeing Jesus shouting at his God: "Open Up. Come on, God, open up and touch this child of yours, this poor, broken man."

I imagine Jesus today as we listen to this reading, hovering over us and praying, shouting for us at the Spirit "Open up Spirit, pour all over this people," and turning and shouting at us, "Open up and let my Spirit in!"

This leads me to my central point today. As we tell the story of Jesus it is never enough to tell the old story over. It is always a new story. It matters very little that this man's ears and tongue were opened two thousand years ago unless my ears are opened now, our tongues unplugged today. What matters is whether we, today, are formed into disciples with ears opened and tongues unloosed.

So as we gather today we long for the messy touch of Jesus. Where do we each and all want Jesus to spit his spirit all over us, shouting "Ephphatha: Heavens be opened! Community be opened!"

I pray for myself to be opened to new ideas, new ways of doing old things. I fear the inclination in myself to shut down, not listen, not share others enthusiasm. As I age and do over what I have done many times before I worry about my hesitancy to join in the collective venture to plan, to dream, to hope. I long to be free to hear what I think I have heard before, freed from a kind of word-weariness that deadens my spirit and crushes the spirit of others.

I pray for us, this community, the ability to to hear the cry of the poor. The wonderful second reading today told the praying community to welcome the poor as much as the powerful to our assembly.

James says:

> "Listen, beloved ones. Has not God chosen those who
> are poor in the world to be rich in faith, to be heirs
> of the dominion promised to those who love God?"

We are not healed to hear just any old sounds, but to hear God's special love for the poor around us, and for whatever is most poor in each of us.

The Story of Jesus is our story. As we move towards the altar we each might be attentive to what we long to hear individually, collectively. We pray to have God's spirit open us in every way to one another, in all our hopes, fears, dreams and needs. Open our inner and outer ears. If the story of Jesus is to continue it must be told through us. When we have heard, like the man in the gospel story today, we will be able to speak, in honesty and truth, the story of Jesus so that story can go on.

49) The Triumph of the Cross

Sept. 14

<u>Scripture Readings:</u> Numbers 21-9; Phil. 2: 6-11; Jn. 3:13-17

(N.B. Some years this feast of the Triumph of the Cross replaces the Twenty-Fourth Sunday of the Year. The Twenty-Fourth Sunday offers the central gospel event of Peter's recognition of Jesus as Messiah (Mk. 8: 27-35) which in Mark's Gospel is immediately followed by a prediction of the passion. Because Jesus predicts his passion in this gospel some of this homily may be transferable. A homily for the Sunday follows)

I bring two vivid personal images to my reflections on this scripture today.

The first happens every time I hear this Gospel text from John. I cannot help but see in my mind's eye a sight that many Americans saw on television all through the 80's at almost every sporting event. Behind the green at the Masters, in the stands at World

Series and Super Bowl, courtside at the NBA finals, always ubiquitously present, a tall African-American man with a Technicolor "afro" holding a sign saying "John 3:16". Like hundreds of others I suspect I looked up the text: "God so loved the world that he gave his only son ..."

I begin so grateful to that young man constantly reminding us of what we so badly need to know.

My second image involves experience of two deaths which occurred within days of each other -- Princess Diana and Mother Theresa. Both women famous, much revered, deeply mourned. One powerful, beautiful, enormously rich who, to her credit cared about the weak, the vulnerable. The other poor, small, fragile who in her constant care for the poor became somewhat powerful.

As we celebrate today a feast called The Triumph of the Cross I find myself asking of these two women, which one was the most happy? Which one had the more serene and grace filled life? Which one, in all honesty, would we like to be?

Though our world says Diana had it all, there is evidence in abundance that her life was deeply tormented, a painful public divorce, a fight for her children, a constant struggle for psychological well-being. The face of Mother Theresa radiated peace and inner wholeness. These two lives demonstrate, with some irony, the clearest imaginable understanding of The Triumph of the Cross.

There is something about following Jesus, becoming a suffering servant, giving everything we have to others that works, it brings life. Jesus was on to something!

God loves us so much, he sent us Jesus.

Jesus loves us so much he shows us the way to happiness.

But because the way of Jesus involves choosing a path of suffering we are not always able or willing to follow it.

The readings today are much like those of Lent, of Holy Week, of Good Friday. Their emphasis is on The Triumph of the Cross, the victory. The central reading today, the Philippians hymn, deserves particular attention. I like to paraphrase it in language that is less churchy.

Paul sings a hymn to Jesus who though he was God did not consider being God such a big deal, something he needed to hold onto, grasp at, cling to. Jesus let go. He emptied himself of everything it was to be divine and entered fully into our human existence. He became a servant. And once he became a servant he went the whole way, the "whole nine yards". He became obedient; he responded to the world the way it was, not the way he wanted it to be. Jesus accepted the suffering that love brought and he did so through suffering, even to the point of death.

Because he went the whole way, was fully human, fully loving, even to the point of a criminal's death, God looked at Jesus with even more than the enormous love God had for Jesus in the beginning.

God reached down and lifted Jesus up, brought him out of the grave, out of death. He placed him high above us and pointed to him saying, "See, that's how to be human! That's what I had in mind when I turned out this human race! That's the fullness and the very best of being human. That's what you all can aim at."

And God, holding this Jesus up invites us to call him "Lord." And we all bow our heads and bend our knees saying, "This is the first and best of us! Praise God!" That's what this reading tells us!

Everything in the world around us invites us to get as much stuff as possible. Everything in the world around us invites us to avoid pain at all cost Buy a faster car, a more powerful computer, a better deodorant and we will be happy. And God lifts Jesus up and says, if you really want to be happy, getting more stuff won't help, and don't be afraid to suffer on other's behalf. Don't avoid serving others, especially those most in need.

The beautiful smiling face of Mother Theresa as she holds a dying baby in her arms tells us this just may be the truth.

Before we move on to the Eucharist I am reminded of a story.

Once upon a time two brothers worked a farm together. They were modestly successful but not rich. Each stored his harvest in a separate barn.

One night one of the brothers awoke. He thought to himself: My brother is all alone. I have a wife and three children to care for me as I age. My children will be sure I am never poor. My brother has no such assurance. It is not fair that we split our harvest in half. I will arise and take half of my harvest and put it in my brother's barn. He got up and took half of his harvest and put it in his brother's barn. From then on he did the same each week.

Just a couple of hours later, the other brother awoke with a thought: I am all alone. My brother has a family to care for and far more responsibilities than I. It is not fair that we split our harvest in half. I will arise and take half of my harvest and put it in my brother's barn. He got up and took half of his harvest and put it in his brother's Barn. From then on he did the same each week.

For years each brother lived amazed that though they freely gave away half of their harvest what they had was never diminished.

One night several years later the two brothers met on the road between the barns, each transporting half of his harvest to the other. Immediately they realized what had been going on for years. With laughter they feel into each other's arms, embraced and wept.

There, on that spot, they built a cross, a shrine
to the God who enriches us by our own giving away,
to the God who loves us so much he sent his son to show us how to be servants,
to the God who lifts up Jesus and tells us
this is how to be fully, joyfully, completely human.

Beneath the shrine they inscribed:

"The Cross indeed Triumphs!"

50) The Twenty Fourth Sunday

Scripture Readings: Is. 50: 5-9; James 2:14-18; Mk. 8:27-35

At the very center of Mark's Gospel, Jesus asks us along with those first followers: "Who do you say I am?"

It is not enough, the gospel today assures us, to acknowledge that Jesus is the Messiah. We are challenged to accept the kind of messiah he will be. The implication of this messiahship is the heart of today's message.

One of the most powerful negative images I have ever seen is in the movie Betrayed. I remember vividly dozens of men in Nazi uniforms, burning crosses, angry, bigoted words and then the entire group standing and singing "Amazing Grace!" As much as anything I have ever seen this raises the question what does it mean to believe in Jesus?

And today, so many who identify as Christians, still burn crosses in racial animosity, still support imprisoning children and families "longing to be free, as they cross our borders, still speak of a" prosperity gospel" in which God's love is shown in material wealth and those who are poor are somehow inadequate in faith.

We spend our lives trying to get straight what kind of Messiah Jesus is. We are enjoined in a collective struggle to respond to the question of today's gospel, "Who do you say I am?" The heart of the readings today lies in the realization that Jesus is not just any old messiah but a Suffering Messiah. Peter didn't want to believe that and neither do we.

Everyone of us when we were baptized were signed with the cross of Jesus, were claimed for a crucified savior. Everyone of us are invited to live and love under the banner of the cross believing such a life will be ultimately salvific. This cross stuff is not an end in itself, but a corrective to the world vision that dominates our surroundings. Jesus invites us into mystery, into paradox, into life. Jesus speaks what he believes and he lives out what he speaks and this life puts him in conflict with his world.

Joy, happiness, fulfillment are found in being poor, in sorrowing, in compassion, in thirsting for justice, in being weak and meek, in turning cheeks, and sharing what one has. This is the path to suffering unavoidable for the Messiah, and for those who follow him.

The most telling aspect of the Gospel today is that Peter tries to talk Jesus out of his path to wholeness. Peter who first recognizes the messiahship of Jesus is then the first to want him to be a different kind of Messiah. In effect, Peter says to Jesus: "Don't do it that way; you're a miracle worker, you're popular, you've got everything going for you. We're on a roll, let's keep it that way."

Jesus flares up, as angry as he appears anywhere in the gospel story. He does not need Peter's negative voice, but his support. I imagine Jesus saying, "Peter, you are my best friend, help me in this! Don't you of all people try to talk me out of this, or ask me to water down the reality of what I am entering into!" Jesus wants and needs human support that we all do to live out the tough choices he will make. He does not need Peter telling him to do it another way.

I think of Dan Berrigan, the Jesuit peace activist. He tells in his biography how painful it was during the Vietnam war when Church and Jesuit leaders tried to talk him out of being a peacemaker, tried to turn him away from challenging the militarism of our national policies. He was not nearly as sad at government persecution as that believers, his own superiors and his brothers in the Society did not support him. To those that did his gratitude to them was immense.

Jesus needed support from Peter and we all need support to be faithful to Jesus.

We Catholic Christians are a community of people who need to support each other in our messianic presence in the world. It is not easy to do so – to challenge each other not to walk away, but to feed those who are hungry, to care for the sick, to shelter the homeless whatever the cost.

Jesus speaks about losing ourselves, taking up a cross if we want to find life. The words are terribly true, but often and easily misunderstood. We need to seriously reflect to get beneath the possible mis-reading of this deeply human truth. Some small ironic part of me wishes that Jesus had had a short course in Jungian psychology. The concepts are similar, but the language of Jung makes the point of Jesus more clear. I imagine Jesus saying, in a contemporary fashion: millennium way:

> Take the risk of letting go, of really discovering your best and truest self. Such surrender will be a cross. Risk giving up your false and superficial ego, not holding on to what your family, your church, your society too easily force on you. Discover your real gifts, real feelings, real convictions. Then you will have something to give to your church and to your world.

Too often we have used these words about "losing yourself" to encourage people to give up themselves before they have a self to give up. These are words for mature believers. When we in the Church invite people to offer their gifts for ministry to parish, or societal needs, we do so out of hope that people will discover what their personal best gifts are and how to use those gifts for others, not just rush compulsively trying to fulfill every imaginable need. There are many, many good things to do; not all of them are good for me to do! We Catholic Christians, disciples of Jesus are a community of believers supporting each other in living that vision, teasing out the best and finest part of one another to be given to others in love.

Finally, when I focus on not merely saying to Jesus: "You are the Messiah!" but accepting the kind of messiah he is and the discipleship required, I get overwhelmed, scared, confused. I love a story by John Shea in which he imagines a very discouraged disciple in his room, depressed, eating popcorn by the handfuls. Jesus shows up in the room. They have a long conversation during which Jesus instructs him on many things, including how to eat popcorn -- one kernel at a time, savoring each bite. The dialogue ends like this:

Disciple: "You walk too fast; I can't keep up!"

Jesus: "Better to be out of breath behind me, than ahead of anyone else."

Disciple: "I need a more moderate master so I can be a better disciple."

Jesus: "You are a perfect disciple. You can't handle my death!, my Father scares you, and you don't know how to eat popcorn. Why live out of something smaller than yourself. You love me because I am large enough to betray!"

This helps me as I struggle for a definition of myself as a believer, and ourselves as a believing community. When I get clear on what it is that Jesus invites us into I agree with Dan Berrigan who says: "We serve a mystery and we serve it badly."

We are a community of people who want Jesus to be central and decisive in our lives, who want to support each other in living out this conviction, who want to know our gifts, our goods, our dreams, our ideas, and offer them to the building of God's reign.

Together, humbly, hopefully, we pledge ourselves to that in Eucharist today.

51) The Twenty-Fifth Sunday

Scripture Readings: Wis. 2:12-17-20; James 3:16-43; Mk. 9:30-37

I am convinced that to the extent that Jesus established a Church at all, he did not establish a hierarchy but rather a "lower-archy". The most important members of the community of Jesus are those who serve others. The most exalted role is the lowest. We give this notion lip service as we call our highest authority, the Pope, *The Servant of the servants of Christ*. But we rarely look at the Church with such eyes.

Just as Jesus "emptied himself," of everything it was to be God, so the follower of Jesus empties self, takes the form of a child, becomes the servant of all. Everything is turned upside down. Still, like those first disciples we have been arguing about who is first or most important all through our two thousand year history.

This saying about discipleship involving service rather than au-thority or power immediately follows a prediction of the passion. Jesus will suffer; so will his followers. The Gospel today seems to invite us to reflect on how becoming like children might involve us in the sufferings of Jesus.

I vividly remember a Eucharist I celebrated with a group of young adults in a parish where I served many years ago. Most of this group of 25-30 year olds were former Jesuit volunteers. Each had spent some time in service, living simply, struggling for justice. Now as they married, got "regular" jobs, were buying houses and worried about bills, they came together to talk about their lives as disciples. They wanted still live out the values of a simple lifestyle, community, and a concern for justice over the long haul and in the real world. They wondered how keep their youthful vision alive? They sought to name the vision they did not want to lose?

It happened almost by chance that the first child of this group had recently been born. After we read the gospel that we listened to today we placed a 5 month old infant on a blanket on the floor in front of us. We asked the question, what does it mean to become the least, like a little child? What would it mean to welcome a little child?

Imagine if you will a child in front of you; what words describe her? What images capture his reality? (pause for a few moments)

Some of those that surfaced in this Eucharist were

Vulnerable .... dependent, ... curious, ... receptive .... uninhibited/spontaneous, ... teachable, ... hopeful, filled with promise, ..

Words and images like this come to us and perhaps many many more.

Do these words and images still describe us, and the Church, the community of the followers of Jesus, of which we are a part.

I want to be vulnerable, able to be hurt, not surrounded by everything that pretends to keep me safe. I desperately want our church and its leaders to be vulnerable also.

I want to be dependent on others for love, for nurture, for wisdom, for direction, and advice; I want the church of which I am a part to be needy with me.

I want to never loose my capacity to ask questions, to be curious, to reach out and touch things, seeing what and how and who they are, never satisfied with what I already know, never closing my eyes to the wonders of the world and its people around me. And how I long for a Church, a Faith community still seeking with the same intensity as that little child!

That child in our midst didn't make decisions about when to laugh, or cry, or even go potty. There is something in that spontaneity, that uninhibited approach to life, that I would like to maintain in the midst of all my pretenses to sophistication and maturity. May I never be too old to cry, never too hardened to the world to laugh!

As we looked at that child and offered other words I cannot now remember, I know the final word was *hope*.

This child before us was filled with promise. Certainly awful things could happen and some tragedy is all but assured, but there before us was all the possibilities of a human life well lived, all the promise of holiness and wisdom and courage and the triumph of the human spirit not yet quenched. Together we spoke of how we would like to look at one another as we age and stumble and never lose the sense of expectation of what we each individually and all together can be. Perhaps our deepest, most moving image of the child, the one we most wanted to maintain our selves involved this sense of hope. We wanted to always believe that the future can be better than the past.

Two parts to today's gospel need to come together:

> First, Jesus predicts the passion and promises each disciple a share in that passion. If we follow Jesus we choose to follow a path of suffering, choose to walk with him to the cross.

> Secondly: Jesus tells his followers not to struggle to be best, or try to be first, but to become the last, the least, like a little child, and to welcome the child in each other.

Before we move to the altar we might pause to pray for a few moments, honestly asking what suffering it will entail for us to hold onto or recapture those childlike virtues, to be --(repeat slowly)

> Vulnerable,
>> curious,
>>> dependent,
>>>> receptive,
>>>>> spontaneous,
>>>>>> uninhibited,
>>>>>>> teachable,
>>>>>>>> a beacon,
>>>>>>>>> a source of hope.

Jesus says: Take up this cross and follow me!

52) The Twenty Sixth Sunday

Scripture Readings: Num. 11: 16,17, 25-29; James 5:1-6; Mk. 9:38-43, 45, 47-48

The readings this weekend have something to upset just about everyone: Mutilation and hell in the last part of the Gospel, warnings to the rich and even the comfortable in the reading from James, and if our conservative tendencies are bothered by anything but the most narrow definition of who really is the Church, we need to skip the entire first reading and the first part of the Gospel.

Since this expanded definition of who is doing God's work touches two readings, let me center on this point.

A few years ago I attended an ecumenical discussion about a bill pending in the state of Washington regarding what we have come to call variously "physician assisted suicide," or "death with dignity." A representative of the Washington State Catholic Conference spoke persuasively and eloquently against the bill. A Methodist

Minister spoke in favor of it, and though I disagreed with him, I found his compassion and pastoral concern quite moving; he gave the best reasons for the bill from a Christian standpoint. A philosophy teacher from a University stood in the middle, critiquing the arguments of both sides.

The discussion that followed ran the gamut of opinion. People spoke and listened carefully. There was at least something of value in every comment . . . until the final speakers. At the end some representatives of what can only be called the militant religious right arose to condemn the Methodist Minister, and the University professor to the lowest rung of hell, attacking their persons rather than their arguments. I was totally embarrassed to find myself even considering the same side as these Zealots. They seemed to condemn anyone who did not use the same words, the same concepts they used, anyone who did not reach the exact same conclusions, anyone who did not have the same degree of certitude.

In the scripture today both Jesus and Moses are very clear. Their followers want to draw very small circles and limit severely who can be called "one of us." Jesus says, let us celebrate our values, service, love wherever they are found.

My point is certainly not that the truth doesn't matter. The Gospel today speaks strongly against an attitude that would imply religious indifferentism:

"Oh, what the heck, do whatever you want, believe whatever you want."

No. The passage about cutting off feet, or hands or eyes, is a strongly poetic way of saying:

"What you do matters. It matters what your eyes see, what your hands touch, where your feet carry you! To be a follower of Jesus is serious, full time work."

But the umbrella is wide. Many people, in many diverse ways, in an almost infinite variety of settings, with different words, passions, understandings can be, together, bringing about the Kingdom.

Jesus is a poet, not a scientist. He speaks in images strong and powerful. The service and care of people is what is important, and this spirit is not confined to one language, or a particular building, or authorized channels. In fact it is better to be maimed, or drowned than to stifle God's spirit.

Frequently in a parish, in these Autumn days people are invited into an active involvement in the life of their community – participation in our liturgical ministry, invitations to singers and musicians, opportunities for teachers to help with catechetics,

Beyond all of this ministry to ourselves and as ourselves to parts of our world, we most especially need to keep sending ourselves into the world where we live. We give a terribly false impression if we seem to believe that it is what we do here at Church that matters the most – as if ministry doesn't count unless it happens in our building, or on our block, or under our auspices. The greatest temptation of the Church, or of any parish is to make us feel that we are only being church when we do things in, around, or sanctioned by the Church. Everything everyone of us does is, or can be, the letting lose of God's Spirit, to work beyond our control, beyond our sanction, wherever that Spirit wills.

The work of the Church is predominantly what we do "out there!" People in this community go from here to work in the university near by, or in Catholic or public schools. We work for the Police Department, the Telephone Company, for Public Utilities. We visit nursing homes, or work in hospitals. We help those with mental illness, or counsel families with difficulties. We parent children, schooling them at home, sensitizing them to issues of justice and compassion. We live in neighborhoods all around this city and beyond, and try to make those places Gospel places, where Jesus is more present because we are.

We may not use religious words at work or home. We may not talk God-talk. We may not even be known as Catholics where we live or work, or have our being. But we bring the Christ that lives and loves in us wherever we go. The umbrella is wide!

If we as Church give or receive the impression that what most matters is what we do here in this Church building we have failed. If what we do here on Sundays, and what happens here all week helps to energize and send us forth, giving birth to a zillion good things happening everywhere, then we are living out who we are called to be.

In the Gospel today a man "not of their company" was casting out demons in Jesus name. The apostles try to stop him and Jesus says:

"Wait! If he is doing our work, if he is helping people,
if he is bringing folks to life, what difference does it
make if he has an office, a title, a degree? If he is not
against us, he is with us!"

I love the final line of the reading from the book of Numbers today. Moses followers are upset that some people are acting like prophets, acting like Moses himself. Moses laughs at their concern. He tells them not to be jealous for him:

"*Wouldn't it be great* if all God's people were prophets,
if God's spirit were given to all, to everyone?"

Well *it is* and *they are.* We are all God's prophets ... wherever we
go, whatever we do.

May our Eucharist here strengthen us all for that prophetic call.

53) The Twenty Seventh Sunday

Scripture Readings: Gen. 2:7,8, 18-14; Heb. 2:9-11; Mk. 10:2-16

(Many Parishes have some sort of Ministry Fair, or recruitment drive, inviting people to offer time, talent, and treasure to the life of the parish. Departing from the readings of this week, a reflection like this might be of help)

Once upon a time,
In a town not far away,
a place quite like our own-- two parishes.
Each parish a deep sense of mission had,
to build a people strong within themselves,
to share their gifts with those outside their doors,
to send their members out to larger worlds
beyond their good, but narrow walls.

Each year, anew, both parishes their Mission
formed and framed and fostered once again,
with endless lists, their names to sign upon,

their services to give, good works to do.

The first, a very Catholic people sure,
at taking guilt upon themselves they experts were.
A million things that must be done at once,
each of them seemed destined to be done by each.
All felt leaned upon
to be some central part of every task.
Angers flared at slackers who their part in every task
they failed to uphold.
This anger, always just beneath the seen,
was quiet, stuffed, and managed most the time,
till councils met, or sessions planning things
began to slice the pie,
and all *their* piece demanded,
Damn the rest!

The people of this parish generous were,
yes, generous to a fault;
They gave unstintingly their treasured gifts of money, talent,
time . . . .
Gave money better spent on children's lunch,
gave time they could have spent with family, friends,
or even taking in-laws out,
gave talents not possessed but wished for.

So those who couldn't sing, the choir joined,
those who couldn't count formed stewardship,
and those who hated kids were catechists.
Since feeding poor, and clothing naked folks
most clearly were good things, all joined in them.
And everyone was always tired!
By Christmas every year they just wore out.

and people rarely stayed for very long,
but limped, or slinked, or ran away
within three years, ... never to return!
So many people good,
so much initial energy,
and, finally, sadly, such little life,
so little laughter flowed.

The other parish not so far away,
did many things the same, but miles differently.
Each year anew their mission
formed and framed and fostered once again,
with lists their names to sign upon.
They also had a zillion things to do.

This second parish found, however, **life**
between the pages of a book they heard,
and heeded, listened to, and loved,
a book filled not with guilt but with Good News,
the news that they were loved *before* they signed
the lists, or did the smallest thing . . . .
Loved by the God inviting them to celebrate
the love within this place, this family.
This book they listened to and tried to live
assured them all that none had all the burden,
that none need care for everything.
For there were within them many gifts,
each one of them had different ones,
and none of them could do what others did,
or give what others gave,
but all could share, vicariously, in all,
So in this parish only gifts were given,
the singers sang, the feeders fed, and counters counted joyfully,

while those who loved to be with kids were with the kids,
and every one knew they needed every other one,
for each could do some thing another could not do so well.

No one ever said "I need you not."
The shoes of one fit every foot,
and one heart beat neath every shirt.

And many knew the parish gladly prodded them,
to live, full speed ahead the work they did
away from there, for God, for good!

The book reminded them that those
who early followed him whose name they bore
had shared of everything.
The world more complex grown, made sharing such as this
more difficult, but still they strove
to share their gifts, their good, their joys
and sorrows all, their hope and faith and love.
They mostly found, it worked.

Their book reminded them that Jesus prayed,
and prayed for them that they be One,
so that a world believed . . .
could see their bonds of love and wonder why,
. . . and ask, . . . and join their band

The loudest sermon preached was how they lived,
and so no teacher thought her words sufficient to convert,
and preachers preached to change, not minds, but hearts,
That all be ONE.

And every year they came, despite fatigue
to start again, and move towards Easter's dawn,
the hope was always there.

So, like them, today we pause
to offer God our gifts, and give ourselves to one another's hearts,
and, then, in Eucharist again,
to share our Easter Hope.

54) The Twenty Eighth Sunday

Scripture Readings: Wis. 7:7-11; Heb. 4:12-3; Mk. 10:17-30

What must I do for everlasting life?

What do I have to do to become part of God's reign going on right now? What do I have to do, Jesus, to be part of everything you are up to? What must I do to live forever?

As with every significant story of Jesus, this is not an old question asked of someone else. This is a personal story about me, about you. Each of us at some moment in our life stand before Jesus and hear him say to us "Are you with me, or not?" Each of us have had times in our lives in which we had to move beyond gloating over the various good things we might have done and get at the root of who we really are, who we wanted to be at the core, in our guts!

If we are to get any real value out of looking carefully at this story we need to first to remember it as our own. When has it all been real, personal? When has Jesus looked me in the eye, asking whether I could let go of this relationship,

this job,

this image of myself,

this myth about the world

--to let go of whatever it might have been that blocked me to begin to follow Jesus?

I invite you to take a moment to recall your biography. When has this story been, in some fashion, yours.

The tenth chapter of Mark's Gospel is central to the entire theme of Mark. It speaks about the challenge, the cost, the call to discipleship. The entire Gospel of Mark keeps asking me the question, Will I join Jesus? Will I be a disciple? Today's gospel begins with the line, "As Jesus was setting out on his journey . . ." This is the journey to Jerusalem, to death. This is the journey into which the young apparently rich, certainly fortunate man in this story enters

The heart of the question put to him is not precisely about wealth. That's the content, the metaphor, if you will. The passage and the entire Gospel story is more a call to relationship. I have heard that if one were conversant in Greek the dialogue would sound something like this.

The Man: Master, what *things* do I need to do to have eternal life?

Jesus: What *things* have you done so far?

The Man: Well, I have done all these things, the pious religious things, the things we are supposed to do.

Jesus: Well there is one more *thing* you need to do; give up *things*, and Follow me!

In the surrounding culture wealth was a sign of God's favor. The things the man possessed showed that God was pleased with him. That's why he and the disciples are amazed – again, its about more than money. It is as if Jesus said:

> "Give up the things that are a sign of God's favor to you, give up your status, your religious identity, your self-understanding. Trust me!"

Quite simply, Jesus asks the Rich man, and asks you and me:

> Are you willing to give up every thing for me?
> Are you willing to so trust me that you will rely on no reputation
> of your own, no institution, no identity, no external sign
> of your significance. Are you willing to follow me wherever
> this following may lead, even if it leads to Jerusalem, to
> suffering, to death, believing that for you, as for me, eternal life will be found right there?

Never was this more clear to me than when, at 62, I had to give up status, reputation, security and begin my life again, if I wanted to follow the Jesus I had glibly spoken of for so many years.

John Shea uses this passage as a fanciful entree into much of Jesus central teaching. He imagines what it was like to be with Jesus in the camp, around the fireside after this man had "gone away sad, for his possessions were great."

Every day Jesus asks "Has that young man come around again? Has anyone heard from him? I wonder what became of him?" Jesus keeps worrying whether he pushed the man too much, too hard, too fast.

Eventually the disciples get tired of Jesus obsessing about this one young rich man. Peter asks "Why do you care about him so much?" Jesus goes on, in Shea's telling of the story, to say how much he cares about every single individual who comes near him, every single one – like the Shepherd cares for the sheep that is lost, like the woman cares the coin she can't find, like the Father for the Son who has apparently died and then returns.

Jesus keeps looking for this young man, keeps hoping he will I come back. We have many, many chances to respond to this invitation to discipleship. The invitation is never withdrawn. Discipleship can always be begun or renewed.

We have another chance today. How do we respond?

55) The Twenty Ninth Sunday

Scripture Readings: Is. 53:4, 10-11; Heb. 4:14-16; Mk. 10:35-45

This Gospel about sitting at the right hand of Jesus came alive for me a few years ago when an amazing event took place the week we heard the reading. This event, captured on the Evening News and seen around the world, had particular poignancy for Jesuits, those of what is called the Company of Jesus.

A candidate for the presidency of the United States was speaking at a Jesuit University about the accomplishments of the previous four years. At his right hand, the most prestigious place, sat a Jesuit priest, a good man, president of the University where the talk took place.

In the back of the room another Jesuit priest rose, speaking harshly to the political leader, questioning how good those years had really been. With intense passion this priest spoke about the plight of people he had cared about all his life – the mentally ill, the homeless, the hungry, the people of Central America. The intruding priest was dragged away by security guards. The other Jesuit remained at the right hand of the political leader who began to ridicule the unwanted interrupter of his speech. Through my particular prism the question was unavoidable:

What does it mean for these two "brothers" to be in the Company of Jesus. Who sits at the right hand of Jesus?

This image from the evening news haunts me as I listen to this Gospel in which the followers of Jesus ask to sit at his right hand when he comes into the Kingdom. What is the place of honor in this Kingdom? Who will be honored in this Kingdom?

Jesus suggests to James and John that they do not understand. He re-defines honor, acclaim. He speaks of drinking the chalice he must drink, and even being baptized with the baptism he must undergo. The line from the Gospel that most haunts me suggests that if we want to be first then we must be servants of all. That seems so overwhelming, so demanding, so impossible really. But it is at the heart of what it means to be baptized into Christ, to be a companion of Jesus. Honor, acclaim, prestige are turned upside-down.

The idea of serving "All" is frightening. But I don't think Jesus means all, as in "every single person," but more all as "without regard to status, wealth, power, amiability, similarity to myself, etc. etc." Jesus speaks of being willing to serve absolutely anyone.

Certainly a president of a University can and should be a servant every bit as much as a priest who lives with and serves the poor. The university president can be a servant to a vast array of people. But in the reign of God he would be honored because of his service not because of the size of his office, or his pay check.

Who is most honored in our parish? It ought to be whoever is most faithful in the servant's role. The Gospel both invites us to serve but also to reflect on where our values are and whom we honestly revere.

Last week the deacon in the parish where I worship was honored for his 30 years of being truly a servant for "all." The man truly is a companion of Jesus, building up the hospital ministry in the diocese, hosting tent city groups to our parish property each summer visiting a prison each week and performing myriad other service roles..

The crunch lines of the Gospel are really ones about "drinking the cup" and "being baptized with the baptism" of Jesus. Each of us has been baptized. We have all plunged into the waters with Jesus, died and come back to life with him with new eyes. The important members of the kingdom are those who have gone through this bath and been changed, put on the eyes of Christ. I was struck by the head of a parish St. Vincent de Paul Society who spends time almost every day taking the resources given to serve the poor, then, one week, serving a breakfast to the entire parish to thank them for letting him serve the poor in their name. Wow!

Each of us, each week, come up and drink from this cup. We say "Amen" yes, to the vision of Jesus – this vision of being open to serving all. Sometimes this may be in big and noticeable ways – even on national TV. But for the most part the service will be small, insignificant, continuous.

- It might be a musician who has a full time job in a university taking hours and hours of his time to help offer a different kind of worship experience to our parish at no recompense to himself.

- It might be a member of the L'Arche Community who stands up almost every Sunday and leads us in singing.
- It might be a parishioner who consistently looks for opportunities to invite people to come back to church and take another look at their faith, or one who notices if people missing from our Sunday worship and thinks to call and see if they are OK.

As companions of Jesus we all want to be with Jesus. Most simply today he suggest that such companionship is not usually on a podium in a place of honor, but rather in a place of humble, sometimes dangerous concern that all be welcomed, all be served.

56) The Thirtieth Sunday

Scripture Readings: Jer. 31:7-9; Heb. 5:1-6;Mk. 10:46-52

I remember vividly how we once celebrated the Rite of Becoming Catechumens and Candidates. Those preparing for the Easter sacraments knocked loudly on our door, then entered at the back of the church. Before inviting them up to join us we asked each in turn: "What do you ask of God? What do you ask of the Church?"

I remembered this moving ceremony as I looked at the Gospel for today. Really our catechumens and candidates, like the Blind Bartimeus, were asked "What is it you want?" That is the question Jesus asks each of us every time we enter into his presence.

Before we look more carefully at this specific passage, I want to reflect on the importance of this question: What do you want?

I believe deeply that creation keeps happening. I believe God continually creates me, creates each of us, moment after moment after moment. God creates us by the desires placed in us. What I want, what I most deeply want, what I struggle for, ache for, live for, die for – this is what keeps me growing, changing, constantly being created! God's will for me is not found outside of me somewhere. If I want to know what God truly wants for me then I need to know what I most truly want myself. What are my deepest, most honest, truest longings?

This approach is far different from what I grew up believing. I used to think that what God wanted for me was just the opposite of what I wanted. Many of us still think that way. Part of us believes in a God who wants pain, persecution, penance, instead of the wine, women/ men and song we think we want. We sometimes present God as one who tortures folks, or who makes up rules just to frustrate us.

I believe, now, quite the opposite. We are created in love, and created continuously. The deepest, truest, most honest desires we have are the creative movements of God acting out of love for us. As we stand by the various roads of our lives our challenge is to get deep down, down to the core, beneath our superficial, selfish wants to touch the deepest answer we have to the question: "What do you want? We get beneath those hopes for fame, fortune, success, good looks, athletic prowess, security and touch those deeper desires to love and be loved, to live with integrity, to live with hope and vision and laughter.

The question Jesus asks Bartimeus is the best, most radical, most creative question possible. As I say so often the Gospel story is never just about someone else a long time ago. It is always about me, about us, a story shaped by the community entrusted with the story of Jesus. This is not the story of a single blind man a long time ago, it is the story of Good News for everyone called to discipleship. A story about the blindness in all of us.

If we look carefully at the story we discover some remarkable things:

- Bartimeus is given a name in Mark, and only in Mark, probably because he was known to this early community. The name disappears as the traditional story is told by the other evangelists.
- The story is obviously shaped by tradition, for the title "Son of David," is a post-Resurrection, messianic title. His prayer "Kyrie Eleison, Christ have Mercy" is a liturgical petition used in worship by the early Christian community.
- The entire Gospel of Mark is about discipleship and this story is about every disciple. Bartimeus meets Jesus on the road from Jericho to Jerusalem, where the paschal mysteries will occur. After the meeting the once blind man, who now can see, follows Jesus along "the Way," a technical term for the first Christians who are "followers of the Way."
- This is perhaps the same blind man we meet in John's Gospel every Lent. Certainly this story makes the same central point. The blind man sees the messiahship of Jesus before those who can see. Though others in power try to silence him he keeps crying out; he trusts in the messiah, and continues to seek a cure no matter how the religious folks try to shut him up. When he can see, he follows Jesus, leaving the sighted folks behind!

This Gospel story invites us more deeply into discipleship on two levels.

First, on the personal level, what do *I* want? What do I ask Jesus to do for me. I need the clarity and the straight forwardness of Bartimeus. I need to be able to know and name and ask for what

I want God to create in me, out of me. On this personal level as I stand by the roadside and recognize Jesus I long for the grace to be faithful to God's love, God's call. I ask not to be sidetracked by the fragility of the Church or its leaders, or of society, or of myself. I ask to be able to "hang in there," to use my gifts, love God's people who pass through my life, and to be, finally, faithful. I need to be able to speak my concerns honestly, humbly, without arrogance.

This is what I ask today.

Each of us must know and name our own deepest longing.

Secondly, we need to do the same thing as a people. What do we want? The first reading speaks of the longing of a people in exile, a people who "went away weeping": needs to know what it wants in order to "come back rejoicing." The deepest longing of a people is also how God keeps creating us as a community. Communally we need to get at our best and truest longings.

Certainly our deepest dreams go beyond a split level home with a pool for everyone. Certainly our longings as a society must be more profound than avoiding an untimely birth or a less than dignified death. I cannot say for everyone what our central creative cry as a people is or should be, but an experience from the past helps me frame part of that collective longing for myself.

In a park just a few block from our church a small group of children were playing. They piled up several cardboard boxes, slabs of wood, some corrugated metal, and were crawling around in and out of this simple construction. An adult walked by and asked the children what they were up to. The oldest child responded, "We're playing shelter!"

That some of the children of our generation, even our very neighborhood are reduced to playing "shelter," the way other children play "house," speaks of something of the deepest longing I have for us as a society. If I, or anyone is too blind to see and be moved by the poverty of children in our midst than we are blind indeed.

Discipleship with Jesus has something to do with letting ourselves be part of God's creation of a more just, more equitable, more far-sighted society, one in which children would never consider playing "shelter."

Before we continue with Eucharist today, let us be still and be Bartimeus, individually and together. We hear Jesus say to us:

> "What is it you want me to do for you? In You? What
> do you need to follow me on the way? What can I do to
> make you more whole, more able to come with me?"

57) The Commemoration of All the Faithful Departed All Soul's Day

Scripture Readings: Is. 25:6-9; I Cor. 15:12-26; Jn. 1:1-5, 9-14

Before we begin our reflections on these readings I invite you to take a moment to do what this feast invites, *commemorate*, remember the faithful departed. Call into you memory, see with your mind's eye some of those whom you have loved who have passed from our midst . . . parents, children, close friends. Let their faces, voices, even their unique smell rest in your heart for a moment . . .

Remember as a community some of the people with whom we have shared our lives in our parish. .

Some famous people, perhaps . . .
Some of the great elders of our community, people who have been here, lived in our neighborhood, and prayed with us almost forever,. . . .

a close friend . .
or unknown, unnamed people who were homeless . . .

Though we have used a short and not very helpful form "All Soul's Day," really this is a day the Church invites us to remember the dead, and celebrate the hope we have for them.

Last week I listened to a young man Talk about his fears for his mother who has cancer. He was afraid she would die. When I said, among other things, "Sooner or later, she will die you know. Everyone you know and love will eventually die," he reacted with a kind of panic. He told me he knew that in a way he never had before and it was shaking his faith. "What kind of God," he asked, with the deepest question we humans have, "would let people suffer, let people die?"

Today we come face to face with the cosmic mystery of death -- not just the death of this person or that person, but the pervasive reality of death – and in the face of that mystery we choose to believe, to trust in, even to love the God who made the world thus.

When I spoke with this young man I realize how focused my own faith is in a particular kind of God, and especially in Jesus. I do not believe in a God who can or does simply take away suffering or death. I do not believe in a God of the gaps who rescues us from being human. The God I believe in rather than taking away human suffering enters into it with us. Perhaps the key line in my entire faith is from today's Gospel, "The Word became *flesh*, and lived among us."

God in Jesus does not stay distant from our sufferings, but shares in it, falls victim to it. After Jesus has fully entered into the mystery of human suffering and death, God raises him up and tells us

"Death is not the end of the story; Suffering and death do not have the final word."

I cannot believe that all of our human desires to love and be loved, to know and be known that are never fully realized in this life are finally and forever frustrated. The story of Jesus assures me I am right.

So today we celebrate that we can entrust all those we know and love who have died before us into the hands of God. This God will raise them from death with Jesus. The images of Scripture this morning are wonderful, vivid, hope filled.

> "God will destroy . . .
> The shroud that is cast over all peoples,
> the sheet spread over all nations . . ."

God will provide

> "a great feast of rich foods, well aged wines,
> . . . and every tear will be wiped away."

That's the promise in which we are invited to trust. And we trust this because Christ was raised from the dead. We touch this morning the very heart of our Christian faith.

I am glad for the person of Jesus. He said such wise things, gave such good direction for how to live a human life. I am grateful for his teachings.

I am glad for the friend we have in Jesus and the companion through life.

But I am most glad that this Jesus entered into the flesh of human existence, that he lived and loved and faced death with courage when his loving and living were not accepted. I am most grateful that this Jesus died as every one I love will die, as I myself will die. I am grateful that God reached down and picked this Jesus from the grave, lifted him up and said, This is what can and will happen to all of you ...

Today as we commemorate the faithful departed, we do not just pray for the Souls in purgatory as I believed when young. What we do is much more profound. We *remember* that everyone we know has died or will die. We know that we will die. And we remember that with faith and courage and hope because we believe that as Jesus was raised from the dead so will they all be. So will you be. So, praise God, will I!

58) The Thirty First Sunday

(Courtesy of John A. Coleman, S.J.

Scripture: Duet:6:2-6;Heb. 7:23-38; Mk 12:28-34

Our first reading from Deuteronomy, called the <u>Shema</u>, is recited every morning and twice more daily by any pious Jew:

"Hear O Israel, the Lord is our God, the Lord alone. Therefore, you shall love the Lord, your God with all your heart, and with all your soul and with all your strength."

In echoing these words in today's gospel, Jesus shows how much of a true Jew he really was (as he did in teaching us the Our Father which is a quintessentially Jewish prayer). So, on the fiftieth anniversary of Vatican II we do well to remember Vatican II's words about our relation to Jews in its <u>Declaration On the Relation of the Church to Non-Christian Religions #4 :</u>

"As the Sacred Synod searches into the mystery of the Church, it remembers the bond that spiritually ties the people of the New Covenant to Abraham's stock. The Church of Christ acknowledges that, according to God's saving design, the beginnings of her faith and her election are found among the Patriarchs, Moses and the prophets. She professes that all who believe in Christ—Abraham's Sons and Daughters according to the faith—are included in the same patriarch's call, and likewise that the salvation of the church is mysteriously foreshadowed by the chosen people's exodus from the land of bondage.

"The church, therefore, cannot forget that she received the revelation of the Old Testament through the people whom God in his inexpressible mercy concluded the Ancient Covenant. Nor can she forget that she draws sustenance from the root of that well-cultivated olive tree onto which have been grafted the wild shoots, the Gentiles. Indeed, the church believes that by his cross Christ Our peace reconciled Jews and Gentiles, making both one in Himself. The Church keeps ever in mind the words of the Apostle about his kinsmen: 'Theirs is the sonship and the glory and the covenants and the law and the worship and the promises; theirs are the fathers and from them is the Christ according to the flesh.'

Re-reading those words I am also reminded of the greeting Pope John XXIII gave upon visiting a Jewish synagogue, referring to Jacob's son, Joseph: I am Joseph, your younger brother."

The question posed to Jesus by the scribe in today's gospel was a typical one put to rabbis in his time. Which is the greatest commandment ? The rabbis often counted 613 different commandments in the Torah—248 of them positive in form and 365 negative in form. They also debated about the distinction between heavy and light commandments. So, the question about what was the first or key to the commandments would have naturally arisen toward Jesus. He answers by appealing to Deuteronomy 6:4-9 which we heard in today first reading and links it to a commandment found in Leviticus 19:17-18 which enjoins us to love our neighbor as our self.

In Luke's version of today's gospel story, the scribe then goes on to ask: well, just who is my neighbor and Luke has Jesus tell the parable of the Good Samaritan (my neighbor is anyone in need). The two commandments are linked by Jesus as one by the word "love": love of God and love of neighbor. By emphasizing inner dispositions (love of God and neighbor) and by going to the root of all the commandments, Jesus provides a help and guide to doing God's will as it was revealed in the Jewish scriptures.

Mark's community of mainly gentile converts living in a polytheistic environment where sacrifices were offered to all kinds of Gods would have taken heart to know that the Father of Jesus Christ is the one and only God and that to love this God and love of neighbor are "much more than all holocausts and sacrifices".

I want to make three brief comments to the texts we heard read today.

In our first reading we heard not only about loving God but the phrase was used about fearing the Lord and keeping his commandments. Father John Endres, Professor of Old Testament at the Jesuit School of Theology in Berkeley, giving his adult faith formation lecture on the Vatican II document on Divine Revelation, pointed out that 'fear' – the Hebrew word – really meant less fear than awe, being dazzled and overwhelmed by the fact that God first loves us into existence and sustains us by his mysterious and inexhaustible love for us.

For, quite clearly, the love command Jesus taught is a response to the Love God has first shown us. As we hear in 1 John 4:19:" We love God because he first loved us." And this love was first revealed to us especially in Jesus:"God's love was revealed among us in this way: God sent his only son into the world, so that we might live through him." (1 John 4:9). Naturally, faced with such love we stand in awe, we are dazzled, indeed we tremble, tremble as the Passion hymn puts it when it reminds us that Jesus died out of love for us: O sometimes I want to tremble, tremble, tremble. That is what fear of the Lord really means: we tremble before God's love.

Ron Rolheiser, preaching on today's gospel, recounts a student-friend of his who teaches high school religion. The student said that his students' idea of God invariably contains too much the notion that God is a kind of petty tyrant, easily offended, threat-ened by our joys and successes and that somehow we have to earn God's love by being good. He tried to present to his students Juliana of Norwich's picture of God as "sitting in heaven, smiling, completely relaxed, his face looking like a marvelous symphony". But then his students ask:" Then why be good ? If God loves us no matter what we do, then why keep the commandments? If we are not to be punished or rewarded for our efforts, then why make sacrifices."

Rolheiser insists that "simply put, we don't try to be good so that God loves and rewards us. God loves us no matter what we do and heaven is never a reward for a good life. Are these glib statements ? No, God's love, as Jesus assures us, is always both unmerited and unconditional; nothing we do can ever <u>make</u> God love us, just as nothing we do can ever stop God from loving us. God loves just as God does everything else, perfectly. God loves everything and everybody perfectly. In fact, part of Christian belief (a dogma in fact) is that God's love is what keeps everything in existence. If God stopped loving anything it would cease to be... Why be good if God loves us anyway? For the same reason that an artist does not deface a masterpiece and a lover does not violate his or her beloved. Ethics follow naturally when truth, beauty and love are properly appropriated."

Finally, Jesus says something worth paying attention to when he tells the scribe:

"you are not far from the kingdom of God." Not far ? How can the scribe be distant in any way if he understands these commandments and accepts them as most important?

Here is the thing to see. Who in fact loves God with all their heart? Who, in fact, loves neighbor as themselves ? If obeying these commandments is the most important thing, what hope is there for anybody ? The answer is—Jesus. He is the Savior. Coming to him in openness to love is the most important thing. All hope for the kingdom of heaven lies in him. And so, the scribe, who is next to Jesus, is not far from the kingdom of heaven since he is not far from Jesus. Jesus implicitly is claiming that in him can be found the love of God and neighbor and the kingdom of Heaven. In the Eucharist, we go to that Jesus who can bring close to the kingdom of heaven and to his father's love.

59) The Thirty-Second Sunday

Scripture Readings: I Kings 17:10-16; Heb. 9: 24-28' Mk. 12: 41-44

Many years ago I spent ten months in a small country in Africa, Lesotho. Two weeks before I was to leave I found myself in a remote, mountainous part of the country to do a workshop. Just after I arrived I discovered that my wallet was missing. In it were my passport, all the resources I had to get out of Lesotho and home again – certainly American Express, I had not left home without it, but some cash too. I was extremely upset especially since I presumed someone had stolen my wallet. I even said out loud my suspicion that I had been robbed since quite a number of people were in and out of my quarters at the mission where we stayed.

Two days later, on a Sunday, we finished the workshop. I said Mass for a group of sisters and waxed eloquent on the Gospel for that day which happened to be the beatitudes ... how blessed are the poor, etc. It was such a good homily people would have been led to believe that I thought it true!

After Mass we went up to the highest part of the Mission, about a mile straight uphill from the original chapel, to have lunch with the parish priest – a wonderful man, now a bishop in that country. During lunch someone knocked on the door. The priest answered the door. He came back to the table and said, to my surprise, that someone wanted to see *me*.

I went to the door and discovered an ancient, gnarled man, barefoot despite the 30 degree weather, wrapped in the traditional blanket of the people. In his hand he held my wallet. He had found it on the road from the airport to the mission. It had doubtless fallen from my coat as I carelessly walked along the road. Through an interpreter the man explained that he had discovered it almost a week before, and then, this Sunday, his one day off from working in the fields, he had walked the two miles to the mission, and the mile almost straight up the hill to the priest's house. He knew the local priest would know how to find this white man to whom the wallet belonged!

In the old man's eyes was a gentleness, an incredible gratitude because he had been able to find the owner of the wallet. He smiled as he gave it back to me. I quickly looked to see if the cash was still there, presuming it would be missing. It was all there. Though only a couple hundred dollars, probably more money than this man would ever see at once in his lifetime. I took a twenty and offered it to him, then another twenty, then another as I realized the implications of his honesty. But he refused them all. He smiled and said, "Bless you, entate (Father)," and withdrew.

I faced the task of returning to the table and explaining what had happened. The local priest smiled, patiently, wisely at my embarrassment.

This wonderful memory now overwhelms me as I read today's Gospel. I feel garbed in splendid robes. I sit on high seats. I pray long prayers, and I can appear to load heavy burdens on others and not bear them myself. And this poor widow is willing to entrust all she has to God!

Once again, the Gospel is not an old story about somebody else. This is my story, your story. In so many Gospel stories there are two people, as there are inside me, inside you. Two people pray in the temple, two sons of a generous father, two men flanking Jesus on the Cross. Always there is the hard-hearted, the religious, the pious, the blind, the closed, the careful, the one who has control. Always the broken one, the wounded, the dependent, the one who knows he/she cannot control the world and so is willing to trust entirely in God. A priest angry at what he thinks has been taken from him; an elderly poor man willing to surrender all his has found.

I picture Jesus. He has spoken to his disciples about his anger at religious hypocrites – those who talk the talk, but do not walk the walk. He comes into Jerusalem where the prophets are slain. He sits down and looks over at the temple. He watches as one of the *anawhim*, God's powerless, God's little ones, God's favorites, comes to put her last two cents in the temple collection. Two very small coins, but all she had. This story is not primarily about money; it is about Jesus who will in the next few chapters be called upon to give up all he had. Thus, his admiration for one who gives him the courage to do so.

A pastor might be tempted to make this a passage about sacrificial giving-- about giving 5% or 10% to the Church or to other needs. But this is a passage about giving *everything*. The reign of God is made up of those who give *all* they have, *all* they are, *all* they can be, like this widow, or like the old man who climbed the hill to give back another's possessions . . . or , like Jesus.

This is a story in which we find God. God isn't in the religious folks, the robe wearers, the long prayer-sayers. God is active in the widow, the old man, the one who risks everything.

We live in a society in which money is a symbol of our value. We tend to feel worth about whatever we earn. Money is a symbol of our values. Our sincerity in faith can, perhaps, be measured by what we give away, what we share with others. The Gospel invites us to give ourselves totally, in one way or another. It can be in a job of service, or as a mother, or even grandparent. We may give as a spouse, a parent, a neighbor. But that wholehearted, non-hypocritical gospel generosity is what we pray for today.

Before we move onto Eucharist we ask ourselves. Who are the widows in my life? Who are the models of faith? Who do I know who gives up everything, and invites me to do the same? And we go on to celebrate Jesus giving himself totally to us so that we can be emboldened to give ourselves completely to others.

Let us be still a moment and wonder what that might mean!

60) The Thirty-Third Sunday

Scripture Readings: Dan. 12:1-3; Heb. 10: 11-14,18;Mk. 13:24-32

I enjoyed this description of one race in a recent election::

> "We have a clear choice between
> going backwards
> and continuing to meander aimlessly."

Everything about these readings in this final Sunday of Ordinary time invites us to consider not just our immediate future in this city, but our ultimate future. How do we envision the future? How does our faith perspective impact the way we imagine the future? What choices does that lead us to make?

Our tradition takes us back to the book of Daniel and the vision of a great Archangel Michael coming finally with the promise of victory out of the greatest possible anguish.

Each of the first three Gospels includes an apocalyptic section along the lines of this reading from Daniel. Today we listen to the first Gospel, Mark. In Mark, as Jesus speaks about the end times, he expects the end to come very soon – before "this generation passes away." The first generation of Christians expected that what we have come to call the Second Coming would be very, very soon. We would neither wander aimlessly, nor turn backwards because <u>soon</u>, in a time of great darkness and anguish (as in Daniel), the Son of Man will come. The substance of Jesus message about this imminent end is this:

The forces of evil in the world, no matter how powerful they seem, will not win. It may look really gloomy, but the Son of Man will come and bring order out of chaos.

That end did not come immediately as the first generation expected. We still look forward to it. I am a firm believer that **our convictions about the future effect how we live in the present.** How will this victory of Jesus finally come? From whence comes this order? It is extremely valuable to reflect on what we think about the end of the World, the second coming. What do we mean when we say "Christ will come again?" How do we imagine this coming? This is especially true when an entire body of mis-lead so-called evangelical Christians base all their political energy around this belief.

Throughout history there have been two very different views about this return of Jesus; many Christians have only heard of one. The prevailing sense has been that we await some dramatic entrance from outside history. We don't know exactly how it will look or feel, but Christ will come from the outside, perhaps born again, but more likely blooming full blown into our midst, ready to call it all over, (ally, ally, alls-in-free) to bring the world to its completion? Christ will come again to judge us!

A more viable image, one perhaps more challenging to live out of, is rooted in the letter to the Romans where Paul speaks of a "World groaning in one great act of giving birth to Christ." This theory of the end would suggest that Christ is already fully present in germ, struggling, moving, (Tielhard would say "evolving") into fullness. Christ is already in the process of coming from the inside out. Christ is coming as we, his body bring to realization the virtue, truth, love, grace of the gospel. When we finally have become who he has called us to be, and already empowered us with his Spirit to become, he will be here finally and fully present.

The first image inclines us to a kind of <u>passivity</u> since the coming is completely outside of our control. The second image invites us into <u>participation</u> – we, the body of Christ, fight to overcome the forces that hold back and forestall the coming of Jesus and build up the loving energy that will foster that fullness of Christ's presence.

This second image connects us more closely with the earthly Jesus. He engaged the world, wrestled with the powers of that world, spoke and acted against dark forces, sought to bring order out of chaos. Jesus did not just announce the coming of the Reign of God, he spoke, loved, healed, cajoled – did everything in his power to battle that Kingdom into being. We his followers, it seems, should do the same.

The elections we just had, at their best, are an effort to put in place public servants who will help advance the values of justice, peace, community..

Here in our city, in our neighborhoods, we look for opportunities to battle poverty, hopelessness, the absence of Faith, or Hope, or Love. We try to engage the world. We struggle to be even a small part of bringing about the second coming of Jesus, believing perhaps that it will only come through the Christ who works in and through us.

Imagine for a moment, before I close, how such a conviction can color our entire lives. A mother teaching and loving her children, involved in their school and all their activities is not just doing a mother's duty; she is building the reign of God. A nurse working at a hospital is not just taking care of the sick, but being part of the long term preparation for the second coming of Jesus where all our ills will be healed. A student doing his homework is building up the body of human knowledge necessary for Jesus to come again. My wife working with others to provide opportunities for at-risk kids and housing for those without any, is building God's kingdom, however slowly. A couple standing together before the altar become a sign of God's love now, but faithful forever. Every human act, every job, every relationship you or I have can be part of the process of helping The Son of Man overwhelm the darkness.

Our convictions about the future effect how we act in the present. As we celebrate this final Sunday of Ordinary Time and come to the end of another liturgical year, we acknowledge that how we image the coming of Jesus, and how we see our part in that ultimate victory has enormous impact on how we live our lives. Jesus will come again only when we have helped bring him fully alive into our world!

61) The Feast of Christ the King

Scripture Readings: Dan. 7: 13-14; Rev. 1: 5-8; Jn. 18: 33-37

This is the final Sunday of the Liturgical Year. Next week, as Advent begins, we start the whole story over again. This is the Feast of Christ the King.

I have been fascinated lately by a prayer said frequently at the end of Mass. In part, this prayer says:

> Loving God, send us from this Assembly,
> Into the Kingdom of this world,
> with the faith to resist it,
> the courage to love it,
> and the wit to transform it,
> into the Kingdom of your Son, Jesus.

Two Kingdoms always:

The Kingdom of Pilate and his Caesars; the Kingdom of Jesus.

The Kingdom of Henry the VIII; the ultimate Kingdom to which Thomas More gave fealty.

The Dominion of Hitler; the martyrdom of Deitrich Bonhoffer.

The power of a Military regime in El Salvador; the courage of six Jesuits and their helpers to challenge it.

The economic values of the world's strongest nation; the vast army of the poor, and people like Dorothy Day and her Catholic Worker followers who stand with thbuilding walls to keep "others" outose poor.

A me first Kingdom concerned with its own power and wealth, building walls to keep o"others" out; a Kingdom of peace, promoting justice for all the people of the world.

A kingdom of dishonesty, even in religious garb, riddled with pomp and power and circumstance; a kingdom of those offering humble service, washing feet, standing with the poor.

In The Spiritual Exercises, St. Ignatius offers a key meditation on the Kingdom of Christ. The meditation occurs at the beginning of the second week, or stage, of the retreat, just as the retreatant begins to consider the life of Christ. Ignatius invites the exercitant to step back from the particulars of the life of Jesus and first consider, in general, the call proffered to him or her, very individually, from Christ the King.

I am invited as a retreatant to consider in imagination what it would be like if the most wonderful earthly leader, with the finest values and the most noble cause, came into my home and invited me to join him in his struggle; the battle involves all that is good, and true and cannot be victorious or even entered into without my help. Will I sign up? Of course!

Ignatius goes on. Then imagine, for example, that Christ <u>the King</u> comes into my kitchen, joins me for coffee, and invites me to join him in a battle to save the entire human race, the whole earth. It will be a difficult battle, but I will not be asked to go anywhere Jesus does not go first. I will never be alone, and, finally, the victory is assured.

Ignatius suggests that "only a slovenly knight" would not join up and go, full speed ahead, promising to endure any hardships just to be with this wondrous leader, Christ the King! I am invited to make an offering, a kind of "blank check," to this king,--a statement of generosity that will be filled in as I look at the mysteries of Christ's life throughout the succeeding days of the retreat.

Ignatius had been a soldier. He had fought for some fairly crummy kings, just for valor and glory, and the pride of a great name on earth. This image of a great earthly king would tap into his soldier's imagination.

For many of us, especially with a feminist consciousness or perhaps a pacifist attitude, this king/warrior/battle imagery may not touch us at all. There is another way to get at the heart of question Ignatius raises.

Who is it in my actual life that gets the best out of me? Who really challenges me to be my best and most generous self? Who is it that could ask anything of me and I would go with them, support them, serve them? When I worked in the Seattle Archdiocese with Archbishop Raymond Hunthausen, I know I was ready to respond to any request he made, so much did I admire him, and his religious leadership.

Perhaps for many this is more a relational question than a heroic one. My spouse, my children, my dad, my best friend – I would do anything for them.

If we can get in touch with what or who on a human level calls the best out of me, invites my deepest, truest, most generous response, then I can switch the image. How much more would Jesus, the Christ, in my kitchen, inviting me to go with him, urging me join him, help him -- for a victory that is assured – how much more this would touch and challenge me. Can I write that blank check for this Kingdom?

Let me return to today's scripture. Pilate wants to know if Jesus really is a King. If he says he is, then Pilate must destroy him, for he is already given to King-Caesar. Jesus, proving again that he is Irish, answers a question with a question!

"Have others said this, or are you asking of yourself?"

That is, is this your personal question? Is your life on the line? Jesus goes on to tell Pilate and us that although the Kingdom is indeed here, in this very place, with these very people, it is a different kind of Kingdom. It is the Kingdom of one born not in a castle, but a stable, one who shows his power by washing feet, and whose throne is a cross. Those who follow him are "fools, for Christ's sake." The kingdom, and the kind of battle involved are very different.

I recall the image of Robin Williams in The Fisher King, leading an army of the poor, the lame, the halt and the blind, coming up to stop an act of violence in a New York alley, not by fighting, but by singing, a kind of 'holy madness'. This crazy King leads his be-draggled chorus singing, "I like New York in June, how 'bout you?" Amazingly, the violence stops! The kingship of Jesus is even more different than the norm!

We have listened for a year to the quite radical gospel of Mark, inviting us more deeply into discipleship. We end the year today, celebrating the victory of Christ the King. In another sense we <u>begin</u> the story today and next week we start all over, entering into the mystery again preparing for birth. Today we ask: Who gets the best out of me? How am I moved to real generosity? Can I write that blank check, open to however Jesus wants me to offer service in his Kingdom?

And we pray:

> **Loving God,**
> **As you sent us into the Kingdom of the World,**
> **give us the faith to resist it,**
> **the courage to love it,**
> **the wit to transform it,**
> **into the kingdom of your son, Jesus.**

Book Three
The C Cycle

Preface: Reflections on Liturgical Preaching

In the first section of homilies, I began with a <u>Preface on Preaching</u>, in general. I focused on what should be the Jesus-centered nature of preaching, the need for stories that touch the real lives of real people. I voiced my hope that these homilies would be useful, not just for homilists, perhaps not even primarily for homilists, but for the "folks in the pews" who frequently are not nourished by preaching as they deserve to be.

It was, and is again, my hope that, individually or on various communal settings, Christian people can use these homilies for their own reflection, use them, in a very real sense, to write their own homiletic on how God deals specifically, concretely, enfleshed, to them.

I begin this volume with a further reflection on preaching, here the need for homilies rooted in the ebb and flow of each liturgical season.

I should not have been surprised but I was. Some years ago, I led an adult Education session in a neighboring parish. The month was October; we were nearing the end of yet another liturgical year, yet another cycle of readings. The session dealt with liturgy, specifically the Liturgy of the Word. I asked the thirty-five people present what "Cycle" we had been on all through this year? No one understood the question. I asked again, which Gospel we had been listening to each Sunday? Again, silence . . . eyes a bit glazed over. I tried again. Do you recall hearing us talk about "The Gospel of Mark, "or "The Gospel of Matthew," or "The Gospel of Luke" more frequently lately? After a few false starts we did identify Luke.

I had already lost any hope of building my entire class on this significant fact, so unknown to my listeners; still, I summoned up the courage for a final question: What are some of the distinguishing characteristics of the gospel we have been listening to this year? How is Luke perhaps different from the other versions of the story of Jesus?

No one had anything to say.

The fault lies not with these well-meaning people, but with how the Word of God, in scripture, has been presented to them.

I introduce this third volume of homiletic reflections from the C Cycle (Luke's Gospel) with some attention to the context and consistency of our preaching.

The Second Vatican Council insisted that the reform of the liturgy should promote an appreciation for the Scriptures by providing the faithful with "more ample, more varied, and more suitable" (SC 35) readings at every Mass. We are asked to do this by opening up the treasures of the bible "more lavishly, so that richer fare may be provided for the faithful at the table of God's Word" (SC 51).

For almost half a century now (since November 29, 1971), fully sixteen cycles with each Gospel, we Catholics have listened each Sunday to readings from the revised lectionary promulgated after Vatican II. Over and over, we have been through the Gospel of Mark, of Matthew, of Luke. Yet I would wager that most Catholic people, like that small group in a single parish one Sunday morning, have very little idea how one Gospel differs from another, no awareness of what the particular nuances of each might be.

Our preaching each individual Sunday has improved mightily in these years but my experience suggests that we still fail to see, and to indicate to the assembly gathered, how Sunday relates to Sunday or how a series of Sundays relate to a season, or how a season relates to the entire liturgical year.

Recently a friend, shortly before his ordination, asked me what I thought was the most important aspect of preaching. He wondered if I agreed that people who listened to our homilies would most remember whether we honestly seemed to care about our message or not. They would remember our passion, or lack of it. They would remember the stories we used to weave our reflections together. They would remember if we touched their very real lives in any way.

I think those things are true.

Still, I find myself more and more wanting to insist that we are not preaching just individual homilies. Nor are we preaching only to a group of individuals. We preach to a community. We hope that, out of our preaching, a community of faith is formed. Moreover our concern is not merely, or even primarily, with what a particular individual or the entire assembly remembers from what we say *each week*. Our task is over time, week after, week, through the repetition of cycles and seasons and feasts, and especially by the Triduum and Easter at the heart of each liturgical year, to help fashion a people. Like the potter with his clay, God's people are shaped and molded by the Word of God, fashioned into a Eucharistic people, ever more eager for the task of building the Kingdom.

The homilist must indeed speak from personal faith, speak with some passion and authenticity, weave stories, and touch lives each week, but the larger challenge is to help form a Christian community over time.

The complexity of this task is compounded by the mobility of our society. The same people will not likely be present each week. Some repetition, referring back to last week, or ahead to next week is frequently necessary so the continuum can hold.

The homily each week matters. It matters more what happens over time, over a year, or several years, or a lifetime. The liturgical life of the Church is a marvelous treasure that, if respected, if given the full scope of its variety and integrity, can instruct and inspire in ways we have barely begun to suspect.

I imagine a parish, to help foster this consciousness, could perhaps begin each liturgical year with some ceremony, blessing those members of the community (priests included) who will preach to us this year. Each homilist would be presented with the Gospel of Luke, or Matthew, or Mark, entrusted to them to be passed on to us over the course of this year. On that same Sunday, in conjunction with this missioning, the parish could offer an adult education session pointing out the particular nuances of each Gospel, what we can listen for and look for in the year ahead.

Liturgical preaching begins in the Gospel ascribed to each cycle, but it does not end there. Various seasons and moods and movements hold the entire year together. No Sunday stands alone; each is part of a pattern.

If we go on to preach liturgically during Lent, for example, no Sunday would stand by itself. Every one who heard the Lenten homilies would avidly long to be present at the Triduum and particularly the Easter Vigil. All would be deeply, dramatically aware that to miss these key events would be to fail to complete the journey they set out on. To miss the Triduum is to somehow miss the point of Lent.

Only in the past forty years, since the Rite for Christian Initiation for Adults (RCIA) began to be implemented in this country in 1978, have we realized the organizational framework for the scriptures of Lent. Each Sunday offers a part of the final instruction to those preparing for Baptism. This is especially true of the third, fourth and fifth Sundays when we celebrate the Scrutinies with the Elect (those preparing for Baptism at the Easter Vigil). If we respect the reason why all these readings were chosen, it is impossible to preach on the Sundays of Lent without relating each specific gospel passage to its Baptismal implications.

The temptation of Jesus in the desert, for example, must be connected with the Baptism of Jesus which it follows. The Gospel is chosen by the Church to heighten the entire experience of exorcism and wrestling with the demons that the Elect (and by extension all of us) experience during Lent.

Liturgical Preaching would help us to hold together the marvelous season of Easter. We now refer to this entire season with its wonderful Greek name, *Mystagogia*. The Church hopes, during successive Sundays, each of them yet another celebration of Easter, to break open the mysteries that the neophytes (those newly baptized members of our assembly) and all of us have experienced through the Triduum. What happened to us in those three days? What happens to someone who dies and rises with Christ? The Easter season is not concerned primarily with what happened to Jesus when he rose from the dead. The concern is far more with what has happened to all of us because of Jesus. What has happened to all of us who plunged into those baptismal waters, who were sealed with the Holy Spirit, who came again or for the first time to the Eucharistic table.

The entire Easter season is linked by this catechetical understanding; the weeks cannot be adequately preached independently of each other. One can give a wonderful homily on "Doubting Thomas" for example, and speak about the struggles we all have to hold onto faith, but unless this is connected with the need to trust the Easter experience we all had in the Pachal Triduum, lest the power and integrity of the season gets lost.

At the end of this wonderful season of Lent-Triduum-Easter we celebrate a Novena from the *Ascension* to *Pentecost*, preparing for our birthday. Jesus leaves, and leaves us behind. Angels admonish us to quit looking up to heaven. The Spirit sends us into the market place. The preaching of this final stage of Easter needs to make the connection with all the forty days of Lent, the three days of Triduum and the seven Sundays of Easter that lead up to them. Pentecost is not a feast all by itself, but the culmination of all the celebrations that have preceded it.

Another example.

Every third summer, during cycle B, we interrupt the Gospel of Mark with five successive Sundays (seventeen to twenty-one) from the sixth chapter of John. One summer, as I traveled around the Western United States, I was in a different Church each Sunday. Essentially I heard the same message each Sunday - a homily about the Eucharist, and the Catholic belief in the real presence. None of those preaching took the specific text of John, though each Sunday differs from the other remarkably. Each took the theme suggested by the reading, but not the specific text. I could not help but wonder what happened on the other Sundays in each Church. Perhaps a different preacher gave another talk on the Eucharist.

Several other aspects of the implications of Liturgical preaching invite comment. We end each liturgical year with the Feast of Christ the King. Though the name is the same this is not the same feast each year. In cycle A, the Gospel is the Final Judgment scene in Matthew. In this most ecclesial gospel we discover we will finally be judged by how we treated the "least" of the disciples of Jesus. We will be part of the Reign of God or not depending on that treatment. This is a culmination of the entire Matthean gospel.

In cycle B the Gospel for the Feast of Christ the King is taken from the Passion account of John, even though most of the year, including the immediately preceding weeks, has been concerned with the Marcan Jesus. The contrast is jarring and perhaps deserves mention. John makes the case that Jesus' Kingdom is not of this world. Commentaries on Mark (I think particularly of *Binding the Strong Man* by Chad Myer) have suggested how enmeshed with this world the Marcan Jesus is. At the end of the year of Mark we are faced with the question whether this kingdom is rooted in, or separate from the World. However we approach the question the issues are decidedly different on this final feast in year B, than they were in year A.

The Gospel on the Feast of Christ the King for cycle C, the scene of Jesus offering his Kingdom to a thief next to him on the cross, is typical of the constant compassion of Jesus in Luke. More than any other Gospel, Luke is filled with stories and words of compassion; we are encouraged to "be compassionate as the Father is compassionate." We hear about the Prodigal Son and the Forgiving Father only in Luke. The cycle C Gospel offers yet another approach to the feast of Christ the King--again this year the culmination of a specific year of our liturgical life. Each year in ways different than the previous one, we are invited to bring together our reflections on who Christ Jesus is, as seen through different prisms, from different angles, in different ways. Good preaching, preaching rooted in a feel for the Lectionary, respects this difference and helps a community to realize the fullness of what it has been experiencing all through the year.

Finally, consider perhaps the most obvious instance of the need for liturgical preaching. The season of Advent always suggests a preparation for letting Jesus be born into our midst. Everything about this season stands in counterpoint to the culture that surrounds us. The darker colors, the quiet music, our emphasis on waiting, preparing, hoping invites us not to start the Christmas parties yet, invites us not to sing the Christmas songs until we are done with this season. To preach Advent is to invite the most counter-cultural experience we can demand of ourselves. We prepare with the Baptist. We wait with Mary. It is not Christmas yet, not till Christmas Eve.

Then, as the world around us dismantles its trees, abandons its seasonal music and gets on with the important business of football bowls, we invite people to continue Christmas for three more weeks and beyond as this child is manifest (*Epiphanied*) to the world. Our world tries to celebrate Christmas before it arrives, then move on to other things. The Christian liturgy, and the preaching that under girds it, invites us to keep celebrating Christmas on and on, into yet another year of looking carefully at Jesus!

The task of preaching can be overwhelming. Consider what is asked of the homilist already--to break open the Word of God, three separate readings and perhaps a psalm, to a community diverse in age, education, ideology and commitment. The homilist is expected to relate an ancient word to the experiences of this varied contemporary assembly, to deepen their commitment to Jesus, and their eagerness to serve God's world, to lead them to the Eucharistic table, and to do all this is ten to fifteen minutes.

When too much is already asked, does this urging to preach with a deeper consciousness of the liturgical feast or season simply add one more unfulfilled expectation? It need not. We need not have a brand new message each week. The task of preaching is, in fact, made easier if homilies are designed in clusters, sets of reflections building on similar themes through seasons.

All the homilies of Lent, or Advent can be seen as a unit, a single extended reflection each week building on and relating to the past week and to the next. One central theme can be the focus of an entire Easter season as we ponder how what happened to Jesus changes us. Even ordinary time can be a chance to grow in an understanding of the Jesus of Luke or Mark or Matthew.

I would dream that ten to fifteen years from now, as our preaching changes, all our listeners come to know, with both head and heart, these few central realities about the mystery we preach: that we have in our rich tradition not one story of Jesus, but four quite different ones, each offering important nuances to our communal faith; that everything in Lent leads to the Triduum, the Easter Vigil; that Advent invites us to stand counter to the department-store-culture that purports to begin Christmas at Thanksgiving; that Christmas starts with the Vigil and goes on for several weeks; that no time is "ordinary," and each Gospel gives us precious and unique insights into the Jesus we seek to follow; and that the way we worship continues to speak volumes about what we most deeply believe.

It is in that hope that the following homilies are presented.

1) The First Sunday of Advent

Rooted in Jer. 33:14-16; 1 Thes. 3:12-4:2; Lk. 21:25-28, 34-36

Christianity is counter-cultural.

The followers of Jesus stand, always, in some tension, some opposition to the cultural world we inhabit.

Nowhere is this tension more evident than in the season of Advent, these dark days before Christmas. Our culture begins to speak of a "Holiday Season," even before Thanksgiving. We celebrate (mostly with abundant commercials) until Christmas Day, when we abruptly stop. Christmas carols surround us. Santa Claus is not "coming to town"; he is already everywhere. Our culture blissfully ignores the gloom of winter, brightening it incessantly with glitz and glimmer, holding back the darkness either with an abundance of "stuff," or the illusory promise of it.

Meanwhile the Church, we Christian people, are invited to enter into Advent. We choose to *experience* the darkness. We acknowledge the misery. We feel the need. We let ourselves be touched by the apparent absence for grounds of hope.

We do this so that we can look forward to celebrating at Christmas a new birth of the presence of Christ in an abundance of ways. We will celebrate Christmas when it comes and we will continue to celebrate the manifold presence of God in our midst in the Epiphanies that spell out the wonder of the feast. Having watched and waited, we will carry our celebration, once it comes, into a New Year, into the beginnings of the story of Jesus, even unto Easter and beyond.

I have two pictures of what we are about.

First, I imagine our culture with a beautifully wrapped Christmas package, just now placed beneath the tree. The package has wonderful ribbons, beautiful paper, and enormous size. We grab up the package and tear it apart in an instant (like a five year old before Midnight Mass). This package, so quickly, so rudely opened, is empty! There is absolutely nothing in it. When we tear hurriedly through all that is supposed to help us prepare for and savor the gift, there is no gift; it becomes hollow, non-existent.

The other image. We carefully consider every fiber of the package. We gaze at every tightly bound ribbon, every heavily taped seam. We look at everything that keeps us from getting at the present. We appreciate the ways we are prevented from seeing the gift.

Slowly, slowly, slowly, we take off the outer wrappings that disguise the gift so that when we finally get inside we will find something (someone?) so precious that we can never not hope again! We find Christ, *the Christmas present* (presence) so eminently worth waiting for, worth Adventing for.

Today I invite us to help each other to slow down and savor our preparation for the offering from our God who really does "Care enough to send the very best."

The readings throughout Advent, every Sunday and every day, help us to experience this waiting. Let me look quickly at today's readings to hint at some of that awareness, that waiting.

Our first reading from Jeremiah speaks of a hope-filled promise to the people, the family of Israel, who right now experience deeply God's absence. This tribe of people knows its pain, knows its longing. And we, in our families in this Advent time would do well not to run away, but to admit the addictions, the alienation, the pains of separation, that we experience.

For example, one out of every four families in our land--likely here in our church today--is touched negatively by alcoholism or drug addiction. Most deny it for a long time and life never comes. Can we, this year, if need be, pause enough to know this darkness, this emptiness, or any other that is that is indeed part of our families, any families.

Jeremiah is speaking about a larger family, really, a people, all who make up his Jewish family of faith. We would do well this Advent to feel our pain as Church. How desperately we need a re-birth of the Spirit of Jesus in our Church both large and small. We do not do well to deny the darkness, the separation, the conflict, the ennui that sometimes overwhelms us as a parish, and as a larger Church. We are inundated with voices urging us to more war, to deeper separation from those different from us in color or culture or creed. We need to prepare to let the deep values of Jesus, with his compassion for the poor, his religion rooted in the heart, his passion for God's Kingdom of Justice be reborn in us as a community of believers this Christmas?

In the second reading Paul invites the Thessalonians to be holy and blameless. As we begin our Advent journey, we acknowledge that we are neither holy nor blameless. Advent will be successful for us if we stop long enough, get quiet enough, to know the various voids in us that only Jesus, re-born, can fill.

Finally, consider the Gospel, with its cosmic sense of disaster, doom. Luke is careful to point out even in the face of darkness that Jesus speaks words of comfort and encouragement. But even for the disciple there is no escape from calamity. We can watch and pray for the power to endure it, to overcome it, but we cannot fully avoid the realization of darkness. So we take the time this Advent to look at our world and admit where the darkness seems to be winning, so the presence of the light of Christ can fill it.

It does not help to deny, for example, that 25% of children in America are hungry and under- educated or that the number of people, especially people of color, in our jails increases every year, more than any other nation on earth.

Our hands feel tied, unable to know how to ease the on-going civil war in Syria without more violence, more refugees, refugees we seem unable to welcome and embrace.

We still continue wars in Afghanistan and Iraq that we don't know how to end or win.

We need to look honestly at the wrappings that hide us from the presence of Jesus if we are to be part of unwrapping Him and letting Him be born in our world and in ourselves this year.

Our culture has already started Christmas. For many, the actual arrival of the feast will be quite empty. Against this we begin Advent. We wait. We experience our emptiness now, our longing, our need. And slowly, together, we unwrap the present (the deep presence) of a light coming into the world that can blot out all darkness.

2) The Second Sunday of Advent

Rooted in Lk. 3: 1-6

We would do well to begin our reflections today in the same fashion as the Gospel:

> As Donald Trump was continuing his presidency,
> When Jay Inslee was beginning a second term governor of Washington,
>
> When Francis struggled to change what it meant to be Pope
> When violent gun deaths occurred in our nation almost daily
> And 500,000 refugees left Syria in a single month
>
> Right then

The Word of God came to us in our various deserts, inviting us to respond,

to say "yes,"
to chose life,
to let our light shine in the darkness,
to help usher in the deeper birth of Jesus in our World!

As Luke points out, it was an unlikely time--Caesar, Pilate, Annas and Caiaphas are not names of benignity, or opportunity, or hope. But it was right *then*, concretely, specifically, *then* that the story of The Good News began with John.

The most important thing about the Readings today is this specificity. God comes to us for a new beginning, for choices, for conversion, *right now!*

If we reflect on our experience most of us can point to a moment in our personal history in which we had to choose. I recall a friend, a recovering alcoholic, telling me about that dramatic moment when he stood on a bridge about to jump. He had an overwhelming experience of the presence of God and he knew in his bones that he had to decide to live, and to live differently!

Most of us have known a moment when:

- We had to return to Church, or leave it all behind,
- or decide to marry this man or this woman,
- or end this relationship,
- or get out of this abusive relationship no matter the fear,
- or take on a new job, a different vocation, to be authentic to ourselves.

We have known a time when we had to let go of everything and trust God, finally and forever.

I remember after I had debated about back surgery for almost a month my doctor said to me "It's time. Shoot, Luke, or drop the gun!"

More importantly I recall the moment I knew I had to depart from the Jesuits, the priesthood I had loved, if I were to live out my final years with any health and hope.

Over and over in my office I met with people in some "crisis," literally a critical time in their lives to move ahead, take a new step, get a new job and I was called to root for them in the name of a whole community I was serving.

Once, I recall, a woman who had been fired from her job came in tears. She did not like the job she had, but it provided security. She had many options ahead of her, but each was scary in its own way. She had a deep sense of God inviting her to a new place in her life and all she needed was a bit of a push, an encouragement that this crisis might In fact be of God

Every Sunday, as we dismiss Catechumens I am aware of the stories of conversion they bring with them. That it is this year, at *this* time of their lives, in *this* specific moment of history that they want to choose to follow Jesus and enter into this community of Faith. Each has a different story, but each invites us to remember the gift that our story is.

Advent is a season in which the Church tries to provide the opportunity, the invitation, the motives to let this be such a time of conversion, of new birth, perhaps in less dramatic ways, for all of us. We are invited to look at Jesus, the promise, the light, the hope, the possibility of new birth and to say "Yes," anew and again.

The central metaphor of the first reading today speaks of "valleys being raised up" and "mountains being lowered"--images eminently worth noticing. We so easily see the obstacles, all the reasons why we should postpone whatever new place we are being invited to.

> The alcoholic cannot imagine life without ever another drink.

> A priest cannot imagine life without the satisfaction of ministry

> The battered wife cannot imagine living without the financial support even of the man who beats here.

> How will we live without that pay check while I am in between jobs? What if we have to move, or switch schools? "To dig I am not able, to beg I am ashamed."

There is always a reason why we cannot act. The entire biblical story is filled with honest excuses: Isaiah can't speak in public, Moses is wanted for murder, Jeremiah is too young, Mary is a Virgin, Peter a sinner – all, initially at least, want to escape God's invitation. The response is always the same. "I will be with you, The Spirit will overshadow you . . ."

The Jewish people in Exile trusted that they would be able to come back to the promised land one day. God will remove the barriers, geographical, psychological, spiritual. God will smooth out the valleys, level the mountains and make it possible to walk back on foot to the land so many miles away.

John the Baptizer, sent to prepare a way for Jesus, proclaimed that this was the time that the obstacles would be removed, the way would be made straight for the coming of our God into history.

This very day, this second Sunday of Advent in the year 2015, I invite us to be aware of choices we need to make. If the obstacles seem overwhelming we try to hear the Advent promise that

If we can say "Yes,"
God can smooth the way . . .

3) The Third Sunday of Advent

Rooted in Zeph. 3:14-17; Phil. 4:4-7; Lk. 3: 10-18

Advent: The word means waiting. On this "Gaudete Sunday," this moment of joy in the midst of Advent, our waiting entails:

> From Zephaniah--waiting for the joy of cosmic victory.
> From the letter to the Philipians--waiting for the peace beyond all understanding.
> From the Gospel of Luke--waiting for the One, who will come after John.

We wait, then, for Jesus, not the baby in the crib, but the full blown adult, wait for Jesus to come more centrally into our lives.

And herein lies a tale.
[Note: I know the basis of the following story is "borrowed" from some-one else, but I've told it my own way and no longer know where I first got the basis of it; my gratitude to the originator!]

Once upon a time, more than two thousand years ago, the devil came to visit with God. He was distraught, for lately the battle between good and evil, between light and dark, had become quite uneven and God was winning. God had become incarnate in Mary's womb and the odds no longer seemed fair. So the devil came to complain.

Well, God agreed that the odds were heavily on God's side, even agreed that the Devil should have a chance to become incarnate too ... anytime, anywhere, in whatever manner he chose!

The Devil rushed back to meet with all his lesser devils and told them his good news. They had a meeting (most meetings are after all the work of the Devil) to decide how and where the Devil should take on flesh, become incarnate.

They first thought of voluptuous women and macho-muscled men, or of the God of Mars, of posing as war, or money or booze, but the Devil decided these would only trap those very few people easily fooled by obvious, if real, human vices.

Finally the Devil hit upon a fresh idea. "I've got it!" he proclaimed. "I'll become incarnate in the world as LOVE." Immediately the very best makeup artists in hell began to transform the Devil with an entire trunk load of Love disguises.

First he put on the red, white, and blue disguise of Love of Country. Many people fell for it, loving their own country more than anything, justifying war, refusing to forgive, blind to any truth but their own, proclaiming: "My Country, right or wrong!" Violence against any other country, violence "in our national interests" could be easily justified. In the name of Patriotism--love of country--so many, many suffered and died! In love's name so many, many died.

He then took out the disguise of Love of Religion, a costume in beautiful stained glass colors, heavy with tradition, and respectability. Many agreed their religion was the one, the true, the only, and they engaged in holy wars to prove it. They hated all religions different than their own, or anything that threatened to adjust the way that their religion had always been. When something new, or bold, or daring threatened their familiar religious ways, the devil whispered, "Heresy, . . . Silence, . . . The Index, . . . The Rack!" Whatever the threat to the religion in sway might be it quickly died and so did those who threatened with it.

As a further disguise, the devil appeared as *Parental Love*, using the sweet juicy gift of guilt as a tool to let parents control their children, long after they had grown. Generation after generation spent entire lives trying to please parents who never would or could be pleased. The Devil created the joke: "How many doting mothers does it take to change a light bulb?" Answer: "None, it doesn't need to be changed, you go on out and have a good time; I'll just stay here in the dark."

But the Devil's most clever love disguise was that of "Love For One Another," so very close to the Incarnation of God, in Jesus. The Devil knew that love makes people blind. He thought to himself: "I can enslave them to the darkness of what they think is love."

Over the centuries, people learned to inflict great pain through words, suspicions, silences, the refusal to forgive, through lies in the name of love. People were oppressed, abused, enslaved, made crazy all in the name of love. This disguise worked the very best of all. It was so very easy, so deceptive! Just use the words, but not the deeds of love!

Eventually the Devil came back to meet with God again, asking if God wanted to throw in the towel, for the Devil was very clearly ahead; his love disguises had been so very good.

But God said, "No, for I know how to make my children see the difference; I know how to let the light break lose and overcome the darkness. I will ask Jesus to show them the difference."

After John the Baptist, as Herald had himself proclaimed, Jesus came into the World. He loved people of every nation, Jews and Greeks, slave and free, woman and man. He loved people of every religion, those who were Jewish and Syrians, and Samaritans, (eventually Moslems and Mormons) . . . even those who worshipped Caesar. Jesus set free those whom he loved, telling them, simply, to "Go and sin no more."

Then, on a dark Friday, in Palestine, in spring, Jesus died on a criminal's cross. At the moment of his death a light flooded the world that was so bright, so intense that no one could mistake the difference between real love and evil disguised as love. Those that cared to look could know what choosing life, choosing love might really mean.

Real love, revealed on a cross, gives unconditionally; evil love takes.

Real love gives freedom; evil love enslaves and owns.

Real love is expansive, embracing; evil love closes the circle and leaves no room for others.

Real love is humble, generous, honest; evil love is riddled with deceit.

Real love suffers; evil love seeks only comfort.

All this was revealed, not so much on Christmas, when those who walked in darkness saw a great light, as on Good Friday and Easter when the darkness could not blot out the light.

So we continue Advent, waiting again, not for the birth of Jesus who is already with us, but for the deeper, fuller re-birth of Jesus as love, in us that will bring that joy of cosmic victory, and the peace that passes understanding--the victory and the peace that only genuine love, God's love incarnate can offer!

4) The Fourth Sunday of Advent

Rooted in Lk. 1: 39-45

The Second Book of Samuel has a marvelous scene in which the ancient Ark of the Covenant--the sign of God's presence in the midst of the Israelite people--Is brought before the tent of King David. The King exclaims, "Who am I that the Ark of the Lord should come to me?" In joy, David dances naked before the ark, to the profound scandal of his daughter.

Today's Gospel is deliberately reminiscent of that historic scene. When Mary, the new Ark of the Covenant, holding the presence of God in her womb, comes to Elizabeth, her cousin asks David's question, "Who am I that the Mother of the Lord should come to me?" Elizabeth's baby dances in her womb for joy. Luke tells us that God is present in a new way in human history and the appropriate reaction is to dance, to rejoice, to celebrate.

Mary, is, in our biblical tradition, the container of God's presence, pervades our Advent journey, is perhaps the central symbol of

Advent. She holds God, her "yes," allows God to be born in humankind. Her trust in God is the means for a similar birth for
us, individually and together. Here on the final Sunday of Advent,
Luke's story about Mary's trust in God is at the heart of the message. Let me step back and share my own profound experience
with this story.

At the end of their training we Jesuits make a thirty day retreat,
considered the formal end to our years of formation. In the late
sixties, a time of enormous transition, I found myself making that
retreat alone in Portland under the direction of a priest friend.
The retreat came at a most difficult time for me. Ordained only
a-year and-a-half, three classmates had already left active ministry,
and many other friends. The initial enthusiasm for Vatican II had
fostered great hope in some, while strong energies fought against
its new Spirit. The encyclical on birth control, *Humanae Vitae*, had
begun to further rend the Church in half. These external realities
played themselves out internally. The mess of the outer Church
was mirrored in my internal life.

I entered this retreat wondering if and how I could possible continue to be a pries t-- to endure, and serve, and flourish in this age
of the Church seemed impossible.

I started the retreat with little energy; it soon got worse. About
6 or 7 days into the retreat the director invited me to pray over
the Gospel passage we heard today. This story of the Visitation
was the only passage he gave me for 5 hours of prayer on a single
day. I tried, but absolutely nothing happened. This story seemed
so familiar. I was bored. I told the director and he suggested I pray
over this same passage again. I spent a second day, worse than the
first, trying to find something new, something fresh, something
even mildly interesting in this passage. Then a third and a fourth.

I look back and while I know my director did not know what it was I might find in the passage, he was profoundly right that my resistance to it, my complete inability to enter the passage was saying something.

Finally, on the fifth day, in what would be the twenty-first hour in which I tried to discover some "fruit" in this selection, it hit me. God hit me. I saw a line I had never seen before. I thought at first that line must not even have been there until this reading. The line touched me to my toes. God said to me, not just to Mary,

> "Blessed is he who can believe that the Lords' words
> to him would be fulfilled."

I cannot adequately describe the gift of that line, but God did speak to me through it. The promise I had made to be priest was not up to me to fulfill. I did not have to figure out how to do it. I did not have to depend on my own wisdom, grace, holiness, cunning or anything. God would be faithful. God can be trusted. God's word to me can be fulfilled by God, not me.

At the very beginning of Luke's telling of our foundation our story, God is said to have entered human history because of one woman's trust in God's promise. Mary is able to say "Be it done," and God can then "just do it." Without her trust, nothing! Without our trust now, nothing!

The very center of our Advent prayer, the final word as it were, this final Sunday of Advent is Mary's trust. "Blessed is she who believed that the Lord's words to her will be fulfilled!"
Mary: you will be happy,
you can be blessed,
you can change human history,

because you trust that God will do what God says God will do. This is worth leaping for joy.

So, in a way, though it came to me with enormous difficulty, the message today is quite simple: Each of us are invited to the same kind of trust that Mary showed in unlikely promises. The heart of our Advent prayer is to trust that the Lord's words to us will be fulfille--to believe this and to act on the belief. With such trust Jesus can come to life, not a long time ago in another place, but here and now, in us, in our world.

Jesus can be born or re-born in our marriage.
Jesus will find ways to use my gifts in work that is meaningful; he gave me the gifts.
With Jesus, I can survive the death of my spouse, or my friend, the death of my self image or my dream.
Whatever seems barren, or impossible in me or around me can come to life this Christmas.

Finally, Advent is not just a time for waiting for God to act, but a time to cooperate with God's action, helping the birth to happen. Our Advent prayer must be, in part: what do I need to do, want to do, these final days of Advent preparation if Christmas is to come.

During Mass, this day, I invite us all to say with David, with Mary, with people of faith throughout the ages: "Who am I that the body and blood of the Lord should come to me?"

5) Christmas Day

Rooted in Lk. 2: 1-14

This Gospel is the most familiar passage in the world. Its familiarity can keep us from appreciating its depth, the masterpiece of carefully constructed theological reflection on the meaning of Jesus whose birth we celebrate. What I want to do tonight is simply to look carefully at the text of the story itself, to invite us to listen, really listen--to let this paradigmatic story into our hearts, our minds perhaps in a new way.

> "A decree goes out from Caesar Augustus." A decree to "the whole world."

Imagine someone being able to count the whole world, and count it as his--under his sway. What power!

Throughout this passage, the power of Caesar is balanced against the weakness of a child and his parents. There is no record outside the New Testament that this census ever happened. It seems a creation of Luke to balance power against weakness, Caesar in tension with God. This emperor who believes himself so powerful becomes only the agent for God's designs to be fulfilled. Caesar, known as one who brought peace to the world, provides the environment from which is born the prince of Peace.

We go on with the text:

From the most remote corner of the Roman Empire, Joseph with his poor family travels 90 miles on foot to Bethlehem--the City of David. This "City of David" calls to mind everything in Jewish messianic expectation, the Kingdom of David, the kingdom that would never end. Luke uses the word *fulfilled* eight times in this chapter. All our human hopes and longings are to be realized in this unlikely event.

Joseph comes with Mary, a pregnant woman not yet his wife. Jewish law as understood at the time required her to be stoned. This woman is most outcast, most lowly, most insignificant in this Reign of Caesar, this family of David.

This birth so understated ...

Out in back, in the place where the animals were. There was no room in the corner of the house where people would put visitors. Can we even begin to imagine Joseph going to his home town ("*He was of the lineage and family of David*") yet, in this culture so deeply rooted in familial roots and family bonds, no relatives take him in, no family welcomes him. The clearest sign that they are outcast, unwelcome, unwanted, unloved--not just turned away by the crowd, but turned away because unwanted. In Luke's telling, our savior enters the world as he will leave it, in disgrace!

Jesus enters our world distained as an illegitimate child and leaves it on a criminal's cross!

It took a divorced Christian woman to "feel" this passage for me. I will never forget this member of a devout religious family telling me what it was like to go "home" for Christmas and no longer be welcomed because of choices she had had to make. Not welcomed in her family's home she stayed in an inn--and not a very good inn because by the time she arrived, expecting a domestic welcome, most of the inns were full. Mary and Joseph have made daring choices and received their reward--banishment to the animal shelter.

Ironically, this outcast child is "first-born" not to indicate that there were others, but to indicate the honored child--that one through whom the religious heritage of Israel will be gloriously transmitted.

Luke goes on, creating details filled with meaning. Jesus is wrapped in *swaddling clothes*--the ordinary clothes of every Jewish child; Jesus shares our human lot completely--not the linen robes of royalty, not the soft bed of kings, but laid in a manger, literally a "to eat" for animals. This *manger* is the first bed of him who will become food for us.

The marvelous details of this story continue: Who first hears about this birth?

Shepherds. The poorest of people, unable to keep the laws of ritual washing; unable ordinarily to attend the temple; people with no income, no standing, the lowly, the outcast. These shepherds presage all those to whom Jesus comes throughout Luke's gospel: the marginal, the outcast, those in need.

In the midst of all of this is a message of enormous joy for everyone--not just for Jewish people, not just for the poor, but for everyone open to the message. Angels, the messengers of God, tell the shepherds and us, even in our poverty, *"Do not be afraid, for a savior is born."* The expected royal leader of the house of David arrives, but by no means in the expected way, or in the expected place.

The sign to the shepherds will be this common lot the child shares with common folk, the swaddling clothes, and his amazing presence in a "to eat," a *manger*, for animals.

The scene ends something like a great Broadway musical with an Alleluia chorus singing about the great glory to God. The word for Glory here is the *Shekinah* or cloud--the cloud that led the Jewish people through the dessert, and hovered over their ark--the sign of God's presence in the midst of the people.

This Glory shines on people of good will, that is, people who experience God's good pleasure. Peace is God's gift of divine choice and mercy to all who will receive it.

What of us gathered here?

We come, at least a little able, to hear the marvelous Good News as if for the first time.

We let the story digest, sift through our minds and hearts:

The power of Caesar, the weakness of God.

The unwelcome, unwanted parents.

The first resting place, with the smells, not of incense and candles and green boughs, but of the waste of animals.

The first witnesses, poorest of the poor.

The song.

Good News.

And we prepare to celebrate the Eucharist, to eat, to share in the life of our God who shares his life with ours, this "manger" God, with us, our Emmanuel.

6) Mary, the Mother of God, January 1, New Year's Day

This feast has so many faces that it is difficult to know where to jump in. It used to be known as the **Feast of the Circumcision**. I recall vividly going with a theology professor of mine to a convent of sisters on New Year's Day and hearing his homily explaining in great detail the physical and ritual meaning of circumcision. He thought they should know. I am glad the title of this feast has changed.

The feast is now called **The Feast of Mary, the Mother of God**.

It is also, in our culture, **New Year's Day** and since the early 1960's under Paul VI, **World Peace Day**. Somehow I think all of these various celebrations fit together.

Let me begin with what is most familiar to us, New Year's Day.

Besides the surfeit of football games New Year's is also the day on which we traditionally make resolutions--a day of new beginnings, of starting over. Collectively we try to begin anew.

I'll quit smoking, or drinking, or eating sweets.
I'll quit complaining all the time.
I'll try to get along better with Joe, or Betty, or Susie.
I'll quit filling my schedule so full that there is no time for leisure, or prayer, or play.

Usually the resolutions don't work. We try to pull ourselves up by our own bootstraps and we fail, often soon, frequently miserably.

Let me shift for a moment and look at this feast as that of Mary, the Mother of God. I suggest that it is the celebration of Christmas, this season of Christmas, that can perhaps free us to change. Mary, through her birth-giving love, places all of us into a new relationship with God that allows us to change.

We hear the ancient, wonderful stories of Mary, pondering this mystery in her heart,
mulling over this new relationship,
this God in our midst,
this God in our arms,
this God, subject to the laws of human nature,
subject to the knife, to the promise--this relationship with God allows us to change.

The second reading today suggests that we, with Mary, are no longer servants of a distant God. We no longer need to make resolutions to better keep a law or rule outside ourselves.

When Jesus becomes not only Son of God, but also son of Mary, then all of us have a new relationship also. We are heirs, children of God, also, related to God in an entirely new way.

Let me step back from this theological abstraction for a moment. Let me talk about human experience. I do not think any of us ever changes just because we make up our mind. Resolutions don't do it. Relationships do. We change because someone loves us and we love them.

When I was young the only reason I ever avoided bad behavior was because I loved my dad and mom and when I did bad stuff I hurt them, disappointed them. As an adult I find that I change because of people who care for, care about me. I take better care of myself than I used to because my wife urges me to do so.

The only resolutions we keep are the ones informed by love.

In the Spiritual Exercises St. Ignatius invites us to use our imaginations and to picture Jesus coming to see us personally and inviting us to join him in his cosmic battle against the forces of evil. Rather than an abstract idea of God, imagine Jesus sitting at my kitchen table, telling me he needs me to get his great work done. He won't ask me to go anywhere he hasn't already gone, or do anything he hasn't done. Such a fantasy (which is not fantasy at all) helps me to respond because I have Christmas relationship, an incarnational, enfleshed relationship with Jesus, now as brother, as face-to-face friend, as companion. Responding personally and in love I want to be my best and truest self.

Mary lets Jesus be born, allows this relationship to happen. This feast of Mary, Mother, and New Year's coalesce marvelously.

It is also a good time to celebrate World Peace Day. Peace is possible precisely because we renew today our relationship with this Christ, the Prince of Peace. Because we love and are loved we can live in peace with one another. We can refuse to see any of our brothers and sisters as "enemies," to be deported, or kept out from the beginning because "not us." We have the resolution and the energy to struggle for peace because Jesus is our brother and our friend.

Before we go on to celebrate Eucharist today, we imitate Mary in the single thing the Gospel says most often about her. We "ponder all these things in our hearts." Look for a moment at the crib:

I hear the small voice speak to me:
>"I am your brother, your friend. I am here because
>I love you. Join me in my vulnerability. Join me in
>my mission. As I grow up, so will you.
>I want to be "Prince of Peace," but you must be brother
>or sister to me in this quest.
>Will you resolve, in love, this New Year, to join me?

7) The Feast of the Epiphany

Rooted in Is. 60: 1-6; Eph. 3: 2-3, 5-6; Mt. 2:1-12

I want this morning to come at this Feast from a variety of directions.

First, the Greek Church had a most intriguing ancient custom in their celebration of this feast of Epiphany. In the cold of a January morning as they prepared to celebrate the sacrament of Baptism, young people gathered with their priest at the edge of the ocean. The priest threw a large cross out into the water as far as he could. The young men then leapt into the water searching under the waves until the winner burst to the surface grasping the crucifix.

This challenging action symbolized the feast. The winner was himself an "epiphany," a witness, a manifestation of what our Christian lives are about--rising from the waters of baptism, holding onto the cross.

The Feast of Epiphany in the beginning was about travelers leaving the comfort of their kingdoms,
moving into foreign lands, foreign customs,
confronting the angry maintainers of the religious status quo,
to discover a new king, new birth, new hope.

The Feast of Epiphany is still about struggle and search,
about openness even to the hidden buried signs of Christ's presence,
about being naked, vulnerable, willing to die to discover the Christ event.

The feast of Epiphany is also about the *Universality* of God's message. This is, in fact, what the readings most stress. When Christ comes into our world, he comes no longer for a small, chosen band, but for everyone, all nations, all people. These travelers from the East symbolize that universality. When Paul asserts that this event is for *Jew and Gentile*, there is simply nothing more universal that he could say. Everyone is included, young/old, man/woman, rich/poor; people of color or none; First-, Second-, Third-, Fourth-World people. Everyone, All.

Thirdly, the Feast is about seeing the manifestation (what the word *epiphany* means) of Christ, to experience the expanding salvation opening up in the most unlikely, even uncomfortable places. I am invited to be like these travelers going to the most remote place outside a small town to find a powerless child, in an animals' feeding trough and to name him king.

I am invited to challenge the Herod in me or all of us that wants to stifle, even kill what is threatening about this presence.

This will mean different things to different people for each of us has a difficult time finding Christ in different places; what is easy for some is difficult for others.

By way of example. We need to appreciate the Christ present in cultures, and religious practices not our own:

- the profound piety of our Vietnamese sisters and brothers,
- the drumming, the ancestor reverence, the nature quests of Native Americans Catholics,
- the effusive singing, *Amen-ing*, clapping, dancing we might find in an African American community.
- I need to understand the religious consciousness of those that hold onto traditions and practices no longer meaningful to me.
- Others need to respect the search for language, rituals, practices that speak to people of a "new age."
- We need as a Church to hear the manifestations of God's presence from women's experience of scripture after centuries of hearing it primarily interpreted by men.
- We need to listen to the experience of single people, divorced people, of dying people, of gay people in our church--of experiences not our own that can manifest remarkable insight into the mystery and complexity of God's love.

On this feast, as we celebrate that "astrologers" from the East found Jesus, we want to ask what is going on in our midst today when people outside the boundaries of any church are drawn to an explosion of books, tapes, psychic phenomenon, spiritual healings, angels, mysticism (as one writer says) "at the boundary of where reason ends and wonder or grace, or spirit begins."

We need to ask whether we have so rationalized, made logical, pinned down our sacred tradition and our sacred texts that millions now turn to superstition to encounter the transcendent, the mysterious, the numinous. This feast of Epiphany invites us to discover what might be real and "of God" in this attraction, this manifestation or epiphany in our time.

So, Epiphany is about strange, intriguing visitors,
coming to call on the Christ child,
with a map made out of darkness,
and the light of a star.
The story, shrouded in myth and legend, captures our imagination and suggest to us that God's manifestation often occurs unexpectedly.
Epiphany invites us to risk a lot,
to dive into cold, dangerous and unfamiliar waters,
vulnerable to the wet and dangerous cross,
to explore the mysterious,
embrace the transcendent,
and praise the God who became incarnate,
and still shares the profound adventure of everything that is human.

8) The Second Sunday

Rooted in: Is. 62:1-5; 1 Cor. 12:4-11; Jn. 2: 1-12

Maturity, I have heard it said, is the growing ability to give up what we have, for what we don't yet have, on the word of someone who loves us.

Imagine that--to give up what I have for what I don't yet have, trusting in the love another shows me. It is as if life were a ride on a trapeze, a series of leaps from one bar to the other. We just get comfortable on one swing and we have to let go of it, and leap to another, with our feet firmly planted in mid-air. We could not make the leap without someone underneath, clapping, shouting, encouraging us, yelling "You can do it!" so we try, we let go, we mature.

This letting go and leaping is a central image of the Gospel today.

Let me step back for a moment, then return to the Gospel text.

Christmas time is over; we begin, today, *Ordinary Time*. But we continue very much in the Spirit of Epiphany as we expand, and expand, and expand the manifestation, the story of Jesus throughout the year. We tell the story over and over. With Ignatius of Loyola we pray from week to week to know Jesus more clearly, to love Jesus more dearly, to follow Jesus more nearly. With every story the question is not "Did this really happen?" or "Did it happen like this?" but "Is this happening still, happening to me? Is this story true in the lived experience of my life?"

The story today, at the very beginning of John's Gospel is an *Epiphany* scene. It is the first miracle, the first public manifestation of Jesus. Almost everything we want to know about Jesus is somewhere contained in this scene. Let's look at it carefully.

First, John presents us with the image of marriage, a dominant messianic image throughout the scriptures. Our relationship with God is like a marriage covenant, a commitment in love of lives inextricably bound together. The first reading from Isaiah speaks of God as "wed" to a people. So Jesus begins his ministry, in John's telling, at a wedding feast. The bridegroom is here. The Love feast begins. The imagery of the story develops this theme of an abundant, never-ending Feast.

Did you notice the amount of wine? All of us have had the experience of running a little short and having to run to the 7-11 store for a jug. But 90 to 120 gallons! This is enormous abundance, the start of a celebration that will never end. This miracle ushers in a whole new creation ("In the beginning was the Word"). This is the first of six miracles in John's Gospel. The seventh is the Resurrection. There are six water jugs -- just on the edge of fullness before the seventh jug, the full flowering of life. The eternal party starts; our faith is feast, a never ending celebration of a love relationship with a God covenanted to us.

Secondly, and slightly more folksy, every marriage, every human relationship, every love sooner or later runs out of wine. When it does it will be helpful if Jesus is at the wedding. It will be good to have Jesus there to help get the relationship, the celebration started again. If he's not there he can't help. And how often the second wine is better than the first.

I invite us to listen to this simple but constant truth with the ear of our honest experience. Be aware of those times we have recovered something, or someone that was lost: a marriage renewed, a parental love restored, a friendship regained. Savor how good, how miraculous that was--the wondrous miracle of starting over again, anew, afresh.

The aspect of the story that most touches me concerns Mary's encouragement to her son to enter a new stage of his ministry, a new maturity. We often miss this; I simply love it. Mary seems the quintessential Jewish mother. She says to Jesus, "Look, these folks are hurting, help them." Jesus initially protests, "What does all this have to do with me, I'm just a guest here at the wedding?" Mary seems to ignore Jesus protests; she turns to the steward and says to do whatever Jesus says.

I picture her walking away with a grin leaving Jesus on the spot. She thinks it is about time this thirty-year-old son of hers gets started on his life's work. The hour is now! She sees in Jesus a promise, a power, a possibility that he appears not to have seen or owned in himself. Mary teases out of Jesus something new, something wonderful. She helps him begin his work.

Theologically it is clearly significant that Mary only appears twice in the Gospel of John. She is here at the beginning helping Jesus get started. She is at the cross, at the end, standing beside him, helping him complete what he has begun. Mary's mission in this gospel is to root, to clap for, to believe in her son, to pull out of him his best, truest, most mature, most salvific self!

Is this not the role of any real love? Any one of us only become what others believe we can become. We only move to new levels because someone stands beneath our shaky trapeze, or alongside our fragile heart saying "You can do it!"

Two important footnotes:

First, this is vocation Sunday throughout the Church, a day we want to encourage people to heed God's call to them to various forms of ministry. I look at my life and I am so grateful for people who have ministered to me over the years, inviting me to be more than I thought I could, challenging me to use whatever gifts I have, correcting me when I wandered from my most mature self. To pray for vocations is to pray for people who like Mary will give their lives to clapping others into life, helping God's gifts to them to be realized.

Secondly, we just celebrated the birthday of Martin Luther King, Jr. This perhaps invites us to have a larger, societal dimension to our reflections today. Out of all the things that Martin stood for, out of all he said and did, I am most grateful to him because he told us all, told us as a people, that we could do more than we imagine to end the violence of our world. The ordinary response to violence in human affairs is more violence. Martin Luther King, Jr. suggested we could end violence by an aggressive and asser- tive non-violence, the non-violence of Jesus. How different our presidential discourse would be should anyone follow this direction! He promised we could do more with passive resistance, with love, with non-violent behavior than with fists or clubs or guns.

Our nation and most of us in it still think that violence can accomplish something worthwhile. We still think force can win. So we need to remember Martin and his challenge every year. We need to let Martin's spirit hover over us. He joins us at the wedding feast, suggesting that things can change from love, can change because we have the courage to believe, and to stand up, and to resist, and not to do so with more violence.

More than anyone in our national history Martin Luther King, Jr. stands with Mary at the feast and says we can do miracles out of love.

We would do well to believe him!

9) The Third Sunday of the Year

Rooted in: Neh. 8: 1-6, 8-10, 1 Cor. 12:12-30, Lk. 1:1-4, 4:14-24

Let me begin with a quiz. I want to discover the best informed old Catholics. Previous to 1963 when were you considered late for Mass? That is, how late could you come and still fulfill your Sunday obligation? (Solicit answers)

The correct answer is "until the priest took the veil off the chalice." This is after the Liturgy of the Word, and just as the Liturgy of Eucharist begins. The Liturgy of the Word did not count!

At Vatican II the Church said that we as a church have always reverenced the Liturgy of the Word equally with the Liturgy of the Eucharist, but this is really not true. In fact, still, fifty years later people come in during the readings, genuflect and make a visit to the Blessed Sacrament while the readings are happening.

What a stark contrast this is with the first reading today, the story of a Jewish people after the Exile as they return to the temple and listen to the word. Men, women and children "old enough to understand" come with incredible reverence, even weeping at this gift of the word of God to them. They hear the word explained and they weep in joy and gratitude. The final lines indicate that they went from this word proclaimed to feed the hungry. This word touched and sent them.

This is the tradition of which we are still a part.

In the Gospel today it is this tradition in which Jesus takes part. He comes into the temple and reads the word with great reverence and begins to explain it to the people. If the word of God is important in general, this word from the prophet Isaiah is especially significant. In many ways this passage from Isaiah has become central to the entire church because it was central to the mission of Jesus. This first sermon of Jesus frames his entire ministry in Luke's gospel, and so it necessarily frames the ministry of the Church of his disciples.

In my imagination I see Jesus taking:
from all the scrolls that make up the sacred books, one author,
and from that author, one manuscript,
and from that manuscript two short verses.
These two verses, read aloud after thirty years of private prayer, outline his ministry to come. Hear again these verses:

> *The Spirit of the Lord is upon me,*
> *for the Lord has anointed me*
> *has sent me to preach good news to the poor,*
> *to proclaim liberty to captives,*
> *sight to the blind, freedom to the oppressed,*
> *a year of favor to the Lord.*

After a moment of stillness he affirms not just that this was an important word centuries ago when Isaiah wrote it, but the word is true, right now, in their very midst.

As we gather today to listen to God's word, the word is still important to us. If we are truly followers of Jesus then this word is still being fulfilled today in our midst. If God's spirit is still with us, upon us, if we are still anointed then this word is still being fulfilled.

Reflecting on the present application of these words, I have found myself paying attention to the second reading this weekend. The image of the Body of Christ, the many members, many parts flows through my mind. No part can say to any other part I do not need you. Every part needs every other part. No one of us fulfills this word by ourselves, but together we are Christ's body. We continue Christ's mission. We live in Christ's spirit. All of us together enflesh Jesus, enflesh this word.

I find myself consoled and excited as I fit these readings together with this community.

The poor are hearing the good news through us,
from those who feed, house, clothe, visit, provide health care throughout our city,
from people in these pews who work in welfare offices,
care for the mentally ill,
work with refugees, or with elderly in nursing homes.
We touch the lives of the poor in many ways.

People here are proclaiming liberty to captives,
through parishioners who work in our jails,
or the many who teach in schools freeing people from ignorance,

or those who live with and serve folks with various handicaps-
-loving them as they are, providing community for them.

People here do provide sight to the blind
literally as surgeons,
but by ministry to elderly--being their eyes, their hands,
through counselors of this parish who help people to see their
lives more clearly,
through the many mothers and fathers, and others who work
with children, helping them see the world with eyes of hope and
laughter and love.

The oppressed are being set free,
by many who work for peace, and justice
by lawyers who provide advice to those who cannot pay for it,
or those who work in drug or alcohol programs helping people
become free of addictions,
of those who advocate for rights of Native Americans.
In many ways this community struggles to respond to this word
of God and make it true today
... to let this be a time of favor to the Lord.

Today, as our national attention is on storms in the East, absolutely bizarre nomination processes for our next president, and still
on football, I am glad we have taken a few moments to ask what
Jesus' life and mission was about, and in that asking to remind
ourselves what our lives and mission are also.

Nourished by the word of God, we prepare to go from here in
the Spirit of Jesus to continue the mission of Jesus!

10) The Fourth Sunday

Rooted in: Jer. 1:4-5, 17-19; 1 Cor 12:31-13:13; Lk. 4:21-30

Despite popular misconceptions to the contrary a prophet is not someone who tells the future, but rather someone who looks accurately at the present and sees the implications.

A prophet does not gaze into a crystal ball to foretell some distant happening. A prophet looks at the reality others may refuse to see, in order to tell us what will happen if we do not change.

A prophet invites conversion.

In the Gospel passage we heard last week and in the beginning of today's selection Jesus returns to his home town, to his home synagogue. He speaks eloquently as the people laud him for doing so. As Jesus continues to look at the people around him, to look into their hearts, he begins to suggest that they will not be able to listen to very much else he will have to say, for "no prophet is accepted in his own land, among his own people."

He reminds the people of painful realities in their collective history. There were more than enough widows in Israel, but Elijah the prophet couldn't help them. He had to go to Sidon to find a widow with a faith that would make his healing possible. There were plenty of lepers among the Jewish people, but Elisha, another prophet, could only help a leper from Syria. Again he had to go outside the Jewish fold. Jesus portends that what he will need to say will not be heard by his own people, a people too wedded to the religion they know to embrace something unknown, something new ... even Good News!

Jesus suggests what will in fact prove true. He looks carefully at the present and sees the implications. Because they do not like the message, his townspeople are ready to shoot the messenger. They rush Jesus from the city and prepare to throw him over a cliff. Jesus escapes, disappears from their midst for now. This inability to listen, to hear his message, on the part of those who should have understood him best eventually leads to his death.

It would be impossible to preach today without acknowledging the second reading, perhaps the single most famous passage in the entire Bible. We hear again Paul's wonderful hymn to love

"... a love that is patient, kind, never boastful or jealous, love that has no end."

I have often thought that this description of love describes no human love I know, but perhaps only the love that Jesus has for us, the love he preached to us, a love to which we shall never measure up. (My mother used to call it "the star we shoot at if we are ever going to hit a thistle top!") Love like this constitutes the religion to which we are called, beyond the narrow religion of the people who seem mired in cold codes and stony tablets. This love is beyond any religion that seeks to codify, control, define.

Paul's hymn suggests that when life is over the only thing we have to bring with us into whatever eternity might be is love. The only thing God can make eternal is love. The only grounds upon which our lives can finally be judged is the depth and extent of our love relationships. Finally, Paul will say, the only gift that matters is love.

Let me stop here and admit that all of my words so far have been the "What" of these readings; where is the "So What?" I have spoken in general about the definition of a Prophet. I have paraphrased what Paul writes about love. What do either of these things have to do with the life of this community today, or any of us in it?

Let me try to think out loud, perhaps in a prophetic kind of stance about the implications of these readings.

Jesus is a religious leader who, like Jeremiah before him, speaks of the need to uproot and tear down the old to prepare for the new. It is not easy to be "church" in the midst of a time of enormous transition. It is not easy to be church when 77 leaders of that church are named as criminals abusing children on the front page of our newspaper.

It is not easy to be a church, a community with no real boundaries, with worshipers coming from everywhere with only loose affiliation depending on a school's success, or a pastor's, or the floundering of neighboring parishes.

It is an enormous challenge to try to be a community that lives and prays from "the side of the poor," a community sensitive to the marginal, trying with everything in us to proclaim the Lord's favor to captives, the blind, the oppressed--a church welcoming gay people while our larger church appears to still marginalize them, a church advocating for the right to life from womb to tomb, pleading for a welcome to refugees in a nation wanting to build higher fences and tighter laws, a church decrying the proliferation of guns in a nation seemingly wanting every citizen armed everywhere, a church seeking justice, education, housing, health care as essential human rights.

But this is what we are called to be, to do, and in so doing to risk suffering the same fate as our founder!

The implications of being a prophetic community of love go beyond our own boundaries. Jesus was not concerned merely about the synagogue. He came to usher in the reign of God in the world, among the nations, to the very ends of the earth. Our prophetic task is "for the world."

I am still being too abstract. When I cut through all the rhetoric what I mean is this.

I hope we see ourselves not just as a kind of spiritual gas station, dispensing sacramental life. I hope we see ourselves as a prophetic community made up of people honestly trying to hear the gospel of Jesus, the call to love, to love no matter what!

I hope we see ourselves as a community trying to support and affirm each other, a community existing not for its own sake but for those whom we serve in the midst of a pain-filled world, a pain-filled city.

The only thing that justifies our existence into the future is that we are called to be prophetic, to look at the way the church is, the way the world is, and to see implications that invite dramatic, radical conversion.

In a church and world continuously changing, the one thing that we know will last, the one thing we value now, as individuals and as a community, is love!

11) The Fifth Sunday

Rooted in Is. 6:1-8 and Lk 5:1-11

Gerald May, a prominent psychiatrist., tells a marvelous story about his personal conversion. He had lost his faith in God after the death of his father when was he was only nine years old. He studied hard and became very successful at a very young age. By the time he was thirty he was responsible for a whole chain of mental health institutions in the D.C. area. At thirty-six he went, somewhat cynically, to a conference at which a famous "faith healer" was present. When she arrived, she "swooped" into the room and came, un-introduced directly up to him, took his hands in hers and said to his amazement: "Gerald, how wonderful to meet you. I can see by your hands that you are a healer also." Then she swooped away saying over her shoulder, "But I wouldn't send my dog to you because you think you can do it all by yourself!"

This unexpected rebuke reached somehow into the depth of May's empty soul; he felt to the core the truth of what she said. He had depended totally on himself, his own expertise, and it wasn't working any more. He was amazed by her sudden, divine-like insight into him, and rendered powerless by her words. This experience began his long journey back to God.

This story leads me to the line in the Gospel today that most strikes me. I love the image of putting out into the "deep water and lowering our nets for a catch." I want to reflect on the task this faith healer gave Gerald May, the task God gives to each of us, to lower our nets into really deep arch-typical waters for a major human truth. I invite us into something really deep, profound, important. I want to see if what I suggest seems true and, if so, not so much to change or cure it as to name and share it, and try to be released from the power this truth has over us!

The truth in question is simply this:

When the power of God gets close to us, we become aware of our own powerlessness.

When God gets close, touches us, even loves us, we get frightened and want to run. Such moments are perhaps the most important moments in our lives as human beings, as religious people!

Isaiah is terrified: "I am an unclean man, living in the midst of unclean people and I have seen God. I am doomed."

Peter sees the abundant catch of fish and cries out, " Depart from me; I am a sinful man."

One evening, years ago, I stood by the bed of a dying man and prayed for his healing; the next morning I called the hospital and the dying man answered phone, fully alert. Though joyful, I was more aware of being terrified.

Someone slips through our ordinary relationships and begins to become an intimate friend, even a fiancée--begins to really know us and love us as we are, and we become frightened. We are afraid that we will fail in this relationship too, and hurt another person we love. We fear that we will not, cannot measure up.

"Wherever love is, there is God" and when God gets close we are in our deepest, most unconscious, most watery depth, afraid we will be found out, unmasked.

Is this true for you? Is this our universal experience of God?

Perhaps we most know God is near when we are most terrified.

Is this true? Has it been true for you?

A retreat director wisely tells a person entering into a time of intense prayer that there are only two things that need to be done in prayer. First, try to go deeply into your heart. Secondly, when you get there, try not to run away!

I am reminded of something Jean Vanier says frequently to assistants in L'Arche, living with a caring for wounded people: "Never forget that what you are trying to do is impossible!" Vanier means that if what they are called to do, finally, depends on their own abilities, failure is assured.

In the scripture readings today, and in every major moment of our lives the most important words are not the call: "I will make you fishers of men and women," but the promise: "I will be with you."

Some years ago I was involved in the funeral of a forty-eight year old friend, the head of our parish council. He had fallen off the roof of his house the day before Thanksgiving. He had a wife, four children, a thousand friends. It would be an enormous funeral with much anguish. I was incredibly anxious about the funeral, and especially the homily. What can one say to ease the pain, bring consolation, make some sense out of tragedy?

Because of the holiday, I had a terribly busy week such that when the planning for the funeral was finished I had only one hour to plan the homily. Just as I began my earnest preparation the man's son knocked on the door. He wanted to talk. He wanted to know if he could go to communion at his father's funeral since he had not been going to church. More than that he wanted to pour out his pain at disappointing his father, at not being able to say a proper farewell. I had to force myself to let go of my anxieties and listen to him. I had a deep sense of God saying to me, "Let go, stop, be with him!" So, for a change I listened to God. I did stop. I did listen.

As the hour ended and the young man walked out the door, in a single instant I knew in detail what I wanted to say at the funeral and how to say it. In an instant the homily was in my heart, on my lips--with absolutely zero preparation.

I gave a really fine homily to about 1500 people and I knew in the depth of my soul that not a word of it was from me.

I walked out of the Church after the funeral shaking, petrified. God had gotten way too close. A "power working in me did infinitely more than I could ask or imagine." Everything in me was saying, "Depart from me, God. I am way too fragile. I can't handle it."

I tell this story because it is not just my own story. The Gospel story of Peter, the story of Isaiah are not just of them. I believe we are in something very deep--the very deep waters of our shared human experience. I believe this is the continued story of each one of us.

I hear this story, this overwhelming fear, from people about to marry,
people starting new jobs, especially in ministry,
people being asked to try something they have never done before,
people facing death--their own or a loved one's,
people changing their lives in response to any call of God.

When God gets very close, we are afraid.

We want to run away, knowing it is impossible for us alone. We wrestle to trust that we are not alone.

More than in most homilies, I want to invite you to enter into your own story and test whether what I have said is true of you--in the past, and still today?

When God is close am I uncomfortable? Do I fear my own powerlessness? This fear constitutes a truly religious moment. Here we will either let God into our lives and trust, or we will run away, will keep God away from us, and leave ourselves open to lives of quiet desperation.

12) The First Sunday of Lent

Rooted in_Deut. 26:1-10; Ro. 10: 8-13; Lk. 4: 1-13

"I am too old to lie anymore."

Year ago I heard a priest say this and I felt in my heart a sense of liberation. I share those feelings. I am too old to lie anymore. I don't mean out and out dishonesty, telling untruths. I mean the subtle masks we wear, the faces we put on, the institutional answers we protect ourselves with. I don't want to try anymore to be what others want me to be, or to say what others believe. I guess I would say, more accurately, I hope I am becoming too old to lie any more.

This seems to me the essential image and central hope of our Lenten prayer and of the readings today. Put more positively, the call of the readings today and the larger task of Lent have something to do with becoming, owning, realizing under God's grace **the truth of who we most honestly are, individually and together.**

The Story of Jesus is true because it is still going on; this story is my story, our story. The tasks Jesus faces are our tasks. The Gospel story today speaks a deep, universally human, archetypical truth. If we are not going to lie, **we need to go into the desert to find out who we really are!**

This story, this archetype is first lived out by the entire Jewish nation. They became who they were in the desert, in Exodus. Moses says "My father was a wandering Armenian. In Egypt we were an alien people ... in a place we did not belong. We went out and were led by God through the desert into a land, a place that was ours. We were formed in the desert by a God who saw our affliction."

Jesus, too, like his people before him, goes into the desert to become who he was called to be, to wrestle with the demons who would have kept him from being his best and truest self. He resists those demons tempting him to lie to himself.

In Lent we imitate our Jewish ancestors; we imitate Jesus. We go into the desert for forty days and nights to wrestle with our demons and discover who we really are.

Let me look carefully at the gospel. First, the context. Jesus has been led by the Spirit to the waters of the Jordan where he is baptized by John. At that baptism he experienced a profound and overwhelming experience of God's love, God's call. He is reminded that he is God's beloved.

Then the same Spirit leads Jesus into the desert, into fasting, prayer, emptiness, to wrestle with that experience, that call. Once Jesus emerges from the desert he will begin his messianic mission. He comes out knowing the truth of who and how he must be.

I read each of the temptations not as if recorded on tape--a video image of what historically happened. Rather each speaks of Luke's poetic imaginings of the kinds of demonic voices Jesus faced if he was to own the grace of that baptismal experience. Every temptation is the temptation to be someone other than who he really is.

> Be a magician; work tricks for yourself, not for others. Turn a stone into bread.

> Be a great temporal leader, achieve power and might in this world. Don't let God trick you with this servant stuff.

> Be a protected, sheltered child, presuming that a God who loves you will not let anything bad happen to you. Don't be one who will suffer, even die for what you say and do.

Each temptation and all three together are finally the same. The temptation to lie, to be someone other than who you are, other than the one God calls you to be.

Jesus will come out of the desert and be led by the Spirit to his home town, his home synagogue, and there he will begin his public ministry. He will begin by showing how he resisted the demonic snares:

> The Spirit of the lord is upon me,
> he has sent me to bring good news to the poor,
> to proclaim liberty to captives,
> give sight to the blind,
> to set the downtrodden free.

Jesus knows what his mission is and he proclaims it out loud. And he will go on to be faithful to this mission. He will live out this mission, speak the truth to power, be hurt, even killed. Through it all he will trust in the faithfulness of God; and when at the end of his Lent, he is killed God will raise him up and Easter in him.

So it is this desert experience of Jesus that we imitate in Lent. These forty days are the final preparation, final instructions days for those among us who prepare to be baptized or to profess their Catholic faith with us at Easter. They come as adults to say we want to join this community; we want to follow Jesus. In some cases their friends, even family, do not understand. Some have tried other paths before--psychological, religious paths, even some very destructive paths--but now this Lent they come in honesty to God and to themselves. They are discovering who they are in Christ.

And each of us begins to renew our own baptismal grace. Every word, every action of Lent prepares us to renew our own baptism at the Easter Vigil and to proclaim again who we are. The faith of the elect, formerly, catechumens and candidates in our midst, challenges us to honesty, to wrestling with our own demons--to let go of the lies we tell ourselves and others about who we are or who we want to be.

I want to remind us here at the outset of Lent that we live out what we started at Ash Wednesday. Through this season, we try, as we prayed as Ashes were put on our heads, to:

"Repent and be faithful to the Gospel."

We will fast and pray and give alms. We will listen to God's word.

We will move through these forty days. Then hopefully all of us will plan to be present at the Sacred Triduum, the three high Holy Days that all of Lent moves towards. At the Easter Vigil we will die and come back to life, putting aside every dishonesty in us and becoming alive again in Christ as who we really, most truly are.

13) The Second Sunday of Lent

Rooted in; Gen. 15: 5-12, 17-8; Phil. 3: 17-4:1; Lk. 9: 28-36

A few years ago, in one of the most profound religious experiences of my life, I was called to the bedside of a woman who had taken an overdose of pills. She had been comatose for several hours; the outlook was apparently grim. Both her parents were Catholics but for a variety of reasons the young woman, though somewhat catechized, had never been baptized. Her parents wanted me to baptize her. My theology told me that it did not make sense to baptize someone unconscious who never asked for the sacrament while awake. To do so went against everything I believe about the sacraments. It was also no time to try to explain this to the parents.

So, against my petty theology, I baptized the young comatose woman. As I did so her eyes opened, she smiled, said "Thank you!" closed her eyes and went quietly back to sleep to awaken in a short while perfectly O.K.

Wow!

An awesome experience of God working outside the boundaries I had established. What a wonderful presence of the healing, loving, Father/Mother God telling this young woman in a way she will never forget that she was cared for, cherished, beloved.

I have questioned often since that moment whether the experience was primarily for her, or for me?

This experience, and this question help me frame the scripture, especially the Gospel today, to reveal the hope and the challenge of this word on this second Sunday of Lent. Is the experience of Jesus transfigured an experience for Jesus, or for his followers?

Let me begin by surrounding this passage, giving its context both in scripture and in our Lenten journey. In Luke's Gospel, Jesus has begun to move towards Jerusalem, where the prophets are killed. In the previous scene his disciples have, for the first time, recognized Jesus for who he is, The Messiah. Now, he begins to tell them what kind of Messiah he will be, to tell them that it will not all be sweetness and light. Jesus begins to predict his passion and theirs, to assure them that becoming his disciples will mean taking up a cross with him.

In this context, Jesus goes aside to pray with his followers and (as earlier at that Baptism scene) he experiences a marvelous touch of God, an assurance of God's deep love for him, call to him. The disciples also experience the closeness of God's glory as they remain with Jesus.

We hear this reading on the Second Sunday of Lent. This Gospel passage is part of the final instruction to those Elect preparing themselves for the Easter Sacraments. As they move forward toward their own death and rising they are reminded, and we are reminded with them, of how, when, where God has been close to them. They remember what has led them to believe, what has revealed Christ to them.

Liturgically, these readings are also addressed to Penitents, to those who in earlier times had broken away from the Church, and sought to return. We imagine them standing outside the Church doors, praying in sackcloth and ashes. They gathered as a group to reflect on God's word as a means of their on-going conversion. They too needed to remember how, where, when God had been close to them in the past. They absolutely depended on this memory to help them return to God's love despite whatever failures, resentments, their angers drove them from the community.

These readings for the Elect and the Penitents also speak to us in our own on-going Lenten conversion. They remind us even in Lent that though we may be part of a suffering, broken, pain-filled, muddled world, in the very midst of it, God is present. And sometimes this God is very close, very dear, touching, bathing us, surrounding us in glory, calling us out of our various comas.

So I ask again, is this an experience for Jesus, or for the disciples?

The answer is clearly Yes!

It was an experience <u>for Jesus</u>. This Transfiguration is an important moment in his ministry and mission. He is on his way to Jerusalem, to death. As so often in Luke's Gospel he goes aside to pray. I have often been consoled that we are often told about the prayer of Jesus, but only twice are we told that "something happened." Most of the time our own prayer is barren, dry, empty, out of faith only. It is consoling to discover that Jesus' prayer may be the same!

But initially, at his Baptism, and here, at the mountain top, before descending to Jerusalem Jesus does profoundly experience the closeness and presence of God. In the midst of the greatest of his ancestors, God reminds Jesus how loved he is. Jesus, like me, like you, needed the profound, tangible, however momentary, touch of God.

This experience is also for his disciples. While Jesus prays, they sleep. They awaken, as if from a dream, to see Moses, Elijah, Jesus surrounded in Glory/*Shekinah*. Peter babbles:

> *"How super it is to be here, this is fantastic, let's build*
> *some tents, like our people did in the desert, and stay*
> *here forever."*

What he says makes no sense. It never makes sense when we try to speak about how God is acting in our midst. The disciples are afraid as Jesus goes, dream-like again, into the cloud of God's presence, and into the glory we will not hear of again until the Resurrection. It is indeed good for them to be here, but it is also terribly scary. They are told that this is God's word to them and they should listen carefully. They too are strengthened for the journey down the hill, into Jerusalem, into death, into the momentary dashing of all their hopes and dreams in Jesus.

As they descend, and in the days ahead, they do not speak about the vision and, sadly, they seem to forget it for a time. They will not be nourished by it when they need it. They will waver, wander, only later coming back, like penitents of every age, to themselves and this touch of God.

Granted this is a strange scene. No vision, no experience of God is "normal." My baptising of that young woman was not normal

Her recovery was not normal. No time when God is close, no glimpse of his glory, no dream of what will come, is normal.

Here, early in Lent, we are invited by this story--and the story of Abraham's encounter with God, and Paul's invitation to let ourselves be charged with God's glory--we are invited to remember where, and how, and when we have been however momentarily touched by God.

Put most simply, I think I find both the hope and the challenge of this scripture to invite me to remember the moments when everything in me said, "It is good to be here; let's stay here, let's set up camp and not go on." We need to go on, indeed. But first we need to remember the moments of grace, the moments we wanted to freeze, to hold, to rest in. We need to let ourselves be nourished by God's touch . . . even Lent, even today. Then, nourished, we can go down the hill, with Jesus, to whatever the future holds.

[NOTE: FOR 3rd, 4th, and 5th SUNDAYS, SEE "YEAR A"]

14) Passion/ Palm Sunday

Rooted in: Is. 50: 4-7; Phil. 2: 6-11; Lk. 22:14-23: 56

A brief homily: The triumphant entry into the Church today and the long, wrenching story of the passion already speak volumes.

It bothers me that we so often lump the four very different gospels together. It is especially true that each account of the Passion and Death of Jesus is unique. When we pray over the death of Jesus we have four very different stories to consider. It is, for example, a mistake to speak of the "seven last words" of Jesus on the cross. Different words appear in different stories, with quite different emphasis. Each narrative gives some special slant to this most sacred event.

Today, I invite you to take just a brief moment to pay special attention to the parts of this most awesome story that are unique to Luke. We do so not merely to know about Luke's Gospel but to help us understand our own relationship to Jesus, especially Jesus in his passion.

My deepest conviction as we move towards the sacred Triduum is that we pray through these paschal mysteries not only to remember what happened to Jesus, but, even more importantly, what happens to us because of Jesus. Luke's Gospel helps us focus on what happens to us, how we are or can be changed by contemplating this mystery.

Three themes especially strike me.

First, Luke "softens," the passion a bit. His telling is neither as stark nor as painful as Mark, nor even Matthew. In the garden Luke only has Jesus praying his prayer of abandonment once, only once returning to his disciples to find them asleep. In Luke's telling Peter's sorrow at his betrayal of Jesus, and his forgiveness begin immediately; Jesus "looks at Peter with love" and Peter "goes out to weep bitterly"--details only found in Luke.

The second theme, quite close to this, is the "compassion of Jesus in his passion." As Luke's Jesus goes to his death attentive not to his own sufferings, but to the sufferings of others. Many details stress this.

Jesus stops to pay comfort to some women weeping along the way; he notices their pain, invites them to look at their own pain differently.

Jesus forgives those who are killing him as they roll dice for his garments beneath the cross.

Jesus speaks a promise of eternal life to a thief crucified alongside him--a detail only found in Luke's Gospel.

The final theme completes a central theme of Luke's entire Gospel. Throughout the Gospel the Spirit of God has led Jesus. The Spirit overshadowed Mary at the beginning. The Spirit led Jesus to the Jordan to be baptized, led him to the desert to be tempted, led him to the temple in Nazareth to begin his public life. At every significant moment in the Gospel Luke tells us over and over that Jesus was "led by the Spirit."

Here, at the end of the Story, Jesus' final words are "Father, into your hands I commend my spirit."

These are not the gut wrenching, pain-ridden final words in Mark and Matthew, "Father, why have you abandoned me," but a more peaceful letting go of a life that had been God's all along.

This giving over of his spirit to God takes on special significance when we realize that the second book of Luke, the book of Acts, the story of the early church, begins with that Spirit of God being poured out on the Church at Pentecost; the entire Book of Acts will then be the story of the Church being led by the Spirit just as Jesus was.

So today, as we begin this most Holy of Weeks moved and pained by the death of Jesus, we are consoled that he pays attention to us, even in his agony. His spirit is showered on us, even as he dies. In this death, we will see at the Easter Vigil, as we already know now, is our life.

15) Holy Thursday

Rooted in: Ex. 12:1-8, 11-14; 1 Cor. 11:23-26; Jn. 13. 1-15

We just listened to an amazing Gospel story. You didn't even blink, or gasp. I was watching your eyes. We have heard the story so often it fails to shock us any more. It sounds like a normal, expected story. We need to reconsider.

Recently, just before I went to sleep, I read something about political perks--all the little things that have crept into the lives of politicians that remove them from the everyday experience, the reality of others. Just before I fell asleep I recalled the old "saw" about what happens when one is elected to high office--never again will he "have a bad meal or hear the truth!"

In the middle of the night, from somewhere deep in sleep, I had a vivid memory of an old experience I had forgotten; I woke with a shock, an absolutely clear awareness. I even said out loud, "That's what Holy Thursday's Gospel is about!"

What I had recalled was an experience from forty years ago. With a Sister of the Holy Names I had gone to Lesotho, in Southern Africa, to offer individually directed retreats to native clergy and religious for a year. Our very first retreat included twenty-two people, eighteen sisters and four priests, all native Africans. As we would have done here in the United States, Sr. Katherine and I put up a schedule inviting people to help clean up after meals. I signed up for the first day to get my turn out of the way so after lunch I helped clean up, clearing tables and eventually washing the dishes. Since we worked in silence I didn't notice anything peculiar.

The following day one of the Basotho priests got up towards the end of the meal and began to help clean up. I noticed Simon; noticed the reaction of the native sisters at table watching him. He looked uncomfortable; the sisters working seemed to give him an exceptionally wide berth.

Fr. Simon just happened to be my first appointment that afternoon. He excitedly entered my room. He told me that he had never before in his life washed a dish, held a broom, cleaned a table. He was proud of having done so for he felt he had crashed through every male, priestly cultural taboo he had. Then I realized the awe and wonder of the sisters who had watched him. Men didn't do such work. Especially, priests didn't do such work.

The memory of this experience with Simon spoke to me in the middle of the night about what we do here this Holy Thursday evening. In this memory I discover a hint of the shock, the cultural upheaval, the power of that serving gesture of Jesus when he washes his disciples' feet. In a culture in which men who were not slaves did not serve, where a rabbi, especially, was waited on, nothing would have prepared his disciples for Jesus' gesture at this meal.

I have often been impressed at our celebration of the Lord's Supper that the Gospel focuses on foot washing rather than on the institution of the Eucharist. We need to recall that at the time the gospel was written it would be every bit as shocking, as radical, for one who was rightly called "Master and Lord" to wash his disciples feet as it would be for him to call bread and wine his body and his blood. In some ways they are the same thing. The washing of feet, this radical act of serving, derives its very meaning from its relationship to Eucharist. Both say, in different ways: to give one's life to another, to be broken, to be poured out, to be consumed--to be a servant and let people use you as they will. I think of Mother Theresa's wonderful line inviting her sisters' service to be a kind of Eucharist: "Let the people eat you up!"

In this understanding, Peter's reluctance to have his feet washed does not arise from a sense of modesty or humility only. Peter resists an entire order of reality in which everything is turned upside down, a world in which the most important people become the servants of all. Peter stands for every one of us who resists the challenge of upsetting the entire order of things--the way things have always been, the way they are supposed to be! Why, it would be like a president shopping at the A.M. P.M. mini-mart, or a bishop or a pastor actually listening to people!

The courage of that Basotho priest, Simon (and now the similarity of name explains my memory), getting up from table and waiting on his sisters, being willing to disrupt a thousand years of custom, says volumes about the kind of man he is. It also gives me a hint into who and what Jesus was and who he invites us to be.

Tonight we celebrate the beginning of our Paschal Triduum. We remember the institution of the Eucharist. We prepare to celebrate death and Resurrection. As we celebrate, some people enter into communion with us for the first time, others will be baptized, others still will celebrate their return to the practice of their Catholic Faith. People come to the table, people come back to the table. And the Gospel we listened to reminds us what this table means: Those who eat and drink here are also those who wash, who serve, who disrupt the order of things, to create a world where the first are last, the least are best and all are for each other.

Personally I have trouble remembering all this. I need to be reminded. I need to celebrate this reminder now.

16) Holy Thursday Alternate

(The bulk of this homily is stolen from John Shea; I am unable to find the reference for this rendition of Shea's Last Supper poem.)

We have just washed the feet of those who will share at table with us tonight for the very first time, and those who will be baptized and Confirmed into our community at the Easter Vigil. We have said in this simple gesture that those who share in this meal are *servants* of one another and the world. A marvelous poem by theologian John Shea reminds us of how much Jesus' ministry surrounds meals, and how that meal ministry leads, easily, to this night.

To Jesus, every person was a guest.
An invitation had gone out from the heart of all life
to every heart within life . . .
His voice was the music of welcome
in the ears of rejection;
his presence, a silver setting in the slums,
with linen napkins on the laps of lepers.

At sunset, Jesus would haunt the marketplace
saluting the unlikely--
    "you there, hurrying in the shadows!
    You there, dressed, without customers!
    You there, with the eyes of Cain!
    EAT WITH ME TONIGHT!"

Now those that know the head from the foot of every table
were offended by his meals.
They regarded God as a knife
which divides the rotten from the righteous;
so they burst into the middle of his meals of forgiveness!
And Jesus welcomed even them;--
"More Guests," he cried!

But the "pure" gathered their robes around them
and went away into a draped room, where they agreed
that it was unpardonable of Jesus to make God
as accessible as a well . . . .

So _on this night_
When one who broke bread with Jesus, also broke bond with him,
Jesus gathered with his friends,
with the last wine before the grape of the Kingdom.

"Who is the Master?" the master asked.
"You are!"
"Who are the Servants?"
"We are," the servants replied

Then Jesus reversed his robe into an apron
and poured water on their feet
--water that ran into the rivers of their legs

and rushed for the home of their hearts.

They, *like us tonight perhaps*, were embarrassed
that he was so poured out,
squandering himself on them ...
So Peter said, "Not me."
"Can so reluctant a guest ever be hosted?" asked Jesus.
"Do not hold back!
Drink! Do not tongue taste the wine of God.
Eat! Do not teeth taste the bread of God.
Give yourself over to my love."

"Then, not only my feet, but hands and head as well."

"Ah, too much," laughed Jesus. "God is here!"

At the meal Jesus said:
"My friends, hold onto life with an open hand,
as I hold this bread and wine.
This bread is our food. This wine our drink.
This meal is our fellowship.
So, we hand over to the Giver of Life
the music that our muscles make,
the kisses that bring peace,
the sounds that swell the heart . . . .

But this bread is my body broken.
This wine is my blood outpoured.
This meal is our sacrifice.
So we hand over to the Giver of Life
the eyes that squint back,
the hands that do not reach out,
the barricaded mind, the hoarding heart.

All we are, we offer.
Life received as gift is given up as gift."

Later that evening there was a garden without fragrance
and a man with cold lips,
and a high priest with a ripped robe,
and a governor with glistening heart,
and a disciple with a labyrinthine lie,
and a carpenter put back to work.

And that is why, tonight
We meet together,
with food and drink between us.

As God would not let go of Jesus
in the hour of his death,
his friends would not let go of him in the hour of glory.

Down to this very day, (this night,)
We break the bread of his absence,
and Hope;
We drink the wine of his presence,
and Live!

17) Easter Sunday

Rooted in: Jn. 20:1-18

We are a people who hunger and thirst for happy endings. I want to start my Easter reflections by remembering for a moment our culture

> After some panic and uncertainty, the doofus gambling speculators reap enormous rewards in The Big Short.

> Rocky's young protégé doesn't win the fight but gains enormous respect and offers great hope for a romantic and pugilistic future in Creed.

> A woman comes to her sense and returns to her quickly married husband in Brooklyn

We human beings have probably always been this way; something in us needs to believe that love can last, that human life is charged with hope, that suffering is not the only truth.

I speak of our culture because we celebrate today *the* Happy Ending. Every other effort to say "things will turn out all right" pales beside the Empty Tomb.

The huge crowds at Church on Easter and Christmas speak to this deep human hunger. Many of us, not sure we believe, or are able to live the implications of this belief day in and day out. Still we desperately want the story to be true. We want the ending to be happy!

With John and Peter we run to the tomb because in Jesus being lifted from death every human failure, every human disaster, every dashed hoped and broken dream can be made new.

If Christ is risen from the dead, people from different classes can make friends, be reconciled. Economic disaster can be ended, or diverted. Bigots can be converted; obsessions can be healed. Even the messy brokeness of my own life, my family, my Church, my world can be mended!

As we gather this Easter morning I suggest the central challenge is to let this Resurrection message be Good News for us. Put another way, we remember and celebrate today not just what happened to Jesus, but more importantly **what happens to all of us because of Jesus.** We who are baptized, we who share in this story need to truly make it our story.

The Resurrection of Jesus says that death is not the end of the story for Jesus or for us. But it says much more than this. We celebrate not only that we get to go to heaven when we die, but the deepest truth all the way along--that God is faithful, God can be trusted, God constantly offers new beginnings, new hope--God offers constantly Happy Endings!

It's all about seeing. We look in the tomb and no body is there. One who was dead is gone. We don't see what we expected to see and now we look at everything else differently.

The second part of this morning's Gospel and other Resurrection stories suggest that Jesus is still alive, still present in our midst, still offering new beginnings. He may look like the gardener, as he does in this story, or like a stranger along the road, or a fisherman at the sea shore . . . but if we look carefully we can see Jesus. He calls us by name, "Mary"--or Bill, or Susie or Pat. He stops our tears.

A bus driver in Tacoma who was part of our RCIA community had this Resurrection approach to life. She drove a bus in the very dangerous Hilltop neighborhood during the evening shift. Inspired by stories like today's Gospel, she began to imagine that every rider on her bus was Jesus in disguise. The more frightening the person, the better the disguise. When a severely drugged or drunk passenger got on she would think, "Boy, Jesus, that's your best disguise yet." This prayerful imagining changed the way she saw each passenger, changed how she approached them, gave her almost endless happy endings!

Let me try to pull this all together.

We come here today because we believe (or want to believe) that God cares about us. God is very near to us. God joins in our human history in Jesus. When God joins us, he joins in the misery, the trial, the pain the disappointment, the rejection--all the suffering that makes up our human condition. He is overwhelmed by that pervasive suffering, indeed, he is killed by it.

But because he was faithful to God, because he loved as best he could, because he spoke the truth and acted on that truth, because he was fully human in his goodness as well as his broken-ness, God lifts him from death and "gives him a name above every other name."

Jesus becomes the hope, the promise, the happy ending offered to all of us in our fragile humanity.

We come to Church today because we want so deeply, so des-perately to believe that "things will be all right!"

And they will. Mary's tears and ours are turned into joy because she and we "have seen the Lord." He is risen and goes before us.

Easter tells us in terms most certain ... Everything will be all right in the end. If they are not all right, it's not the end!!

18) The Second Sunday of Easter

Rooted in: Acts 5:12-16, Rev. 1:9-19; Jn. 20:19-31

Easter is a big event, the biggest event of human existence, the biggest event in our Christian lives. So we spend forty days getting ready for it, three days celebrating it, and fifty days getting over it.

We continue to celebrate Easter for fifty days. Seven Sundays. These weeks are not the second, third, fourth Sundays *after* Easter but *of* Easter. We keep celebrating Easter Sunday over and over and over. Many things go on during this time.

We deepen what happened at the Easter Vigil.

We explain the faith, the mysteries, to those baptized--they just had hints before; now we tell them what we are about. We explain our faith. We call it *mystagogia*.

Perhaps most importantly we test out the truth of what we celebrate. Is it true? Does it matter? Deep down in our guts?

Thomas becomes a perfect minister for that testing. Thomas wants to believe this new reality of faith--Jesus risen from the dead--but he needs evidence. Thomas is a paradigm of the post-Easter Christian asking in what shape or manner, in what place can we meet and know the Risen Christ? Where and how does Jesus show himself now? How can we touch him, be touched by him now?

The Easter question that matters to us is not what happened to Jesus--what happened in that tomb, that upper room so long ago. The question is rather what happens to us now because of what happened then.

I suggest that, with Thomas, we ponder for a few moments where we meet Jesus now?

I admit that I share something of the frustration of the other apostles with Thomas' absence. "Doggone it, Thomas, if you had been here, you would already know what we are talking about."

The Easter Vigil has become for me *the* experience of the Risen Christ, in word, story, song, symbol, community, tears, hope, laughter. If someone, like Thomas, was not there when we celebrate we cannot explain it afterwards. Many, many people come together faith-filled, celebratory, illustrative that Christ lives in our midst.

If we missed the Vigil, if we were not there when Jesus came into our midst in so many wonderful ways ... or if we were there but it didn't touch us, or if it touched us but we have since forgotten, we still do ask what are the ways, the reminders, the signs the pointers now to Jesus' presence?

The readings today give us excellent clues.

First, the Acts of the Apostles story: We hear of "signs and wonders" that the apostles worked among the people--precisely the signs and wonders of the Risen Christ. Jesus' Spirit entered into the lives of people to make them a new creation. I am struck, for example, that Peter in these stories is a *hero*. People struggle just to stand inside his shadow! This is the same Peter who last week said "I don't know him," who ran away. Peter has been transformed.

One of the continual great signs of Christ's presence is the transformation of people who have been touched by Jesus. Every year catechumens, now neophytes, are in our midst--people changed by Christ this year! I know how different I and my life would be if it were not for Jesus. I know the long history of our church of people changed because of their relationship with Jesus, from Augustine to Oscar Romero, from Magdalene to Dorothy Day. Every such saint is a sign of Jesus in our midst.

We say, sometimes so glibly, that the Church is the Body of Christ; but we really do affirm that this Church, alive in Christ is the Risen Body, the agent for the Transformation of the World. We get glimpses of this truth. We glimpse this presence in every one of our heroes or heroines.

Let me be more specific. Look at the first part of the Gospel today. Jesus blows his Spirit of forgiveness on his followers. The disciples are given the power to forgive. From that day to this, whenever forgiveness happens in our midst we see the unmistakable sign of the presence of Jesus. It is not easy to forgive. Jesus would not have talked about it so much if it weren't so difficult. Whenever forgiveness happens Jesus is with us.

> (As an aside, I do not mean by forgiveness some nam-by-pamby victim stance--"go ahead, walk all over me." Forgiveness is not about being a victim, a martyr. Forgiveness rather means "not defining someone by what is weakest in them." To forgive is to remember the hurt, to acknowledge that it may still hurt, but refusing to make this hurt the only truth. To forgive means to see the possibilities still present, to affirm that the future can be better than the past, to expect more than I have seen so far. To forgive means to love the way God does ... in Hope!)

This is the way the Church best witnesses to the Risen Christ, alive in us. We witness by being willing to expose again our wounds, our hurt hands, our broken hearts, our stepped-on feet and to love again. Whenever anyone in their suffering searches for Christ, hopes to put a finger again into his side, this community of Jesus--to the extent that we are forgiving--offers the wounds again.

There is perhaps nothing more powerful that we can do during this Easter season than to celebrate forgiveness in our midst over and over again. A healing, loving community showing signs and wonders of forgiveness, proves that Jesus is alive.

19) The Third Sunday of Easter

Rooted in Jn. 21: 1-19

We continue to celebrate Easter. We tell the early stories of the Risen Jesus. These stories are an effort of the early disciples to capture a mystery. They had seen Jesus dead. They experienced that he was still alive. But the experience of the Risen Christ is not easily put into words.

This is not so different from our own experience of believing that Jesus lives still. It is very difficult to explain, to put into words why and how we trust this to be true.

I suggest that we look at the Resurrection stories in the Gospels to help us understand our own stories. The Christ we meet today is the Risen Christ met still in ways similar to those first disciples.

We meet in the breaking of the bread.
We often do not recognize him at first and have to look carefully.
We meet him when are wounds are shown,

when peace if offered,
when comfort comes.

In today's Gospel we discover four mysterious ways in which the Risen Christ was manifest to his first followers--four ways we might also look to see where he is present in our lives.

They met Jesus, we meet Jesus, when the catch is far beyond the cast--the results are disproportionate to the effort, in the miracle of abundance.

They met Jesus, we meet Jesus, in a meal shared, a sacred meal--Eucharist--or any honest meal of love.

They met Jesus, we meet Jesus when forgiveness is given, healing happens, and a sense of mission is renewed.

They met Jesus, we meet Jesus when lives are surrendered to another, to the Other.

This wonderful story begins with the disciples afraid, confused by life, returning to something familiar. They go fishing. Through their own efforts they fish all night and catch nothing. A stranger appears and suggests they try the other side. Reluctantly they cast their nets again and the catch is larger than they can hold—seemingly every fish in the sea of Galilee. They recognize "It is the Lord" precisely because the catch is beyond their own efforts, their own imaginings. Peter overcomes his fear, puts back on his robe (of baptism?), and leaps into the waters to come to Jesus!

This conviction that it is indeed Jesus grows as they share a meal; the sacred character of the meal is suggested by the language of breaking bread, but this is also any meal with loved ones after a long night's work, a deeply shared success, a hope restored.

After the meal Jesus takes Peter aside. Jesus gives his dear friend an opportunity to recover from his denials of a few days before. More important, out of his great affection for Peter, Jesus longs to hear that this affection is reciprocal. Jesus affirms again his commission to Peter, despite his failures, tells him again that he is to lead Jesus' community. Peter, himself healed, loved, forgiven is still invited to love, heal, feed others not because of his gifts, but because of his very weakness . . . he is to be leader of a community of screw-ups!

The story ends with Jesus inviting Peter ever more deeply into this relationship, into imitation, into surrendering his life to God as Jesus has already done. "Go where another will lead you." Peter meets the Risen Christ most personally in the invitation to surrender. Note that today we hear the final words of Jesus in this final Gospel, spoken both to Peter and to us: "Follow me!"

There is too much here. The story is too rich, too detailed to be captured in a few brief reflections. I can only hint at the ways this resurrection story leads us to look for the Risen Christ in our lives here and now, this Easter Season.

We find Jesus still when things are multiplied beyond our expectations, the catch exceeds the cast! I think of people I have known who run feeding programs for the poor. Without exception when asked where all the food comes from, they respond "I don't know, it just comes!" The miracle is repeated day after day. Closer to our experience here I find Jesus in the phenomenon of parish life. We ask people to help us celebrate Easter, for example, and everyone first says "yes," then does a more careful conscientious job than could have been imagined. Notice in your own community, the complete care with which the music was offered, the cross was carried, the church was decorated, the word was proclaimed? We meet the Risen Christ in a community that maximizes and multiplies its gifts beyond belief.

We meet Christ in meals shared. Sacred meals. Family meals. The faces of children receiving Eucharist for the first time on Holy Thursday, show me the risen Christ. The tears of a candidate receiving for the first time after more than a year of being "dismissed" Sunday after Sunday assure me Jesus is present in that bread. But I have the same experience Easter evening sharing a meal and honest, warm, convivial conversation with a community of friends.

One Holy Saturday morning I sat with all those celebrating the Easter Sacraments that year, some thirty-three adults, children, babies, with their families and their sponsors. I looked at the almost incredible spectrum of racial, educational, social, political diversity in that room. Nothing but a shared faith in Jesus would bring this group around a common table, breaking bread. And I knew Jesus was here, alive and well.

Christ is alive when those who have stumbled are given a chance to start over, to begin again, to be healed--and not just healed but commissioned to bring the good news to others. I once worked with three people in one year who had come to a church community after imprisonment, starting over. Jesus was so very present in this new beginning. I worship in a parish where I once served as pastor; I had to start over in an entirely new way and I still meet the Risen Christ there.

So many others whose marriages have failed, whose original vocations have crumbled, who have been beaten by the forces of life, people part of any one of many twelve-step groups, others devastated by a child's death, a failed business, an adoption that fell through. Others whose wounds are not visible, are carried inside in ways that only a handful might know. The Risen Christ is surely present, working, throbbing, pulsing new life into old veins in the courage to begin again.

The final lines of the gospel are the final lines of the Jesus story. The final word of the Risen Christ to Peter, who always stands for all of us. These words are repeated each Sunday in our midst, especially in this Easter season. Jesus stands with us, individually and together, and says:

"See, I let go. I loved. I suffered and I died. And God raised me up. And God will do, God does do, the same for you.
You used do things your own way, go where you wanted, run your own life.
How far did it get you?
Now, at Easter, look at me. Let God lead you. As you grow older, grow wiser.
Follow me!"

20) The Fourth Sunday of Easter

Rooted in Acts 13, Rev. 7, and Jn. 10:27-30

In 1975, I was outside the chapel of Bellarmine Prep high school where I taught. Surprised, I saw two young men in flowing robes and sandals knocking on the glass door; I opened and invited them in. They told me they were evangelizing, telling people about Jesus Christ and they wanted to speak to some or all of our classes. I tried to tell them we already told our students about Jesus. But that was not nearly enough. When, after a few minutes of relatively heated conversation, I ushered them out the door; they astounded me when they took off their sandals and, to my chagrin, literally "shook off the dust from their feet" in protest against my stubborn blindness..

Despite the silliness of it all, I felt terrible for most of the day.

The reading from Acts today always calls this strange experience to mind. During the Easter season, coupled with our other two readings, it leads me think about Jesus, about knowing him and being known by him, being called by name, being loved by a God who never gives up on us, never shakes dust from his feet even when we err, as Pope Francis' encyclical "The Joy of Love" reminded us.

I would rather think of so many catechumens over the years passing through this baptismal font, bathing in Jesus, wearing white robes, "washed white in the blood of the lamb." I prefer to remember the lamb who will shepherd them and all of us baptized like them who Jesus "leads through springs of life-giving water." I prefer to recall the promise that Jesus rather than shaking dust off feet will "wipe every tear from our eyes."

Another memory. The brief gospel about Jesus as a shepherd who knows us and whom we know and follow and from whom nothing can separate us.

My only personal experience of shepherds came nearly 40 years ago when I spent a year in Lesotho, a small mountain nation inside the Republic of South Africa. There were many shepherds in that country, but they were not the men we imagine. They were almost always small boys 8-12 years old. Grown men were mostly in South Africa earning money for their families. It was left to boys to take turns with other boys in their family, or other neighbors, spending nights in the hills, watching the small herd of sheep most families grazed to survive, both for eating and for the wool from which they shaped their incredibly lovely blankets.

To my eyes, the sheep looked healthy. It was the boys I worried about. Lesotho had frequent thunder and lightning storms; frequently small boys were brought to the clinic next to my little house having been struck by lightning, sometimes dead, always at least badly burned. Had they not been barefoot, been grounded even by simple tennis shoes this would not have happened. These boys missed school for days, even weeks while out in those hills searching for food for their flocks.

They did this because the lives of themselves and their families depended on the sheep, not just that the sheep depended on them.

All of which leads me to a simple thought. We often reflect on how we depend on Jesus, his knowing us by name, his caring for and about us deeply and personally.

I wonder if Jesus the shepherd doesn't also depend on us. Just a small thought, but doesn't the Christ who lives still in a Church, a community depend on his sheep.

His human family cannot be housed and fed and protected without us, his sheep. The wars that abound in our world will continue until this shepherd's sheep can stop them. Every day some 90 people are killed by gunfire in our nation--other slaughtered sheep. The Shepherd, Jesus, needs us to do whatever we can to stop this needless tragedy.

We are the sheep who have passed through the waters and been washed clean. We say we have "put on Christ," have become his body. He, as Theresa said, has no hands now, but ours.

My eyes can still tear up when I remember those lovely small Lesotho boys with big smiles and scrawny bodies, wandering the hills all around the nation tending their little bands of sheep. But I am grateful for the reminder they still offer me. The shepherd not only knows and loves his sheep; he also depends on those sheep. That's why He cares so deeply.

21) The Fifth Sunday of Easter

Rooted in: Acts. 14: 21-7; Rev. 21: 1-5; Jn. 13: 31-5

We celebrate again today Easter Sunday. It is a bit difficult to realize that, after a few weeks, and with a Gospel that seems to be
about something else entirely. Still, this is the fifth Sunday of Easter,
the fifth time we celebrate Easter together this year. Once we
have heard the stories of the Risen Christ, the Church seems to
wander randomly through other issues until we get to Pentecost;
but each issue is connected with inviting the recently baptized-
-and all of us with them--to understand their new-found faith, and
to renew that faith in our midst.

First, Easter.

Every Sunday of Easter tells us something more, not just about
what happens to Jesus, but what happens to us because of Jesus.
The reading from the book of Revelations is the clearest about
this. In this final book of our bible, John sees a vision of a new
heaven, a new earth: God dwells with us, we who are God's people

through Baptism. At the end God finally wipes every tear from our eyes, takes every care away; there will be no more weeping or mourning. Jesus sits upon his throne and promises, "Behold I make all things new!"

The promise and the glory of Easter for us, as for Jesus, is that God makes everything new.

The Gospel itself fits into the Easter themes because it lies at the very heart of the Gospel message. It helps to recall the context of this Gospel passage that takes us back to the Triduum, to Holy Thursday, to the celebration of the Lord's Supper.

The Gospel on Holy Thursday included the verses just before today's passage. We recall Jesus getting up from table, washing his disciples' feet, and asking them if they understood what he had done. If he, Jesus, who is master and Lord, has washed their feet, they must do the same for one another. We, the followers of Jesus, are to be washers of one another's feet. This is the Easter message. The followers of Jesus are servants.

The very next lines are those we heard today in the gospel.

> A new commandment I give to you, that you love
> one another; even as I have loved you, you must
> love one another ... this is the way that people
> will know you are my disciples, by the love you
> have for one another."

The followers of Jesus are those who have so experienced God's love for us in Jesus that we are set free to love each other without reserve.

One week these readings fell on Mother's Day, so I hear these readings in connection with Mother's Day. It strikes me that no one washes as many feet as mothers; it's almost the job description! I recall a profound personal experience. Let me tell a story that brings together this Gospel story, Mother's Day and our own Easter call.

A woman came to me once to make a retreat. She was at a turning point in her life, divorced, a mother of several now-grown children. She came searching for direction to the next stage of her life.

On the third day of retreat, for no reason that I can recall, I suggested she pray over chapter 13 of John's Gospel, the story of Jesus washing his disciples' feet. The next day she told me she hadn't found anything in that passage and she read a number of other passages, and part of a book. I invited her to pray over the same passage again, wondering if she were not avoiding something.

The next day she entered my room in anger. She threw the bible on my desk, saying she never wanted to read that passage again. She hated that passage. She had served, loved, washed endless feet all her life. If there was a foot around she washed it. She never wanted to wash another foot as long as she lived.

Apparently we had touched a nerve.

With trepidation I invited her to pray about the same passage for yet another day.

The next day she came in calmly, quietly, honestly. Her prayer had revealed to her an enormously important truth. She spoke about the ultimately discouraging reality of washing feet when someone else demanded or expected it, of serving out of guilt, out of *should* and *ought* and *must*, and the great difference service can be when chosen. When one allows oneself to choose who and how and when and where to love, the service becomes rewarding and life-giving.

It is so easy to lose our center, our perspective, our balance. More than one authority has said that the biggest risk for women (and indeed a great risk for men, too) is the tendency to give and give, and give without any center, without holding onto any core of oneself. Since something seems to lead women to believe it is their job to keep the peace, women are apt to try to hold together the whole world, single-handedly, to make everything peaceful, to keep family, school, neighborhood, and world all in one piece, all by oneself. Finally, often only after falling apart, the poor woman discovers it cannot be done.

This particular retreat went on for three more days, unremarkably, but prayerful, consoling.

The final time I met this retreatant, as we finished talking, I paused and closed my eyes for a moment of prayer. Suddenly I was aware that she was kneeling at my feet, taking off my shoes and socks and beginning to massage my feet with a sweet smelling ointment. I did not want her to do this. I was uncomfortable, embarrassed. I wanted to stay "in charge" but she was doing this because *she wanted* to.

When finished, she put my shoes and socks back on, put her ointment away and left the room with a quiet "Thank you."

I believe this woman heard the Easter message. She could become a deeper better mother than she had ever been before,

loving because she was first loved,
serving because she had been served,
laying down her life because she chose to.

And in her insight and conversion we all discover something about traps and joys of motherhood and every kind of love.

22) The Sixth Sunday of Easter

Rooted in: Acts. 15: 1,2, 22-29; Rev. 21: 10-14, 22-23; Jn. 14: 23-29

One Sunday after Mass I said hello to a young family with two small children. I know they have had trouble making it to Mass lately so I said I was glad to see them. They responded a little sheepishly that they had arrived very late, and told me, finally in laughter, the entire story. They got up and started in plenty of time for Mass, but just before they left they realized diapers needed changing. After the diapers, they went to the car and remembered the need for some crayons and paper to keep the five year old busy during service. As they got in the car, the baby's nose began to bleed, and they went back to take care of that. Then mom remembered something she needed to give to someone at church and rushed to find it. Finally they arrived, quite late--in fact just as I was inviting the Assembly to offer each other a sign of peace. The last thing they felt like doing. On the cosmic level, on the personal level, or, as here, on the familial level, the peace of Christ is hard to come by.

In the key lines in today's gospel Jesus says:

"Peace I leave with you; my peace I give to you ...
not as the world gives. Do not let your hearts be
troubled or afraid."

And hearing this we touch that part of all of us that is not at
peace, that is indeed afraid. We become overwhelmed with the
absence of peace in the church, in the parish, in our world, even
inside ourselves.

I am helped to hear in Acts, as we do all through the Easter season, the story of the early Church. Today we heard a reminder of
the first big battle in the Church, a battle resolved today in what
we have come to call "The Council of Jerusalem." Somehow it
helps me to hear of the struggles of the Church from day one.
In the first twenty years of the Church life, they had a violent
disagreement. Some said that new Christians outside the Jewish
household needed to become Jews as they became Christians,
needed to be circumcised, needed to be bound by the entire
Mosaic law. Others said "no." The fight apparently went on for
several years. Even our hero leaders disagreed. Peter believed that
to be a Christian one also had to be a good Jew. Paul who had
worked with gentile converts, and seen God's grace working, tells
us in the letter to the Galatians that he "had to rebuke Peter to
his face."

Finally, in the passage we heard today, after years of struggle, much
pain, many arguments, the dispute is ended, the law is eased, the
Spirit is freed, and the Good News continues to spread.

I am strangely consoled that the early believers, like ourselves,
lost sleep, worried, were fearful, forgot the promise of Jesus that

the Spirit was with them, working in them. Some of them were probably even late for church.

These readings remind me that the Spirit is given to the whole church, and works in us. We need not be afraid. Here, between Easter and Pentecost, we are invited to remember the image of that Spirit given to the Church. Not as on a pyramid, given to Peter, and filtered down, but, as in a circle, given to all and filtered in. The Spirit is given to the whole family of the church, and every family in it. We can resist for a while, but finally the Spirit will penetrate, we will listen, the Spirit will live in us, and peace will be possible.

Remember, I tell myself, this peace is not "like the peace the world gives." This is the peace of a man going to his death. This is the peace of integrity, of being in touch with God, of being faithful through suffering. This is the peace that is possible in the midst of conflict and division, peace in the midst of pain, because God has overcome all pain, in raising up Jesus.

Most simply put, this is the peace of Jesus--the peace of one who knows in every fiber of his being that he is loved by a God who will be faithful. The peace Jesus gives us is the peace of knowing we are loved!

Jesus' peace does not mean no conflict, no struggle, everyone is "cool" all the time. What this peace promises is that struggle, and growth, and change can all happen in the spirit of Jesus, with peace.

My image of any parish, and this one in particular, is of a hundred balls thrown into the air, none ever completely coming down. Things never quite finish,, they just stay up there floating, vibrating, alive, unsettled.

We struggle to adequately care for the elderly in so many nursing and retirement homes, or in their own homes, and people keep falling through the cracks.

We struggle to relate as a single mission with a university next door and each of us still operate individually and forget to involve one another in our ministerial lives.

We direct a very large part of our budget to our Catholic school, hoping to pass on the faith to the next generation, but we often fail to include the school in our worship lives, or other parts of our planning.

We have four very distinct Masses, and are unsure how to bring these communities together and realize that the more open or liberal part of our community is neglected even in these offerings.

And what I love, what seems to me the sign of Christ's presence in it all is that we keep at it, keep all these and other various balls up in the air and do it maintaining a certain peace, a certain love for each other. My conviction is that we are able to do this because everyone is right. There is a portion of truth in every person, every position. Every parishioner invites us to share their position, their convictions because they are rooted in the gospel. Each voice here is concerned not with selfish personal things, but with the values of Jesus.

The voice that speaks for justice and care for the poor is right.

The voice that says we need to be financially solvent in the parish is right.

The voice that says Catholic schools are terribly important is correct; so is the voice that insists that we support the public school system.

I sympathize with those that worry that the university is encroaching into our neighborhood, and with those who rejoice that we have become a university neighborhood.

Every voice is true and all are passionate. The balls all stay in the air, and in it all, Jesus is with this community, giving peace. In the very midst of our struggles I find Jesus in this community because we do not run away, deny, or minimize the conflicts. We just try to face them in the Spirit of Jesus. This Spirit tells us all, in our uniqueness that we are loved just as we are!

We need to keep celebrating and believing this truth, so now we move towards the altar where we share a common meal, a common body.

23) The Feast of the Ascension

(N.B. This feast, celebrated on Sunday, takes the place of the 7th Sunday of Easter)

Rooted in: Acts. 5: 1-11 Eph. 1: 17-27; Lk. 24: 46-53

Years ago a pastor friend of mine answered the phone one evening. A man called to ask the priest to come to his home and anoint his dying wife. The pastor said, "I'll be right over and I'll bring Jesus," meaning he would bring the Eucharist with him for the sick woman. The husband told his wife that the priest was coming and bringing Jesus.

As he moved towards the door a newly ordained priest asked if he could come with him. The new priest in the style of the seventies was a big handsome man, with a long flowing dark beard. The pastor knocked on the apartment door and when the husband opened the door his wife was on a couch directly in front of the door. She rose up on her elbow, saw the familiar face of the pastor, and just over his shoulder the very unfamiliar face of a tall, young, handsome, bearded man.

As they entered the room the woman cried out in joy,

"Oh, you did bring Jesus with you."

Then, with apparent great peace, she died there on the couch.

I don't know, really, if you hear this story as joyous or tragic. The husband was overwhelmed with joy at the peaceful, faith-filled passage of his wife from life to death, to life again.

I thought of the story as I prayed about the feast of the Ascension, along with Pentecost, its companion feast next week. Both feasts celebrate the birthday of the Church. Both remind us of the central truth of our faith that *wherever we go we do bring Jesus with us.*

The history of our Faith is a sort of eternal relay race. For centuries on end God ran the race, created the world, choose a people, fashioned a future. Then, in the fullness of time, Jesus came and took the baton, became God's runner in our world. Jesus ran fast and well, to death and beyond. Then the Spirit of Jesus, risen from death entered into a community of faith, into the believers in Jesus, into us.

On Ascension and Pentecost we celebrate that this baton, the task of God, the Spirit of God is passed on to us. We run, with the Spirit of Jesus in us.

Wherever we go we carry Jesus with us. We continue his work and pass on his message.

All of the scripture of this feast seem to me included in the single line: "Men of Galilee, why are you standing looking up to heaven?" (Ironically, I am always struck that the opening prayer invites us to keep our eyes always on heaven--exactly **not** the point!) The focus of this feast is to quit looking up to the sky where Jesus has gone, and turn our eyes out towards the world Jesus loved, and invites us to serve.

The story of the two priests with which I began feels to me a kind of symbol of this feast. It says that if we truly bring Jesus with us we will overwhelm people. We will have a dramatic, even cataclysmic effect on others.

People would rather see a sermon than hear one, so what would it mean for us to "bring Jesus," not just our words, but his deeds? I hear Jesus say:

> "I pray that they be one, that they be so completely
> one that the world can believe."

I hear him say:

> "By this will people know that you are my disciples,
> by the love you have for one another."

And I wonder aloud:

Do people say that about me, about us? Is this what the people of our neighborhood or of our city say about this parish community?

In our families as our children look at us, listen to us, is this what they children most notice--our love for each other?

In the classrooms where we teach, in the parks where we play, in the houses where we gather, is this how we are seen?

In our work places, in the clubs and boards and stores and markets we attend, is this how we are experienced?

I wonder when I die will they write on my tombstone, he lived like Jesus, he loved like Jesus, he brought Jesus with him wherever he went.

Ascension just begins our birthday celebration. Thank God, next week we celebrate Pentecost; the Spirit of Jesus comes to us to live in us. The Church offers these two feasts as a kind of single celebration, an octave of prayer. We spend this week aware of how and where we need the spirit of Jesus to come if we are to indeed carry him with us wherever we go!

24) Pentecost Sunday

Rooted in Acts. 2: 1-11; 1 Cor. 12:3-7, 12-13; Jn. 20: 19-23

I begin today reflecting that my wife reminds me that yesterday I had my 35th hospital visit since our marriage not yet 16 years ago--kidney stone removal in which, so far, the cure is worse than the disease. But this does make me a bit of an authority on getting up and starting over during my nearly 80 years of life. And that's what Pentecost is about. Starting over, with God's spirit breathing us to life.

Three more different images, impressions, all of which seem to come together through the scripture readings for this feast of Pentecost.

First, I have a vivid memory of a television image during the riots in Los Angeles, after the verdict at the Rodney King trial. Somehow the television crews had located two women who lived in the middle of the riot area. They were huddled in their home in the midst of the city, surrounded by fire and shooting. Throughout the day the television station spoke with them. They were philosophical, even wise, but grounded. They were like the apostles in the scripture today; they reminded me that we are all a little like that at times. All of us hide in our various houses, surrounded by violence and danger, waiting for the Spirit of Jesus to inspire us out of our hiding into a fearsome, uncertain world.

We gather here today and often, waiting, praying, longing for a spirit not our own to help us enter into a world that desperately needs us, but can terrify us.

The second image. I once did some spiritual direction with a woman who had recently given birth to a severely handicapped child. The mother was overwhelmed by the feelings of responsibility that lay ahead of her. She was afraid, insecure, feeling woefully inadequate. She told about a marvelous experience she had in prayer. She was sitting before God speaking words like "I can't do it; I'm not strong, or holy enough. I'm not that heroic kind of person." Suddenly she felt overwhelmed with a deep realization of what her prayer, really any prayer, was all about. She realized that she needed the Spirit of God to do what she could not. She could not do it alone; but she was not alone!

Again as we come to our Pentecost prayer we are all, at least at times, just like her. We feel overwhelmed by this or that part of our life, feel powerless. All of us cry out in some form or fashion, "I can't do it." And then we let God's spirit enter us, let our imaginations be converted, and see ourselves as radically not alone, but filled with a spirit, and as parts of a body, members of a larger body of Christ, that can, together, do infinitely more than we can ask or imagine.

The third image is a continuing nagging question about who we are, who I am, really. So often we hear that religious folks are hypocrites, coming together for church on Sunday, acting all pious and good, forming community, singing songs with one voice. Then we spend the rest of the week just like everyone else, split up and divided into various factions, by color, gender, class or race. There is some truth in the accusation. I have often felt the hypocrite in saying anything about god, or love or life. But maybe we need to turn that image around!

It strikes me today that perhaps *who we really are* is the people we want to be here, together, as one on Sunday. Here we are indeed our best and truest selves. The rest of the week we forget, wander, lose ourselves and we come back again next week to celebrate who we really are. Rather than feeling like we should quit coming because we don't live up to what we celebrate here, we realize we need to come more often, come more deeply, for it is here that we proclaim who we want to be, who we hope to be!

With these images as a backdrop, let me look at the marvelous scripture for this feast.

The first reading from Acts, the story of the Spirit descending on the Apostles in that square in Jerusalem, is even more wondrous than it appears. To understand it we need to know the books that preceded it. We need to know especially the story of Babel, one of the stories of the *origins of sin* in the first book of Genesis. At Babel the people built a tower in their prideful desire to reach up to God. In their pride, the people became for the first time divided from one another. They could no longer speak to one another, no longer understand each other, no longer communicate with people different from themselves.

The story of Pentecost is very deliberately crafted not necessarily in fact, but in poetry, proclaiming a story of overcoming division, overcoming the power of sin and separation. In the Spirit of Jesus the apostles go to the central religious city of the world and speak in one language to all the peoples of the earth. And everyone understands them. Ancient divisions are healed, the people of the earth are one again!

The very meaning of this feast is that
we don't have to remain hidden in isolation,
we don't have to rely just on our own gifts and talents,
we are not, really, the divided separated isolated people we think.
We really are one because Christ is one, and we are "in Christ."

The Gospel repeats a story we heard just a few weeks ago, the Second Sunday we celebrated Easter. In this passage Easter and Pentecost are one event. Easter Sunday night Jesus appears to his closest friends, breathing on them his Spirit.

As he breathes this Spirit he says, "Forgive, forgive, forgive... If you forgive, people will know they are forgiven by God." This power is not given just to a select few, to priests, but to the Church, to all of us, to the disciples of Jesus. We are called to extend to everyone the forgiving spirit of Jesus. There is no greater challenge to us as disciples than to continually "unbind" each other from the terrible weight of our failures, the sense we all have of not being good enough. Only in community can we change our worst and weakest selves into our best and truest self, only by supporting and challenging each other can we help one another to hear the voice of Jesus say:

> "You are good enough;
> this is who you really are;
> don't stay huddled, hiding;
> bring the Spirit of Jesus that lives in you,

and lives in all of us together out into the world
that so desperately needs it!"

There is perhaps too much here. Let me make a final simple suggestion that may bring all this together.

At communion today on Pentecost Sunday, I invite everyone to focus on the "Amen" we say when we receive the Eucharist--the bread, the wine, the body, the blood of Jesus. We mean always, at least two things by this *Amen*.

We say "Amen" to receiving the risen Jesus into our Body, so that we become his body. We say "Amen" to a power that comes to us, a Spirit we receive that frees us to do far more than we could do alone. We say an individual "Amen" to becoming our best and truest self in Jesus.

But we also say "Amen" to this Church Body,
this body of many members.
We say "Yes, Amen" to one another;
we receive into ourselves all the many members of this body-
-all those messy, imperfect, confused, people--and all the gifted, graced, incredibly Christ-filled people.

We receive each other so that what we cannot do alone, we can to together.

I invite us today at communion time to come up here singing in one voice, and when the minister says "Body of Christ," "Blood of Christ," let each of us say loudly and with conviction "AMEN" so that **Amen** echoes through the Church over and over and over again as we accept one another and the Christ that lives in us.

25) Trinity Sunday

Rooted in Prov. 8: 22-31; Ro. 5:1-5; Jn. 16: 12-15

The temptation on Trinity Sunday is not to talk about God, and God's love for us, but rather abstract truths, about dogma. I have been subjected to Trinity Sunday sermons in which the priest tried to explain the carefully crafted conclusions of the early centuries of Church dialogue, language about *processions* and *relationships,* the inner working of the Divine Nature, which I doubt that anyone really understands.

In fact I am tempted to recall (and I willingly give in to the temptation) my summary of Church dogma.

> There are twelve apostles,
> eleven faithful ones,
> ten commandments,
> nine choirs of angels,
> eight beatitudes,
> seven sacraments,

six precepts of the Church,
five decades of the rosary,
four Gospels,
three person in God,
two natures in Christ,
one God,

And no proof!

The feast of the Trinity is not a time to explain dogma. That is the task of a theologian. The homiletic task is to somehow stand within a community pointing out the various presences of God, and pointing the community out to God to look at our world, our lives, our struggles, our joys and say, "See, there is God." This is where God is present. This is how we touch God.

Then we turn, in prayer, and we ask God to keep looking at us, keep loving us, keep seeing us as we say thanks to you for the past and long for your presence more in the future.

As we look at the scripture today we see it is entirely about the Trinity, about the mystery of God.

In the first reading God is the creator, making a wondrous world, but the Spirit is always there, God's craftsman, God's delight.

The second reading reminds us that we are saved because of our faith in Jesus Christ, who leads us to God by the power of the Spirit that is in us.

Finally, the Gospel reminds us of this Trinitarian flow--Jesus getting everything from his Father, and the Spirit of Jesus passing it on to us.

In all of this we are speaking of a God who has many faces, many diverse interactions with us. We cannot capture them, explain them fully, or explain them away. We stumble for a language, words to try to "eff" what is essentially ineffable.

I find it helpful to look at how the different "persons" of this Trinity interact with us, and to use the language of "Life-giver," "Pain-bearer," "Love maker."

God is not static, unmoved, unmoving. God relates to us.
God creates and sustains life in us--Life-giver.
In Jesus, God enters our life and shares our struggles--Pain-bearer.
God binds us together in love with God, and with one another--Love-maker.

This feast invites us to name, and to celebrate, some of this interaction with God.

God keeps giving us new life, creating us, day by day, moment by moment:
This year tons of new people joined our Catholic Christian community at Easter; a plethora of new Christians were created.

Perhaps too frequently at Eucharist, we baptize new infants into our community; more than 50 children in the parish I attend this year.

Every week new parishioners come here and enter into our communities.

And every time we get up in the morning grateful to be alive, every time we have been moved by a sunset, a rainbow, the birth of a child, the gift of a friendship, we have known God as Life-giver.

God keeps creating us in so many ways.

And God shares our pain.

Recently we stood with a family whose son ended his own life. We have said a celebratory farewell to another man who died by inches from multiple sclerosis, and helped his family mourn his passing. We have supported a family whose husband and father finally died after 8 years of fighting cancer.

Every week folks in a community visit the sick, struggle for equal rights, help out a neighbor, feed the hungry, shelter the homeless and simply care for a friend, a neighbor, a family member in some kind of pain.

And every time any of us have personally been lifted out of the waters that are drowning us, or lifted up from mats where we were paralyzed, or faced with unexpected hope any kind of suffering in some personal garden of agony, anytime we have forgiven another and been able to start again, in all these times and so many others, Jesus is present.

God shares our pain.

And God's Spirit is with us as "Love-maker." The Spirit of God binds the unlikely together, forms new relationships, deepens old ones.

I recall vividly experiencing the Spirit of Jesus at a golf course when a group of parishoners, many of whom did not know each other, shared life and laughter as new friendships were formed.

The Spirit of Jesus moves in the couples married in our communities each year forming new families of faith.

Every weekend someone comes and finds a new home, a new sense of belonging here in this parish community,

Every time one of us experiences a sense of belonging, of being held and loved and cared for, whenever we experience the profound sense of being loved, God is in our midst as Love-maker.

Life is not just a succession of one darn thing after another. It is not true that stuff just happens. No, God is present, the Trinity lives in our midst.

I will keep trying to point it out, not just for you, but for myself. And whenever we notice that God is with us, we can turn together to this altar and celebrate, say "Thanks," offer Eucharist together to this God among us.

26) The Feast of the Body and Blood of Christ

Rooted in Gen. 14:18-20; I Cor. 11:23-26; Lk. 9:11b-17

To help us enter into this feast of the Body and Blood of Christ I invite us into a fantasy of imagination--one of many possible future scenarios.

Let's place ourselves about ten years into the future; what we had half expected has become doubly true. There are now only 5 full time priests serving in all the inter-city parishes.

Our own parish, like many now around the world, is only able to celebrate Eucharist about once a month.

Because of the vitality of our community, however, many things seem the same or even better. There is still a spirit of community and service in our midst. Folks, almost as many in number as ever, still gather here each weekend to celebrate together. Many people are involved in the life of the community.

When we gather to pray, excellent homilies are given by five different people on a regular basis; each homilist is wonderful in his or her unique way. The music is still excellent and we have learned to sing and move and pray together very well.

Many different cultures are incorporated into our worship and we celebrate all kinds of events in people's lives.

When we gather, after the liturgy of the Word, we share in simple communion from the hosts consecrated in large numbers by the priest who comes infrequently. Among us, as with others, anger grows at the rigidity of the institution that still refuses to ordain any but single, life-time celibate men, but, by-and-large we have learned to cope well. One would have to say that we are thriving.

We have learned to celebrate weddings with couples witnessing the vows of those they had helped prepare for marriage. Funerals are simple honest farewells presided over by someone on the parish staff who best knew and can speak of the deceased. Weddings and funerals are almost always done without the Eucharist.

We are still a people rooted in the Gospel of Jesus, still sharing frequently in communion, still gathering in various small communities during the week, still trying to love, to serve, to be faithful to Jesus.

The least satisfying experiences we have as a community are those weeks when the priest comes – an older, overworked, kind priest, but disconnected from us, our life, our struggles, our joys.

My point on this Feast of the Body and Blood of Christ, is not to predict the future by offering this scenario, but only to raise questions about the present! In this *one possible scenario,* a rather rosy one indeed, has anything essential to us been lost? We are no longer really a Eucharistic Community, for Mass is a rare, and less satisfying event . . . but we are certainly a Christian community. Does Eucharist really matter?

This is a serious question, today, before anything like this becomes true. The question is precisely that: Would we be any different without regular Eucharist? Does Eucharist, the Body and Blood of Christ, matter?

We need to admit that it may not matter. We may not now realize what we have, such that we would not miss it in the future. We may have already for too long simply used left-over hosts from a tabernacle, from the Mass of yesterday or last week, or even last month. We may have for too long focused only on the words of consecration or institution, the magic moment when a miracle happens, to the detriment of the action, the poetry, the larger transformation of a community that Eucharist is about.

We may have affirmed an importance we could not name, and did not always experience, such that its absence becomes relatively insignificant, as least in our conscious Christian life.

I want to imagine again, this time not the future but the past. I hold deep in my heart the memory of a funeral Eucharist I once celebrated; certainly other celebrations could make the same point but let me recall just one.

It was, indeed, a Eucharistic funeral. After the word was heard and reflected on, we placed bread and wine on the altar, along with the hat and a picture of the mildly handicapped young man to whom we were saying farewell--a young man, John, killed suddenly, tragically, run over by a bus. John's life was offered; we who knew him offered also <u>our</u> loss, our brokenness, our pain, our memories, our love.

We thanked God for Jesus, and took, blessed, broke and gave not just our bread and wine, not just the life of John, but our lives, our loves, our hopes, ourselves. Grief was transformed by hope as we shared the life, death and resurrection of Jesus.

Another young man had wandered into that funeral by accident. He had not been to Church for eight years. He came that night in his own brokenness because he had nowhere else to turn. Addicted to drugs, grieving a parent who had just died, lonely and lost, he needed to be touched, healed, changed. He did not know John, but this funeral was the most profound experience of his life. He found himself, in words he did not have, taken up with those gifts, with John's life, with the pain of John's family, and he discovered himself changed, transformed in ways he could not explain. He only needed to thank John's mother for the effect this celebration had on his life.

In Eucharist we do not simply watch as God changes bread and wine into the body and blood of Christ.

We are not mere spectators at a renewal of Calvary, of what happened to Jesus long ago.

Bread and wine are not brought to the altar just as bread and wine. They are the sign of our offering of ourselves. And it is ourselves, the new body of Christ, that is transformed!

We are not thankful (Eucharistic) only for the life, death, resurrection of Jesus, but for the ways, right now, that this mystery is played out in us – the ways we die, and rise, and become, like the bread, like the wine, something we have never been so fully before.

The scripture readings today use the same language, describing the miracle of Jesus and the enduring miracle of Eucharist. Jesus *took*, he *blessed*, he *broke*, he *gave* ...

In Eucharist these words are said, not simply over bread and wine, but over us. We are the bread. We are the wine.

Jesus *takes us*, where we are, how we are, as we are, this day, this moment and throughout our lives.

Jesus *blesses*, consecrates us, renews in us our baptism, calls us by name, tells us we are special, loved, chosen.

And Jesus in diverse and awesome ways breaks us, out of our own separate individuality. Out of whatever pain is ours, we are somewhere, somehow broken, brought to our knees, forced to recognize the unmanageability of our lives if left to ourselves.

We hurt and do not die.
We suffer and do not lose hope.

We are the Body of Christ, overcoming pain and death and now risen to new life with him.

And when we have been taken, blessed, then broken, Jesus can *give us*, give us back to our loved ones, our family, our Church, our world, now no longer just ourselves, but with Christ living in us.

Certainly God can and does work the transforming love, this transforming action in our lives in many other and mysterious ways. Certainly the Eucharist half-heartedly done, certainly mere ritual adherence to empty forms acted out by priest or community not really present, does not magically make all the above transpire. Sometimes, I'm sure the Eucharist has very little effect towards doing what at its best it signifies. We do not need cynicism or despair as we face our future; it may well be better than our past. But there is reason on this feast of the Body and Blood of Christ to look at the possibility of losing what most can make us who we are. And there is reason for appreciating what we have now.

There is reason for renewing our desire to come to this celebration that we do have now, ready and willing, not just to witness some miracle happen to bread and wine on the altar but to be changed ourselves, to be made new.

There is reason to put ourselves into that cup, and on that plate, knowing it is ourselves, each of us, all of us, giving ourselves both to God and to each other.

There is reason for letting go of our fear of being broken, and poured out, reason for really thanking God with full heart and voice for all we have and are together.

And there is reason, at the end of our time together today, to let ourselves go into the world, transformed, renewed, more able to love and serve the Lord because we have indeed experienced that WE ARE THE BODY OF CHRIST.

27.) The Tenth Sunday

Rooted in Lk 7:11-17

Luke is a great story teller: the story of the Prodigal Son, the story of the Good Samaritan, even the way the story of the birth of Jesus is told, are great pieces of literature, aside from their faith content and context.

The short, simple story today of the healing of the son of the widow of Nain is wonderfully well told. It is easy to visualize, to be in the scene as we hear again the story.

We see a big crowd walking through street . . . Jesus . . . his disciples and a whole bunch of other people . . . so visual. Then, the gradual introduction of the characters as each small step reveals a slightly more sad story: A dead man is being carried . . . the only son of his mother . . . the mother is a widow . . . and she has a ton of friends. We can see a second large crowd meeting the first large crowd following Jesus.

In the midst of this double crowd, Jesus, is moved by pity.

He doesn't just say something, or wave his hand; he moves through the two crowds and touches the coffin . . . and everybody halts, stops dead. The hustle and bustle comes to a stand-still. Jesus speaks: "Young man, I tell you, Arise!"

Then Luke offers a peculiar detail. The man sat up and *started talking*. We are not told what he said. What does one raised from the dead say? We aren't told the words. Jesus then, apparently takes the man by his hand and gives him to his mother. WOW. If we can visualize this we are as moved as was that crowd.

I got stuck on wondering what he said.

I could not help but remember a somewhat similar event in my own ministry. Once I was called to the bedside of a young woman who had attempted suicide. Her dad, a close friend and coworker, had not want to tell anyone of the suicide attempt, so he had remained silent for almost two days; but after a day and a half in coma, he and his wife were deeply concerned about their daughter's survival. My friend called and begged me to come to the hospital and pray with her, even to, please, baptize her since, though twenty years old, she had never been baptized.

I knew the girl a bit. Knew she had attended Gonzaga U. Knew that if she had wanted to be baptized she could very well have made the choice herself and wondered if baptizing her now would not be against her own wishes. But standing in the hospital room with mom and dad in tears, I was also "moved with pity," and knew this was no time for theology. I took some water from the sink in the hospital room, and baptized the young woman "in the name of the Father, and of the Son, and of the Holy Spirit." To my and to her parents amazement, the young woman after 36 hours of coma, opened her eyes, sat up and spoke!!

What she said was very simple. "Thanks, Pat!"

So, bringing this lovely story of Jesus to an end, I imagine this young man sitting up and saying, simply, "Thank you, Jesus." And returning to his mother's arms.

The point of listening regularly and praying over the story of Jesus is not just to remember what happened a long time ago. The point is to let it happen still, in us and around us. The story lives.

This so vivid story can live in us in different ways. We can be the crowd, watching, waiting, in the midst of any tragedy small or large, waiting to see what happens.

We can be, and are frequently, the weeping mother, experiencing the tragedy of our world, or a deeply personal tragedy; we find ourselves hoping, praying, longing for Jesus to walk by and bring healing.

And we have many opportunities to be like Jesus ... to see human suffering and do what we can to heal and help. We can, almost every moment of every day, be moved with pity and the suffering surrounding us just reading the obituary pages in the morning paper, or the tragedy piled on tragedy on the front page. We can see the sleeping women in the doorways of downtown offices, or men in sleeping bags along the side of our freeway exits. We can see the pain of refugees fleeing Syria or Sudan. We have numerous opportunities each day to be moved with pity, and, though we may not be able to cure a dead young man or even baptize a comatose young woman to life, we can imitate that "pity," and do what we can. We can reach out and touch whatever coffin there might be, and leave the results to God.

And, often enough, we are the young man. Each of us in our own ways have been brought back to life, had second chances, large or small. Every one of us has been placed in the arms of a loved one with a new start, a new hope. Like the young man placed in his mother's arms, we can say "Thank you, Jesus." We can live in gratitude.

We can come to this altar, this day, this Eucharist saying thank you for all the marvelous ways healing has happened in our lives. We can look around, right now, at family with us, friends around us, even strangers *in this crowd* and say "Thank you, God, for letting me be alive again today . . ."

28) The Eleventh Sunday

Rooted in: 2 Samuel 12:7-10, 13; Luke 7:36 - 8:3

Forgiveness is a difficult thing. It's really hard to forgive someone who hurt you, even difficult to forgive ourselves. It's even a deeply human challenge to ask for forgiveness.

Forgiveness is also a constant theme in religion, in Hebrew and Christian scriptures and spread throughout our Sunday liturgy from "Lord Have Mercy," to "Lord, I am not worthy . . . speak the word and I shall be healed."

The Gospel the Sunday after Easter presents Jesus breathing his spirit on the Apostles, giving us his spirit; the only thing he says about this spirit is "Forgive!" The same Gospel is repeated on Pentecost. It seems as though the only distinguishing characteristic of a Christian is the (perhaps supernatural) ability to forgive.

The first reading today tells of David--not the handsome shepherd, or the brave warrior, or the great King, but David the abysmal sinner who has taken his general's wife and had him killed to cover it up. David recognized as "The Man" in a story of the need for forgiveness. David purported to be the psalmist who wrote:

Have mercy on me, O God,
according to your steadfast love;
according to your abundant mercy
blot out my transgressions.
Wash me thoroughly from my iniquity,
and cleanse me from my sin!
For I know my transgressions,
and my sin is ever before me.
Against you, you only, have I sinned
and done what is evil in your sight,

The gospel story is about many things but essentially forgiveness, including the ease with which Jesus forgives whatever the woman's sin might be, but also the terrible time Simon and others had accepting his forgiving because they cannot really "see" this woman and recognize her great love. I love the ambiguity of the language. We tend to read it to say that the woman is forgiven because she has loved much; I think it far more clearly mean she loves a lot because she has been forgiven a lot . Forgiveness comes before we earn it, deserve it, do anything to "merit" it.

I want to think out loud about forgiveness for a moment: what it means, what it doesn't mean.

I don't like the notion of forgive and forget. I think forgiveness, to be real, has to remember, has to hold onto the hurt, the injury, acknowledge another's mistakes . . . or my own. Essential to forgiveness is remembering . . . then refusing to make whatever fault involved the whole truth!

I think forgiveness means the adamant refusal to define someone by what is worst in them. Forgiving myself means I refuse to make whatever stupid or terrible things I've done the whole truth.

David, you did some terrible things, but you can still be the King you are and have been. Get it together and be again your best self, not this petty, cruel lustful man you let yourself become.

Woman, washing my feet with your tears, you may have done something awful in your past but you still have the ability to love, to serve, to let yourself be ridiculed by a crowd of people, to be your best and truest self. This is who you are . . . keep it up.

My husband drank too much and said some awful things last night. This morning, I remember and I tell him I remember and I don't ever want that to happen again, but I forgive. I refuse to define you by that stupid, insensitive behavior. You are still a man I have loved and believed in and cared for over many years. Be that man, be the man I love.

You gave into greed and cheated me out of what was rightfully mine and I am hurt and confused by that behavior, but that is not all I know of you. You have been generous and kind to me for many years, have welcomed me into your heart and home. I am deeply hurt by this action but will not define you by it. I forgive, and hope you will again become your best and truest self.

Forgiveness does not, cannot, mean leading with your chin. "You hurt me, but that's OK; do it again and again, if you wish." To really forgive we confront the hurt, the one who hurt us, or hurt our community, or hurt our nation, and we say: Don't do that any more, ever. But that is not your best and truest self. I won't define you by what is worst in you. I will not say that action, that word, that betrayal is the only and final truth. I will hope for, expect more of you . . . for your sake and for mine.

I invite us to sit with that a moment.

Remember when we have been at our worst . . . and someone, or some community, called us to start over, to be bette--refused to define us by that weakest moment, or by our worst behavior.

Remember hurts that you have experienced and wonder what it might mean to forgive, that is, to not let whatever hurt us be the only or the final word.

Then, together, let us come to the altar to accept a great love that keeps forgiving, keeps inviting us to be our most true and very best selves.

29) The Twelfth Sunday

Rooted in: Gal. 3:26-29; Lk. 9:18-24

Recently I watched again the incredible Robin Williams in *The Dead Poet's Society*. Interesting in itself, the movie is also a kind of parable that points to the heart of today's gospel.

Robin Williams acts as teacher/prophet to a group of high school students in an upper class boarding school--students being prepared to take their rightful place in a programmed, upwardly mobile, financially secure, humanly depressing world.

Through literature, especially through the Romantic poets, Williams holds out to these students the possibility of a more human life, one not based on power, or conformity to what is, but on things like:

individual expression,
personal gifts,
relationships,

the exciting discovery of one's life,
and the courage to live that unique life.

This message, in *this* school, is not acceptable.

The students' fumbling efforts to live out such personal values in a conservative environment are crushed. One boy dies; the others are disillusioned; the teacher is dismissed.

The film ends with one glorious moment as the entire class defiantly stands up and acknowledges their dismissed teacher as "Oh captain, my captain," from a poem by Walt Whitman. The gesture probably is ineffective either in the lives of the boys, or the direction of the school.

Freedom is difficult to come by. Preaching or acting in freedom brings a cross!

Though couched in purely humanistic terms, with less than (to me) fully human values, the film works as a parable of the human struggle for fullness, providing a parallel to, perhaps a sub-text of, today's gospel.

The film speaks of the human struggle discovered this very day in any place where people struggle to change a rigid and unjust system, a system that crushes the human spirit--gay people in Orlando, rebels in Syria, young people who are here illegally but have never lived in any other nation, on death-row in Texas . . . or even a woman in our Catholic church!

The film speaks of the cross involved in any effort to change systems, to make any organization, civil or religious, more human, more life-giving, more faithful to the gospel of love, equality, free-dom--the Good News of Jesus.

Let me look carefully for a moment at the Gospel.

After a time of prayer, Jesus asks his followers, and all of us, a question. The question comes midway in the story in each of the synoptic Gospels. His followers have listened to Jesus for some time, have felt the surge of hope that he has brought to them, to all. Now comes the crunch question:

"Who do people say I am? Who do you say I am?"

And they answer--perhaps we answer with them--"You are my friend, my savior, our path to truth, our way to God, our source of life. You are the answer. You are the Messiah of God!"

Great answers.

But the second part of the Gospel is disturbing. To recognize the truth of Jesus as Messiah, to make this act of faith, is to take a stance that is challenging, frightening, liberating, disturbing,

Jesus warns his followers immediately that the powers in control, the elders, the scribes, the chief priests (the principal, the board of directors, the boss, the bishop) will reject, kill him.

To accept Jesus as *The Way*, and to follow Jesus to freedom (in a way far more profound than Robin Williams can capture) is to choose The Cross!

Jesus is the way to life, but to pursue this way with him is to accept hardship, rejection, misunderstanding, to pass through death--the cross!

It is never easy to change what is oppressive, unjust, death dealing--in a classroom, in Syria, on the streets of our city, or even in the Church.

To follow the path to life, to walk with Jesus, to really say he is Messiah, and to proclaim that his path is true means to reach for his dream, and to risk the wrath of those with other, smaller dreams.

Because of the second reading today, I cannot avoid making one obvious application. Paul speaks of the radical equality of the baptized, an equality such that there is no longer Jew or Greek, slave or free, *male or female*. All are one.

Yet two thousand years later we still make such distinctions.

Recently at church I saw woman wearing a button that captures the clash between Jesus' vision and the reality. The button said, simply:

"If you won't ordain me, why do you baptize me?"

Simply put, to say that Jesus is Messiah is to accept the cross of pursuing his ideals of equality, and to struggle for this ideal is to embrace the cross--and to make that cross explicit, this is the kind of thing that strikes me; this is the suffering a follower of Jesus will endure if we pursue the freedom, equality, balance he sought for his community:

The cross of women who stay in the church and keep struggling, loving, serving, speaking out while their gifts are not fully recognized.

The cross of women, mothers, girls who rarely hear the gospel preached from their vantage point, out of experiences similar to their own,

The cross of losing jobs, having no voice, being given the results of deliberations in which women had no part,

The cross of a handful of bishops who have tried to affirm this equality and were silenced, or a priest who spoke out and was removed from his priestly ministry.

The cross of seeing more and more people throughout the world unable to share in Eucharist because we so limit who can preside at that celebration,

The cross of a priest today--to constantly feel responsible and guilty when doing what he loves to do while knowing that what he does is inherently discriminatory, and having to cover two or three or four parishes, filling the gaps in ministry at the same time!

The Dead Poet's Society was merely a bridge to get at the much deeper and more pervasive message of the Gospel, challenging all of us today to recall that we cannot be complacent with whatever is unjust, oppressive, inhuman in any system of which we are a part.

To be faithful to Jesus, we need to accept daily the pain, the cross of struggling to make justice, equality, and peace not just the dream of Jesus, but the reality of his followers.

30) The Thirteenth Sunday

Rooted in Lk. 9: 51-62

Jesus sets his face towards Jerusalem.

Luke's gospel is, in part, a travel narrative. Jesus has been travel-ing in and around Galilee, then to the immediately surrounding regions. But now, right after his disciples recognize him as "The Christ," The Messiah of God, he puts his face towards Jerusalem. From this moment on in Luke's Gospel, Jesus is on his way to Jerusalem, where the prophets are killed. This is the geographical, and religious turning point. He will never turn back. He will go to Jerusalem, to death and to new life.

We, his disciples, are invited to put our heads down and go with him. We may have a million excuses. We may think we have to go home and help take care of things until our parents die. We may think there are farewells to be said, but the invitation is to go with Jesus now, to go totally, to go without looking back.

It's summer. Rather than go on in the abstract I thought I would just tell a story. A story that captures this gospel perfectly. A story about all of us.

"Once Upon a Puddle"

(Adapted from <u>Along the Water's Edge</u>, by Daniel Juniper, Paulist Press, 1982, p. 9-14).

Once upon a time some fish lived in a very small puddle of water. They swam around in circles, often fighting with each other:

"Give me that Waterbug!"
"No, I saw him first!"
"Get your dirty fins off my supper!"

Every day the fish swam in small circles, cramped quarters. Not much to do but swim and hunt for waterbugs. Life didn't change much for these puddle fish.

Their puddle lay next to a giant oak tree just beside a flowing river

One morning there was a sudden noise. SPLASH. A beautiful, brightly colored fish jumped into this riverside puddle. This fish had blue and red and golden scales, and what was even more unusual for this puddle, the fish was smiling. The puddle fish were frightened.

"Where do you come from?"
"I come from the sea."
"The sea; what's the sea?"

"The sea? Well it isn't like this little puddle. It's endless. A fish doesn't have to swim in circles all day. A fish can dance with the tides. Life isn't

lived in the shade–why the sun arches over the waves in silver and crimson. And there are many sea creatures, so many you could scarcely imagine. The sea is endless and sparklingly clear. The sea is what we fish are made for."

"How would we get to the sea?"

The sparkling fish smiled and pointed to the Oak tree and to the river just beyond it: ""It's really simple. You jump from this little puddle into that river, and then <u>you trust</u> that the river will take you out to the sea."

Great consternation followed . The sparkling fish was immediately confronted by three of the fish.

The first was a REALIST fish. He knew that reality was swimming in circles looking for waterbugs. He announced: "This story of the sea is pie in the sea nonsense!"

The sparkling fish smiled: "But you don't understand. I've been there. I've seen the sea."

The realist fish swam away.

The second fish was SCARED FISH. His tail twitched; he began to stutter. "If I understand you we're supposed to jjjjump into that river?"

"Yes. If you want to go to the sea, the way lies through that river."

"But that river is ddddeep, and sss....swift and has a strong ccc...current, and I'm just a little fish. If I jumped out of this ppp...puddle and followed you I wouldn't have any control. I just ccc...can't."

"Trust me; trust that the river will take you someplace good."

But the scared fish swam away.

The third fish was a THEOLOGIAN FISH. He took out a sheaf of notes, adjusted his glasses, and leaned on a podium: "My friends, sparkling fish has made some good points and deserves a listening. But the puddle fish have also made some good points. We can work this out. Let's form a study group, have a meeting every Tuesday at 7:00."

The eyes of sparkling fish grew very sad. "No, this will never do. Talking is important, but in the end the matter is simple: You jump. You jump out of this puddle and trust me, trust that the river will run to the sea. Besides don't you know that summer is coming? This puddle will very soon have no water! No puddle lasts forever!"

The puddle fish were stunned. REALIST FISH shouted "There you go, you religious people...when you can't convince, you try to scare. You're just an end of the puddle fanatic!" She swam away in disgust.

All the colors of the sparkling fish shone and whispered: "It's a simple matter. You come with me and jump from this little puddle and trust that the river will take you to the sea. Who will come with me? Who will follow me?"

At first no one moved. Then a few puddle fish swam to the side of sparkling fish. Together they jumped into the river and the current swept them away.

The remaining puddle fish were quiet for a long time. Then, once again, they began to swim in circles and look for waterbugs.

Jesus sets his eyes on Jerusalem and never turns back. Do we go with him?

31) The Fourteenth Sunday

(Fourth of July Weekend)

Rooted in Is. 66:10-14; Gal. 6: 14-18; Lk. 10:1-12, 17-20

(With appreciation to William Bausch, Storytelling the Word, Twenty-Third Publications, 1996)

As in each of the preceding weeks we continue to hear to a call to discipleship. On his way to Jerusalem Jesus sends his followers in pairs ahead of him into every place he will eventually visit. He still does this today. We, still today, bring a message of evangelization to our world.

On this Fourth of July weekend we bring a Gospel message of good news to a nation and a world filled with more than enough bad news--from riots to child abuse, almost constant multiple gun killings in our own land or France or Turkey, from drunken driving to drug dealing, black kids killed by police, or an election between an unpopular politician and a scoundrel.

Today, near Independence Day, I want to insist that the message of Good News is one of wonderful *dependence* on God and one another if we are to truly be free.

Yes as we celebrate a Declaration of Independence, we need to be concerned lest our declaration be so independent as to leave God and all the other people of our lives out of the picture. To do so would be to court disaster and invite bad news.

The evangelization theme of the Gospel calls to mind the story of a famous bishop from Notre Dame Cathedral in Paris from the last century. This bishop was a great evangelizer. He was committed to spreading the gospel message especially to unbelievers and those most cynical towards religion.

The bishop often told the story of a young man who for several weeks stood outside the Cathedral, shouting derogatory slogans at the people entering to worship. He called them fools, naive, stupid at the top of his voice. The people tried to ignore him but it was almost impossible to do so

Finally the parish priest went outside to confront the young man directly. The young man ranted and raved against everything the priest said to him. Finally the priest suggested a deal to the young man:

> "Look, let's get this over once and for all. I want to offer you a dare and bet that you will be unable to do it!"

The cynical young man retorted that he could do anything this white robed wimp proposed!

The priest made this suggestion:

"All I ask is that you come into the sanctuary of the church with me and stare at the figure of Christ on the cross. I want you to scream at the top of your lungs, as loud as you can,

> 'Christ died on the cross for me, and I do not care one bit.'"

So the young man began. Initially he cried out in a somewhat muted voice,

> "Christ died on the cross for me and I do not care one bit.!"

"Louder," the priest suggested. The man screamed again, somewhat more loudly.

"No," said the priest, "I dare you to scream it out at the very top of your lungs."

The young man raised his fist defiantly, kept looking at the crucifix, but now the words would not come.

He just could not look at the face of Christ and say that any more.

The real punch line of this dramatic story came after the bishop told this story; the bishop added: "I was that young man. That defiant young man was me. I thought I did not need God, but found out that I was wrong and I am here to tell you that today."

When Jesus sends out the seventy-two disciples to proclaim God's love to every town towards which he intends to go, he is essentially trying to let every person on his path know their dependence on God.

Today I think of them, as I do this bishop; I think of us as we live our lives in this very nation, this very year, this Fourth of July Weekend. We keep trying to say that we as individuals and perhaps even as a nation independent of God. We can think we do not need God. But like the restored bishop we are here to say as American Catholics, "But we do!"

And this Declaration of Dependence may be our greatest contribution to our land.

So in this Spirit I invite us all to stand now, square our shoulders, shake loose the dust from our feet, our minds, our hearts. I invite us to look at the crucifix before us here and declare our Declaration of Dependence, as we recall our deepest faith!

32) The Fifteenth Sunday

Rooted in Lk. 10: 25-37

A priest friend of mine used to say he only ever prayed for one thing, "A smart heart!"

That's what the readings this weekend are about, having a smart heart. The first reading reminds us that "The word is very near, not in the heavens where we can't get at it, not written on stony tablets, separate from our human experience . . . but written in our hearts. Very, very near."

The second reading speaks of Jesus as the Word of God, the image of an otherwise unseen God. Jesus makes the Word near, gives God a human face, puts God into our hearts in relationship of love that we can get at.

The Gospel gives a heart-felt summary of the entire Gospel message. "Love God with your whole heart--and the way to do this is to love your neighbor as yourself."

The message is so clear we'd have to go out of our way to miss it ... yet sometimes we do.

Let me look in some detail at the Gospel.

The lawyer who comes to Jesus is dealing with law. What rules do I have to follow to be "good," to win the award of eternal life. Jesus summarizes the *smart heart* of the law for him. Then he tells a story.

In the story two of the characters carefully follow the rules--the priest and the Levite. The rules say don't touch a dead man or you become unclean. The man who had fallen among thieves looked dead, so they did not touch him. They walked by him on their way to Jerusalem, to the temple, to worship God. They did what the rules said they were supposed to do. They were good people. They were correct. They knew well the laws written on stony tablets; a distant law, a long ways away.

They would never let child go to communion without first receiving reconciliation.

They would never let a divorced person enter a second marriage without following all the
canonical norms,

They would never allow a woman to preach, or change a word in a canonical prayer,

or let a gay person actively living in a relationship with another go to communion.

The rules are very clear. They may be distant, not relating to real persons, or to the heart, but clear. And there is certainly a bit of them in me--perhaps in you.

Jesus' story goes on to tell about a Samaritan, an outcast, not one of their kind, or our kind. A Samaritan, the butt of all ethnic jokes of Jesus' day. A Samaritan who may not have been of their kind, but who was *kind*. In fact, the story suggests that we let every kind be our kind, so we be kind, so we react with our hearts, where God's word is found, where God's word is near.

In response to the question, *"Who is my neighbor?"* Jesus says, *"Let every kind be our kind."*

It is not in the New Testament as we have it, but I have heard a rumor that shortly after this event in the gospel Jesus was sitting around with his followers one day and he asked them the question:

"How can you tell when night has ended and day is about to begin?"

His friends argued among themselves for awhile, until finally one of them, probably James, piped up:

"Could it be when you look off in the distance and see two trees, and are able to tell that one is a fig tree, and one a palm tree?"

Jesus answered: "No!"

So they argued a bit longer until Peter spoke up and said,

"Could it be when you look off in the distance and seeing two animals are able to distinguish that one is a sheep and one a dog?"

Again, Jesus answered, "No."

Finally, frustrated, the disciples said:

"All right then Jesus, you tell us. How do we know when the night has ended and the day is about to begin?"

Slowly Jesus looked at each of them, looked them in the eye, and with a smile said:

"It is when you can look on the face of any man or woman and see it is your neighbor, because if you cannot do that, then no matter what time of day it is, it is still night."

33) The Sixteenth Sunday

Rooted in Lk. 10: 38-42:

Sometimes the timeless insight of the Gospel overwhelms me-
-never more than in this Gospel, the story of two sisters. This
ancient story could have been written last week in Seattle, or
anywhere. I suspect it could have been written about me, or you.

An important visitor comes to the family home, a man of great
reputation as a charismatic religious leader and a gentle loving
companionable man besides. Two sisters welcome him in entirely
different ways. One is concerned that this important guest should
be well fed and cared for. She spends the day, even the time after
he has arrived, getting the home and meal ready. The other sister
is concerned that this might be her last chance to hear, to come
to know and be inspired by his presence. She lets all the practical
things go and simply sits attentively at his feet.

I imagine both Mary and Martha pursuing their chosen approach
to their esteemed visitor wondering what on earth the other is

doing. Mary couldn't figure out why Martha was so compulsively busy about cleanliness and food instead of enjoying the wonderful presence of this Jesus in their home. Martha was confused, and eventually angered by Mary's insensitivity to all the myriad things that had to be done if his visit was to be a "success."

If only they had known Jesus was going to be coming through their town and staying at their house on his way to Jerusalem. They could have had a family meeting and decided who would do what and when, instead of each of them taking their accustomed approach to every situation.

Mary always seemed to let people be more important than things, a conversations always preferable to caring for the practical matters of life. Martha always took over and did what needed to be done.

So here they were again. Martha busy about many things. Mary quiet, contemplative in the presence of Jesus.

For years I was troubled at the normative interpretation of the story. Contemplative life superior to the active life. Those who are able to sit quietly, prayerfully in the presence of Jesus all the time are seen as somehow more lauded than those who plow the fields, kneed the bread, or even preside over the funerals and the weddings.

Only after many years did I see the operative word that Jesus uses to describe his praise of Mary. Mary "has chosen" the better part. I always noticed the "better part," but only lately have I seen the "chosen." Jesus seems to honor Mary's choice, not because it is a better thing to do but because she has chosen it. If Martha is not doing what she "wants," what she "chooses"--if Martha is slaving away in the kitchen because she thinks she "should be"--then why pick on Mary who is only doing what she wanted to do?

When I call this story "contemporary," " applicable" to any time of place, it is precisely because I think we human beings have always had trouble knowing what we *want* to do. We have trouble because we are pretty sure that what God wants us to do is not what we want to do. We have to guess what God wants and then do it whether we want to or not. But if the "Kingdom of God is within" then what God wants us to do and what we want to do are perhaps the exact same thing. If we can get way down deep at what we really want we will probably get as close as we can to what God wants for us.

On one level I want to play golf every day, and have not a care in the world. But on a more honest and deeper level, I really want to help build God's reign, want to bring God's word to the troubled places in people's lives, want to connect the Jesus story with the stories of Jesus' people. What God wants is what I want at the best and deepest level of that "*I*".

It is not necessarily better to pray than to work. It is not necessarily better to sit and listen than to clean and cook. It is not necessarily better to go to Mass than to run a food bank, or to pray than teach the third grade. It is not necessarily better to quietly read scripture and ponder God's word rather than sell a house, or drive a truck, or mend a sweater or a broken heart. What is better is knowing what I really, truly, deeply, honestly want to do and then having the courage to do it, trusting that this is what God wants for me.

What makes this simple story so wonderful is that it is so true--then and now. How often I see people, women especially, trying to fill all the needs of everyone else, having lives riddled with "oughts" and "shoulds," unable to get down at the core of their own deepest desires where God abides. Psychologists suggest that women are prone to breakdowns, both psychological and physical, trying to care for every problem, to keep every thing peaceful, to avoid all conflicts, to make everything work, paying insufficient attention to what is truly in their own hearts. They may even become impossibly impatient with everyone who is not as compulsively attacking every need as they do (Mary, don't you care that I am slaving in the kitchen?). Eventually they just collapse, inclined to stop doing anything for anyone ever again.

Far better to know that there are a million feet to wash and only one me. I need to know which feet I want to be responsible for, and to be sure that those, at least are washed.

There are a thousand social issues needing attention; only one or two of them touch my life and my gifts and need my attention.

A hundred people are always in need and some of those, some few, I cannot and do not want to escape from attending to.

Lord Jesus, help us to choose--out of some deep inner core of knowing you are with us, loving us, calling us to be our best and truest selves. Help us to choose.

34) The Seventeenth Sunday

Rooted in Lk. 11:1-13

Recently I re-read *Children of God*, Maria Doria Russell's follow-up book to *The Sparrow*. Two books about Jesuits in the future involved in space exploration and life on other, terribly unfriendly planets. I hope you've heard of them, even read them yourselves. They are indeed about the Jesuits, and space travel, and people of other planets. More deeply they are about Good and Evil and, like the scripture readings today, about prayer. These two books raise the questions about the usefulness of prayer in the face of the overwhelming mystery of evil.

The gospel reading is about praying continually and the apparent, eventual fruitfulness of that prayer and about the things worth praying about.

On one level both these novels undermine the readings we have just heard. They present a picture of God who, if not absent, is certainly not benign. The very best people, with the very best motives for the very best causes suffer incredibly--unbelievable physical pain, incredible degradation, near despair. Whether the protagonists' suffering, like the suffering of Jesus, is redemptive we are left to wonder.

These books simply will not let me be naive about the efficacy of prayer.

I thought and taught and wrote about prayer all my professional adult life. I have pondered this passage and others like it all my adult life. I still have more questions than answers.

Do we pray--whether alone, or here at worship--to give glory to God?

Do we pray to get God to change, like a man asleep who will finally wake up and give us what we want if we ask loudly and long enough?

Do we pray to prove we are sincere in our faith, performing our duty, going to church, saying our prayers dutifully, as good people?

Maybe we pray, as Elie Weisel suggested, just to get the questions right!

If God answers all our prayers then

> why do good people suffer so much?
> why does the praying wife's husband keep on drinking?
> the child dying of brain cancer still ever so slowly die?
> our children's marriage still end in divorce and tragedy?
> Why do the Israelis and Palestinians still battle

when more prayer is said in these two places than perhaps anywhere else on earth?

If there is only one God to whom all our different religions are praying why do people fight most over religion and kill each other in God's name?

Further, I don't know anything that disturbs me more than the way we can make people, already suffering, feel worse by believing they just don't believe enough, or pray enough or surely things would be much better. "You will do better getting over your cancer," "your kids would come back to church," "your nation will no longer be at war," "just pray more, pray better!" Ugh!

I can tell you why I pray.

I pray to "let God love me." I pray because I need to know ever more deeply that I, that we who pray together here at Eucharist, are loved by God. I pray because I need to keep being touched by that God's love. I need to keep trusting in and affirming this love even when I don't feel or experience it.

In that spirit I understand the Gospel.

"Lord teach us to pray."

And Jesus does. In Luke's shorter version of the Lord's prayer Jesus suggests what we should pray about

> for the coming of the reign of God,
> for what we need to survive each day,
> to forgive and be forgiven,
> and not to be overwhelmed by evil.

That's not much but it is really all I need. Perhaps, if I pray faithfully, if we pray faithfully, eventually, little by little

> God's kingdom will be built.
> I'll have enough to survive each day.
> I'll keep forgiving and believing that I am forgiven
> and I won't be overwhelmed by the evil that surrounds
> me, inside and out!

And I need to keep pounding on the doors, crying out my needs, my hopes, my desires-- however mistaken or wrong-headed, or trivial they may be--because I believe as much as I believe anything the final line of this Gospel.

> *If we, with all our sins,*
> *know how to give our children good things,*
> *how much more will the heavenly Father*
> *give the Holy Spirit to those who ask.*

I believe that no matter what we ask for, God will give us the Holy Spirit, the Spirit of Jesus. I may not get what I want, or think I need, but I will get God's Spirit. We might not get what we think we want, but we will get God's Spirit!

In the novels I mentioned nothing is solved, no one gets what they think they want, things consistently go from bad to worse-- The Sparrow seems to be crushed. But underneath the pain, the struggle, the broken dreams, the Spirit of God prevails, even wins, despite all odds.

The story of Jesus himself is one of apparent defeat, misunder-standing, and finally a torturous death. But he is raised in the Spirit of God.

I pray. I think we need to pray. I believe we come to this Eucharistic Prayer today because we need God's Spirit. It doesn't take away the pain of human life; this Spirit does not provide an answer, especially an easy answer to all life's questions, but this Spirit does continually remind me, remind us that I/we are loved by God and finally nothing else matters, for this love will finally and forever prevail.

35) The Eighteenth Sunday

Rooted in: Eccl. 1:2, 2:21-23; Co. 3: 1-5, 9-11; Lk. 12:13-21

The readings today, especially the so straight forward Gospel passage, do not need a lot of explanation. The point is quite clear. I can express it simply with two contemporary aphorisms.

In a world which says to us in a million ways

"The One who dies with the most toys wins!"

Jesus affirms:

"There's no U-Haul behind a hearse!"

If we invest all our energies, all our efforts, our hopes our trust in the material goods we can accumulate in this life we are ultimately foolish.

As simple as this is to say I honestly doubt if it is very relevant to most of us. Surely there are people whose entire life is concerned with "getting and spending," people for whom "mall-ing" is a favorite sport, but not many of them are here in this assembly. Most of us, I think, are getting by, perhaps working hard to care for ourselves our family, making do with our pension checks, our retirement funds, our teacher's salaries, our student loans. We may get overly concerned with preparing for retirement or having something to pass on to our kids, we may sometimes become disproportionately concerned about "security," but I do not see greed as a major fault of most of us. If we leave this gospel only on the material level--"you can't take it with you"--the passage will not challenge most of us very much.

I invite us to take this gospel passage to a somewhat deeper place.

Philosophers say mental--I would add and spiritual--health demands that we include the reality of death in our understanding of life. We have not made real sense out of human life, we have not laid out all of our cards, until we factor in the reality that we will die. Everyone of us will die. Everyone we love will die. If our hopes, dreams, expectations, all involve only this present world we can see we are doomed to despair and emptiness. As the first reading suggests, all would indeed be *vanity*, empty, meaningless.

Today's parable of the rich man and his barns is only part of the story, only a hint at the deeper reality inviting us to look at all the barns we build, all the ways we expect to hold on to the "goods" of this world, all the ways we try to push back the mystery of finality. As difficult and even unpleasant as it may be we are invited today to consider deeply, without flinching, the honest- to- God truth that most of what we are concerned about in this life will end!

The obvious thing seems to be to ask what doesn't end? What *do* we take with us? What from this human experience might indeed be *eternally* valuable. Again, at least from our faith, our biblical perspective. the answer is simple.

Love.

Love alone endures. Only the love that we have received and given do we bring with us into whatever comes next.

Faith becomes knowledge; hope become fulfillment. Only love lasts.

If I honestly face the reality that I will die, but the love in my life will not, that realization cannot help but have profound impact on how I live, on my day-to-day values. Jesus tells us in many ways, but especially at the end of Matthew's gospel, the success or failure of this life will be based on. . . did I feed those who were hungry, clothe those who were naked, visit those who were sick or imprisoned? Did I love? We will not be asked how much money we made, what our profession was, what kind of house or neighborhood we lived in. We will not even be asked whether we went to church or believed a particular dogma, or said a particular prayer. We will, Jesus suggests, only be asked if we loved him in all the wounded forms in which he came to us.

Another parable about the farm and storing in barns brings out the truth. Once upon a time two brothers farmed the same land together. Their farm was modestly successful and every day they took the fruits of their labors and split the yield fifty-fifty into each brother's barn.

One night the older brother awoke and thought:

*This is not fair. I am a single man; my brother has a
wife and three children. His needs are far greater than
mine. I will get up and take half of what I got today
and put it in his barn.*

He arose and did this very thing. He continued to do the same thing, every night for many years. Every night he took half of what he had put in his barn and took it to his brother's barn.

The very same night the younger brother awoke and thought:

*This is not fair. My brother is all alone. I have a wife
and three children to care for me when I grow old. My
brother has no such security. I know. I will get up
and take half of what I received today and put it
secretly back into my brother's barn.*

He arose and did this very thing. And he did it every night for many years.

So both brothers, over many years kept giving away half of what they acquired and yet their supply never seemed to diminish.

One night one brother was late, the other early. They met in the road, half-way between the barns. Each brother saw the other, their flatbed truck laden with goods, going towards his barn. They laughed; they cried. The next day they built a monument to the God who gives but is never diminished; a monument to love that never ends.

36) The Nineteenth Sunday

Rooted in Lk. 12: 32-48

Once upon a time, a young priest was told by his senior pastor to be careful when preaching never to go beyond a half-hour after Mass started. For example, at 8:30 Mass the homily is over by 9:00, at 11:00 Mass, it's over by 11:30. On the priest's first sermon Mass was late starting, the assembly practiced a song or two, the readers were slow, the psalm was long and by the time the poor young priest finished reading the Gospel (the very passage we just listened to) it was just two minutes before the half hour. Perplexed, he paused for a moment, read the Gospel line over again: *The Son of Man will come at an hour you least expect!!"*

Then gave this one-line homily: *"So when this happens, you can't say I didn't warn you!"*

We are inclined to hear today's gospel this way--as a warning. Be ready, watch out, you don't know when it's coming.

I have first-hand experience. Twenty-one years ago while saying Mass on the *seventh* day of a retreat in Missoula, Montana, without warning, my heart suddenly stopped. 95% of the time such an experience results in death but I was surrounded by doctors and nurses and across the street from a hospital, so here I am still. Still that: "Be ready, for you don't know the day or hour" has become much more literal and vivid than it was.

In all honesty that experience of instant death has helped me to hear the words of this Gospel about the surprising coming of Jesus less as a warning than a whoopee! Not as a threat but as a promise. I hear especially *the very first words* of the Gospel coloring the entire passage: "Do not fear, little flock, it has pleased God to give to you a Kingdom!"

All those words about waiting, watching, being ready is not so that I won't get "caught with my pants down" but so that I will see, hear, feel life as it comes. If I am not ready, not looking, I will miss the coming of Jesus, and Jesus does not want any of us to miss out on the promise.

Part of the promise of today's gospel suggests that if the servant is ready, working, watching, when the master comes, the order of things will be flip-flopped--the master will become the servant, and we will be seated at table while the master serves us, so glad will he be that we were ready for him.

The early Christians believed that Jesus would come again at Passover. This parable has overtones of the Passover meal where the Messiah returns and serves the meal. When Luke's gospel was written down the community had already been celebrating Eucharist for about forty years, indicating that this promise was already realized, over and over again at every Eucharist. The community then, and we today, celebrate our "staying ready," by the Messiah serving us at table with his life, his body and blood. We celebrate today that same being awake, attentive, ready--to find Jesus here in this Eucharist waiting on us. If we really did experience that, how enthusiastic would be our praying, how loud our singing, how awesome our silences!

The third part of the Gospel tells us that if we are watching, ready, waiting, and if we are good ministers of some of the master's stuff, he will put us in charge of all his property. Everything will be ours.

The entire gospel is about promise, about wonder more than woe!

Underneath the promise is the invitation to us to be ready, waiting, watching. What does that mean? I don't think it just means being ready to die. I don't think it is primarily about the end, but more about all the way along. Jesus does not only come at the end, but is incarnate, enmeshed in our life every moment. The Gospel invites us to be attentive to the life, laughter, love, promise, the possibility all around us.

I was privileged to live for several years with Fr. Gary Smith, who worked on the streets in Tacoma and Portland for years, then in several African places with refugees. Now, at 79, with prostate cancer, Gary has returned to that Mission in Greece, working with Syrian refugees. In Gary's three books, beginning with Street Journal, he shows how he lives and looks at life all the time. Gary has the ability both to see and to translate the experiences of those most marginalized in our society with the eyes of faith. In every story he tells the master is there, the kingdom is present, the servants are those who get served. Every story speaks of a

Divine Milieu because Gary was attentive, was ready, was watching and is graced to see the story that way.

In what could arguably be the pain-filled, most joyless, most desperate situations some eyes will see God's beauty. This sight can happen anywhere. A drug-abusing prostitute whose life is turned around brings the joy of the Kingdom. A possible fist fight turns into a celebration of friendship. A stuffed up toilet becomes a community project, a badly burned soup the finest meal someone ever ate.

This Gospel is not a warning about being ready to die. It is rather an invitation to be more fully alive, more attentive, more aware. The Son of Man will come when we least expect it, in a cardiac arrest, in an encounter on the street, on a golf course, or around a breakfast table, in the question of a child, the loving touch of a spouse, the surprise of a rose.

In this Eucharist right now.

In the hospital in Missoula after my cardiac arrest I was not aware of anything from noon on Saturday until about 3:00 Monday afternoon. At that time my brother John, my only living immediate relative, came into my hospital room. John and I share a common birthday. We have shared our entire lives but we have always disagreed on just about everything--politics, religion or the chances of the Mariners.

But as John walked into my room that afternoon I awoke and began to cry in joy. I was alive. I knew to the depths of my fragile heart how much I loved him and always had. I am grateful today for the entire cardiac episode if only that it told me how fond I am of my brother, how deeply grateful I was for his place in my life. I always had been but did not know it.

I wonder ever since then how many other entrances of Jesus into my various rooms have I taken for granted, not noticed, missed? How many other ways has the promise of the kingdom been given and not possessed, not enjoyed? How many ways has Jesus come and waited on me and I missed it?

I pray for myself today, and for all of us, to live with awareness, intensity, with passion, with laughter, with life.

If we see Jesus here in bread and wine we can perhaps see him everywhere.

37) Twentieth Sunday

Rooted in: Jer. 28:1-2a, 4-6, 8-10; Heb. 12:1-4 and Lk. 12:49-53

This is not an easy week to proclaim what the scriptures say, partially because I do not live up to what I believe to be true. But we must say it, if only to call ourselves to such truth.

Jesus, the Prince of peace, comes, not to bring peace but the sword, to bring division.

This most confusing statement brings me a series of random thoughts that lead slowly to my homily today.

My first thought: I found myself reciting a great poem of Gerard Manly Hopkins about peace. He directs questions at Peace . . .

> When will you ever, Peace, wild wood dove, shy wings shut,
> Your round me roaming end, and under be my boughs?
> When, when, Peace, will you, Peace? I'll not play hypocrite

to my own heart; I yield you do come sometimes; but
that piecemeal peace is poor peace....

The peace of Jesus is not external, but some kind of internal conviction. *It rarely feels like peace.*

Second thought: Whatever happened to the sweet and gentle
Jesus of my youth? How different this man restless for the cross,
this "baptism with which he must be baptized." If it must come,
let it come quickly. Like a man waiting for cancer surgery! This
restlessness of Jesus to get the suffering started and over, warns
us to reflect on what we signed up for in our own baptism.

My third thought in the face of this Gospel text: How challenging,
how disturbing, this entire concept of a savior that brings division
is for me. My preferred personal life stance is to look good, to
get along, to make friends, to have people like me. And I am told
it cannot be done. If we speak and live the Gospel it will upset
people, set them at odds one with another.

Which begins to lead me into the heart of a homily.

I have heard it said that the only thing that upsets Christians more
than having the Gospel message doubted is seeing it practiced!
Whenever someone actually lives the gospel, really sets about following Jesus, others are unsettled, order is upset, families, nations,
the whole world are in tension. The Gospel makes a mess!

Let me root today's readings in their history, their context.

Jeremiah lived and spoke as a prophet in a most dark time of
Jewish history. The people were notoriously unfaithful to the covenant with Yahweh. Jeremiah was compelled to tell the people

what was in store for them if they continued their sinful ways. In a world in which everyone was saying, "Don't worry, be happy," Jeremiah spoke to them a truth they did not want to hear. So they threw him down a well!

The Gospel we heard today is rooted in the actual happenings of the time it was written. By the time Luke's Gospel was written down the words we heard this morning were not a prediction but a fact. Jesus had brought enormous division.

Jewish converts who became followers of Jesus had to leave their families, their synagogues, their identity. Families were, in fact, torn apart, brother against brother, father against son . . . Paul spoke agonizingly about the great pain it was for him to leave behind his Jewish roots in order to pursue The Way.

For Luke himself, whose Gospel is addressed primarily to Gentile believers, those Roman citizens who became Christians left behind the civil religion of their family and friends. They said, in effect, the Emperor is not God, the state is not divine. Only Jesus is Lord. In doing so they risked alienation, persecution from the state, and even from their own family members.

Right from the beginning Jesus brought not peace but the sword, division.

That same division can be seen in every moment of Christian history.

For example most of the Churches in Nazi Germany supported Hitler. The dean of the Madeburg Cathedral said in 1933 that "The Swastika flags around our altar radiate hope." Only a small handful like Karl Barth or Diedrich Bonhoffer said "No." In 1933 they drew up the famous Barman Resolution saying clearly that Jesus is the Word of God, not Hitler, inviting Christians to stand against the Nazi tide. Only a few did and most of them were killed.

The annals are filled with Christian witnesses against the powers that be . . . Desmond Tutu speaking against Apartheid in South Africa, Archbishop Romero, four American Women martyrs, six Jesuits and their companions standing with and for the poor in El Salvador, Dorothy Day or Dan Berrigan in our own country decrying war and the weapons of war. An elderly priest killed by ISIS just for being a priest. Speaking for peace brings the sword, division.

And if we want to risk continuing such division now we continue to speak out on behalf of the values of Human life. We speak for peace in ways that often bring division:

Decrying Abortion and struggling to find alternatives,

Being voices against Capital Punishment in the only nation that continues to favor it,

Advocating for universal health care as a basic human right, insisting that gay rights and women's rights are human rights!

Insisting on a living wage for anyone working full time and lamenting the lack of care for the truly poor in our own nation.

Proclaiming to some that Black lives Matter, and to others that Blue lives do also.

Voting for common sense gun regulations and doing everything possible to get weapons capable of mass destruction out of the hands of anyone who might use them on our citizens.

Seeing the plight of refugees and immigrants, driven from their homes by violence or poverty, and wanting to welcome them to our land!

If we are the voice for the voiceless, a voice on behalf of the sufferings of our world, many will not want to hear that voice and we will bring division, the sword.

The message in the Gospel today is as simple as it is disturbing. To go with Jesus, to view the world through his eyes, to speak with his voice, and to act with his love and compassion is to take a risky stance. It is to face the cross of separating ourselves from some loved ones, some relatives who do not understand, even some members of our communities of faith--to risk putting a sword between brother/ sister/ father/ mother, as the Gospel so clearly suggests.

Finally, one thing the Gospel does not say but certainly hints at.

Jesus longs for the baptism with which he must be baptized. We who are baptized with him, we who stand with Jesus may find alienation within our families, but we, through that baptism are given a new family, now bonds of affiliation. All who struggle to follow Jesus become our brothers, our sisters, our family. We are promised that, in Jesus, we will discover new communities, supporting, loving, standing with us. Through this Eucharist to which we now turn we become one bread, one body--a new family.

There is enormous strength in being part of great cloud of witnesses who like Jesus, having joy set before him, choose the cross.

May I--and all of us--have the faith and courage to hear and proclaim the gospel truth!

38) The Twenty First Sunday

Rooted in: Is. 66:18-21; Heb. 12:5-7, 11-13; Lk. 13:22-30

During the summer lots of people go on trips. In my experience people travel in two very different ways. Some folks just get in the car and drive to their destination, passing up everything to get where they are going. I know a family that didn't stop to see the Grand Canyon because that is not where they were headed.

Others take a more leisurely approach, going somewhere, but seeing the journey as just as important as the arrival. Where they are going is in part wherever they are.

Central to the Gospel of Luke is the journey of Jesus to Jerusalem. Though he stops frequently along the way, and each encounter is significant in itself, from chapter nine on the sense that Jesus is going to Jerusalem is always present, always important in understanding the individual text.

Today's Gospel happens "on the way to Jerusalem," and this journey narrative provides a sub-text for understanding what surely are harsh words--"with me or against me," "cast out," "first and last."

The notion of coming to Jerusalem is expanded from the Gospel to the entire history of God's people, beginning with today's passage from Isaiah.

The first Reading today suggests the universality of the Kingdom. Finally everyone from every tribe and nation will "come to Jerusalem." Everybody is invited to join the journey; everyone can come. But you have to really join up!

In the Gospel Jesus is on his way to Jerusalem--to the fulfillment of his mission and of all that was prophesized about him. He suggests that many who were part of the Jewish family took their "being chosen" for granted and when the end comes they will be left outside. Others, again from every direction, will come in their place to the Kingdom of God, warning them that being "children of Abraham" was not necessarily enough; you can't merely have your name on the list, you have to join the journey.

The language of the text takes Jesus' words beyond the Jewish context and puts it in our own. The words in Luke are addressed to those Christians hearing the word right then, people who have been celebrating the Eucharist for 40-50 years already. People not unlike ourselves.

"You taught in our streets," suggests people who have listened to the word, heard the scriptures proclaimed in their midst for many years.

"We ate and drank with you," suggests people who have shared the Eucharistic table.

Jesus does not respond to the question asked about "many" or "few," but suggests to the asker and to us to worry about ourselves--worry about the door being shut in my face because, having been given every opportunity for experiencing God's love, I missed it.

All this is pretty abstract. Let me tell a story. A minister in the Church noticed one day at Mass a woman he had worked with fifteen years before. After Mass he eagerly went up to her to greet her and began to give her a hug when she looked at him with deep scowl and said "I can't believe you are so friendly; you treated me with ridicule all the time when we worked together." Immediately he felt a deep hole in the pit of his stomach, a recognition he had buried and forgotten, but which he knew to be true.

I imagine the man whom Jesus addressees in the Gospel today feeling that same pit of the stomach ache. He is pretending a fidelity he does not live up to and he knows it. We have all been there. We have all tried to get by because we go to church, we follow the rules, we do what is expected. We have been baptized. We are part of the family. We have listened to the word and eaten at this table. We don't rob or kill people. But we have not truly invested in the journey.

In the context Jesus says, "But I am on my way to Jerusalem, will you come with me." Jesus says I will speak the truth and act with integrity and I will suffer and die because of that. Are you going to join me on this journey? People from every geographical area, every religious conviction, every corner of the earth will gather in that love and risk being persecuted for it in love and their suffering will be redemptive. Will you be part of that?

That "going to Jerusalem" is what matters, nothing else. Will I be a voice for justice, will I be poor in spirit, will I make peace not war, build bridges not walls?

The journey Jesus goes on and invites us to join is the very heart of the Gospel today.

39) The Twenty-Second Sunday

Rooted in Lk. 13:22-30

In the light of this Gospel I have found myself remembering and treasuring my mother. She died when I was only twenty-one during my early years in the seminary. I never got to know her as an adult, but I have vivid and fond childhood memories. One memory in particular, today.

I remember often when our family went out to dinner, usually at some small "Denny's-like" place, seeing my mom's eyes begin to drift around the room until she spotted someone eating alone. She would wait a moment, appear to be thinking, then get up and go talk with this stranger, frequently inviting him or her to come and eat with us. We met a lot of strangers that way.

Many years later I ran into an elderly priest who told me my mother had literally saved his life. He had come by our house many times in the years after that, but I had forgotten how we initially met him. He reminded me that he had been sitting alone in a restaurant, massively depressed, considering suicide when my mother invited him to dine with us. He did, and that shared meal began his journey back to health.

I don't think my mother made such invitations to be holy, or nice, or to live out the Gospel specifically. I don't think she was pretending to be humble. I think my mom extended such invitations for two very simple reasons. She liked people, any people--our milkman and our garbage man were among her best friends. She also knew what it was like to be alone; she had known isolation, and she never wanted anyone else to feel that!

I'll come back to my mom.

The gospel today tells us how to have a dinner party, how to go to a dinner party. The injunctions sound like rules, quite different from Miss Manners, but rules nonetheless:

> Invite the poorest people.
> Even if you think you are important, take the lowest place,
> even if you don't like people invite them so you'll be rewarded.
> The humble will be exalted,
> the exalted will be humbled.

Sounds like a game. Play humble and you will get good stuff. Trump has it all wrong. Uriah Heep had the right idea.

Such an understanding misses the point. Luke says that Jesus "told them a parable." These are not rules, but rather something to "roll around," to "play with," parables. We are invited to throw this around in our mind, our hearts, to let our categories be disrupted, our perceptions confused and hopefully re-ordered.

Parable suggests that we look at something from another angle, to see a truth that might otherwise escape us.

I want to comment on one line of the Gospel--"the humble will be exalted, the exalted humbled"--but I think this captures the truth of the entire passage.

Jesus turns reality upside down, and gets it right.

We think love is founded on shared strength. Really, the basis of love, of true intimacy, is shared weakness.

People love each other because they are screwed up, not because they are perfect. My wisest teacher once said, "Always put your clay foot forward." We have some bizarre quirk in our makeup that tries to escape this truth--it's only clear when we are forced to face it.

If I meet someone who is really smart, really wise, really has it all together, I might admire that person, even respect her or him. But only when a person shares with me their fears, their foibles, their history of brokenness can I love him or her. Only then do I know that they are like me.

We all know, deep down, our own fragility. We all have a part of ourselves that we hide and hope no one will notice. Only when I can share where I am blind, or crippled, or lame, and still be invited into your friendship, can I know I am loved. Only when you share your messiness with me, and I receive it gently, can you know that you are loved. Only then are we both lifted up, only then do we truly lift each other up.

We have all been at dinner parties where everyone walks around trading business cards, talking about the most recent book they have read or written, where "have a nice day" is the high point of the conversation, but everyone there is terribly important. And we have all had meals with friends, people we love, with whom we share our sorrows and dreams. We know which party we prefer.

So, Jesus is not making rules, passing laws, giving Emily-Post-like hints for Christian social decorum. He is reminding us of something terribly important about life.

In the Gospels whenever a meal is spoken of we suspect it says something about The Meal--the Eucharist, the banquet we are celebrating together right now. We do not come to this best banquet, this table of the Lord, wearing our best duds, looking important, trying to impress one another with our worthiness to be here. We do not come because each of us is so terribly important in the life of the Church.

We are here in our shared brokenness, longing even for this hour to be lifted up, brought to the very right hand of our host, Jesus, and to be fed with his life. We do not come here, any of us, because we deserve to be here, but because we need to be told again and again that we are loved despite ourselves. This is no game; it's truth.

We remember how he loved us to his death;
we celebrate that he is with us still.

We are the poor, the blind, the lame that Jesus invites to his banquet, and we can never afford to forget it.

When we ourselves have a party, a dinner, if it be a real party, a Eucharistic Party, no matter who we invite, we know on some level we are inviting the poor, the lame, the blind, the outcast. We are, indeed, inviting people just like ourselves, people with whom we can grow and love. On the best and most true level it is the wounded part of others that draws us for it is that very woundedness we share with them.

My mother knew this a long time before I did; I am grateful for what she taught me.

40) The Twenty-Third Sunday

Rooted in: Wis. 9:13-18; Lk. 14: 25-33

Let me think out loud for a few moments about "Prudence." That's what this Gospel is about, Prudence--"Exercising sound judgment in practical matters."

I think first of that wonderful movie "Field of Dreams," in which Kevin Costner built a baseball field in the middle of an Iowa wheat field on the chance that a deceased baseball player, Joe Jackson would come. "If you build it he will come." The field was built and Jackson came. Maybe it wasn't so imprudent.

It sounds imprudent to me for young people just out of expensive Jesuit colleges to forget all about the loans they've built up and spend a year or two as Jesuit Volunteers, making $10 a month to work with the poor. But, again this year and for a half-century about 100 Jesuit Volunteers do exactly that. And they seem happy!

I can't imagine why a young man with a business background and three children--all of them in Catholic Schools--would work for the Church for about a half a real salary. Is that sound judgment in practical matters?

Paul tells a friend to think about letting his escaped slave, Philomen, go free rather than punishing him. He maintains that they are not slave and master, but brothers in Christ. But slaves cost a lot of money. That isn't prudent.

My father and my brother were insurance men--the ultimate American Prudence; we even name them that way: Prudential Insurance! We live in a world where we hear advertised every day things like "The Club"--a device to keep your car from being stolen. (The alternative of course is to have a really cheap car, say a Geo Metro, that no one would want.)

Prudence and questions of sound, prudential judgment surround us.

Jesus bursts onto the scene and disturbs all our categories about what is prudent.

Let's take a careful look at today's Gospel.

Jesus is still "on his way to Jerusalem." A large crowd follows him. The Gospel sounds almost as if he turns on them and tries to drive them away, to discourage them from following him.

> "If you follow me you will have to fight with your
> parents, your family. If you follow me you'll have
> a cross. You'll have to suffer. Do you really want
> to come? Are you sure?

Words not calculated to encourage a plethora of disciples.

Then Jesus tells two simple, almost inexplicable parables about prudence:

> Nobody should try to build a tower without enough money to finish it.
> No king should go to war unless he has enough troops to win.

Obvious statements of prudence--sound judgment in practical matters.

Then, such a strange prudential statement:

> In the same way, you cannot be my disciples unless
> you are willing to give up everything you have!

Listen to that--it is imprudent to follow me unless you are willing to give up everything. It is imprudent to walk with me now unless you can look ahead and see that you are willing to let everything else go.

Wow! Jesus turns the world upside down. He changes everything. In a world where we protect ourselves, hedge our bets, cover our rear ends, Jesus says, in effect:

> It is imprudent to be prudent!

And we wrestle with this teaching. Is it true, does it fit our experience? Can we reach into our lives and see this apparent paradox as Good News?

I know I am by nature rather afraid of new and changing things. I don't like to spend money or take risks. Friends tell me my initial reaction to almost anything is "No." When I think about it I may change but faced with a challenge or a new idea my first response is usually very cautious.

But I also know that when I do risk everything even for a short while before I start taking it back, I am most happy. Leaving the active ministry at 62 years old was the most scary thing I've ever done, and perhaps the least prudent, but it has borne much fruit, much joy and an extended life in which to learn to love better than I had before.

I invite you to reflect. I suspect you experience the same thing. When you have most risked, you have felt most secure. I don't mean the little stuff like having a bank account, or insuring your home. I don't think Jesus resents your saving money for your kids' education, or planning ahead how you'll use your resources. But the really main point--to risk putting God absolutely first in your life--when you have done that hasn't it brought joy, and life?

This is the point of the passage. To be prudent as a Christian I have to put God/Jesus/the Kingdom first--not let them fit in later. I can't decide what kind of work I'll do, what kind of neighborhood I'll live in, what kind of education I want, what kind of person I'll marry, and how many children I will have first--then try to fit God in. That won't work! That's imprudent! I have to decide first to fall in love with Jesus, to follow him to Jerusalem, to let his Spirit lead me to every important decision.

This may disrupt my life. This may disrupt my family. But it is the only way the war gets won, the tower gets built, the slave goes free.

I invite you to wrestle with this paradoxical truth.

Finally, years ago G.K. Chesterton, one of my favorite all-time authors, talked about *madness* and *sanity*. He made an observation that came back to me as I pondered this Gospel. Chesterton suggested that *madness*, insanity, is to have all the answers, all the logic, to have everything all figured out. The man you visit in an asylum has great certitude, excellent logic. But the circle is too small. We might have all the answers, but we don't have all the questions. The mystery is lost. Truth is not something we can draw a circle around and lock in.

On the other hand, Chesterton suggests, *sanity* is cruciform, extending out in all directions, stretching us farther and farther from a comfortable center. (Use gesture to support this image)

Finally what is reasonable, sane, prudent, "good judgment in practical matters," is, as Jesus said, what reaches out in four directions at once--like a cross, like following Jesus, like being willing to risk everything to walk with him wherever that leads.

41) The Twenty Fourth Sunday

Rooted in Lk. 15: 1-32

"This Man Welcomes Sinners and Eats with them"

I look at myself and our whole Assembly gathered this Sunday morning and repeat:

"This Man welcomes sinners and eats with them ... with us;"

Everything else in my remarks this morning simply develops this truly amazing realization.

The Gospel today and our Eucharist are all about table fellowship, about with whom Jesus shares meals, about with whom we share meals.

A wonderful Jesuit mentor of mine told us, more than 60 years ago, that all we needed to know as followers of Jesus were two passages of scripture; John:15 and Luke:15. We have just listened to Luke:15 in its entirety, a chapter sometimes called "The Good News of the Good News of Luke." Everything we could want to know about Jesus, and especially about the God that Jesus believed in and served, everything we need or want to know about how we should conceive of and respond to God, everything we need or want to know about religion--all is in this chapter. We can return to this chapter over and over and over again, year after year and never fully finish relishing it.

Today I want to simply take a glimpse at some of the more startling, easily missed details in this great passage.

First, we cannot understand this chapter or any of its three stories without noting the context--how the chapter begins. Religious folks, the keepers of the law, Pharisees are scandalized that Jesus hangs around with sinners, especially that he eats with them. Each of the three stories addresses this scandal, and the question of welcoming at table. The final story ends with a party, a banquet--and a son who may or may not go into the party.

Jesus' image of God is of one who celebrates everyone, good or bad, being invited to the table as long as they be willing to be there together.

These three stories are deliberately, progressively more outrageous stories of the unimaginable love of God--unreasonable love, foolish beyond bounds.

The God of Jesus is like a foolish shepherd who would risk losing ninety-nine safe sheep to rescue and recover just one who was lost. This shepherd is happier about the one found than about the ninety-nine never at risk. That seems pretty foolish.

The God of Jesus is like a woman who has a few coins, none of them worth very much. It would be unusual for a peasant woman to have any coins at all; normally everything would be purchased by barter. Having these coins the woman loses one, then turns the entire house upside down to find the coin. When she finds it she invites the neighbors over and throws a party that would cost more than all the coins together were worth. That seems pretty foolish.

Thirdly, the God of Jesus is like the father who allows both of his sons to abuse and insult him, but still invites each to party with him. He loves them both as sons, not servants, no matter how they treat him. That is especially foolish.

But that's how the God of Jesus is!

This extraordinary chapter aims, <u>partially</u>, at convincing the listeners that God loves us no matter what, no matter how lost, how bad we've been. But <u>more</u>, the chapter aims at convincing the Pharisees (and the pharisaical, righteous part in each of us) that we need to be celebrating sons and daughters, children (not just servants) of this loving God!

Other details we might easily miss:

Did you notice how Jesus asks the Pharisees, "Which of you, having a hundred Sheep…?" Well no Pharisee would have *any* sheep. Sheep are dirty, and shepherds have to work on the Sabbath. Shepherds don't keep the law, don't say their prayers at the right times. A Pharisee would not have sheep, nor spend a single moment looking for a lost one either! Nor would they, with their many coins, appreciate the plight of the woman in the second story.

They would not easily understand the third story either. Like us, perhaps, they would be inclined to hear it as a story about two sons, one who was bad and another who was good. We need to look at the details here also.

The issue for each son is the same--to accept that he is a son, not a slave.

It is not easy to be a son, a daughter, part of a family. If we belong to a family we are loved just because we *are*, and we have to love back. Being in a family raises all kinds of relational obligations and expectations. Sometimes it's easier to just work, earn our keep, be a servant. That's the issue of the parable.

When the younger son returns to his senses, and to his father, he says "treat me like one of your hired servants,"--that is, let me earn my keep, pay you back, stay at a distance. But the father insists, "You are not a servant, you are my son." He showers the wayward son with unearned and undeserved gifts and throws a party.

When the older son returns from the field he tells his father, "I've always worked like a slave for you and you never threw me a party." The father says, "You're not a slave, you're my son--every party I have is your party, every guest, your guest. My friends are yours. Don't try to separate yourself from me. Quit acting like a slave around here!"

A further detail; both sons seem to want their father dead, this relationship over.

The first son essentially says, "You've waited too long to die, old man, give me my inheritance now." He takes that inheritance and wastes it. He insulted his father, and the entire community, breaking away from all Jewish custom in a foreign land. He sunk as low as possible both as a son, and as a Jewish boy--feeding pigs, unable to eat the food the pigs eat (and, remember, being Jewish, he couldn't eat the pigs either)! Still the father welcomes him back, treats him as son and invites the entire community to welcome him too--the son who was dead is alive.

The older son also wishes his father dead so that he could party with "his friends," in a place that was his own, not his father's. In that culture, the older son's refusal to come into the party, forcing his father to come out to him rather than coming in to his father is a terrible insult. But, again the father comes out to meet his son.

We can miss it but Jesus' parable does paint the older son, the righteous religious servant, as just as sinful, if more deceptively so, as his brother. Remember the story is about sharing table with sinners. The parable is addressed to the Pharisees. The older son treats his father scandalously, disdains his father's love, wants to be his own person, not his father's son. He separates himself from the family--says "your son," not "my brother." He has worked hard, like a slave, but he has totally missed the fact that he is "son."

This chapter, these three stories, are about grace, about the unearned, undeserved love given freely to God's children.

In response to the shock of seeing Jesus welcoming sinners and even eating with them, we are reminded:

> None of us has earned the honor of being God's children.
> No one else has to earn it either.

The final detail of the story is extremely important.

The story doesn't end. We want to hear a final line like "So the older son went into the party with his father, put his arm around his brother, and the feast went on." But it doesn't say that. We know what Jesus did: Jesus welcomed sinners and ate with them.

We don't know what the older son did.

We do know what the Pharisees who heard the story did--they killed the messenger.

We don't know what we will do.

42) The Twenty Fifth Sunday

Rooted in: Lk. 16: 1-13

We live in an age of addictions and those working for their healing. From addictions, often in one or another twelve-step programs. (Did you hear about the twelve-step group for compulsive over-achievers? They have thirty-six steps. Or the group I've been advised to join for compulsive talkers? Called "On-and-on!")

I have been told that the most difficult addiction for people to work on is an eating addiction because it is an addiction that cannot be entirely abandoned. A person can live, perhaps live better, without alcohol or gambling, or tobacco or other narcotics. A person can even live without sexual expression. But we cannot live without eating.

But eating is not the only thing to which this difficulty pertains; the same thing is true about money. And the point of the gospel today is that our relationship with, our desire for, or our spending of, money can be addictive; nor do we really have a choice whether we will deal with money or not.

I find the line of the Gospel quite disturbing:

You cannot serve God and money!

We try to do so; we almost have to try to do so. We have to serve money at least a little bit. Most of us need to have jobs, need to have a bank account, an insurance policy or two, a mortgage payment. We simply have to pay attention, serious attention, to money to live in this real concrete world. This is quite specific for my wife and me today: our 16-year-old car that we have cared for, loved, kept up, expecting to drive it until we died was rear-ended while parked two days ago--probably totaled. Its face value is only a fraction of what it is worth to us and we are worried sick about how we can afford to replace it. We have real money worries. How to serve both God and money is a real question.

Jesus tells a story and the story comes at the question from a different direction. The parable today praises a person who was wise, cunning, devious in dealing with wealth and security. He deals with his financial addiction very creatively. To dig he was not able, to beg he was ashamed, so the manager undermined his boss but did a great job of taking care of himself in the calamity that was about to come.

The point of this strange parable is that we ought to take at least as much wit and cunning to our service of God, ought to be as wise in building the Kingdom of God as developing security in the here and now, ought to learn the tricks needed to promote justice, peace, and love.

I find the gospel sadly silent on some things we would really like to know. How much money is it all right to have? How much security can a Christian legitimately strive for? How much service can we give to the material world without becoming its servant? The gospel raises the question but doesn't answer it. Maybe because it is the wrong question.

The first question always has to be the Kingdom question. What does this decision have to do with building God's reign? How will this insurance policy help me to promote justice? How will this new job, with better wages and better benefits really help *me* be better, more loving, more gentle, more Christ-like?

Strange as it seems when we put together the entire gospel today it suggests that all of our decisions about money, wealth, security need to become questions about a very different kind of wisdom--the wisdom of disciples.

Before I conclude let me invite each of us to pause and think of a very real financial decision, recently made, big or small--maybe selling or buying a house or a car, maybe just grocery shopping, or renting a movie. For us right now it involves how to replace our car.

Stop and think of some recent transaction. (pause)

I invite you to honestly reflect quietly to yourself, did the reign of God enter in anyway into the decision? How could it have? What difference would such a reflection have made?

Was this tennis shoe made in Taiwan? Will our moving make this neighborhood better or worse? Will this extra tuition really help my youngster to be stronger in his or her faith? Does this car consume more fuel than necessary? Such questions, and a thousand like them, speak of the centrality of God's Kingdom more than my own well-being or security.

I am told that the word we have often heard in today's Gospel, the word *Mammon* (remember hearing, "You cannot serve God and Mammon?") has the same root as the word *Amen*. *Amen* means "Yes" it is true, I give assent to this statement, this truth. Money and wealth are such strong realities in our world that we can give assent to them, can give a kind of final *yes* to their centrality in our lives.

We are asked this morning to deal with the question: When we get up each morning and begin our day, when the day is finished and we retire exhausted, to what do we give our loudest and most central "yes": the Goods of this earth, or the God of this earth?

It cannot be both.

43) The Twenty Sixth Sunday

Rooted in Lk. 16: 19-31

I want to approach the so-clear story of the rich man and the poor man, by telling of a dream a woman friend told me about some years ago--a dream amazing for its luminosity and its universality. The dream has seemed to me ever since to capture the quintessential experience of most middle- to upper-class American Catholics.

In her dream the woman and her husband are visiting with Mother Theresa, in India, in a huge ramshackle mansion. The woman knows, even while dreaming, that Mother Theresa is a symbol of God. The couple present themselves to Mother Theresa to work with her as volunteers. The holy, aged sister smiles at them and says "If you really want to help you are welcome, but if you cannot, or do not really want to, that's all right. I want you to be free."

In her dream the woman had, indeed, a deep sense of this freedom. While they spoke, the woman heard and had a sense of the sounds of many rats running around upstairs in the mansion.

She and her husband then went outside to think about their choice. In the streets the atmosphere was more like Aleppo than Calcutta--lots of shooting, violence, bombs, even people fist-fighting. She and her husband ran through the streets avoiding the pervasive violence until they stopped by the side of a building. They looked in the window of an exquisite French restaurant. She remembered looking at the price list and seeing something she would love to eat for about forty dollars. They saw in the restaurant, in the midst of all the violence, beautiful white tablecloths, huge wine goblets, with fluffed napkins, about six small tables. She looked at her husband, they nodded, then entered. When they entered the restaurant, however, the discovered the table cloths were very old, falling apart, the wine glasses were covered with dust, and...there were many rats running round on the floor. The dream ended.

Perhaps the meaning is quite clear, at least in outline, on levels that touch, somehow, most of us. We are good and caring Catholics, with some resources, some social conscience. We struggle to hold onto some sense of our life-style in tension with the needs of the world around us. Each of us, perhaps, feels some nudge to real generosity, some total risk--like running off to join Mother Theresa. But we are afraid--afraid of the rats upstairs which we cannot quite see, but know must be there.

At the same time we are aware enough that we cannot return, nor can we charge into a life of comfortable luxury. The world of French restaurants has turned to dust, and we see the rats there quite clearly if we are honest with ourselves.

Usually as I preach I want to break open the world and make it clear. Today the Gospel is so clear immediately. That dream makes the experience more contemporary, but the challenge is the same.

How do we live with a social conscience in such a pain-filled and complicated world?

I am sure that not a single person in this church would live comfortably with a single beggar on our doorstep. If there were only one beggar there, one Lazarus, we would do everything we could to help. The tragic reality is that there are always, everywhere hundreds of beggars, the poor, the fragile, the weak the needy. It is difficult to get through a day without some variety of Lazarus presenting himself to us--on the streets of our city, on television, in the newspaper, or even in our neighborhood--homeless in droves on our city streets and visions of Syrian refugees searching for a safe homeland.

Every day I may touch a wound here, a symptom of poverty there, but the sheer volume of human suffering and inequity is overwhelming. I feel, as I'm sure you must at times, like that woman in the dream, scurrying around, jumping from one fight, one battle, one round of gun shot to another.

The breadth and extent of human suffering is immense and we, good people, want to see Lazarus at our door step. One has, indeed, come back from the dead to tell us.

Another image helps me get inside this parable in a way larger than the single beggar and myself. Sometimes I imagine myself in the square outside a beautiful Cathedral. I want to go to the church to be with my God, but between me and that Church is an entire Church square filled with the poor. Everywhere I look between myself and the beautiful Church I see a hand out for help, a baby nursing a shriveled breast, crippled men, their crutches at their side, shaking a tin can for change, lepers with open sores sitting slightly apart from the group.

I look at this sea of poverty and I am faced with a variety of choices:

I can turn away and look for other Churches, in other squares.

I can put my head down, charge through the crowd, and try to get to God, to pray. But ignoring the needs of the Incarnate God before me, I will find no God in that Church.

I can begin to try to help each needy Lazarus I meet as I walk towards this church. If I give a little to each person I pass I will, long before I get to the Cathedral, become one with these beggars. This is the choice of some in our tradition who have cast their lot totally with the poor.

I can, perhaps, pick out one beggar, one cause, one issue, and make them my beggar. I can do something to help at least in one arena, can make the world a little better in at least a single area.

Perhaps, in a larger picture I need to gather with other pilgrims and look for the cause of all this poverty, and see how we can get at whatever systems help create the mess.

To face this parable today we do need in some fashion to make the issue bigger than the single beggar at our personal doorstep. I invite each of us before we move to Eucharist--that is before we share in the death and Resurrection of Jesus again--to let this Lazarus story be ours. What does this really mean in my life, and how might I respond to one "come back from the dead"?

44) The Twenty-Seventh Sunday

Rooted in: Habakkuk 1:2-3, 2:2-4; 2 Tim. 1:6-8, 13-14; Lk. 17: 5-10

I love the image of the first Reading this weekend from the prophet Habakkuk. I wish we read it every week.

Write down the vision ... make it plain, there is still a vision ...

It reminds us what we are doing here each week, is the reason for
our coming together, our homilies, our prayers:

And Paul writes to Timothy this morning in the same vein:

Rekindle the gift of God that is within you ...

We come each week to recapture our shared vision of faith in
Jesus and to build our lives on that shared faith, even if be as tiny
as a mustard seed.

If you have faith as small as a mustard seed, you can say to this mulberry tree, 'Be uprooted and planted in the sea,' and it will obey you."

Let me tell a story that may help in this rekindling of faith.

Years ago a great circus performer, a tight rope walker, declared that he was going to set up a wire and walk across Niagara Falls from Canada to the United States. The event was widely advertised. On the day of the daring walk thousands came to watch, perhaps to witness a tragedy.

Before the eyes of thousands the performer walked almost casually across, over the wildly raging waters, to the United States, and then returned across the wire back to Canada. Then, almost before the people caught their collective breath, he put on a blindfold and made the two-way trip again, this time only slightly less steadily. A third time he loaded up a wheelbarrow with sand and, with much more wobbling and hesitating, but still quite steadily, he took the wheelbarrow back and forth over the falls. People were awe-struck at both his balance and his courage.

As the exhausted performer dumped the sand out of his wheelbarrow a young man broke through the crowd, rushed up to him enthusiastically, complimented him profusely for his courage and confidence. The tight-wire walker looked at the man in the eye and said, "Thank you for your compliment. If you really mean it why don't you let me put you in this wheel barrow and I will take you back and forth across the Falls?"

The man panicked, turned white, backed quickly away refusing the offer. "But why?" the performer asked, " If what I do is so wonderful and you really think I am so gifted, why won't you trust me? Why won't you get in the barrow?"

To appreciate the Gospel today I invite all of us here to ask ourselves whether we would have gotten into the conveyance and trusted ourselves into this man's hands?

Then I ask the deeper, further questions, can I entrust myself into the hands of the real wonder worker, the real man of balance, the real risk-taker who walks across the waters?

The Gospel today, and really every day, is about Faith--not faith at a distance, not faith as in admiration of another, but faith as "giving my heart" to another, to Jesus.

Can I trust the one that I believe passed through death to life, trusted in love beyond even the grave, and was lifted up by God? Can I trust that if I put my hand, my heart into his keeping that I can get through this present trial, this awful moment, this stage of my story with safety and love?

Whatever it is that I bring to this Eucharist that troubles or frightens or holds me back, or hangs me up--Jesus asks me this morning "Can you get into my hands and trust me?" Every person present here comes with some challenge, big or small, to our faith. How will I ever get through this time of incredible humiliation? How can I ever trust my husband, or wife, my brother, or son or daughter or parent again? How will I live without that job, or any job, or that house, or my health? Almost everyone at almost every moment of our lives has some precipice to cross and we don't see how we can cross it.

The Gospel begins with a request from the apostles, "Lord, increase our Faith!" They, like us today, wanted to believe more deeply, more honestly. Jesus tells them just a little bit of faith can do great things.

Perhaps the most amazing aspect of the Gospel today is the way that Jesus underplays such trust. He speaks about a servant just doing what is expected, "working in the field, waiting at the table"--just doing the obvious tasks before him. Not expecting any big reward for doing one's job! Just believing and acting on that belief. Certainly the person who admired that tight-wire performer would have the sense, the courage to trust him with his life. Certainly someone who believes in Jesus and entrusts his or her life to Jesus would be willing to follow him through any kind of death to life. It seems obvious, simple.

But it is not so easy, so simple, we know. And Jesus knows, too. That's why we are invited to come here week after week to renew our vision, to rekindle the gift of God in us.

As we go on with the Eucharist I invite us each to pause a moment--first to be in touch with that feeling in the pit of our stomach when we are invited to be rolled across the tight-wire, over the Falls, risking death. Then reach beneath that feeling and notice what happens when Jesus invites us to believe, to trust, to put everything in our life into his loving hands.

Then let us pray!

45) The Twenty-Eighth Sunday

Rooted in Lk. 17:11-19

Ten lepers are healed; one returns to give thanks. Where, indeed, are the nine? What keeps us from giving thanks?

Today, with this wonderful Gospel story, aided by the imagination of others, I want to reflect on blockages to God's Spirit, on things that keep us from being and living in gratitude.

This will only work if we begin with the realization that we--each of us--are in this story. It is not told to us today as a story about a bunch of lepers 2000 years ago. We need to hear it as people who have ourselves been healed, cleansed, gifted, as people who have abundant reasons to give thanks to Jesus.

We are the lepers. Where indeed are the nine? Borrowing from a book I read many years ago, adapted over the years, let me reflect with you on these lepers for a few moments--all ten of them.

One leper came back to give thanks. A very good thing to do. Now as a Samaritan he wasn't much interested in going to the temple and showing himself to the priests anyway. He was not welcome in that temple, but he did come back and say thanks to Jesus. And that is a good thing to do.

We may be this leper. But this gratitude thing is more complicated than we sometimes think. We may find ourselves in the stories of other lepers who found it difficult, if not impossible, to let God's Spirit work in them. Or work in other ways!

One of the lepers just *forgot*. He forgot to come back and say thanks because he was so excited. he shouted, laughed, danced, skipped down the road and was so incredibly excited to be healed that in his excitement he forgot to thank the one who healed him. He just forgot.

One leper was *afraid*. She had always found it difficult to stand out, to be noticed. If all ten had returned to say thanks she would have doubtless gone with them, but she was too afraid to go alone, to be embarrassed before Jesus, or the crowd. Her shyness hade always curtailed her life.

One woman did not return. She didn't even consider returning. She had *duties* after all--her children, a husband she had not seen or cared for in two years. In deep joy, and with real gratitude in her heart, she rushed back to those who needed her, to be with them to care for them again.

One of the lepers, a Pharisee, was *offended by cheap grace.* He did not return because he was upset at Jesus' approach to God. He did not, like Naaman in our first reading, even have to go wash seven times in some pool. He did not have to do penance, did not have to say a thousand prayers. The God he had always believed in asked so much more, demanded so much more, much fasting, long trials. This man would not believe in such abundant, unearned, undeserved love. He could not say thanks to Jesus who made God's love so cheap!

Another leper was very angry. He realized too late that he did not want to be cured. He knew how to be a leper, had become a good, successful beggar, and experienced a kind of perverse enjoyment in forcing others to listen to his complaints. Now he had no reason to complain. He had to be on his own, support himself, be responsible for his own joy or misery. He had turned his wheel chair into a throne. He did not want to be well. He did not want to say thanks.

One leper did not return because there was *nothing to be grateful for*. Jesus had done nothing, really. He just told them to go away. He was now healed, but Jesus had nothing to do with it. There was no evidence of that. There was undoubtedly some scientific explanation, some natural reason they all found themselves suddenly clean. Why return to this itinerant preacher to say thanks; Jesus had nothing to do with it. There was no miracle here.

One leper just *dawdled*. He intended to go back, he meant to say thanks, but he was so alive with this new health. He jumped into the creek for a swim. He sat and smelled the flowers. He chatted with people along the way who used to avoid him. He just dinged around, enjoying the beauty of life and by the time he got back to where Jesus had been, no one was there.

One leper did not return to say thanks because *he could no longer say thanks* to anyone for anything. He had said "Thank you" to so many, for so long, for so little--the piece of bread begrudgingly given, the sip of water from a horse's trough, the stable out back to sleep in. He was supposed to be grateful for these ridiculous tokens. Years ago, he had vowed never to say thank you again. No more, no thank you, never again. He had already used up a lifetime of gratitude for little nothings so that when a big one came along he was unable to feel or extend gratitude.

The final leper is perhaps the most interesting, and most important for us. While a leper he had been for a long time around the edges of Jesus' ministry. He had stood just behind the crowds and listened. He had heard the words of Jesus, seen the actions of Jesus.

"Since I have loved you, you ought to love one another."
"By this will people know that you are my disciples, by the love you have for one another."
"This is my commandment, love one another."

This leper did not go back to Jesus to say thanks because he believed such an action would not be what Jesus wanted. Rather he went off to look for other lepers, for others to heal, as he had himself been healed. He went off filled with love and hope, to continue the mission of Jesus.

That's where, that's how the other nine might be; and there could doubtless be many others. There are reasons not to come back to give thanks, some of them far better than others. But enough to look for ourselves in the story, enough to reflect on our own gratitude and our response to all the gifts God has given us.

The Spirit of Jesus is God's gift to us, breathed on us in Baptism, deepened in us in Confirmation, regularly nourished here in Eucharist.

I invite us to enter this Eucharist with an honest self appraisal. If we live lives filled with gratitude, wonderful. If we do not, where is God's spirit blocked in us?

46) The Twenty-Ninth Sunday

Rooted in Ex. 17:8-13 and Lk. 18:1-8

The image of Moses in today's first reading fascinates me. It offers a primitive, even ugly image of God, but the story of Moses is great! Picture him with his arms up as the battle goes on. When he keeps them up, the good guys win. When he lowers his arms they start to lose. He needs to get props, people, use anything or anyone he can to help keep those arms up.

Can we keep our arms up when things get difficult?

This question meshes with the gospel words *"When the Son of Man comes will he find any faith on earth?"*

Can we hang in there, believe, hope, struggle, be faithful in the face of the suffering, hardship, apparent failure? Can we plead to the ear of an apparently deaf God? Can we show faith as persistent as a nagging widow seeking her due!

The focus in the scriptures today is not so much on the God who answers our prayers, but on our keeping praying, believing that our prayers will indeed be answered.

Let me look with some care at the Gospel.

One morning, I was about half asleep when I heard a slightly crazy neighbor, Daphne, out looking for her dogs--at about 6:30. Her screeching voice awoke me. I thought of the judge in this parable. I too would have done anything I could to stop the screaming. This story of the widow asking for help is taken by Luke from a similar story in the Wisdom of Ben Sirach, a passage in which a widow prays persistently and God answers her prayer.

Luke's Jesus changes this story in two significant ways. First, the widow is screaming. She won't stop screaming. She is a "nag," not just faithful. She leans dangerously close to obnoxious.

Secondly God is strangely imaged as a very negative character, a rascal of a judge. This judge has no respect for God or anyone, has no shame. The implication is that he does his job by taking bribes, helping whoever most crosses his palm. He makes no pretext of fairness, of justice. He is in this just for the money (very difficult for us to grasp in our era, because so unlike any judge, or lawyer these days)!

The widow does indeed have a case, but she is a woman in a man's world. As a woman she cannot even get into the courtroom. She has no money, certainly no man in her life, or he would be interceding for her. She has no power. She cannot bribe the judge. She cannot get a hearing.

So she stands outside the courtroom and screams her head off; she keeps yelling hour after hour, day after day. I love the image and I hear Daphne out in the street below my window.

"Wears me out," I am told, is in original language, a boxing term. It means literally, she "has opened a cut under my eye." "Made my eye open" is obviously a pun we miss in translation!

Read from one vantage point the story is about "hanging in there in our prayer," because if this corrupt, unscrupulous judge will respond, how much more will God. But the deeper point of the story is more subtle. The sub-text is that "it might not look like it." It may well seem that God is not listening, hearing, responding. Can we keep on asking even then?

To grasp this parable it is important to hear the final line. "When the Son of Man comes will he find any faith on earth?"

Some have read this as Jesus saying something about the end time, the so-called second coming. I prefer the reading that suggests the centrality of the title *Son of Man*. The *Son of Man* is precisely a Messiah who will, who does suffer. When the messianic presence you have waited and hoped for turns out to be a suffering messiah--taking on himself the vulnerability, fragility, pain of the entire history of humanity--will your faith persist? Jesus asks that when he scandalizes the religious folks, the civil authorities by being arrested, crucified, killed, when he is "lifted up," will faith still persist?

Will you keep believing in me when I come precisely as "*Son of Man?*" Will you keep your arms up then?

This was a question for the disciples who in fact <u>fled when it occurred.</u> It is a question still.

I read this parable as a challenge to persistent faith, to keeping our arms up, to continue to shout about Justice and Peace when it doesn't seem to happen--when things even get worse.

I remember my dear friend Fr. Bill Bichsel, who spent his life fighting for nuclear disarmament, for justice on many levels, who lived with former felons, saying once, with a huge smile, that everything he had ever worked for always got worse ... but he kept praying, kept struggling.

Can I keep my faith active when so much poverty abounds in our land, when so many are not cared for, when children still suffer, mass killings continue, our earthly home is being destroyed and all of these concerns are barely mentioned in a national election? Can I keep trusting, praying, hoping when my life seems to fall apart into little pieces and I can give no concrete reason for my hope?

When Jesus comes as the Son of Man, overwhelmed in suffering, can I keep praying, keep my arms up, keep believing in the face of the cross because I trust that God is faithful, God will answer, will be more benign than that unjust judge?

Some days more than others this seems like the right question to bring to Eucharist, where we are caught up into the death and resurrection of Jesus as we celebrate the fidelity of God--no matter what?

47) The Thirtieth Sunday

Rooted in: Sir. 35, 12-14, 16-18; 2 Tim. 4, 6-8, 16-18; Lk. 18, 9-14

I have a friend who asks me with frustrating regularity, "How's your heart?" Each time I'm asked I have to stop and consciously pay attention. I do not always know how my heart is. I suspect we all need to pay more attention to our hearts. In today's Gospel passage we hear part of a large pattern of Jesus inviting us to pay attention to our hearts, and let them be healed.

Jesus loved the human heart in its fear and panic; he exposed the divine heart in its overwhelming love. Jesus invited us to come to him, to learn of him, for he was "meek and humble of heart." Theologian John Shea suggests that Jesus sought in myriad ways both to challenge and disrupt the hardened heart and to mend the broken heart. How many stories and scenes, especially in Luke's Gospel, have characters like the two in this parable--a parable told to those whose hearts were self-righteous?

We hear of a broken-hearted woman taken in adultery, confronted by those with stones in their hands and hearts.

A woman known as a sinner come to wash the feet of Jesus who had touched her heart; a Pharisee who did not want her in his home, or heart.

Two sons, one broken, feeding the pigs he could not eat, estranged from his father's heart; the other angry at the brother, refusing to eat the banquet of his father's generous heart.

A Samaritan stops to help a fallen stranger by the side of the road; a priest and Levite walk by.

At the end, two thieves--one with a sorrowful heart, repentant, the other holding onto the aggressive stony heart that brought him there.

In today's story two people offer prayers--one struggles to convince God that he deserves to be loved for all his good deeds, the other laments that he has no good deeds, deserves no love.

And how is my heart? If I can penetrate these broken hearts, these hardened hearts, I can learn something of my own.

If I speak about myself it is only so that each of us may do the same. There is in me something of the envious, the hardened heart. There is a part that is not sure of God's love and so sets out to be not just good but perfect, desperately hoping that God will look on me with love. Flannery O'Conner speaks in one of her stories about a man who had "stuffed his own emptiness with good works, like a glutton."

This do-good position in my heart only works in comparison. I need to look around and find someone who is less good, less holy, less upright than myself, so I can feel superior: "Look at that tax collector there"; "I may not be the best priest in the world, but I'm a lot better than that other guy who only talks about money or the one who plays golf four times a week, or the one who can't keep any staff people to work with him." I'm OK in my little hard heart if I am better than someone else.

I suspect each of us has known, too, a broken heart. All of us, no matter how we have tried to avoid it, have had moments, periods, perhaps a life-time in which we knew we were not OK, were not good. We have had times when we looked in the mirror and our lives and said "Yuk!" We touched our hearts and they were broken.

We have all been Charlie Brown forever kicking a football that wasn't there. We have been so down on ourselves, so aware of our brokenness that we accelerated our destructive behavior--we drank more, or spent more, told even more lies, or entered into yet another doomed relationship--just to prove our unworthiness to ourselves, to others and to God.

The gospel today is one of many scenes in which Jesus speaks to such hearts, touches such hearts. He challenges the pretended complacency of the hardened heart, and lifts up the brokenness of the wounded heart. The first becomes last; the last becomes first. Then everyone can be in the center!

My experience, perhaps yours, reflects this truth about Jesus, this loving God who crashes through our defenseless hearts. I have felt most close to God, believed most in God's love when

I have felt totally broken, unworthy, and yet been touched
with a compassion beyond belief, or
when I have done something really well, really successfully-
-so well that I had to admit in my heart that I did not do it,
but it was from the power of God working in me beyond
what I could ask or imagine.

As I pray with this parable, and the others like it, as I try to let
Jesus heart speak to my heart, I find myself the past few years
recognizing the need to hold together in my heart two apparently
contradictory truths. To be whole, to be healthy, to be holy, I need
to own both the destruction and the creation of my life. I need, at
the same time, to stand in the back beating my breast, owning my
failings, and also to stand in the front, owning my goodness. I need
to deny neither, nor to exaggerate either.

In my life I have failed. I have let people down. I have hurt people I
love. I have broken commitments. I have caused scandal. I have not
written the great American novel, or become the saint I intended
to be. My heart has large broken chunks of which I am ashamed.

But I have also loved, cared, been faithful in my fashion. I have
helped some people grow and blossom. I have spoken well of
Jesus. I have helped create some small, but lovely gardens in God's
kingdom. I have done some things quite well.

I am at the same time both sinner and saint. My heart is both
proud and broken. If I forget the broken part I will inevitably continue the same mistakes, continue to hurt people. If I forget the
parts of which I can, in Christ, be proud, I will despair.

The truth lies in holding together the tension, the paradox, the
ambiguity--acknowledging again the Cross.

For a few moments, before we go on with Eucharist, let's consciously locate ourselves _in this temple at prayer._

Take a moment to acknowledge the part of myself that crawls to the back, hides my face from God, weeps in my woundedness.

Notice too those things for which (because God works in us) we can acknowledge ourselves as good and loving and lovable—maybe not because we earned it, but because it is given to us as gift.

Then we move _with our whole hearts_ to this altar in prayer.

48) The Feast of All Saints
Nov. I

Rooted in: Rev. 7: 2-4, 9-14: I Jn. 3:1-3; Mt. 5:1-12

A friend of mine told me about going to Verdi's opera, <u>Falstaff</u>, on Halloween--the night before this feast of All Saints. Verdi's opera is a version of Shakespeare's <u>Merry Wives of Windso</u>r in which Falstaff, the wine-guzzling sack of an improbable mixture of virtues and vices, tries to seduce two sisters in Windsor. They lead him on to teach him a lesson and he gets thrown into the Thames in a dirty linen basket. Later he gets his come-uppance in a wood where he thinks he is going to have a tryst. The opera ends with a kind of repentance on the part of the fumbling, lovable rake. Falstaff and all the company sing and point not just to themselves but to the whole audience:

Life is but a jest,
but a jest,
we are all fools.

My friend turned to his companion and said, "Tonight we are all fools, and yet tomorrow (all Saints Day) we shall all be saints."

That's what this feast is about. *We are all fools; we are all saints.*

As we look around this Church in every corner, in each window we see the array of saints, all in a sense minor to the Cross, the tabernacle, the images of Jesus, but all reminding us of the great cloud of witnesses to Jesus' power and goodness and mercy that are with us as we worship. Our Eucharist is so much more exalted and powerful than our paltry moral celebration. This earthly liturgy is intimately connected to the heavenly liturgy we hear about in Revelations. The saints--especially the martyr saints who bear witness to Jesus suffering--stand before the throne and worship and praise our God.

Who are these saints? Certainly the canonized ones of the past, Ignatius and Aloysius, Francis and Catherine. Above all, Mary. Those who embodied in their lives the works of mercy, the beatitudes. But we think, too, of those we have known. I think of Leo Eckstein, a marvelous Jesuit pastor with whom I lived and worked many years--a gentle, joyful, compassionate man who spoke constantly of and invited all to trust in God's eternal love. Or I think of Dorothy Day who fed the hungry and refused to accept a distinction between the worthy and unworthy poor. She spoke and acted against the validity of war long before it was an apparent Gospel mandate to do so. Dorothy will never be canonized because she had an abortion in her early years, yet she might be more saint than all the others. I think of many I knew at St. Leo's who lived and worked among the poor and now have gone to join them around God's throne: Bill Bichsel, Keith Hagen, and just lately, Lyda Flannagan

St. Thomas Aquinas had it right when he said that "Saints are really friends of God." Aquinas knew we become like our friends, we take on the virtues and good qualities of our friends, so saints-- God's friends--become like God. The have God's own love infused in their lives and see the world and love the world and its people as does God.

This is the point of that second reading from the letter of John. We are already children and heirs of God and Christ, and later we shall see him as he really is. As friends of God the saints can and do intercede for us. Being very Irish I talk with the dead, those I have known and loved and who I believe still love me. I talk to Ignatius and Xavier, the martyrs of El Salvador, and both my moms and my dad, and some other heroes of my life now gone to God. They have not disappeared into thin air but live on with the Lord. This intercession of the saints is part of the communion of saints, part of acknowledging who we are. We are not alone in this universe of mortality.

Returning to my Falstaff theme, that saints are stumbling human beings like ourselves, I am reminded of Dorothy Day's response when people called her a saint. "Don't trivialize me!" Don't put me aside by making me different from you. If I am a saint it is because I am messed up as you are, only trying harder to be faithful to God.

Saints are real, people with faults, with tempers and fears and foibles. St. Jerome said lots of things no one would want their mother to hear. Francis of Assisi walked naked through the town square. John Berchmans was so uptight that he didn't know where the rector sat in the dining room because he never looked up! But each saint, like each one of us, struggled to become who God calls them to be. Not to become like another, but to be the one they are as God wants it.

The worst way to try to become holy is to be a perfectionist, or to imitate someone else's way. I love Ignatius, but I am not Ignatius. None of us is called to be Francis of Assisi. We will never become the saints we are called to be unless we first take Falstaff's words to heart; we are all fools, all mortals, all stumbling, stuttering beings in need of God's mercy and goodness. Only a stance like this allows the openness to God's grace to work, transforming us daily into the new creatures our baptism calls us to be.

So now we turn to Eucharist, and we know we are with a great cloud of witnesses more sweet smelling than any incense, more powerful than our paltry prayer, more loving than we could hope for. Though fools we may be, we celebrate our communion with those witnesses today.

49) Thirty-First Sunday

Rooted in: Wis. 11:22-12:1; 2 Thes. 1:11-2:2; Lk. 19:1-10

Every once in a while, I remember that prayer is about God, not about me. Frequently enough, I get all caught up in *my* mistakes and failures, and *my* needs and hopes then remember that prayer is about paying attention to God, and God's love and God's power--not focusing on myself. I bring that reflection to today's readings.

In the second reading today from the letter to the Thessalonians, Paul prays for the early Christians and for us:

> May *God make you* worthy of the call, and fulfill every good resolve and work of
> faith so Jesus may be glorified in you.

I cannot imagine a better prayer to bring to this Eucharist and to our reflection on the Gospel. This prayer "to let God make us worthy of the call" is somehow at the center. The first reading from Wisdom reminds us that it is God who does the work, makes us worthy, overlooks our stumblings, loves everything. God works in us, as Jesus did with Zacchaeus, not because he deserved it--quite the opposite: because he needed it.

Put simply perhaps, the point of the Zacchaeus story is "Always put your clay foot forward!"

We get loved and cared for by God in our weakness, not because of our strength. It is in the place where we are most needy that we are most loved. God makes us worthy; we don't.

Zacchaeus was rich in material goods, but he was poor. He was a social outcast, small in ethics and in stature. He needed Jesus.

A few years ago I directed a year-long retreat with a man in his early forties trying to put his life together. He had been making more than $100,000 a year, had a wonderful condominium, a fine car, time for golf three or four times a week, much influence and many friends. He also realized he had been through two marriages, was an alcoholic, and miserable. Joel took a year off work to evaluate his life, go through treatment, rediscover God and begin a new life. He came to God in weakness, powerless, knowing, as people in twelve step programs do, that his life was unmanageable. And God found and loved him in that place to some wonderful new beginnings. He got out of the way and God made him worthy!

There is something of Zacchaeus' story in all of us if we acknowledge it. He was outwardly successful, but hated by his people. Small of stature he felt inferior. But he needed Jesus so much he was willing to appear the fool, to climb a tree to get a glimpse of him. He was willing to let his life be changed if he could sit at the table with Jesus.

My favorite section of that quintessential men's book Iron John, by Robert Bly, suggests that every man (and I suspect every woman in her own way, too) needs to forget about being the king's son sometime, go work in another man's castle, work in the basement, shoveling out the coal dust ashes. Metaphorically we all need to grovel in the ashes, acknowledge our brokenness, feel our emptiness, and out of that unmanageability, powerlessness, really turn to God, to Jesus and then for the first time be found.

So I come to this Eucharist, this celebration of gratitude not bringing all my wonderful gifts to God, but offering my need. I am aware of whatever in me is "tax collector," that is whatever separates me from my sisters and brothers, whatever ways I use them for my benefit, whatever ways I collect from others' misfortune.

I come to Jesus in my shortness of stature--those places where I feel inadequate, unsure, immature.

Everyone I know has at least some small part that wears the bumper sticker "They'll never know you're swimming naked unless the tide goes out."

Every man I know has a scared little twelve-year-old boy inside. We all feel at times like we are bluffing it, and if the world, the boss, the pastor, or even my wife and children find out it will all be over. It is that terrible sense of inadequacy that we bring to Jesus today.

The beginning point of healing in the various twelve step programs is the admission that I am powerless, that left to myself my life has become unmanageable. Out of this awareness we come to discover a power greater than ourselves that can restore us to sanity, to wholeness.

The Christian tradition says the same thing. Unless I am a sinner, I do not need a savior.

Every truth has an opposite and equally important truth. The reality of our weakness and our need does not deny the good that is in us, and the grace God has already bestowed. But today, with Zacchaeus we are invited to stand before God as we do at every Eucharist, saying "Lord, I am not worthy, but you speak the word and we'll be healed."

As I said at the beginning the purpose of this is not to focus on my weakness, my stature, my failings but to be overwhelmed by the love of God that overlooks and reaches beyond and loves me fully, anyway!

If we do that, like Zacchaeus we can be invited to climb down out of our tree, to follow Jesus, to join him at this table, to become his disciple.

50) Thirty Second Sunday

Rooted in; 2 Mc. 7:1-2, 9-14; Lk. 20:27-38

I begin my reflections with two general truths that usher us into the scriptures today. First, the constant problem of life is death. We need to have some understanding of the mystery of death in order to wrestle with the mystery of life.

Secondly, with scripture, as in life, it is sometimes possible to miss the forest for the trees. We can get bogged down in details and miss the point. That seems especially true of the readings today.

In the reading from the book of Maccabees we are tempted to wonder why eating or not eating pork should result in so many deaths, or we can be distracted by the gruesome character of those deaths. But the heart of this reading is that we hear today the first, clearest full statement in the bible of a belief in eternal life. The young man, going to death, speaks his trust in the faithfulness of God, and the hope that he will be restored to life. We who gather here have heard such words, we have grown accustomed to the concept, but this is the very first such statement of hope in biblical history!

In the Gospel we may get trapped, as the Sadducees hoped to trap Jesus, by the absurd example they used to deny the possibility of Resurrection. "Yes," we may ask, "whose wife would the woman be in eternal life if she married all seven brothers in this life?" Again, the point is Jesus' absolute belief in the faithfulness of God, the hope of Resurrection and the firm belief that God is the God of the living. Even after the death of Abraham, Isaac and Jacob, God remains their God; he does not abandon them--more importantly, God will not abandon us, in death.

As we approach the end of another liturgical year we consider again, final things. We consider death, and what happens after death and what that means for how we chose to live our lives. Our Jewish ancestors wrestled with the questions and they simply could not accept that the death of a martyr for the sake of faith could be the end of the story. They had to assert that life must extend beyond the grave to make sense of life now.

More importantly, our own Christian faith is rooted in the belief of Jesus that God would be faithful beyond death. Jesus--whom we must see as human like ourselves to make sense of all of this--refuses to change what he believes, or how he acts, or what he says. He faces rejection, misunderstanding, enormous suffering, and an absurd death because he trusts in God's fidelity. Jesus' hope is rewarded by resurrection, by being lifted out of the tomb to new life. God is indeed faithful! Jesus "being raised up" is the foundation of our entire faith.

Christian faith is rooted in fidelity to the words and example of Jesus. We want to love as he did, speak as he did, trust as he did.

It is terribly difficult to do so if our experience is limited only to what we can see and hear and experience in the here and now. We cannot follow Jesus unless we trust as he did, in God's fidelity beyond the grave.

I do not pretend to know what heaven is, nor to explain exactly what happens after death. But I can trust that what we have here is not the final story.

I maintain that we come to trust in life coming, in whatever form or fashion, finally out of death because we experience this truth at the heart of all human reality. We trust it is the final word because it is the word all along. Life comes out of death. Life comes out of various deaths.

Every birth of every child begins in pain, birth pains.

Every other significant birth in our human life has its own birth pains. We say glibly, "No cross, no crown." But we do experience life that way. We have to do your homework to pass the course, from the first grade till the funeral. We have to do the work to get the check. We have to struggle with a marriage to let that initial love come to fruition. We have to work hard at being parents if we expect our children to grow into meaningful adulthood. We know we cannot help our children grow by protecting them from the pains of life, but by helping them live through them.

Such examples are the outline of life. Each of us has our own more convincing stories. I think of the many alcoholics I have known who tell stories of their unique "hitting bottom," before they began a second and fuller life. I think of some of the best couples I've known who knew profound disillusionment with their marriage, felt die what they started with, but out of that death fought to recover not something old but something new and put life again into their love.

Pause for a moment and feel, admit, acknowledge your deepest failures, your most profound hurts. (Pause)

But here we are, upright and sometimes smiling. We can say yes to what will be, only if we can say thanks to all that has been. We are who we are out of what we have been through, what we have overcome. We come to trust in the fidelity of God beyond the grave because we experience that fidelity first on this side of the grave. We are able to incorporate the mystery of death into our understanding of life only if we reflect on the experiences of death that occur at every juncture of life.

As we move to Eucharist today, as we prepare again to enter into the life, death and **resurrection** of Jesus, we do so conscious of how we have already shared in that mystery. I invite us into a moment of silence to savor and own whatever truth this all has in our lives. (Pause for a moment or two).

And as we move to the table now, we trust that what we have already experienced in miniature in life, will be the biggest truth imaginable when this life ends.

51) Thirty-Third Sunday

Rooted in Lk. 21: 5-19

Today is the final Sunday of Ordinary Time. Next Sunday we end the liturgical year celebrating the Feast of the Christ the King. Then we begin the story again with Advent. This final Sunday we hear about final things, ultimate things, earthquakes, plagues, famines, omens, and the followers of Jesus manhandled, persecuted, put to death. Serious stuff. Ultimate stuff.

Before we look at the scripture passages we might recall that from the beginning, from Jesus on, what is foretold has been fact. Our very best people have always been persecuted, even martyred. Often they suffered even at the hands of the Church.

Peter and Paul both died for their faith.

My patron, St. Lawrence, who gave the Church's money to the poor, killed on a gridiron by the Romans who wanted the money.

Thomas Aquinas spent years on the Index before being named a doctor of the Church. John of the Cross, Theresa of Avilla, Francis of Assisi, Ignatius of Loyola--all honored now, but only after great persecution in their own time, often by their own communities and Church.

Thomas More defied a King and died for it.

I think of the movie *The Mission*, about the Jesuits in Paraguay, and how this incredible work with the indigenous poor was scuttled, the people slaughtered by those who would colonize them. The great work of selfless missionaries undermined, the missionaries killed or scattered.

Dorothy Day in jail for her Pacifism during the Second World War.

The four American Women killed in El Salvador for their work with the poor. Oscar Romero, killed for siding with the poor.

I think even of Archbishop Raymond Hunthausen, the holiest man I have personally ever known well, so questioned and persecuted by the very Church he sought to serve.

It's not just today, not just this week that things appear to turn out badly for those who want to help the poor, care for refugees, the immigrant, the sick. This is a prophecy continually being fulfilled.

When Luke's gospel was written Jerusalem had already been de-stroyed, Peter and Paul and many others already martyred. Those who expected an imminent end to the world were forced to have second thoughts and prepare for the long haul. Whatever the ac-tual words of Jesus were when he entered Jerusalem, Luke shapes them for his own contemporary purpose. The words fit his day, any day, our day--for any followers of Jesus.

Luke presents a Jesus warning us not to trust in buildings, temples, institutions, governments, structures. They will collapse, disappoint, let us down.

Jesus insists that we not try to predict the end of time, or of this period or of this persecution. There will be all kinds of signs that everything is coming down. These signs will always be present. Don't trust those who say "This is it"--even though there are wars, tensions, insurrections in the Church and outside it. Even though there may be earthquakes in Haiti, floods in Central America, plagues like the Zika virus spreading, or total devastation in Syria, or Mosul.

Such signs will occur in every time, and in our own, but they do not necessarily signal the end. Hang in there, live it out.

Luke's Jesus says that in his own time, in every time, in our own time and even in our own backyard, there will be persecution, and judgment before religious and civil courts, for people who dare to speak and act in the name of Jesus, who live with the message and compassion of Jesus. Civil and even religious people with power, prestige, position will not like what Jesus' followers do and say and will attack them.

Jesus says this will always be true. You will have to give an account of how and why you have acted in my name.

Jesus encourages those of the first generation and us, not to worry a whole lot about defending ourselves. God will give us "words and a wisdom." Even should you be delivered up by friends, family members, people of your own Church or synagogue (or diocese, or religious community, or parish), don't worry.

Amazingly, don't worry even if you are persecuted or put to death--the strangest line of the passage: even if you are killed your hair won't be messed up! Your life will be saved! By patient endurance you will save your life!

It is a most uncomfortable but most true realization that people who proclaim the Gospel, who live, act, love in the name of Jesus will always be persecuted. Rarely will they be vindicated, validated, recognized by those in power. They will be revered by the little people, the powerless, the outcast, the broken, God's *anawhim*, and perhaps by the broken part in the hearts of all believers.

So what do we do with this so challenging word? What is asked of us today? I suspect each of us has to ask that question ourselves, but I end with two reflections.

I remember the poster from the sixties that has always challenged me. It asked, "If you were arrested for being a Christian would there be enough evidence to convict you?" This Gospel forces me to wrestle with the question.

Secondly, for many years on the wall before my desk I had two pictures. One a formal portrait of Archbishop Oscar Romero, killed for his faith and his care for the poor in El Salvador. Above his picture was a smaller one, a photograph of the small house in El Salvador where six Jesuits and two companions of theirs were killed by the same forces a few years later. The world's first glimpse of this same house pictured butchered bodies and ex-ploded brains of people who had spent their lives proclaiming the ideas, the vision and values of Jesus. But here, before my desk, the picture was quiet, serene, simple, with a rose bush, carefully tended by the husband of one of those killed, blooming to the right side.

The picture of the house, this serene white house where death rampaged, this composed picture of Oscar Romero, hold out the promise that nothing can kill us, finally and forever. Nothing can really harm us for we are the white-robed army of those washed in the blood of the lamb.

The challenge of the gospel today, here as winter surrounds us and the liturgical year draws to a close, is to live in that hope, refusing to lose heart, to despair, to be cynical. As bad as things might look in our nation or our world today, or any day, we are invited to join in this task of Jesus--however that task presents itself to us--with passion, patience, endurance, despite whatever risk might come.

52) The Feast of Christ the King

Rooted in Lk. 23: 35-43

I would like to start my reflections today with a simple exercise. Take a moment, close your eyes, and picture the word I give you: Tree (pause after each word)...

Mountain ...
Mother ...
My friend ...
God ...

What did you see, visually, for God? Pay attention to that for a moment.

How do I see, how do I picture God?

In the first reading of this feast of Christ the King the hymn from Colossians reminds us that Jesus is "the image of the unseen God." Jesus gives God a face. Jesus shows us what God is like toward us. Jesus is the best entree into the face and features of God. We enter into the reign of God through Jesus.

When you pictured God, was Jesus in the picture? I hope so.

Throughout this year we have entered the reign of God, of Christ the King, through the eyes of Luke. In today's Gospel, at the end of the liturgical year, the year of Luke, we look at Jesus on his throne, the cross. I invite us to reflect on two features of Luke's Gospel that we have seen all through the past year, features that "crown" our image of Jesus as King, crown our picture of God.

The first feature is the theme of *Compassion*. Luke's Gospel is a gospel of compassion. Jesus gives face to the compassion of God. In the word of Pope Francis, *MERCY*

All through this Gospel Jesus touches people with compassion, with mercy, in ways unique to Luke. Stories of the Good Samaritan, the ten lepers, the prodigal son, Jesus weeping over Jerusalem, all are found only in Luke.

Luke changes a key line of the Gospel and makes it his own. Matthew's Gospel in the midst of the Sermon on the Mount invites us to "Be perfect as God is perfect." Luke says, rather, "Be compassionate as God is compassionate." The face Jesus gives to God is one of mercy, compassion. And it is far more possible to imagine being compassionate than to be perfect!

This compassion theme culminates as Jesus ends his life on the cross. Only in Luke does Jesus meet the weeping women along the way and comfort them. Only in Luke do we hear Jesus speak to those who crucify him: "Father forgive them, they do not know what they are doing." Only in Luke do we see the scene of today's Gospel, and hear Jesus say to one next to him on the cross: "This day you will be with me in paradise."

On this Feast of Christ the King, here at the end of our long liturgical year, we see the face of God in Jesus and the face is filled with compassion. The reign of God is a compassionate reign, celebrating God's compassion towards us, inviting us to have compassion towards one another. In this year of mercy, we celebrate the central virtue of God's reign.

It is not easy to show compassion from a cross, not easy to care for others when we ourselves are suffering, from headache or heart-ache, but we are truly living in the kingdom of Christ when we do. I recall sitting, more than once, with people slowly dying whose concern was for their loved ones left behind more than for themselves. "Be sure my wife will be OK, Father," was been for me one of the surest signs of God's presence in death.

The ability of anyone to get out of their own "stuff," and see the needs of another gives sign of God's Spirit:

> A high school athlete with his broken arm cheering on his team when he can't play,

> A paralyzed woman who continues surviving by always paying more attention to those who came to visit her than to herself,

> A homeless person working the line at a food bank,

Signs of the reign of God, of people living alongside Christ the King!

The second big theme in Luke that flows through the entire Gospel focuses here at the cross with _two_ men next to Jesus. From the beginning to the end of Luke's gospel there are two people in almost every story.

In the beginning of the Gospel story, Simon in the temple after the birth of Jesus sees in this child a sign that the messianic time has come. He looks at the child and says, "This child is destined for the rise and fall of many in Israel." Some will *rise*, some will *fall*. In almost every scene of Luke there are two people present; one rises, another falls. One has a hard heart that somehow cannot be touched, remains disturbed and threatened. One has a broken heart that can be mended, can be given a promise of hope. One can be loved and enter into God's reign; another resists.

A woman of the town who was a sinner, washes Jesus' feet with her tears; Simon, the Pharisee, accuses in his blindness.

Two people go to the temple to pray, one acknowledges himself as sinner and is saved; the other justifies himself, does not need God.

Two brothers, one broken and returning to the father's home and heart; the other has always been there and never enjoyed it, self-satisfied, angry, vindictive.

Here, finally, in today's gospel for the Feast of Christ the King, two men hang next to Jesus on the cross. One admits he deserves what he is getting and asks for mercy. He can be loved and changed. One taunts him, asks for unearned miracle, and is hardened in his sin.

Throughout this year with Luke's Jesus, and here at the end, we have a choice about which person we will be, which part of ourselves we bring to this Cross, this Kingdom. Luke proclaims that the reign of God, the Kingdom of Jesus is offered to those who most need it and least deserve it.

The values of society and every other kingdom on earth are turned upside down:

> Those who think they have nothing, have the kingdom.

> Those least likely to believe in and feel worthy of God's love, have first and fullest access to it.

We are tempted to turn God's reign, the Kingdom of Jesus into one that apes the kingdoms of this world. We build palaces instead of crosses, have offices and officials instead of servants, are more like an army than a circus, climb ladders rather than dance in circles. We are tempted to exclude those we think do not measure up--the tax collector, the leper, the wayward son.

If we bring these central themes of Luke's Gospel together here this final Sunday of the year, we look at the face of Jesus and see our God. We know that God's reign is in our midst as we face a simple disturbing fact. The reign of God, the Kingdom of Christ, awaits those who acknowledge their need for it!

As we enter into Eucharist today, the feast of the Kingdom, I invite us to reflect on our very own communal and personal tickets to being here.

What emptiness, what brokenness, what deserved punishment, what need for compassion do I bring with me, demonstrating my ticket for admission to this banquet?

Bring that, as we offer our bread and wine to our God.

CPSIA information can be obtained
at www.ICGtesting.com
Printed in the USA
FFHW020442220119
50249748-55247FF